HIGHER
EDUCATION
IN AMERICAN
SOCIETY

HIGHER EDUCATION IN AMERICAN SOCIETY

edited by
Philip G. Altbach
and
Robert O. Berdahl

⌶⌶ Prometheus Books
700 East Amherst St. • Buffalo, New York, 14215

Published by Prometheus Books
700 East Amherst Street, Buffalo, New York 14215

Copyright ©1981 by Philip G. Altbach and Robert O. Berdahl
All Rights Reserved

Library of Congress Catalog Number 81-82204
Cloth: ISBN 0-87975-165-7
Paper: ISBN 0-87975-166-5

Printed in the United States of America

Contents

1. Higher Education in American Society: An Introduction
   Robert O. Berdahl and Philip G. Altbach

Part 1: The Setting

2. The University and the State: A Historical Overview
   E.D. Duryea

3. Autonomy and Accountability: Some Fundamental Issues
   T.R. McConnell

4. Academic Freedom in Delocalized Academic Institutions
   Walter Metzger

5. Political Action, Faculty Autonomy and Retrenchment:
   A Decade of Academic Freedom, 1970-1980
   Sheila Slaughter

6. Happenings on the Way to the 1980s
   Verne A. Stadtman

7. Current and Emerging Issues Facing American Higher Education
   Clark Kerr and Marian Gade

Contents

Part 2: External Forces

8. State Government
   John D. Millett

9. The Federal Government and Postsecondary Education
   Aims C. McGuinness, Jr.

10. The Courts
    Walter C. Hobbs

11. Private Constituencies and Their Impact on Higher Education
    Fred F. Harcleroad

Part 3: The Academic Community

12. Stark Realities: The Academic Profession in the 1980s
    Philip G. Altbach

13. The College Student: A Changing Constituency
    Arthur Levine

14. Presidents and Governing Boards
    John W. Nason

15. Stress and the Academic Dean
    Donald J. McCarty and I. Philip Young

Part 4: Concluding Perspectives

16. The Insulated Americans: Five Lessons From Abroad
    Burton R. Clark

17. Conclusion
    Robert O. Berdahl and Philip G. Altbach

Bibliography

Contributors

1

Higher Education in American Society: An Introduction

Robert O. Berdahl and Philip G. Altbach

For a time in the 1960s, when student activists received daily television coverage and a book a week seemed to be published concerning the "academic crisis," higher education was, according to public opinion polls, the key concern of the American people. Now, a much less dramatic crisis engulfs higher education. While few headlines are generated, America's colleges and universities face an unprecedented situation. Stimulated by demographic changes, fiscal stringency, and a major intrusion of government involvement in all aspects of higher education, the 1980s are a period of considerable stress. In this book, we are concerned largely with the relationship of this crisis to higher education, particularly to how colleges and universities relate to their external environments. We are especially concerned with the key questions of autonomy, accountability, and academic freedom in this context. Our contributors, all experts in their respective fields, have brought their expertise to aspects of these complex relationships.

Basic and time-honored concepts in higher education have undergone substantial transformation. The history of academic freedom, for example, considered the evolution of the concept.[1] But Walter Metzger has argued

1

that the 1915 definition of academic freedom, propounded by the American Association of University Professors, is no longer adequate to cover the complexity of external relations now confronting the contemporary college and university.[2] Arguing that academic institutions have become "delocalized"—removed from their traditions of being relatively small, isolated, inexpensive, and fairly self-governing—they have been transformed into today's large and costly academic systems, interacting extensively with society and much influenced and/or controlled by some of these social forces. We need to think carefully about the cumulative impact of these changes. This volume tries to understand the complex relationship of higher education to society. This introductory chapter provides some basic definitions and a conceptual framework for the following chapters.

Some General Cautions

First, we should confirm what our title implies: this book is essentially about *higher* education, rather than the broader term, postsecondary education, and it is mostly about *American* colleges and universities, although the historical chapter and the Clark essay in the conclusion make reference to comparative material. Our focus on traditional colleges and universities does not mean that we ignore the importance of emerging nontraditional institutions, but we felt a prior obligation to help clarify the substantial changes already taking place in long-standing units.

Second, in dealing with a university's or college's (hereafter we will use the generic term "college" for short) relations with society, it is easy to err in one of two directions: on the one hand, it is possible to exaggerate the golden glow of the past when colleges supposedly operated without social intrusions; on the other, one may overreact to grim pressures of the present and assume that all is now lost for higher education.

In fact, neither response seems fully warranted. In describing Metzger's "localized" college, we purposefully qualified the description of its size, isolation, cost, and self-governance with the term "relatively" because, as Duryea's following chapter on historical perspectives indicates, colleges were never totally isolated or self-governing. From their start, colleges have had an ambivalent relationship with their surrounding societies: involved and withdrawn; needing and being needed; serving and criticizing. Yet, and this is important to keep in mind, American higher education has never strayed too far from the mainstream of American society—criticism has been within the acceptable standards of the day. Throughout most of its history American higher education has been more a transmitter of culture than a creator of divergent cultural or ideological norms. The links between higher education and the state, church, and in general the Establishment have traditionally been strong.

Academic institutions have nevertheless pursued their own goals and have often jealously guarded their internal independence and their commitment to autonomy and academic freedom. In a way, this sense of mission and commitment that allowed colleges to survive and prosper in earlier adversity may well see them through even the admittedly difficult conditions of the present and near future. Yet, it would seem that the contemporary academic institution, the "delocalized" college in Metzger's terms, is faced with a trio of potentially threatening external factors—enrollment decline, fiscal austerity, and increased governmental pressure for accountability. These challenges add up to new relationships between higher education and society that may constitute changes *in kind* rather than *in degree*. Nevertheless, in observing the reactions of the main internal constituencies—the faculty, students, and administrators/trustees—we see ample signs of continued vitality and adjustability.

A Few Definitions

Although our authors will offer their own working definitions of key terms, we think it wise to pause here briefly and outline the *general* usage of some concepts which play a fundamental role in this volume.

Academic freedom will mean the freedom of the scholar in his/her teaching and research to pursue a scholarly interest wherever it seems to lead and without fear of termination of employment for having offended some political, religious, or social orthodoxy.

Professional autonomy will mean the extent to which control over immediate working conditions of the faculty member (whether or not some of the conditions also pertain to academic freedom issues) has been decentralized to the working level professionals.

College autonomy of a *substantive nature* will apply to the power of a college to determine its own goals and programs—the *what* of Academe.

College autonomy of a *procedural nature* will apply to the power of a college to determine the means by which its goals and program will be pursued —the *how* of Academe.

Although all four concepts are inevitably blurred in real academic life, we suggest that it will be helpful in analyzing a college's relations with its environment to keep the four terms conceptually distinct. Academic freedom, as here defined, is an *individual* protection; professional autonomy applies to a *collegial* process; and substantive and procedural autonomy constitutes *corporate* concepts relating to the legal entity, whether it be a single campus or a multi-campus system.

Thus, intrasystem decisions could deny autonomy to a local campus but such actions would not qualify for this volume's focus on relations between the corporate structure of colleges and their *external* constituencies. As another example, there might be a "professional autonomy" decision by a dean, college president, or board of trustees concerning an internal curriculum issue, or a "substantive autonomy" decision by an external, statewide board of higher education concerning a disapproved field of study —and neither of these would necessarily involve an "academic freedom" issue unless the grounds for the decision had to do with orthodoxy of the curriculum in question. Or, along another dimension, one could envisage a set of external *procedural* controls so severe (e.g., pre-audits of budgets for propriety as well as legality of expenditures) that they have serious impact on a college's ability to achieve its self-chosen *substantive* goals.

Some of these terms are further explored in Baldridge, et al.,[3] Berdahl,[4] and Dressel,[5] but we raise them briefly here so that readers may consider how they evaluate the proper balance between each of these dimensions and their opposite concept: accountability.[6]

A Possible Conceptual Framework

Assuming the rough validity of these definitions, the chapters of this book may yield more significant insights if viewed across the categories of analysis used by Martin Trow to understand the interrelationships of the various aspects of college life as higher education expanded in the postwar period. Although current problems point in the opposite direction, it is still highly instructive to consider Trow's analysis of the impact of expansion on purposes, structures, access, curriculum, teaching styles, degree standards, research patterns, modes of financing, and internal and external governance systems as American higher education moved across the spectrum from "elite" to "mass" higher education and poised on the brink of "universal access." Though "universal access" may not be fully realized in the near future, Trow shows how the three "ideal" categories may be used to understand the linkages between and among the various specific consequences as higher education systems grew.

For example, Trow deals with the varying nature of the "locus of power and decision-making" as follows:

> With respect both to ultimate power and effective decisions, elite institutions are dominated by relatively small elite groups: leaders in significant institutions—political, economic, and academic—who know one another, share basic values and assumptions, and make decisions through informal face-to-face contact. An example of this would be the small number of leading civil servants, government ministers, university vice-chancellors, and members of the University Grants Commission who shaped the face of the British univer-

sity system for many years in small committee rooms or around tables at the Athenaeum Club.

Mass higher education continues to be influenced by these elite groups, but is increasingly shaped by more "democratic" political processes and influenced by "attentive audiences." These are parts of the general public who have special interests and qualifications, and develop a common view about higher education in general or some special aspect, such as the forms and content of technical education. Higher education policies increasingly become subject to the ordinary political processes of interest groups and party programs. One kind of attentive audience is the employers of the products of mass higher education, who are interested in the nature of their skills and qualifications. Another attentive audience is the body of "old graduates" who retain an interest in the character and fortunes of their old university. These groups often develop political instrumentalities of their own, such as associations with an elected leadership, and develop lines of communication to the smaller groups in government, legislatures, and the universities themselves who make the actual decisions, both day to day and over the long range.

When the system moves toward universal access, increasingly large portions of the population begin to be affected by it, either through their own past or present attendance, or that of some friend or relative. In addition the universities and colleges—what is taught there, and the activities of their staff and students—come to be of general interest, leave the pages of the serious press and magazines, and are reported in the popular journals and on television. They thus attract the interest of mass publics that increasingly come to see themselves as having a legitimate interest in what goes on in the institutions of higher education, if for no other reason than their enormous cost and obvious impact on society. And these mass publics begin to make their sentiments known, either through letters to public officials or through their votes in special or general elections. The change in the size and character of the publics who have an interest in higher education and exert an influence on higher educational policy greatly influences the nature and content of the discussions about higher education, who takes part in them, and the decisions that flow out of them. The claims of academic men to a special expertise, and of their institutions to special privileges and immunities, are increasingly questioned; much of what academic men understand by academic freedom, and the significance of the security of academic tenure for the protection of their pursuit of truth regardless of political interests or popular sentiment, all are challenged by the growing intervention of popular sentiments into these formerly elite arenas. [Paragraphing added.]

Growth itself stimulates prescriptive planning: the more higher education grows, the more money is needed for it, the more interest there is in it among larger parts of the population, the greater demand there is for tight control over its shape and costs. The growing demand for "accountability" of higher education, for its ability to demonstrate its efficiency in the achievement of mandated and budgeted goals, inevitably translates itself into tighter controls and prespective planning....The growth of higher education, given a prescriptive control system, places ever greater demands on that system to maintain and increase its control over numbers and costs, structures and standards.

The pressures for uniformity or convergence associated with central governmental control over higher education, are several:

- The uniform application of administrative forms and principles, as in formulas linking support to enrollments; formulas governing building standards and the provision and allocation of space; formulas governing research support, etc.

- Broad norms of equity, which prescribe equal treatment for "equivalent" units under a single governing body;

- Increasingly strong egalitarian values, which define all differences among public institutions—in their functions, standards, and support—as inequitable.

There are counter forces that help to sustain and even increase diversity in higher education. In some places there is a multiplicity of governmental bodies involved in higher education: the United States is an extreme case in this respect. More generally, there are variations in the degree of diversity of sources of support, both of public and private funds. The growth of institution and systems toward mass higher education puts a strain on administrative structures designed for a smaller, simpler, elite system, and activities begin to elude the controls of an overburdened and understaffed administration. The near monopoly within the academic world of specialized knowledge about the nature of the academic fields and their needs and requirements is the ultimate basis of academic autonomy, and slows (though it may not prevent) rationalization and the application of standardized formulas governing admissions, academic standards, support, workloads, etc. (This is, of course, the more true where the knowledge base is greater and the intellectual authority of the academics concerned is higher—which is why academic autonomy is defined more successfully in elite institutions.)[7]

Another Conceptual Framework

Although some of Martin Trow's discussion of the inevitability of college expansion now sounds a bit dated, his analysis of the linkage of consequences across his different categories continues to furnish valuable insights into current conditions, since we are living with the implications of the past several decades of growth.

Howard Adelman, a Canadian philsopher, provides us with another perspective from which to analyze developments in higher education. His analysis is not directly related to the growth syndrome, but it is complementary to Martin Trow's views and useful to help in understanding the nexus of relationships between higher education and society.[8]

Adelman argues that North American higher education has gone through a number of different phases in the past two centuries, and that these phases shape a whole series of relationships. Such factors as curriculum, finance, and governance are all altered by the different phases. He posits four models of academic development:

1. *The Sanctuary of Truth,* in which absolute moral truths are taught to certain special students with the aim of turning out high moral character;

2. *The Sanctuary of Method,* in which professional education inculcates high professional skills in the search for infinite knowledge;

3. *The Social Service Station,* in which the college agrees to "serve" the community with products and services recognized to be appropriate to the collegiate tradition; and

4. *The Culture Mart,* in which the boundaries between the college and the community are progressively blurred, and all "educational activities," whether on campus or off, whether by formal colleges or other institutions performing educational services, get validated and legitimized by colleges acting as educational brokers.

Adelman identifies Jose Ortega y Gasset as the philosopher of the first model,[9] Abraham Flexner as that of the second,[10] Clark Kerr as that of the third,[11] and the Wright Commission Report on Postsecondary Education in Ontario as the articulation of the fourth.[12] According to Adelman's analysis, we in North America are now deep into the dominance of the Social Service Station model, now, with elements of the first two still existing here and there, and with governmental planning systems trying to assess the values and costs of moving on more fully toward the last model.

These analytical models are by no means the only ones which might be called into play to explain the postwar development of higher education in the United States. For example, Samuel Bowles and Herbert Gintis argue that education, including higher education, has responded to the changing needs of the labor market and that colleges have increasingly been brought into the capitalist sphere.[13] In this framework, it is not surprising that government authorities have moved increasingly to control higher education—hence, the growth of accountability. They argue that the links between government, industry, and higher education have grown stronger as the need for highly trained manpower in a technological society has grown in the postwar period.

This volume does not posit any uniform framework of analysis. As editors, we asked only that our contributors deal with specific topics that related to the higher education and society nexus. Each author provides an analysis of his or her specific subject. Each, naturally, comes to the topic with a range of implicit assumptions. What has been provided in this volume, then, is a range of perspectives concerning the key elements of the relationship between higher education and society.

The Organization of the Book

We have tried to select topics that focus most directly on the important
issues relating to higher education-society questions and that are relevant as
we enter the 1980s. We have not been able to deal with all topics. But we feel
that this volume provides the basis for an analysis of contemporary
American higher education.

The first part of the book elaborates on the fundamental concepts by including a chapter on the historical background to the current scene, one on
the origin and evolution of academic freedom in the United States, one on
more recent developments concerning academic freedom, and an essay on
the broad concepts of accountability and autonomy. Then, as a slight
change of pace, we conclude this part with an account of college
developments in the 1970s and a treatment of the emerging issues for the
1980s.

Part Two then treats the major *external* constituencies of universities and
colleges: state and federal governments, the courts (treated as a separate
dimension of external power), and so-called "private" constituencies
(meaning those without a governmental base, such as foundations, associations, consortia, regional groupings).

The third part then presents analyses of the reactions of the major *internal* constituencies to the increased roles of the external forces. Chapters
cover the faculty, students, deans, and presidents/trustees.

A final chapter offers our concluding perspectives along with some comparative material drawn from other higher education systems; for we all
need to be reminded that problems facing American higher education are
not necessarily unique to this country, and that we could profit much from
increased knowledge of foreign systems. But this is a subject for another
volume!

Notes

1. Richard Hofstader and Walter P. Metzger, *The Development of Academic Freedom in the United States* (New York: Columbia University Press, 1955).
2. Walter P. Metzger, Sanford H. Kadish, Arthur De Bafdeleben, and Edward J. Bloustein, *Dimensions of Academic Freedom* (Urbana, Ill.: University of Illinois Press, 1969).
3. J. Victor Baldridge, David V. Curtis, George Ecker, and Gary L. Riley, "Diversity in Higher Education: Professional Autonomy," *Journal of Higher Education,* 48 (July/August, 1977), pp. 367-388.
4. Robert O. Berdahl, *Statewide Coordination of Higher Education* (Washington, D.C.: American Council on Education, 1971). See also Carnegie Commission on Higher Education, *Governance of Higher Education* (New York: McGraw Hill, 1973).
5. Paul L. Dressel, *The Autonomy of Public Colleges* (San Francisco: Jossey-Bass, 1980).
6. Kenneth P. Mortimer, *Accountability in Higher Education* (Washington, D.C.: American Association for Higher Education, 1972).
7. Martin Trow, "Problems in the Transition from Elite to Mass Higher Education," *Policies for Higher Education: the General Report on the Conference on Future Structures of Post-secondary Education* (Paris: Organization for Economic Co-operation and Development, 1974).
8. Howard Adelman, *The Holiversity: A Perspective on the Wright Report* (Toronto: New Press, 1973).
9. Jose Ortega y Gasset, *The Mission of the University* (New York: Norton, 1944).
10. Abraham Flexner, *Universities: American, English, German* (New York: Oxford University Press, 1968). Originally published in 1930.
11. Clark Kerr, *The Uses of the University* (New York: Harper Torchbooks, 1963).
12. *The Learning Society: Report of the Commission on Post Secondary Education in Ontario* (Toronto: Ministry of Government Services, 1972).
13. Samuel Bowles and Herbert Gintis, *Schooling in Capitalist America* (New York: Basic Books, 1976).

Part I
The Setting

2

The University and the State:
A Historical Overview
E.D. Duryea

Looking back on the relations between universities and society in Western culture, one can discern a similarity between the institutions of the current century and their ancestors in the twelfth and thirteenth centuries. Both have reflected what Marjorie Reeves highlights as "a tension between two impulses: one, the drive towards a search for 'pure' knowledge, and the other, the acquisition of knowledge and skills for specific social ends."[1] Both have evidenced a combination of legal and *de facto* obligations to an external sovereignty and a measure, at times extensive and at times limited, of internal autonomy.[2] The commitment to extending human learning inherently and inevitably brings to the fore the critical importance of what we know today as academic freedom. The service to society implemented by educational programs directed toward socially significant knowledge and skills—historically, the combination of a common learning and preparation for one of the "higher" vocations or professions—and the exportation to the external society of a professional expertise responds to the broader implications of accountability.

A further observation suggests that in this perception the modern and the medieval draw together in form and function after an intellectual hiatus of about four centuries, during which the medieval era waned and the universities in Western culture were converted to handmaidens of state and church, both Catholic and Protestant. To my thinking, it is most important to understand this historical evolution in order to understand contemporary tensions between academic freedom and institutional autonomy, on the one hand, and accountability to the state, on the other. To convey such an understanding, at least in its more manifest aspects, constitutes the purpose of this brief historical essay.

At the same time, wisdom requires a sense of perspective in reading an interpretive essay such as this, which constructs a historical montage covering several centuries of complex developments. Relationships associated with academic freedom and the nature of the autonomy-accountability dualism are relative. One would look hard to find a perfect condition of freedom, obviously, and similarly, one would be hard put to identify either complete autonomy or full accountability. The most accountable institutions of recent times, the nineteenth-century German universities, allowed professors a high degree of autonomy to handle internal affairs and press their academic interests within a system that assured the final authority to the state through its educational ministry. Also, while this paper rests on the thesis of an intellectual decadence and subservience to church and state during the fifteenth through eighteenth centuries, it does not mean to imply that what we call the eras of the Renaissance and Enlightenment left the universities to lie fallow. They remained, in fact, significant establishments to which, especially in England, an expanding middle class, deriving a livelihood from commerce and industry, turned as vehicles for social and political mobility. Sons of the new gentry of Renaissance England learned their classics and manners at Oxford and Cambridge; those of the burghers of the German states found in the universities there a curricular response to their needs. But the balance suffered and the scales dipped sharply in the direction of an accountability of service performed in accord with theological and political postulates held by the religious-political governing authorities.

To develop this historical analysis, therefore, requires an initial, brief survey of the medieval era that sets a general pattern for the development of the university in Western culture. Then, it serves to review, succinctly at least, the transition from medieval to modern associated with the Renaissance and, particularly, the shift to a secular orientation associated with classical humanism and with the origins of modern knowledge in the "Enlightenment" of the seventeenth and eighteenth centuries. Finally, one must come to grips with the drastic changes in higher education that led, during the nineteenth century in this country, to what Laurence Veysey describes as "the emergence of the American university."

From this perspective, the concept of the university as an autonomous institution within a society evolved early in the middle ages, in close company with the use of the corporate form as the basis for the government of universities. However, one must recognize that the medieval universities could not escape from their societal context, either in terms of accommodation to the prevailing values and medieval power structure (primarily in terms of religious beliefs and the authority first of the Roman Catholic Church and then of secular kings and emperors) or of the performance of an educational function relevant to their times. Conflicts over scholarly independence and restraints upon it do not lack medieval precedents. Likewise, while the idea and form of institutions of higher learning draw from experiences in the twelfth and thirteenth centuries, both underwent thorough change during the progression of secular knowledge. Contemporary conceptions of academic freedom and autonomy derive from the professionalization of the professoriate accompanying a swing toward specialization and investigation during the late nineteenth and early twentieth centuries.

Medieval Background

The medieval centers for higher learning gained their institutional structure in the course of the twelfth century in conjunction with the intellectual fluorescence of that era, stoked by the penetration into Western Europe of the learning of an earlier era, especially that of ancient Greece. By the beginning of the thirteenth century they had evolved into formal institutions, of which that at Paris created the prototype for the universities in northern Europe and set a pattern for institutions in this country. Paris stood out among these medieval centers as a consequence "of the particular intellectual achievements of the galaxy of outstanding scholars who raised it to the forefront of academic life in northern Europe,"[3] and as a universally recognized source for interpretation of ecclesiastical doctrine within the Catholic Church.

The formation of the University of Paris following the turn of the thirteenth century created that dual relationship, now expressed as autonomy and accountability, that has remained throughout the centuries a particular tradition of universities. Paris, as a formal institution, congealed from the informal associations of scholars—masters and students—who gathered around the cathedral school of that city. Its development "was determined by, and reveals to us, the whole bent and spiritual character of the age to whose life it became organic."[4] The success of the Paris center, confirmed through the influx of teachers and students, inevitably led to conflicts with the local church officialdom and Parisian citizenry. As head of the cathedral school around which the University was taking its particular form, the Bishop of Paris and his representative, the Chancellor, sought to maintain their control of the burgeoning educational center. The expanding mass of scholars inevitably proved an abrasive element at times disruptive of town life and led to retaliatory efforts by secular officers to maintain their law over a turbulent mass of strangers. The scholars did not lack their own aspirations for separate jurisdiction. For protection and authority, they turned to an external but superior power, that of the Papacy. Without elaborating the course of events, the University achieved a local autonomy for the price of submission to a more distant sovereignty, that of the Church. The form of this autonomy came as papal bulls or charters that granted to the University power over its internal affairs as a Church corporation that owed its legal existence to the Pope. This arrangement adhered to medieval practice, which supported corporate associations holding an inherent right of existence separate from that of members, and served a wide range of activities, ranging from religious orders to mercantile and craft enterprises.

In the centuries that followed, as national kings pushed aside the popes and grasped power as a divine right, the University of Paris (and European universities in general) lost not only its preeminence but its independence, as it ineffectually sought to maintain medieval religious prerogatives within "a state already modern, national and territorial."[5] In effect, what the king gave by charter the king could withdraw; the university had become an institution authorized by and obligated to the state. Yet, there had been established and still remained a general acceptance, "of the principle that the essence and core of a university was its autonomy,"[6] leading to a dualism between political reality and academic tradition carried on in an uncertain equilibrium.

Similarly, the origins of the ideal of scholarly freedom can be viewed in association with the medieval universities. One can perceive a parallel between the twelfth century and the nineteenth in the sense that both stand out as critical for Western thought. The former presents us with an era during which scholars in the West "became aware of the vast corpus of classical material which hitherto had been but dimly glimpsed."[7] A new learning reached Europe from the pens of adventuresome clerks (for only in the monasteries and other Church agencies were there literacy and some pretense to knowledge) who found in Arabian manuscripts the writings of the Greeks, especially of Aristotle. Supported by a social stability consequential to the unifying force of Christianity, these medieval scholars undertook the task of understanding and communicating this past learning and did so in the lecture halls of the nascent university centers. Among them, creative thinkers such as Peter Abelard, Roger Bacon, Thomas Aquinas, and William of Ockham grappled with the implications of this new knowledge for the revealed truth of the Christian faith. In the process they began to apply human reason to ecclesiastical doctrine.

This latter tendency, the application of reason to faith, raised the hackles of the orthodox Churchmen; it led to a response from them that sought to eliminate what they viewed as heretical thought and to what well may be the first great case of academic freedom. The famous case in point involved Abelard, who was brought to trial by the Church. In the words of his accuser, Saint Bernard, he was guilty of "trying to make void the merit of Christian faith, when he deems himself able by human reason to comprehend God altogether."[8] It was the controversy of realism vs. nominalism that stood behind the trial; whether there was a source for understanding (or truth) independent of human thought or whether reality constitutes what the senses perceive and the mind interprets, a controversy that gave to Western culture a gleam of intellectual light so tantalizing that it could not be ignored. While it moved outside the vision of medieval scholars and their successors in the universities in the following centuries, the application of reason to comprehend reality reentered Western thought as the basis for secular, and especially scientific, knowledge. In time, it returned also to the universities, and therein lies the modern concept of academic freedom and its association with nineteenth- and twentieth-century specialized knowledge.

Finally, while the fame of the medieval universities may well have rested upon the excitement of its speculative theology and heady exposure to new philosophical ideas, their sustenance derived from a more mundane function. According to A.B. Cobban, "their roots were extricably bound up with utilitarian values. They evolved as institutional responses to the pressures to harness educational forces to the professional, ecclesiastical, and governmental requirements of society."[9] They provided educational opportunity and appropriate training for students who looked to careers within the administrative hierarchy of the Church or civil government or as legal or medical practitioners. For the majority of students, the universities served as an entree to rewarding careers, no matter how attendance might be cloaked in the guise of their clerical status. More than one contemporary master complained about the worldliness of students and their commitment to a quick passage through the lower arts courses so that they might enter the advanced faculties into a chosen career. Learning was pursued in an active relationship to the social order, as an essential service to its society.[10]

In summary, the Paris model formed an institutional pattern antecedent to that of the twentieth-century system of higher education in its major components. It drew to its halls creative intellectuals who pressed hard on the borders of the then existing conceptions of reality, which, while speculative rather than empirical, constituted a commitment to the extension of knowledge. Their efforts inevitably led to major conflicts over the intellectual or academic freedom of creative scholars. It set clearly the condition of the institution as a corporate body owing its existence to an external sovereign, but possessing a degree of autonomy to manage its internal affairs, including the nature of its educational program. It served as a passage to "higher" or professional careers. The English universities evolved in the Parisian pattern and set a general pattern for the early colleges of this country, along with the Protestant institutions of the continent and Scotland. The essential point, of course, is that the pattern of government, in terms of its relationship with church and state, remained in the English-United States tradition: that these institutions maintained a corporate form, that scholars of these universities retained a tradition of internal autonomy, and that the higher learning continued to serve as the gateway to significant roles in society.

Transition from Medieval to Modern

If the nature of the medieval university carried over to the higher education of this country in the twentieth century, what about developments during the intervening centuries? In responding to this query, it is important to note two cultural or intellectual streams that flowed into higher education in this country. One led to the eighteenth-century and early nineteenth-century colleges through influences associated with the Protestant Reformation and the humanistic ideals and studies of the Renaissance. The other lay with the development of secular knowledge attendant with the growth of science and related philosophies, which motivated European intellectuals during the Enlightenment of the seventeenth and, especially, the eighteenth centuries. It becomes important, therefore, to give some attention, albeit briefly, to the forces at work in connection with the university and higher learning during this intervening era.

Western culture passed from the medieval era into the Renaissance and the Enlightenment as the Roman Catholic Church suffered a loss of its hegemony over European affairs. At the turn of the fifteenth century the Great Schism had left the papacy dominated by secular power; it was barely recovering its ecclesiastical authority when, a century later, Luther inaugurated the Reformation that broke northern from southern Europe. However, one senses that the problems of Christian orthodoxy accompanied and participated with other forces at work that set a new social context for the universities. Their essence was a secular turn in the interests and values of Europeans, away from what has been called that "principle of a single and uniform but articulate whole...based upon the conviction of a solidarity of mankind as the beloved children of God, united through God's infinite charity."[11]

It is important to remember that the Renaissance is a historical conception and not a specific historical epoch. It designates a number of related and interacting changes that entered European life as the authority of the Roman Church declined during the fourteenth and fifteenth centuries. Its origins intermingled with the intellectual movements of the middle ages; its spokesmen never broke with the essential tenets of Christianity. Historically, one probably associates the Renaissance primarily with the flowering of culture expressed through the rebirth of the classical literature from Greek and Roman sources and inspiring artistic and literary achievements. It does not serve, therefore, "to speak of the Renaissance as though it were a single age or single force..." but rather the name serves to identify that flowering of intellect and culture that accompanied "the great fundamental economic growth of European society and its rising middle class."[12]

One has to recognize also that probably the most fundamental aspect of this cultural change lay in the secularization of Europe. Without casting aside Christian beliefs and doctrine, the people of Europe were accepting and acting upon values more closely associated with the affairs of this world and reacting less to the consequences of their actions for the life hereafter. The Renaissance emerged in part as a consequence of the growth of trade and commerce that established new, commercial sinews across Europe, replacing the theological ties of the Church and breaking down the locally oriented economies of the previous era. The commerce and, to a degree, industrialization in such trades as weaving and metallurgy intermingled with the formation of national states. Temporal power shifted into the hands of national kings who grasped control from the pope and Holy Roman Emperor to carve up Europe geographically; papal sovereignty gave way to divine right; filial loyalty for the Father in Rome to national patriotism. Finally, the Protestant Reformation culminated these inroads upon European homogeneity. It represented, in the words of historian Preserved Smith, "the natural, though unconscious, adaptation of religion to the needs of a new social situation." "The individualism, the nationalism, the commercialism of the new age were all reflected in the Protestant church."[13]

In the evolution from medieval to modern, it is important also to recognize that, in company with the breakup of theological unity and the secularization of thought and culture, one finds the gestation of contemporary knowledge and relationships between education and society. The former emanated as a major aspect of modern civilization with the gradual development of science and the emergence of a whole system of new knowledge, knowledge that looked to the future rather than the past, knowledge completely secular and permeated with the idea of progress. Pending the fluorescence of knowledge, however, a mercantile nationalism, accompanied by the ready acceptance and thus dispersion of Protestant theology, impacted upon European universities and created conditions that strongly influenced the role of the early American colleges in our society. A humanistic tradition in education based strongly on the Greek and Roman classics framed the ideal of an educated man, which in turn served as the criteria for service in the courts of kings and the establishments of the Renaissance elite. Concurrently in the Protestant realms, political and religious leadership formed an alliance that set out to combine the church,

state, and education into one coordinated effort built around the propaga-
tion of the faith and preservation of theological orthodoxy.

For education, and especially the universities, the social and political
restructuring of Europe introduced a new constituency and new studies that
strengthened accountability to society but undermined commitment to
creative thought and new knowledge. What we view today as the great
minds and pioneering thinkers[14]—the counterparts to the provocative
medieval intellects who pressed beyond orthodoxy—found their destinies
outside the halls of the universities with few exceptions. Conditions of the
times supported submission to royal and religious authority. In the first part
of the seventeenth century, for example, English philosopher Thomas
Hobbes stressed the obligation of the universities to the good of the king,
and the great German mathematician, Leibniz, rejected the very idea of
academic freedom.[15] Within the broader parameters of the Renaissance, a
segment of educators known as humanists promoted educational reforms
that stressed Greek and Roman antiquity and the ideal of Cicero, which
conceived of an education for the man who would serve as the humane and
just leader. Education stressed "in the spirit of classical antiquity and of
Christianity" to the end of "training in virtue and good letters" and "of the
learned, responsible gentleman who devotes himself to the tasks of government."[16] Histories of the English universities confirm that the inroads of
the humanistic, classical studies achieved a position alongside of the rem-
nants of medieval scholasticism. Whatever our view of such learning today,
it responded and thus was accountable to the power structure of a social
order; and, as such, it carried over into the curriculums of the early colleges
in this country.

Protestantism imposed obligation to church and state. To achieve doc-
trinal hegemony within their domain, Protestant leaders allotted a primary
role to the schools and universities. In contrast to Catholicism, in the
reformed churches "the external and institutional side was subordinated to
the heart and conscience of the individual."[17] Whatever their sectarian differences—at times critical for the individual's relations to God—both
Luther and Calvin concurred on the supreme authority of the Bible and on
the access of individuals to the scriptures. As a consequence, their creed required the translation of God's word into the vernacular, the literacy to
enable its reading, and an educated and informed clergy to lead their flocks.
Protestant reform in the German universities, to illustrate, "meant a broad
attack on the autonomy of academic corporations by demanding the subordination of academic affairs to the needs of the territorial-confessional state
for trained administrators, ministers, and teachers."[18] It led to a system of
educated cleric and lay officials. As the German historian Freidrich Paulsen
observed, "about the middle of the seventeenth century there was hardly a
single village in Germany without a clergyman who had received his education at a university."[19]

Similarly, the maintenance of the English church, of which the crown was head, required an educated and conforming clergy. With their corporate existence dependent upon royal authorization, the universities proffered the available and essential means to this end. One finds that during the reigns of the Tudors and Stuarts of the sixteenth and seventeenth centuries the pressures for religious conformity mounted within the universities in support of an educated ministry. Therefore, it was not surprising in the controversy over tithes upon local communities to support an appointed clergy to find the rhetoric, "no universities, no ministry...no learning, no confutation of heresy."[20]

The age of the Renaissance, therefore, marked a shift toward the latter in the balance between autonomy and accountability. As one thinks about this period, however, it was not so much that political and theological leaders viewed education as a bastion of orthodoxy. This same view held in the medieval period as well. Rather, the shift inhered in the authority of secular state administrations, committed to one church or another, designed to achieve conformity and support through direct control. This contrasted with the ideal and reality of the university as a place apart, an autonomous institution in which the acceptance of sovereignty from the more distant papacy buffered it from the immediate force of local and national powers. Whatever the occasional deviation, as in the case of the Puritans in their resistance to the national church of England, the church-state-education triad translated into a conformity that accentuated responsibility over any pretensions of autonomy.

Formation of Contemporary Higher Education

This discussion has proposed that the present system of higher education evidences in many important ways a regeneration of its medieval antecedents. Obviously, our current scene presents a far greater diversity of institutions and certainly displays an accretion of services carried out across the spectrum, from community colleges to research universities, and from vocational, training courses to advanced graduate study and research. Yet, the essential functions of extending knowledge, of instruction, and of service through professional preparation and professorial expertise do parallel medieval centers of learning in dimensions not present during the Renaissance. The governing trinity of the Reformation weakened during the nineteenth century, a consequence of the secularization of society. Accompanying this was a renewal of the medieval conception of the university as a center for learning and of the belief, at least among its intellectual leaders, that "the essence and core of a university was its autonomy."[21] That dualism referred to before in this commentary between academic tradition and political reality once again began to characterize relationships between academe and the society. The nineteenth century, therefore, proved to be a metamorphic period as the Reformation college was transmuted into the modern university.

The first colleges of this country were formed in the spirit of the Reformation, as the colonists carried over into the new world their old world experiences and beliefs. Consequently, in the words of Jurgen Herbst, it was to be expected that the "traditional theme of the trinity of church, state, and college found expression in the New World."[22] The leaders of the churches held parallel roles in church and government and as overseers of the colleges in a kind of interlocking directory. They could and did insist upon religious orthodoxy and educational conformity despite the fact that the corporate basis for the colleges were separate from the agencies of government and committed to secular, humanistic studies.

For the trustees and presidents of the early colleges—and indeed for those who taught with them—questions of academic or intellectual freedom simply did not surface. A prescribed curriculum in the Renaissance tradition accompanied a sectarian commitment to Christian morality, within which the teachers had limited freedom for the pursuit of personal intellectual interests in instruction or scholarly interests. In the main, the colleges responded to a public need for an educated clergy and proffered an accepted entree into mercantile, political, and professional careers. Governors, legislators, and the general public as well—to the extent that they thought about the colleges—viewed them as performing a public function; and, although chartered with private, self-perpetuating boards of control, they remained subject to legislative will. As late as 1812, for example, the Overseers of Harvard College accepted without judicial protest changes in their charter made by the Massachusetts legislature. Thus, while this conformity was by no means perfect in either curricular or organizational dimensions, there the issue of accountability versus autonomy in either intellectual or organizational dimensions did not exist.

In the course of the nineteenth century, the Renaissance triad disintegrated, as both the nature of the society and advanced learning changed. By the turn of the twentieth century higher education had achieved a position of broad significance for the development of a culture becoming dependent upon science and technology and committed to educational opportunity. Professors were gaining status as specialists and experts and were beginning to view themselves as professionals worthy of special professional freedom in their research and instruction and a voice in the decisions affecting the conditions that impacted upon their employment. The secularization of higher education, the specialization of faculty members in their academic endeavors, and the new premium placed upon research afforded a basis for relations with society, one attested to in 1915 with the formation of the American Association of University Professors.

The consequence was a renewed vigor in the perception of the university as a place apart, a center for learning holding a right to a special and autonomous role within the society.

Thus, by the early twentieth century there reappeared the disaccord inherent in the two pressures for an autonomous role and the necessity for society to control an enterprise increasingly essential to its welfare. To grasp the essence of this issue, it becomes important to give attention to two developments. The first extends from medieval origins but arose more directly from what is known as the Enlightenment of the seventeenth and eighteenth centuries in the form of the growth of knowledge based upon secular interpretations of reality, especially those of a scientific nature. The second inheres in the organizational structure of higher education associated with the establishment of colleges and universities under the control of corporate governing boards manned by private individuals separate from the direct agencies of government. Each will be discussed briefly.

Knowledge and Its Social Importance

The inception of scientific thought as we know it today probably lies with the *New Atlantis* of Francis Bacon; if so, its gestation goes back through Copernicus certainly to William of Ockham.[23] But, after Bacon, if not entirely as a consequence of him, scientific thought does take off on the road to the twentieth century in company with a stress upon human reason via the seventeenth and eighteenth century Enlightenment of the intellectuals who constituted a kind of international association, a "loose, informal wholly unorganized coalition of culture critics, religious skeptics, and political reformers from Edinburgh to Naples, Paris to Berlin, Boston to Philadelphia."[24] "Inheriting from their ancestors the bel.ef in absolute truth and in a reasonable and comprehensive universe, these philosophers of the Enlightenment found a new standard of truth in science, and a new scheme of the universe in the astronomy of the seventeenth century."[25]

For American higher education the passage of reason bifurcated during the Enlightenment. One stream flowed directly to the early colleges. The intercourse between Adams, Jefferson, Franklin, and their associates and counterparts in Europe is well enough documented. Enlightenment ideas came to this country through France and England and, probably most influentially, Scotland. The new studies of the sciences had begun to enter the colleges before the Revolution and achieved a general acceptance, although one tertiary to Christian ethics and mental discipline, in large part because they did not appear to challenge established religion but were viewed as a further elaboration of the great work of God. In general, scientists may have agreed upon the importance of analysis based upon observation but remained committed to the view of John Locke that reason and experience fitted with divine revelation.[26]

The other Enlightenment stream moved through the German universities as in the early nineteenth century they solidified and expanded scientific and philosophical studies that originated in the new conceptions of "the world and man" accompanying the eighteenth-century awakening to the powers of observation and reason. In the years before the Civil War when the colleges of this country joined in support of the Yale Report's commitment to piety and humanistic, classical learning, the Germans were fashioning new disciplines and were gaining prestige for their scholarship. Until about the 1870s, German universities were virtually the only institutions in the world in which a student could obtain training in how to do scientific or scholarly research. German academicians had achieved the prospect and in large part the reality of "a full-time occupation role, that of the university professor whose professional duties explicitly included research."[27] They received appointments on the basis of formal qualifications and achievements. "The right to lecture at the university was the right of the recognized scientist."[28] In the course of the century, they offered a lodestar to adherents of educational reform in the country, discontent with the constraints of their college regimes and desirous of changes that would place their own institutions in line with advances in the intellectual realm. In the four decades following 1870, they succeeded in this endeavor and fashioned an academic reorganization spearheaded by a university model of specialized disciplines grounded upon advanced, graduate study in tandem with research and scholarship. In this country, as previously in Germany, the professor began to achieve status associated with a new role. Less and less a teacher and disciplinarian, he became, at least in the first-rate institutions, a person of professional substance in terms of a role as an academic specialist regarded as an expert and consulted in the mundane world. The engineer, agriculturalist, purveyor of veterinary medicine, economist, psychologist, and political scientist had something to contribute that gained by the First World War respectful, if at times tenuous, recognition amplified in the decades that followed.

This new role also carried with it a pressure for autonomy. Professional expertise set a scholar aside from the more direct intrusions of the uninitiated and allowed at least a partial monopoly on those admitted to profession. Specialization accompanying expertise gained organizational structure in the form of disciplinary and professional departments that had unto themselves the knowledge necessary for not only the recruitment of new staff but the formation of courses of study and determination of research priorities and extended, through constellations of related departments in the form of schools, to the curriculum itself. Whatever the influence of the donor, the legal authority of the state, or the formal power of trustees and regents, it became less and less possible for them to extend this external influence into the basic academic substance of the higher learning. Harvard President A. Lawrence Lowell was to write in 1921 of the faculty

as a "society or guild of scholars,"[29] and a 1924 report of a committee of
the American Association of University Professors was to complain that
professors had come to look upon the university "as a place where their
own departmental specialties can be practiced without let or hindrance."[30]

The intellectual transformation of Western culture identified with the extension of knowledge had a correlate in the industrial revolution and the
prominence in the American society of an egalitarian ideology. For the
nineteenth century, this meant an alteration of political, economic,
religious, and moral components of life and the passing of the mercantile
economic and political systems of the republican era that had been attuned
to the European-oriented culture of the eastern seaboard and headed by an
educated elite who had led the nation to its independence and set it upon its
course in history. In this context, advocates of accommodation to the new
knowledge had counterparts who promoted an applied orientation in
tandem with expansion in opportunity. As the industrial system matured in
this country (in agriculture as well as in the factory and commerce), higher
education took on a responsibility for preparing students for roles that
covered a spectrum from applied engineering and agriculture to
psychologically-based personnel services. "The industrial system," as
economist John Galbraith has observed, "by making trained and educated
manpower the decisive factor of production, requires a highly developed
education system....Modern higher education is extensively accommodated
to the needs of the industrial system....The great prestige of pure and applied science and mathematics in modern times, and the support accorded
to them, reflect the needs of the technostructure."[31] In effect, the nineteenth-century reforms combined commitment to the extension of
knowledge with service of direct usefulness to society.

The growing recognition of the value of a college or university education
and the egalitarian sentiment for opening up opportunity for all to move
toward economic success in life stimulated the growth of public higher
education. The initiative for a system of public colleges and universities
came largely after the Morrill Act of 1862 provided for the land-grant colleges. The act reaffirmed a national commitment to support education by
assigning the proceeds from the sale of lands to support in each state a college designed to promote programs in engineering and agriculture along
with the more traditional studies. The importance of the Morrill Act lies
with the impetus it gave to increased state assistance to higher education.
Public support necessitated greater responsiveness to public needs and
desires expressed through legislative appropriations that accentuated a curriculum geared to "useful" programs in engineering, agriculture, home
economics, veterinary medicine, business administration, and other more
applied areas. Perhaps as significantly, it made going to college an accepted
part of the American middle-class tradition.

However, the popularization of public colleges and universities inevitably meant an enlargement in their supervision on the part of public authorities. One finds this clearly etched in founding statutes. Nearly two-thirds specified educational programs of one type or another. Those for the University of Oregon, for example, required "instruction and complete education in all departments of science, literature, professional pursuits, and general education" and those for Kentucky, for programs in law, medicine, and surgery. Commonly, statutes prohibited political and sectarian tests for admission and "sectarian affiliations or beliefs" as criteria for faculty positions. It was a common practice to include requirements for annual reports to the governor and/or legislature covering financial affairs and internal management. Legislative restrictions upon educational programs, admission policy, and financial affairs were uniformly upheld by courts.

For private institutions, philanthropic support intruded its own type of control, perhaps more subtlely through personal rather than legal pressures, not without parallel to federal funding for students, research, and plant that brought with it policy constraints as effective as legal ones. By the turn of the century, however, courts did impose some limitations upon institutional control over students—for both public and private colleges—on the basis of reasonableness in rules and regulations and due process and proper hearings in suits brought in response to perceived injustices related to admissions and the award of degrees. Although reluctant to intrude judicial judgement in place of that by college faculties and administrators, courts did accede to a limited supervision. However, it does not appear that such appeals to the courts set precedents for the plethora of cases in more recent decades; rather, courts recognized that boards as corporate bodies held ultimate authority for the management of their institutions in the context of what delegations were made to faculties for educational affairs and to administrators.[32]

Thus, by the turn of the twentieth century the concept of higher learning had acquired a broadened context of its role within the general society and an institutional basis for its application to an increasingly wide swath of social activity. That central impulse of the transition from medieval to modern—the progression and extraordinary elaboration of knowledge— had fueled a commitment to greater access to formal education. For relations between higher education and society, it brought with it a combination of increased autonomy within the academic structures at the level of the professoriate in departments and schools and an increase in the basis for governmental control that accompanied the amplification of public support. With reference to the first condition, Walter Metzger has written: "There can be no doubt that secularization, specialization, and the new premium placed upon research improved the status of the profession, both in domestic ranking and on the competitive world exchange."[33] For the second condition, although an active turn toward centralized systems of state colleges and universities did not come into being until more recent decades, precedents had appeared in a half-dozen states prior to our entry into World War I and, certainly, legislators and governors did not hesitate to intrude their desires upon institutions when an occasion arose.

Corporate Basis for Government

The corporate form in the medieval university created an autonomy from local authority within the sovereignty of the papacy that established its right to existence by means of papal bulls or charters. This conception of a corporate association separate from government yet obliged to it for its establishment carried over to the early colleges through precedents associated with the English universities and with English legal custom in general. By the eighteenth century in England the corporation had become an accepted legal conception, a distinctive social unit holding designated rights in law similar to those held by individuals. In this regard, English common law set a pattern for similar arrangements in the colonies and served as a starting point for the development of a more indigenous conceptualization in this country. Colonial leaders used the English tradition of the corporation as a mechanism for conducting certain public services, such as the colleges (and toll roads and bridges, public wharves, canals, parish organizations, towns, etc.), separate from agencies of government. As corporations, the early colleges owed organizational existence to the sovereignty of the state but functioned as relatively autonomous societal agencies. Apparently as a consequence of precedents in Holland and Scotland, although clearly concomitant with the Reformation trinity, corporate authorization went to a board composed of nonacademic members. This arrangement assured control to the religious-political leadership of the early Protestant church-state and, in the course of the nineteenth century, to the succeeding power elites more secular in nature.[34]

The point here is not that the establishment of the nine colonial colleges as chartered corporations provided them with the same kind of institutional autonomy we have known in the present century. Quite the contrary, until the Dartmouth College Case decision of 1819, they were viewed as public institutions subject to direction and even control as appeared necessary from the colonial and state governments. Yet, the corporate form of organization in time did carry with it a degree of autonomy, clearly greater for private institutions, inherent in the delegated control of internal affairs. In the Dartmouth College Case decision the Supreme Court under Chief Justice Marshall defined the College as a private, eleemosynary institution and interpreted its charter as a contract as binding upon the state of New Hampshire as on the trustees, "a contract, the obligation of which cannot be impaired without violating the constitution of the United States." As a consequence the autonomy of private colleges gained a legal barrier to intrusions from governmental sources. It also led to a reexamination of the state-college relationship and to the establishment of public colleges during the expansion of higher education following the Civil War, rather than to the provision of state funding for existing private ones. By the Civil War the practice of establishing colleges through boards of trustees or regents holding corporate powers, although by no means a legal necessity, had fixed a generally observed practice "of delegating immediate responsibility to a special corporation."[35] The state university derived its form of control from precedent in the early colleges through what can be viewed as a public corporation. Thus, even though clearly regarded in the legislatures and courts as agencies of state government, public colleges and universities retained, in most of their features, the corporate structure; their boards controlled internal affairs.

Nevertheless, it must be recognized that during the later decades of the nineteenth century limits upon the authority of public boards, limits that founded precedents for the expansion of supervision and control by state governments in the latter half of this century, did exist. Courts in general, for example, recognized the legal sovereignty of legislatures and governors in ways that deprived boards in the public sector of managerial freedoms enjoyed by their private counterparts. As noted above, this included directions in founding statutes over who was to be admitted and what educational programs were to be offered. Even more significantly, an existence based upon statute could terminate by legislative action, a condition that carried important implications for intrusions into internal affairs by state agencies. The exceptions to this were the eight or nine constitutionally-based universities whose mandate lay with popular referendum, which placed the institution beyond direct legislatural control.[36] Notwithstanding legal limitations occasionally enforced in practice, as Alexander Brody points out in his 1935 survey of the legal basis for public higher education, "even after the universities came to be regarded as agencies of the central government, they were permitted to retain, in most of its features, the corporate structure that they had acquired during their development."[37]

In summary, the reorganization of the colleges into a system of higher education at the close of the nineteenth century brought together two mutually supportive conditions. The ascension of specialized knowledge drew the professoriate back to a commitment to the advancement of learning and, in turn, to a segmentation of institutional organization into separate and frequently inner-directed departments. Expertise and the professional status of academic service placed a premium on self-direction in teaching and, especially, research. The corporate form carried with it the medieval tradition of the university as a place apart, a bastion of learning protected by a delegation of limited sovereignty to carry out a mission for learning. It provided for an institutional autonomy respected in general, if violated from time to time in the specific. By the First World War, higher education had achieved a reasonable, if at times uncertain, balance between intellectual freedom and institutional autonomy *and* accountability for an educational service and accompanying public control. An examination of the elements of this balance provides the focus for a brief concluding discussion.

Twentieth Century

By the first decades of the present century, therefore, the medieval conception of the university as a place apart, a sanctuary for scholars, had a renaissance. Through the corporate form of government derived from its medieval creation, higher institutions secured legal status separate from agencies of state government. Through their acceptance of the extension of secular knowledge and its use in the service of society, the universities, and in turn other institutions, had achieved a status that afforded to the professoriate a professional status that supported their intellectual freedom and control of academic affairs.

As in the case of their medieval precursors, the universities and colleges of this country in the twentieth century did not enjoy total autonomy but functioned within a myriad of societal constraints that accompanied the various forms of support essential to their maintenance. Regents and trustees intruded into internal affairs their own values and priorities, frequently reflective of conservative forces at work within the society. Administrative officers and, indeed, many professors as well adjusted their academic preconceptions to the desires and needs of the marketplace. Although undergirded by traditions associated with private institutions, those in the public sector could hardly ignore the financial and legal sinews that tied them to legislatures and state executives. Freedom and autonomy by their very nature signify relative conditions, and the point here is that, relatively, higher education in this country had acquired an independence in many ways parallel to that of its medieval progenitor as a consequence of parallel functions.

Yet, whether illustrative of some pervasive historical pattern or simply idiosyncratic to the times, social forces have entered into the educational arena in the course of this century to shift the balance away from professorial freedom and institutional autonomy toward accountability to and control by public governments. As the century progresses, one senses that in many ways higher education begins to find itself enmeshed in the Reformation trinity of church, state, and education without the church, an enterprise subject to the determinations of governmental instrumentalities as to what its proper functions should be. In concluding this historical overview, therefore, it makes sense to very briefly identify the forces at work that give weight to both sides of the balance.

On the side of freedom and autonomy, several conditions had continued to weigh the scales and may prove ultimately of sufficient heft to keep higher education as at least a distinctive enterprise worthy of special status. Overall, they associate with the linking during the last century of the colleges with the extension of specialized knowledge and its applications. The higher educational system that ensued served as the institutional instrument to this end, and the graduate school emerged as a fountainhead from which the values associated with specialized knowledge and its extension were dispersed throughout the enterprise. More importantly, the extension of knowledge and derivative applications complemented the requirements of an expanding industrial economic system dependent upon a science-based technology. The resulting professionalization of the professoriate and their segmentation into departments and professional programs brought within their purview, and control, the critical academic decisions having to do with selection and promotion of members and the organization of and criteria for instruction and research. This specialization combined with increasing institutional size and complexity to construct an effective barrier against direct supervision from administrative and external sources. Initially, this concentration fitted with perceptions of board members about their role and limitations upon their supervision. It was bolstered by an influential system of accrediting agencies, both regional and specialized, through which the professoriate has assured the primacy of its judgments regarding the quality of departments and programs, libraries, and instructional and research facilities. Finally, the American Association of University Professors gained strength as as influential advocate for the cause of academic freedom and professorial role in institutional decision making.

However, the professional strength of faculty members during the course of the century came up against contravening forces that have augmented the role of state and federal governments in affairs of higher education. These counterforces rest upon two conditions: the legal bases for the existence of colleges and universities and for an increasing supervision of the society in general; and the power of financial support that flowed increasingly from governmental sources, first through the expansion of state colleges and universities and secondly through federal and, to some extent, state funding of higher education (to students, institutions, and research activities).

There are many specific reasons for intrusions by the public polities into the internal affairs of academe. However, viewed as a whole, they demonstrate that the success of colleges and universities in achieving a significant role in the society has made increasingly clear that they cannot stand apart from the main currents of the society. American higher education during the course of this century has steadily become a critical resource for an increasingly sophisticated and complex culture. It mans the portals to careers in a wide variety of occupations and professions, provides expertise to government and industry as well as other societal entities, and generates knowledge essential for a wide swath of affairs, ranging from personal and social health to the maintenance of the economic system to space exploration. Through the expansion in size and number of its institutions, it has itself become a significant sector in the local, state, and national economy. In an era—most clearly demonstrated in the post-World War II years—during which government has extended its supervision and direction across the entire economic and social spectrum, it could hardly be otherwise than that colleges and universities would find themselves similarly treated.

For the colleges and universities, having no prospect of the security of isolation from the activities of the society—except perhaps for the small church-related colleges—because of the very nature of the services they provide, efforts to maintain a balance between autonomy and control come hard against influences that simply outweigh them. Institutions in their need for research support, physical plan development, and students cannot remain aloof from the federal financial trough. And financial support does not come unencumbered but rather brings with it rules, reports, and sanctions. Although percentages of total state expenditures may not have risen dramatically, the amount of money involved has; and state governments simply have to create budgetary and control systems that provide a proper accounting for the use of public funds. A variety of social improvement programs, primarily at the federal level, have led not only to an aggravation of controls by administrative agencies but have opened the way to referrals to the judiciary in increasing numbers and led to a pattern of decisions that subject institutions to a great deal more legal accountability than possible previously. This latter condition has its affirmation in the emergence in recent years of a new professional area, that of legal counsels for colleges and universities, a professional group with its own national association.

Perhaps the most salient aspect of the changing nature of relations between academe and society is characterized by the title of a paper by Gellhorn and Boyer, "Government and Education: The University as a Regulated Industry." "As the influence of regulatory procedures, programs and techniques spreads throughout higher education," they comment in summary, "there will be fundamental changes not only in the way the university interacts with the outside world but also in the way it governs itself internally."[38] A parallel assertion can be made in respect to financial support. In effect, the balance between autonomy and control, which indeed rested in large part upon the pivot provided by the corporate status of governing boards, tips steadily toward the latter. The prospects of a restoration of the balance are no more promising in the late twentieth century than were those for regaining the independence of the great medieval universities in the sixteenth century as the Reformation swept over northern Europe. Rather, higher education will have to come to terms with government and devise the arrangements and develop the attitudes that at least facilitate a constructive interaction. At best, one suspects that the remaining strength of academic freedom and professional autonomy may shift to disciplinary and professional departments, not unlike the nineteenth-century German universities in which the professors exercised control over academic affairs within the domination of the education ministries.

Notes

1. Majorie Reeves, "The European University from Medieval Times," in *Higher Education: Demand and Response,* W.R. Niblett, ed. (San Francisco: Jossey-Bass, 1970), p. 61.

2. E.D. Duryea, "The Corporate Basis of University and College Government: A Historical Analysis," 1973.

3. A.B. Cobban, *The Medieval Universities* (London: Methuen, 1975), p. 78. The universities of northern Europe of that era, of which that at Paris was preeminent, contrast in many distinctive ways to those that originated in Italy and in general appeared in southern France and in Spain. The former derived from associations of masters, while the latter initially sprang from gatherings of students seeking instruction in civil law and other medieval studies and in time came under the control of the local principalities. Those in Spain were founded by the kings. The influence of the southern university centers seems to have flowed into Spain and Latin America. Certainly, they exercised minimal influence upon the northern nations, such as England, Holland, and Germany, which served as precedents for the college foundings in this country.

4. Hastings Rashdall, *The Universities of Europe in the Middle Ages,* ed. F.M. Powicke and A.B. Emden, 3 vols. (London: Oxford University Press, 1936), 1:3.

5. Jacques Verger, "The University of Paris at the End of the Hundred Years War," in *Universities in Politics,* ed. J.W. Baldwin and R.A. Goldthwaite, (Baltimore, Md.: Johns Hopkins University Press, 1972), p. 48.

6. A.B. Cobban, *The Medieval Universities,* p. 75.

7. Ibid., p. 7.

8. Quoted in John H. Randall, *The Making of the Modern Mind* (New York: Columbia University Press, 1976), p. 94.

9. A.B. Cobban, *Medieval Universities,* p. 8. The decline of the medieval university intertwined intimately with the decline of the Roman Church that interfaced with the emergence of industry and commerce and of the rise to importance of economic interests. Even in the thirteenth century secular rulers—the Holy Roman Emperor and the kings— also participated in the founding of universities by secular decrees and acts. But throughout the thirteenth and fourteenth centuries secular or national kings slowly gained preeminence and power as the Church floundered increasingly in the problems associated with its loss of temporal power and with internal corruption. The Great Schism of 1378 to 1447, during which two popes competed for control, marked the end of the Church's domination of Europe and the shift of European power to national kings. An interesting footnote to this era was the influential role played by the doctors of the University of Paris in the final solution to the papal conflict. But this also marked the end of the University's preeminence in European affairs.

10. It should be noted that in addition to the value for vocational ends, the arts or lower faculty of the study of the medieval university did require a learning common to all students that contained "certain forms of knowledge which...all educated people ought to have, together with the basic skills necessary to the arts of communication." In doing so, the medieval institutions established the concept of an educated person that has persisted in Anglo-United States culture. Marjorie Reeves, "European University from Medieval Times, " p. 64.

11. Anton-Hermann Chroust, "The Corporate Idea and the Body Politic in the Middle Ages," *The Review of Politics* (1947), p. 423.

12. John H. Randall, *Making of the Modern Mind,* pp. 111, 143.

13. Preserved Smith, *A History of Modern Culture,* 2 vols. (Gloucester, Mass.: Peter Smith, 1957), 1:357.

14. Francis Bacon and his concept of the inductive method, deriving axioms from observations; Kepler and Galileo in astronomy; Descartes' rational philosophy; Pascal's studies of the atmosphere; the investigations of Boyle into combustion and the atmosphere, leading to the mathematically-based synthesis of Newton; and Newton himself, as the creator of a system of physics that lasted as the conception of reality until the end of the nineteenth century—examples of the pioneering scientists who set the foundation for modern thought.

15. Preserved Smith, *History of Modern Culture*, 1:343.

16. Fritz Caspari, *Humanism and the Social Order of Tudor England* (New York: Teachers College Press, 1968), pp. 256, 279.

17. John H. Randall, *Making of the Modern Mind*, p. 52.

18. Jurgen Herbst, "The First Three American Colleges: Schools of the Reformation," *Perspectives in American History* 8 (1972), p. 19.

19. Freidrich Paulsen, *German Education Past and Present* (London: T. Fisher Unwin, 1908), p. 90.

20. Christopher Hill, "The Radical Critics of Oxford and Cambridge in the 1650s," in *Universities in Politics*, p. 112.

21. Frederick Rudolph, *The American College and University* (New York: Alfred A. Knopf, 1962), p. 26.

22. Jurgen Herbst, "First Three American Colleges," pp. 14-17.

23. Richard M. Weaver, *Ideas Have Consequences* (Chicago: University of Chicago Press, 1948), p. 3.

24. Peter Gay, *The Enlightenment* (New York: Vintage Books, 1966), p. 3.

25. Preserved Smith, *History of Modern Culture*, 2:20.

26. Merle Curti, "The Great Mr. Locke: America's Philosopher, 1783-1861," *Huntington Library Bulletin* 11 (April 1937), p. 114.

27. Joseph Ben-David, "The Profession of Science and its Power," *Minerva* 10 (July 1972) p. 369.

28. Ibid., p. 370.

29. A. Lawrence Lowell, "Faculty and Governing Boards," *School and Society* 13 (February 19, 1921), pp. 236-7.

30. Committee T, "Place and Function of Faculties in University Government," *AAUP Bulletin* 10 (May 1924), pp. 27-8.

31. John K. Galbraith, *The New Industrial State* (Boston: New American Library, 1967) p. 377-8.

32. This discussion of statutes and the courts derives from a study under way by the author examing the corporate authority of governing boards from 1870 to 1910.

33. Walter P. Metzger, "Origins of the Association," *AAUP Bulletin* 55 (Summer 1965), p. 230.

34. The English pattern of awarding corporate authority to academics did influence the original arrangements at Harvard and William and Mary, however. But neither college set the precedent for those that followed; that fell to Yale, which was formed with a single board of nonacademic members. Both Harvard and William and Mary subsequently shifted control to nonacademic boards.

35. Alexander Brody, *The American State and Higher Education* (Washington, D.C.: American Council on Education, 1935), p. 112.

36. Other exceptions to this situation existed for normal schools and state teachers' colleges established by or under departments of education. The idea of constitutional authorization for a college or university appeared first in Michigan in 1850 when the University was placed under a Board of Regents elected on the basis of judicial circuits. In all, "twenty-seven of the states make explicit reference to higher education in their constitutions. The remainder of the states, through exercise of policy powers have legislative provision for higher education" (Kern Alexander and E.S. Soloman, *College and University Law* [Charlottesville, Va.: The Michie Company, 1972], p. 26). Of the states with constitutional provisions, according to Alexander and Soloman, at least nine guarantee constitutional autonomy for universities: Michigan, Minnesota, California, Colorado, Georgia, Idaho, Oklahoma, Nevada, and Arizona.

37. Brody, *American State and Higher Education*, p. 115.

38. Gellhorn, Ernest and Barry B. Boyer, "Government and Education: The University as a Regulated Industry," *Arizona State Law Journal* (1977), p. 593.

3

Autonomy and Accountability: Some Fundamental Issues
T.R. McConnell

In characterizing their so-called binary system of higher education, the British have ordinarily referred to the universities as the "autonomous" sector and the polytechnics, together with certain other institutions of advanced further education, as the "public" sector. It is true that the British universities have had a long and distinctive history of relative independence. Yet, as they have become more and more dependent on government funds —now reaching something like 90 percent of their financial support—they have become increasingly subject to external guidance from the University Grants Committee, and through the UGC from the government itself. The public sector is more directly controlled and financed by the Department of Education and Science at the top and locally by the education authorities and is subject to much more external control than the universities.

Autonomy and Academic Freedom

Autonomy not absolute

The British universities have come to recognize that autonomy cannot be complete or absolute. A scholar and administrator in British higher education, who served as vice chancellor of one of the newer technological universities, put the issue as follows:

> Absolute autonomy is of course impossible: a network of relationships with both national and local Government to determine how the needs of society and individual citizens should be met is inescapable. There can be no formal set of answers, only an ever-changing balance of interests within which the maximum degrees of freedom must be strenuously maintained.[1]

If a college or university is effectively to define its goals and select or invent the means of attaining them, it must have a high degree of independence. Bowen has observed that the "production process" in higher education is far more intricate and complicated than that in any industrial enterprise.[2] Turning resources into human values defies standardization. Students vary enormously in academic aptitude, in interests, in intellectual dispositions, in social and cultural characteristics, in educational and vocational objectives, and in many other ways. Furthermore, the disciplines and professions with which institutions of higher learning are concerned require different methods of investigation, diverse intellectual structures, different means of relating methods of inquiry and ideas to personal and social values, and variable processes of relating knowledge to human experience. Learning, consequently, is a subtle process, the nature of which may vary from student to student, from institution to institution, from discipline to discipline, from one scholar and/or teacher to another, and from one level of student development to another. The intricacy and unpredictability of both learning and investigation are factors that require a high degree of freedom from intellectually limiting external intervention and control if an institution of higher education is to perform effectively.

On first thought one might identify academic freedom with autonomy. Certainly a high degree of intellectual independence is necessary for faculty and students in choosing the subjects of study and investigation, searching for the truth without unreasonable or arbitrary restrictions, and expressing their scholarly conclusions without censorship. Some forms of external control or even some kinds of subtle efforts to influence teaching, learning, or research may endanger intellectual freedom. However, Berdahl has pointed out that "academic freedom and university autonomy, though related, are not synonymous...academic freedom as a concept is universal and absolute, whereas autonomy is of necessity parochial and relative."[3] Berdahl was writing about the statewide coordination of higher education through such agencies as state coordinating boards and consolidated or system-wide (such as the University of California Board of Regents) governing boards. Presumably designating the missions of sectors or particular institutions after appropriate studies and consultation would not be an unwarranted invasion of autonomy by such boards. Specifying the academic programs, academic organization, curriculum, and methods of teaching for the attainment of designated missions is likely to be considered an unjustified form of intervention. A coordinating or governing board might phase out a doctoral program at a particular campus (after appropriate study and consultation) without unwarranted invasion of institutional autonomy or violation of academic freedom. The federal government might impose antidiscrimination procedures in admitting students, or appointing and promoting faculty members, without interfering unjustifiably in academic affairs provided the means do not make unreasonable demands on the institutions or violate necessary confidentiality of records. If appropriate safeguards are followed, no invasion of academic freedom need be suffered.

Requirements for accountability may impose onerous procedures on an institution, e.g., accounting for the use of research grants (as noted later in this chapter), but even these restraints may not endanger academic freedom. Whether restrictions on DNA research, referred to below, put an undesirable limit on choice of problems for investigation remains to be seen. In this case public protection may justify what seems to be an infringement on academic freedom.

In any event, Dressel, in a recent analysis of the autonomy of public institutions, came to the following conclusion: "Academic freedom is not ensured by institutional autonomy, and recent restrictions of institutional autonomy have had relatively little effect on academic freedom."[4]

One may agree that the absence of external controls does not guarantee academic freedom, and that certain elements of external control do not endanger intellectual independence. But an institution's right to mobilize its intellectual resources—and, within reasonable limits, even its financial resources—toward the attainment of its agreed-upon purposes is at least strongly fortified by a relatively high degree of autonomy.

Nature of Accountability

As this is being written, intellectual freedom in colleges and universities is not under special threat, but autonomy is being steadily eroded. Financial austerity causes legislatures, statewide coordinating boards, and even consolidated governing boards to look more critically at institutional roles, at the availability and distribution of functions and programs, at effectiveness, and at educational and operational costs. As the federal government extends support for higher education it prohibits discrimination in the admission of students and in the appointment and promotion of faculty members. This is an example of the fact that the public at large is becoming more conscious of its institutions of higher education. States and localities are more demanding of education and service, more critical of what they perceive institutions to be doing, more vocal in expressing their criticisms and desires. Public institutions, always answerable to the general interest, will no longer be excused from defending what they do or don't do. No longer can a university shunt public criticism aside as a mere expression of intellectual shallowness. It will increasingly have to explain itself, defend its essential character, and demonstrate that its service is worth the cost. It will become increasingly answerable, i.e., accountable, to its numerous constituencies for the range of its services and the effectiveness of its performance. "The extension of substantive autonomy to an individual, organization, or group implies responsibility and accountability," Dressel wrote recently.[5] He went on to outline the elements of accountability as follows:

> Responsible performance, then, involves using allocated resources legally and wisely to attain those purposes for which they were made available. Responsible performance requires continuing accumulation of evidence of the extent to which purposes are achieved; reviewing the evaluation evidence to clarify the avowed goals and their interpretation; consideration of the relevance, effectiveness, and costs of the processes used to achieve the goals; and continuing effort directed at improving the educational processes used or finding more effective processes.[6]

Relationships between the federal government and research universities have recently become strained as the former has attempted to impose techniques of accountability for federal research grants that the institutions have considered unreasonable, onerous, and unnecessarily expensive. In 1978 the National Commission on Research was organized for the purpose of proposing means of resolving the differences between the two parties. The Commission recognized three forms of accountability: financial and administrative, involving evidence of financial propriety and compliance with administrative regulations; scientific, concerned with achievement of results and progress toward scientific objectives; and social, referring to the extent to which specific social goals have been fulfilled. The Commission concluded that "When well designed, the system of accountability involves an appropriate balance between independence and control, between incentives and constraints, and between the costs and benefits of the various procedures and requirements used."[7]

Accountability and intervention

Accountability is not confined to an institution's external relationships. Internally, a college or university is a complex of mutual responsibilities and reciprocal pressures for accountability. Important as these bases of accountability are, this chapter will be devoted to a discussion of accountability to external agencies. External accountability often emanates from external intervention, but intervention often goes well beyond reasonable requirements for accountability. In any event, intervention and accountability should be discussed together. The first subject is higher education's accountability to the public interest.

Accountability to the public

Ultimately, public institutions of higher education are broadly answerable to the people who support them. After California voters had failed to approve a state bond issued providing large sums for the construction of medical school facilities and had given other evidences of disaffection, the president of the University of California recognized the ultimate public accountability of the University when he said to the Assembly of the Academic Senate:

> Make no mistake, the university is a public institution, supported by the people through the actions of their elected representatives and executives. They will not allow it to be operated in ways which are excessively at variance with the general public will. By various pressures and devices the university will be forced to yield and to conform if it gets too far away from what the public expects and wants.[8]

At one time the people were relatively remote from their public institutions, but citizens now find their future economic, social, and cultural life increasingly influenced, in some cases virtually determined, by their colleges and universities. Consequently, the public university has had to become responsive to a wider range of economic interests and to a more diverse pattern of ethnic and cultural backgrounds and aspirations. Minority groups are pressing for financial assistance, for remedial programs when necessary for admission or attainment of academic standards, and for academic programs that will meet their interests and perceived needs. As special interest groups have pressed the university to provide the services they believe they need, students have organized to promote their interests. With the prospect of declining enrollments, many colleges and universities have responded to the student market by establishing new vocational and professional programs of study, and most institutions are struggling to redistribute faculty, equipment, and resources as students shift from liberal arts courses to vocational and professional curricula. This trend has been especially observable in the community colleges, and the effect will change the pattern of enrollment in four-year institutions to which community college graduates have transferred in large numbers in the past.

Serving the public interest has become a complicated process; not all institutions will undertake the same missions or serve common purposes. Accountability is still further complicated by a question of what special interests should be served and what should be put aside. Only when an institution's goals are defined, the groups to be served are identified, and the relevant programs of teaching, research, and public service are determined can an institution's effectiveness be estimated. Thus, accountability is both general—to the broad public interest—and particular—to more limited constituencies.

Accountability to the public is mediated by operation of several layers of representation between it and the institutions in question. Colleges and universities are answerable immediately to their governing boards. Most boards have statutory status. They were created by legislatures and are in nearly all respects under legislative control. Seven or eight states have given constitutional status to their public universities. This unusual situation has been characterized as follows:

> The idea was to remove questions of management, control, and the supervision of the universities from the reach of politicians in state legislatures and governors' offices. The universities were to be a fourth branch of government, functioning co-authoritatively with the legislature, the judiciary, and the executive.[9]

The purpose in creating their constitutional position was to give the universities a much greater degree of autonomy and self-direction than statutory status would provide. Their autonomy, however, has been materially eroded over the years. A study of statutory and constitutional boards showed that the supposedly constitutionally autonomous university "is losing a good deal of its ability to exercise final judgment on the use not only of its state funds but also of those derived from other sources. It now undergoes intensive reviews of budgets and programs by several different state agencies, by special commissions, and by legislative committees, all of which look for ways to control."[10]

Government Interference

State government intervention

Whether an institution has statutory or constitutional status, or even whether it is public or private, it is moving into the governmental orbit. As Clark put it: "In the changing relation between higher education and government, higher education...moves inside government, becomes a constituent part of government, a bureau within public administration.[11]

Most students of university governance believe that government officials should not serve on governing boards, since this identifies the institution too closely with political and governmental agencies. In California the governor, the lieutenant governor, the superintendent of public instruction, the president of the state board of agriculture, and the speaker of the legislative assembly are among the ex officio voting members of the Board of Regents of the University of California. A governor may also use his appointive power in attempting to influence governing boards. For example, it was charged recently that in appointing four new Regents, Governor Jerry Brown of California chose persons who would follow his opposition to the University's connection with the Livermore (California) and Los Alamos (New Mexico) atomic weapons laboratories. Whether that was true or not, the Regents voted to renew management contracts with the Department of Energy. Governor Brown's outspoken and blunt opposition to the weapons laboratories evoked critical comment, an example of which is the following excerpt from the editorial page of the *San Francisco Chronicle:*

> Throughout his time in office, the Governor has shown contempt for the University and for what it represents....As a veteran observer of the Regents says, "He's there on his own issues, investment in South Africa, farm mechanization or nuclear politics, the topics he feels appeal to his followers."[12]

The new members of the Board of Regents whom Governor Brown appointed may prove to be open-minded and judicious in their attitudes and votes on University matters. In any event, it would seem more appropriate for a governor to appoint to a university governing board persons who investigate issues thoroughly, consider the interests of the institution and the public open-mindedly and objectively, and vote independently of political figures and political biases.

Although he may influence institutions via their governing boards, it is "...through the executive budget process that the governor makes his impact and gives significant leadership on major issues of higher education policy."[13] The state finance or budget officer, who is ordinarily responsible to the governor, may also exercise an important element of authority by controlling shifts or changes in line-item budgets. Some state finance departments conduct pre-audits of expenditures that not only pass on the legality of the use of itemized funds, but give the state officer the opportunity to rule on the substance or purpose of the expenditures. In recent times the long arms of state finance officers have reached into academic affairs by conducting program audits or even program evaluations.[14] The question of external program audits will be discussed at a later point.

Important as the understanding and support of executive officers of state government may be, public colleges and universities are even more directly answerable to the legislature. The institutions are dependent on legislative understanding of their broad missions and programs, the legislature's financial support, and the lawmakers' judgment of the institutions' educational effectiveness.

As noted above, even a constitutionally autonomous public university is ultimately accountable to the legislature for the ways in which it uses its state-appropriated funds and for the effectiveness of its educational services. For some years certain leaders in the state legislature have criticized the

University of California for neglecting undergraduate education. One of the persistent critics has been the chairman of the powerful Assembly post-secondary education committee. The University's legislative critics were recently given more ammunition by studies that revealed that Berkeley campus faculty members were devoting less time to teaching and other contacts with students. A new chancellor who took office in 1980 at Berkeley responded to legislative criticism by appointing a vice chancellor for undergraduate education. The president of the University called on the faculties of all the campuses to increase their teaching loads and to spend more time with students. The actions of the president and the Berkeley chancellor were open recognition that the University is accountable to the legislature and the people of the state.

Program auditing

State agencies including legislatures have begun to move into program evaluation. Dressel has outlined what is involved in program auditing:

> Issues raised in program evaluation include the consistency of the program with the assigned institutional role and function; the adequacy of planning in regard to the objectives, program structure, processes, implementation, and evaluation of outcomes; the adherence of program operation to the objectives, structural features, processes, sequence, and outcome appraisal originally specified or the presentation of a sound rationale for any deviations from the original prescription, an evaluation of planning and operation and use of feedback for alteration and improvement, and provision for cost benefit analyses.[15]

After investigating legislatively-mandated program evaluations in Wisconsin and Virginia, Berdahl declared that "Academic programs, quality considerations, course content, faculty evaluation—these had always been considered too close to the heart of academe to be subjected to normal state accountability measures."[16] Berdahl warned that if institutions, systems, or statewide coordinating boards, in company with colleges and universities under their surveillance, do not keep their academic programs under periodic appraisal, external agencies will take over this function.[17]

Federal intervention

With increasing federal financial support and numerous federal laws and regulations governing use of the funds, both public and private educational institutions find themselves increasingly accountable to agencies of the federal government. Total federal support recently reached about 15 billion dollars awarded and controlled by a variety of governmental bureaus. It was inevitable—and appropriate—that higher institutions should be held accountable for the way in which they expand these funds. However, tension between universities and federal granting agencies has steadily increased as the institutions have been subjected to regulations and accounting procedures they consider unnecessarily extensive, expensive, and often inappropriate.

One of the major causes of strain between the federal government and the universities is the failure of government agencies to recognize, in the words of the report of the National Commission on Research, that "Universities carry out teaching, research, and service as an integrated whole, not as separate functions." The Commission went on to say that since teaching, research, and perhaps public service are closely related, accurate costs cannot be assessed to each of the related outcomes.[18] Nevertheless, the Commission recognized the necessity for accountability. What is needed, said the Commission, is a joint effort between research universities and government bureaus to devise methods of accountability that recognize the peculiar characteristics of the academic enterprise.

A clash of interests between the federal government and higher education characterizes a dispute over federal investigators' right, not only to inspect, but also to remove confidential personnel files from the Berkeley campus of the University of California in determining the University's compliance with federal antidiscrimination laws. The University was afraid that if the files were permanently maintained in federal offices they might be subject to access by other parties for other purposes under the public information provision and so lose their confidentiality. Nevertheless, a Labor Department official threatened that if the University did not comply with the Department's insistence on removing the files, the Secretary of Labor would cancel immediately about 25 million dollars in contract funds and ultimately cut off a total of 75 million dollars that the Berkeley campus received in federal aid.

Just before the deadline the University and the Department of Labor came to an agreement that although files might be removed, they would be returned to the University upon the conclusion of the federal government's investigation for compliance review.[19]

One of the most recent examples of the federal government's demand for accountability is its regulation of DNA research. After an international group of 150 scientists met to discuss how DNA research should be conducted, the National Institutes of Health appointed a committee that promulgated regulations governing the safety of recombinant DNA research done with NIH funds. It was not long until a university faculty member experienced first hand the new strictures on DNA investigation. A bio-safety committee of the University of California at San Diego forbade a faculty

---

*The NIH Committee found the faculty member guilty of violating the federal guidelines. (Daily Californian, March 26, 1981.)

member in biology to conduct any more cloning experiments after it was charged that he copied genetic material from a virus then banned from use in such investigations. The University's bio-safety committee reported its action to the National Institutes of Health and the NIH said that it would form a committee to study the University's report and consider what action it might take against the University or the professor.[20]*

It would be an exaggeration to say that research universities have become departments of federal and state government, but it is not too much to say that they have become more directly accountable to government agencies in manifold ways and that it has become difficult to distinguish governmental *intervention in university* affairs from reasonable governmental requirements for accountability. It is clear, however, that recent issues and events have accelerated invasions of university autonomy. Senator Moynihan has gone so far as to say that "universities must now expect a long, for practical purposes permanent, regimen of pressure from the federal government to pursue this or that national purpose, purposes often at variance with the interests or inclinations of the universities themselves."[21]

As this was written the U.S. Supreme Court agreed to decide whether the federal government has the legal authority to cut off funds to colleges and universities that do not conform with Title IX of the Education Amendments of 1972 (in this case equal pay requirements for both sexes). What changes, if any, in federal government-university relations may occur during the Reagan presidency cannot be predicted at this writing. It will be interesting to see whether intervention and control will be reduced.

Governmental accountability of private institutions

Although governmental intervention, regulation, and incipient control of certain activities may threaten public more than private institutions of higher education, the latter are increasingly held accountable by governmental agencies. Private research universities, as are publicly supported ones, are accountable for the way in which they use federal grants. Furthermore, private institutions are required to comply with other federal regulations, such as those prohibiting discrimination in employment.[22] The Carnegie Council on Policy Studies in Higher Education recommended that "Financial aid to students should be the primary (though not necessarily the exclusive) vehicle for the channeling of state funds to private institutions."[23] Some state governments, however, do make direct grants to private colleges and universities. An Illinois commission recommended that as a means of avoiding government intervention in private higher institutions, direct state grants should be channeled to them in the form of contracts administered by the statewide coordinating board.[24]

Judicial Intervention

Recourse to the courts

Increasingly intimate relationships between government and higher education mean that colleges and universities are in and of the world, not removed and protected from it. Toward the end of the period of student
disruption on college campuses this writer observed:

> Judicial decisions and the presence on campus of the community police, the
> highway patrol, and the National Guard symbolize the fact that colleges and
> universities have increasingly lost the privilege of self-regulation to the external
> authority of the police and the courts....it is apparent that colleges and univer-
> sities have become increasingly accountable to the judicial systems of the com-
> munity, the state, and the national government.[25]

A recent book on higher education and the law summarized legal conditions
bearing on higher institutions and gave numerous examples of court decisions involving trustees, administrators, faculty members, and students, as
well as cases involving relationships between institutions and both state and
federal governments. Recourse to the courts to settle disputes has increased
greatly during the past decade. Faculty members may sue over dismissal,
appointment, tenure, and accessibility to personnel records. Students may
sue to secure access to their records, over discrimination in admissions (e.g.,
the DeFunis case at the University of Washington and the Bakke case at the
University of California in Davis), and over failure by an institution to
deliver what it promised from the classroom and other academic resources.
Institutions may take governments to court for the purpose of protecting
their constitutional status and as we have illustrated above, in contention
over the enforcement of federal regulations.

The traditional aloofness of the campus has been shattered. Kaplin has
pointed out the "Higher Education was often viewed as a unique enterprise
which could regulate itself through reliance on tradition and consensual
agreement. It operated best by operating autonomously, and it thrived on
the privacy which autonomy afforded."[26] The college or university sanctuary was once considered to be a necessary means of protecting the institution and its constituencies from repressive external control and from invasions of intellectual freedom. Now other means must be devised to protect
an institution's essential spirit while it bows to the world of law and
tribunal.

Accountability to Other Agencies

Accountability to coordinating boards

Financial austerity, the need to diversify opportunities for higher education, governmental demands for accountability, and other influences have pushed decision making upward in the authority structure both internally and externally. In the course of this development, statewide governing and coordinating boards have come to play an influential, often critical, role in the evolution of higher education.

Three broad kinds of agencies have been organized for statewide or systemwide planning and coordination. These are (1) the advisory coordinating board, (2) the regulatory coordinating board, and (3) the consolidated governing board. In 1979 there were ten advisory boards, eighteen regulatory boards, and twenty consolidated governing boards.[27] Consolidated governing boards are powerful bodies. Regulatory coordinating boards, with which we are mainly concerned here, have also become influential agencies. Where does the coordinating board fall between institutions or systems and the state government? Millett, who once served as chancellor of the Ohio Board of Regents, a statewide coordinating board, believes that such an agency is a part of state government and as such "will inevitably be identified primarily with state government officials and processes," while the consolidated governing board is identified with state institutions of higher education.[28]

Another view of the status and function of statewide coordinating boards is that they should not be "identified primarily with state government officials and processes," as Millett asserts,[29] but that they should be "suspended at a strategic—and extremely sensitive—point between the institutions and sectors, on the one hand, and the public and its political representatives, on the other." The function of coordinating boards as intermediaries has been expressed as follows:

> Coordinating agencies have the responsibility of helping protect institutions (and sectors) from ill-advised influences and incursions by the legislative and executive branches of government and from unwise public pressures, and the responsibility of leading the system of higher education to serve demonstrable and appropriate public needs—all the while retaining the confidence of both sides.[30]

This view brings the nature of the coordinating board more nearly to that of the consolidated governing board, although the latter will in most cases be more intimately identified with the institutions. The primary function of coordinating boards is to plan the development of higher education in their states in cooperation with institutions of postsecondary education and their basic constituencies. Then, according to Glenny, the board should provide a thorough analysis and evaluation of systemwide or statewide academic programs in relation to long-range strategy. Proposed budgets should be appraised in relation to educational priorities, differential institutional functions, and relevant allocation of financial resources.[31] Thus the boards may exert their influence and authority by holding institutions or systems accountable for the effective performance of the functions for which they have accepted responsibility. Dressel has declared that coordination is here to stay and that it will continue to confront institutions of higher education with issues of autonomy and sometimes debatable requirements for accountability.[32]

Accountability to accrediting agencies

Accreditation is a process for holding postsecondary institutions accountable to voluntary agencies for meeting certain minimum educational standards. Recently, however, both federal and state governments have entered this arena too.

Institutional and program accreditation are the two types usually noted. Six regional agencies are responsible for accrediting entire institutions with their schools, departments, academic programs, and related activities. Program accreditation, extended by professional societies or other groups of specialists or vocational associations, is extended to a specific school, department, or academic program in such fields as medicine, law, social work, chemistry, engineering, or business administration. A variation is an agency for accrediting single-purpose institutions, such as trade and technical schools. These kinds of accrediting bodies are independent, voluntary agencies. A recent list includes nearly seventy such accrediting bodies.[33]

Two of the principal factors that have brought accreditation to the fore in discussions of accountability are the consumer movement and the allocation of state and federal aid to postsecondary education. Certain federal laws require the secretary of education to publish a list of nationally recognized agencies considered to be "reliable" evaluators of academic quality as a basis for distributing federal aid. An account of the federal government's attitude toward voluntary accrediting bodies recently noted that the head of the Division of Eligibility and Agency Evaluation of the U.S. Department of Education had urged that federal oversight of accreditation should be strengthened. "Stressing the need for greater public accountability," said the report, "he and his supporters say it is more important than ever for the government to know how its money is being spent, especially in light of some institutions' widely reported abuses in handling student-aid funds."[34] Representatives of higher education, on the other hand, have urged that instead of using its own criteria for identifying acceptable accrediting agencies, the federal bureau should use those proposed by the Council on Postsecondary Accreditation, an organization of voluntary accrediting agencies.

In the meantime, state governments have become parties to the debate as they determine eligibility for state aid to both public and private post-secondary institutions. Most states charter and license degree-granting institutions, but some observers believe that in most instances the standards specified are insufficient to assure quality. At its annual meeting in 1979 the Education Commission of the States declared that the states should establish minimum quality standards for all postsecondary institutions.

Accountability for Student Development

A complicated process

It is apparent that educational institutions are increasingly to be held answerable for the attainment of their professed goals in the form of demonstrable changes in students. Bowen had declared that "The idea of accountability in higher education is quite simple. It means that colleges and universities are responsible for conducting their affairs so that the outcomes are worth the cost."[35] This view may be simple in conception, but it is also extremely difficult in implementation. First of all, it is difficult but essential to translate goals into relevant outcomes. An even more complicated task is to devise means of determining the extent to which students have attained these outcomes. The first question to be asked is, how has the student changed at a given point in relation to his characteristics at entrance? This requires information on how students vary at the starting point, not only in previous academic achievement, but in general and special academic aptitude; intellectual dispositions, such as a theoretical or pragmatic orientation: and interests, attitudes, values, and motivations, to mention only some of the dimensions of personality that are relevant to the educational process. These attributes not only establish base lines for estimating the amount of change over stated periods, but some of them are indicative of students' educability.

Studies of the influence of institutions on student development also require means of measuring or describing college characteristics, "the prevailing atmosphere, the social and intellectual climate, the style of a campus," as well as "educational treatments."[36] One of the complications involved in describing college environments is that student characteristics and institutional qualities are by no means unrelated. Student attributes are significant determinations of institutional character. Furthermore, most institutions are not all of a piece and the "total environment" may have less influence on particular students than the suborganizations or subcultures of which they are members.

It is even more difficult to determine the impact of the environment on students. I have mentioned some of the difficulties elsewhere:

First, environmental variables probably do not act singly, but in combination. Second, changes which occur in students may not be attributable to the effect of the college environment itself. Developmental processes established early in the individual's experience may continue through the college years; some of these processes take place normally within a wide range of environmental conditions, and in order to alter the course and extent of development, it would be necessary to introduce fairly great changes in environmental stimulation. Third, changes which occur during the college years may be less the effect of college experience as such than of the general social environment in which the college exists and the students live.[37]

For these and many other reasons it is extremely difficult to relate changes in behavior to specific characteristics of the college or to particular patterns of educational activity.

Studies of change in students' characteristics have revealed wide differences from person to person and detectable differences from institution to institution. One example, an investigation of changes in intellectual orientation, has been summarized as follows:

An index of intellectual disposition was constructed from the following tests of the Omnibus Personality Inventory: thinking introversion, theoretical orientation, estheticism, complexity, autonomy, and religious liberalism. Students' scores on the index were distributed among eight categories. At one extreme (categories 1-3) were students with broad intellectual and esthetic interests, openness to new ideas, intellectual independence, and sufficient freedom from traditional patterns of thought to permit imaginative and creative responses. Students at the opposite extreme (categories 6-8) had little interest in ideas, were more concerned with the concrete and practical than the general and abstract, were relatively more conventional and less flexible in their thinking, and had few if any artistic interests. We studied differential change in intellectual disposition in eight institutions that embraced a wide range of both student and institutional characteristics. Three colleges—Antioch Reed, and Swarthmore—were highly selective, small, residential, elite institutions. Three church-related institutions—St. Olaf, the University of the Pacific, and the University of Portland—were in the sample....St. Olaf and the University of Portland had relatively close connections with their sponsoring denominations. The sample was rounded out by two large public institutions, San Francisco State and the University of California at Berkeley.

With the exceptions of Reed (where the proportion of freshmen in the three top categories was so large that little change was possible) and the University of Portland, there were higher proportions of seniors than freshmen in the highest three categories at all institutions. Thus, one could conclude that the world of ideas was more appealing to seniors than to freshmen....Twenty-four percen. of Swarthmore students (the largest proportion among the eight in-

stitutions) shifted from categories 6-8 to categories 1-3. The colleges with the
next largest proportions were Antioch and St. Olaf (8 percent). The percentage
change at Reed was zero, but there were only nine students in the three bottom
categories as freshmen. Of the seventy-six students who could have changed at
the University of Portland, only 1 percent did so.[38]

Bowen has summarized the evidence on changes in students in both
cognitive and noncognitive outcomes, and also differences in the effects of
different institutions. "On the whole," he wrote, "the evidence supports
the hypothesis that the differences in impact are relatively small—when impact is defined as value added in the form of change in students during the
college years."[39] Nevertheless, institutions are accountable for stimulating
the development of students in ways which give evidence that colleges and
universities have attained their professed goals in reasonable measure.

To date, the research on changes in students has been done mainly in
undergraduate education. Fundamental studies on the attainment of outcomes also need to be made in professional and graduate education, as well
as in research and public service. Bowen has discussed at some length the
social benefits that flow from professional training and the social outcomes
from research and public service. He also has emphasized the interaction of
liberal and professional studies, and the contribution of research and public
service to education of various kinds and levels. Learning is an integrated
process which may involve scholarship, investigation, and the relationship
of knowledge to personal enrichment and social welfare.[40] Although the
definition and measurement of outcomes are especially difficult at higher
educational levels and the environmental forces involved are hard to determine, studies of student development in such fields as professional training,
graduate education, and research should be pursued.

Educational costs

After summarizing the available evidence on the outcomes of higher education, Bowen observed that "a tidy dollar comparison of costs and benefits is
conspicuously absent." However, he summarized the financial value of
higher education as follows:

> First, the monetary returns from higher education alone are probably suffi-
> cient to offset all the costs. Second, the nonmonetary returns are several times
> as valuable as the monetary returns. And third, the total returns from higher
> education in all its aspects exceed the cost by several times.[41]

It is usually said that institutions should be accountable for both effectiveness and efficiency, the latter having to do with the cost of the outcomes
attained. But costs arc extremely difficult to compute in analyzing differences in student change both within and among institutions And, as

pointed out above, it is extremely difficult to relate changes to significant features of educational environments. Nevertheless, as enrollments in postsecondary education level off or decline, institutions will be increasingly held accountable for the attainment of goals inherent in their assigned or professed missions. "Accountability accentuates results," wrote Mortimer, "it aims squarely at what comes out of an educational system rather than what goes into it."[42] Perhaps it would be more telling to say that accountability aims squarely at what comes out of an educational system *in relation to what goes into it.* The outcomes to be attained must be more explicitly defined and the means of determining accomplishment must be more expertly devised. Then resources must be distributed among institutions and among academic services in accordance with chosen educational values and defensible costs of their attainment. Bowen has made a significant contribution to the analysis of institutional costs including expenditures per student, cost differences among institutions, and the implications of cost data for administrative policies and decisions.[43] But we have a long way to go before sound means of determining cost-effectiveness are developed.

Summary

Although autonomy cannot be absolute, only a high degree of independence will permit colleges and universities to devise and choose effective academic means of realizing their professed goals. First of all, institutions must assure academic freedom to faculty and students. Autonomy does not guarantee intellectual independence, but some forms of external intervention, overt or covert, may undermine such freedom.

While intellectual fetters must be decisively opposed, institutions may legitimately be expected to be held accountable to their constituencies for the integrity, and so far as possible, for the efficiency of their operations. Colleges and universities are answerable to the general public, which supports them and needs their services. Responding to the public interest, federal and state governments are increasingly intervening in institutional affairs. At times government pressure may induce an institution to offer appropriate services; at other times government agencies may attempt to turn an institution, or even a system, in inappropriate directions. Only constructive consultation, and requirements for accountability that recognize the fundamental characteristics of academe will effectively serve the public interest and give vitality to the educational enterprise.

Most institutions, including those supported by legislatures, are not immediately controlled by the general public. Public accountability is mediated by several layers of representation. Institutions are directly answerable to their governing boards. They may be responsible to a consolidated governing board. They may be first responsible to institutional or systemwide governing boards, and these in turn may be in certain regards under surveillance of statewide coordinating boards. Institutions thus may be controlled by a hierarchy of agencies, an arrangement that may complicate their procedures for accountability, but provide a measure of protection from unwise or unnecessary external intervention.

Colleges and universities are moving into a period when they will be expected to provide, not only data on the attainment of defined outcomes, including changes in students during undergraduate, graduate, and professional education, but evidence that results have been gained at "reasonable" cost. Institutions of higher education will have to specify their aims, stand ready to justify activities by demonstrating their contribution to objectives, and defend the cost of the enterprise.

Notes

1. Peter Venables, *Higher Education Developments: The Technological Universities 1956-1976* (London: Faber and Faber, 1978), p. 305.

2. Howard R. Bowen, *Investment in Learning* (San Francisco: Jossey-Bass, 1977), p. 12.

3. Robert O. Berdahl, *Statewide Coordination of Higher Education* (Washington, D.C.: American Council on Education, 1971), p. 5.

4. Paul L. Dressel, ed., *The Autonomy of Public Colleges* (San Francisco: Jossey-Bass, 1980), p. 13.

5. Ibid., p. 5.

6. Ibid., p. 96.

7. National Commission on Research, *Accountability: Restoring the Quality of the Partnership* (Washington, D.C., 1980), p. 17.

8. C.J. Hitch, "Remarks of the President" (Address delivered to the Assembly of the California Academic Senate, Berkeley, Calif., June 15, 1970).

9. Lyman A. Glenny and Thomas K. Dalglish, *Public Universities, State Agencies, and the Law: Constitutional Autonomy in Decline* (Berkeley, Calif.: University of California, Center for Research and Development in Higher Education, 1973), p. 42.

10. Lyman A. Glenny and Thomas K. Dalglish, ibid., p. 143.

11. Burton R. Clark, "The Insulated Americans: Five Lessons from Abroad," *Change* 10 (November 1978), p. 30.

12. *San Francisco Chronicle,* 23 September 1980.

13. John W. Lederle, "Governors and Higher Education," in *State Politics and Higher Education,* ed. Leonard E. Goodall (Dearborn, Mich.: University of Michigan, 1976), pp. 43-50.

14. Paul L. Dressel, *Autonomy of Public Colleges,* p. 40

15. Paul L. Dressel, *Autonomy of Public Colleges,* p. 43.

16. Robert O. Berdahl, "Legislative Program Evaluation," in *Increasing the Public Accountability of Higher Education,* ed. John K. Folger (San Francisco: Jossey-Bass, 1977), pp. 35-65.

17. Ibid.

18. National Commission on Research, *Accountability,* p. 3.

19. Letter from Chancellor Ira Michael Heyman to the members of the Berkeley faculty, 2 October 1980.

20. *Chronicle of Higher Education* 21, September 8, 1980.

21. Daniel Patrick Moynihan, "State vs. Academe," *Harpers* 261 (December 1980), pp. 31-40.

22. Robert O. Berdahl, "The Politics of State Aid," in *Public Policy and Private Higher Education,* ed. David W. Breneman and Chester E. Finn, Jr. (Washington, D.C.: Brookings Institution, 1978), pp. 321-352.

23. Carnegie Council on Policy Studies in Higher Education, *The States and Private Higher Education* (San Francisco: Jossey-Bass, 1977), p. 63.

24. Commission to Study Nonpublic Higher Education in Illinois, *Strengthening Private Higher Education in Illinois: A Report on the State's Role* (Springfield, Ill.: Board of Higher Education, 1969).

25. T.R. McConnell, "Accountability and Autonomy" *Journal of Higher Education* 42 (June 1971), pp. 446-463.

26. William A. Kaplin, *The Law of Higher Education* (San Francisco: Jossey-Bass, 1978), p. 4.

27. Elizabeth French and Robert Berdahl, *Who Guards the Guardians?* Occasional Papers Series, Department of Higher Education, State University of New York at Buffalo, 1980, p. 3.

28. John D. Millett, "Statewide Coordinating Boards and Statewide Governing Boards," in *Evaluating Statewide Boards,* ed. Robert O. Berdahl (San Francisco: Jossey-Bass, 1975), pp. 61-70.

29. Ibid., p. 70.

30. Kenneth P. Mortimer and T.R. McConnell, *Sharing Authority Effectively* (San Francisco: Jossey-Bass, 1978), p. 225.

31. Lyman A. Glenny, *State Budgeting for Higher Education: Interagency Conflict and Consensus* (Berkeley: Center for Research and Development in Higher Education, University of California, 1976), pp. 148-150.

32. Paul L. Dressel, *Autonomy of Public Colleges,* pp. 99-100.

33. *Chronicle of Higher Education* 20 (June 16, 1980).

34. Ibid.

35. Howard R. Bowen, "The Products of Higher Education," in *Evaluating Institutions for Accountability,* ed. Howard R. Bowen (San Francisco: Jossey-Bass, 1974), pp. 1-26.

36. C.R. Pace, "When Students Judge Their College," *College Board Review* 58 (Spring 1960), pp. 26-28.

37. T.R. McConnell, "Accountability and Autonomy."

38. Ibid.

39. Howard R. Bowen, *Investment in Learning,* p. 257. Other evidence on changes in students over the college years is presented in Alexander W. Astin, *Four Critical Years* (San Francisco: Jossey-Bass, 1977).

40. Howard R. Bowen, *Investment in Learning*

41. Ibid., pp. 447-448.

42. Kenneth P. Mortimer, *Accountability in Higher Education* (Washington, D.C.: American Association for Higher Education, 1972), p. 6.

43. Howard R. Bowen, *The Costs of Higher Education* (San Francisco: Jossey-Bass, 1980).

4

Academic Freedom in
Delocalized Academic Institutions
Walter P. Metzger

Editor's Note: This essay, written in 1969, provides a relevant historical perspective to many of the issues discussed in this volume. We reprint it because the issues it raises are so relevant to contemporary debates and because it considers how American higher education developed at a crucial historical period.

The gist of the argument that follows is that the theory of academic freedom as it has been articulated in this country has become, in critical respects, outmoded. By this I do not mean to imply that the value of academic freedom has diminished; it is not only relevant to the modern university, but essential to it—the one grace that institution may not lose without losing everything. A theory of academic freedom, however, goes beyond an affirmation of its value to a description of the forces and conditions that place this desired thing in peril, and a prescription of the norms and strategies that may offset those specific threats. It is in this latter sense, as a mode of analysis and advice concerning the realities of social power, that I believe

Reprinted with permission from Walter P. Metzger, et al., *Dimensions of Academic Freedom* (Urbana, Ill.: University of Illinois Press, 1969), pp. 1-33.

the inherited canon has, to a large degree, outlived its day.

One should not suppose that the American theory of academic freedom owes its staleness to senescence. Though it draws on an ancient legacy of assumptions, it did not become crystalized in this country until as late as 1915, when Arthur O. Lovejoy of The Johns Hopkins University, E.R.A. Seligman and John Dewey of Columbia University, and a number of other academic luminaries wrote the *General Report on Academic Freedom and Academic Tenure* for the newly founded American Association of University Professors. To call this report a classic is to comment on its quality, not its venerableness—a document only two generations old hardly qualifies as antique. But a short period in the life span of ideas may constitute a millennium in the time scale of institutions, especially American institutions, which have been known to change at breakneck speeds. What has happened in the half-century since 1915 is that American universities have been remodeled while the ideas once consonant with them have not. The result has been a growing discrepancy between milieu and theory—an ever widening culture lag.

By the lights of 1915, a violation of academic freedom was a crime designed and executed within the confines of the university. Dissident professors were the victims, trustees and administrators were the culprits, the power of dismissal was the weapon, the loss of employment was the wound. Concentrating on this stage and scenario, the authors of the 1915 statement concluded that the key to crime prevention lay in the adoption of regulations that would heighten the security of the office-holder and temper the arbitrariness of the "boss." So persuaded, they persuaded others, and in time these institutional regulations, known as academic tenure and due process, came to be widely adopted if not always faultlessly applied. It should be noted, however, that by defining a violation of academic freedom as something that happens *in* a university, rather than as something that happens *to* a university, these writers ignored a set of issues that had caused their foreign counterparts much concern. Nothing was said in this document about the relations of the academy to state authority. Except for brief allusions to the class obsessions of wealthy donors and the populistic foibles of local legislators, nothing was said about the external enemies of the university, though history made available such impressive candidates as the meddlesome minister of education, the inquisitorial church official, the postal guardian of public morals, the intruding policeman, and the biased judge. Finally, nothing was said about threats to the autonomy of the university that were not, at one and the same time, threats to the livelihood of its members; indeed, it was not even clearly acknowledged that a corporate academic interest, as distinct from an individual academic's interest, existed and had also to be preserved. In short, 1915's criminology (and the criminology operative today—cf. the policing efforts of Committee A of the AAUP) was wise to the ways of the harsh employer, but it lacked a theory and vocabulary for dealing with the outside offender and the nonoccupational offense.

Along with this definition of the crime went a recommended rule of good behavior: a university, the report declared, should never speak as an official body on matters of doctrine or public policy. In the lengthy history of universities this gospel of institutional restraint had not had many preachers or practitioners. Indeed, there were many more examples of commitment: e.g., the adherence of the continental universities after the Reformation to the confessional preferences of the local rulers, the involvement of Oxford and Cambridge in the dynastic struggles of Tudor England, the proselytizing efforts of the church-built colleges in America prior to the Civil War. The authors of the 1915 statement took aim at this tradition by attacking some of its basic premises: that truth is something to be possessed rather than endlessly discovered; that truth-questions yield to the edicts of institutions rather than to the competitive play of minds. Intellectual inquiry, they insisted, had to be ongoing and individual; organizational fiats defeat it because organizations are mightier than individuals and fiats are inevitably premature. In support of their brief for neutrality they likened the true university to an "intellectual experiment station" where new ideas might safely germinate, to an "inviolable refuge" where men of ideas might safely congregate, and—most simply—to a "home for research." By no stretch of analogy was the modern university to be considered a missionary society, a propaganda agency, an arm of a political party: it was a residence, a hothouse, a sanctuary—the figures of speech were adoring, but they left the university with nothing of substance to proclaim.

How was this no-substance rule to be effectuated; what were the means to this lack of ends? Here our near-yet-distant academic forefathers made another enduring contribution. Conceivably they could have argued, taking a cue from the independent newspaper with its balanced display of editorials, that an academic institution achieves neutrality by appointing men of varying opinions to its faculty. Or they could have argued, with an eye on the renunciative code of conduct common in the military and civil service, that an academic institution achieves neutrality by prohibiting its members from speaking out on public issues, especially on those foreign to their specialities. Significantly, the authors of the AAUP report did not accept either of these possibilities, but instead set forth a formula possibly suggested by the economic market: let the university disown responsibility for everything its members say or publish and then let it permit its members to say and publish what they please. This formula, which was to be made more explicit in later decretals, had obvious advantages over the others. Neutrality by disownment was easier to administer than neutrality by selection, harder to abuse than neutrality by proscription. But it also created a peculiar asymmetry: it asserted, in effect, that professors had the right to express opinions but that their colleges and universities did not.

By including the concept of personal freedom under the rubric of academic freedom, these writers made their doctrine even more asymmetrical. Traditionally, academic freedom had merely offered on-the-job protection: freedom of teaching and research. These, it had been supposed, were the main arenas where professors exhibited special competence and where they deserved a special latitude; beyond lay a terrain of utterance which professors, like any other citizens, were presumed to enter at their own risk. The authors of the 1915 report would not accept such zonal ordinances. Academic freedom, they asserted, protects professors in all of their identities—as teachers, scholars, scientists, citizens, experts, consultants—and on every sort of platform. It applies not to a category of speech but to a category of persons.

The first and most important thing to be said about the college or university of 1915 was that it possessed and exercised impressive powers within a demarcated area. This attribute, which I shall call its "localness," derived in part from the clarity of that demarcation. The lands of the college of that period usually made up a contiguous property and were often marked off by fences that kept the students in corral and warned the outsider of the line of trespass. Usually they were located in sequestered regions either on the outskirts of major cities or in the bucolic settings of college towns. Spatially these institutions lived apart, and this apartness contributed to their autonomy.

In addition to acreage and location, style and organization fostered localness. Administratively, with the exception of a shrinking number of ecclesiastically controlled institutions, each unit was entirely discrete, with its own board of regents or trustees, its own executive figure, its own sublieutenancy of deans, its own budget, its own rules and regulations. Legally each was endowed by charter or statute with a vast amount of discretionary authority. Extensive in the management of property, that authority was virtually without limit when it came to the regulation of persons. In 1915 neither outside law nor internal dissonances restrained the exercise of student discipline. It was common in those days for students to live under rules they did not fashion and to be expelled for infractions without a trial. When students asked the courts to intervene they usually were disappointed, the courts generally taking the position that students had, by implied or explicit contract, consigned themselves to the mercies—quasiparental and therefore tender—of those who had initially let them in. It should not be supposed that students submitted gladly to this regimen. The annals of these institutions disclose too many revels in the springtime, too many rebellions in the fall and winter, to support the view that, uniquely in America, 18 to 22 were the docile years. Yet it is also clear that few in this febrile population challenged the legitimacy of that regimen. Students sought to outfox, not unseat, their elders, they made a game of the rules, but accepted the rules of the game. This kind of popular acquiescence, together with the virtual absence of serious judicial review, gave the academy the appearance of a foreign enclave, ruling indigenous peoples with laws of its own devising, enjoying a kind of extraterritoriality within the larger state.

Of course institutions calling themselves academic came in many different shapes and sizes. The grandest institutions of the period—those that had gathered into their custody the tools of modern scholarship and research—were much more involved with the world around them than colleges that were little more than *écoles*. But the worldliness of the Harvards and Wisconsins did not yet undercut their localness. For one thing, research tools were on the Edison scale of cost: Brookhaven magnitudes were not yet imagined. By means of the usual fund drives and appropriations, these institutions could sustain the cost internally and thus keep control of what their members did and spent. For another thing, the scholars and scientists they assembled were still burdened with heavy academic duties. At this point in time, while there were many teachers who did no research, there were practically no researchers who did not teach—and teach assiduously and regularly. In a much more than *pro forma* sense, men who worked *in* the university also worked *for* the university and were responsive to its interests and requirements.

Even in their transactions with their patrons the colleges and universities of 1915 had a great deal of decisional independence. It is a convention of academic history to deny this, to conclude from their chronic neediness, their perennial courting of the legislatures, their incessant wooing of potential donors, that they were the most obsequious of creatures. But I suspect that those who assert this take as their implicit model of comparison the English university of the nineteenth century, an institution that owed its aplomb and self-reliance to ancient clerical endowments, enormous property holdings, and the privileges of the class it served. Without that invidious comparison, the American college would seem to have been made of sterner stuff. For one thing, the bulk of collegiate instruction was still going on in private institutions which, despite many resemblances to the public ones, had a narrower constituency to account to, and far more discretion in defining that constituency. Some were dependent on very rich patrons, and not the braver for it; still, very often, behind the captains of industry who invested fortunes in universities, there would be a charismatic president who told them how their money should be spent. In the public sector, the whims of the men who held the purse strings had to be catered to more consistently, and presidents of state institutions were often chosen for that capacity. Yet even here the processes of negotiation that took place between legislators and administrators left considerable discretion in local hands. Members of appropriations committees seldom developed the educational expertise needed to initiate novel policies. Far from being sources of innovation, these committees were political arenas where administrators would bargain with their counterparts for public monies and where the essential educational decisions would concern the division of the take. Nor was there much regulation of the system, either in the public or the private areas. Large-scale private philanthropy, though it had worked important reforms in such limited fields as medical education, was not yet a ubiquitous improver; agencies for self-regulation, like the regional accrediting associations, tended to be self-protective bodies, shielding the run-of-the-mill establishment against its fly-by-night competitor. Far less than in railroads or in banking were the firms in academe made to conform to specific standards. And the reason for this is not hard to find. Serving a small segment of the population, not yet central to the economy, taken more seriously for its fun and frolics than for its earnest devotions, the college or university of 1915 was regarded as a public ornament and curiosity, not yet as a public utility.

Above all—and this is what makes the period seem an age of innocence, our own academic *belle epoque*—the organs of the central state were not intrusive. For years the federal government had given land to universities without conditions, or had laid down conditions (e.g., the furtherance of agriculture and technology) without imposing very strict controls. In 1915 Washington did not even have an apparatus for dealing systematically with academe. The federal interest in education, which was at that time almost negligible, could be contained in a lowly Bureau of Education whose primary task was to get statistics; the federal interest in (nonagricultural) science, which was even at that time quite considerable, could be met by governmental agencies like the Geological Survey and the Naval Observatory, and did not impinge on the universities. Americans tended to attribute this phenomenon—substantial federal assistance without a significant federal presence—to the genius of their Constitution and their history. Doubtless a literal reading of the Tenth Amendment, plus the hold of Jeffersonian prejudices, did erect barriers to state intrusion. Where such barriers did not exist, as in Great Britain in the nineteenth century, universities felt much more statist pressure. Thus, for all their vaunted independence, Oxford and Cambridge were compelled to submit to extensive changes suggested by royal commissions in the 1850s and 1870s and enforced by parliamentary decrees. But there was still another explanation, albeit one less visible to contemporaries, for the special state of American affairs. In large part our federal government was undemanding simply because it had no urgent demands to make. A nation that had just entered world politics but had not yet become a world power, that lived in the Edenic security of a miniscule army and a safe frontier, lacked one of the principal motives for intermeddling—the motive of martial necessity. Let that motive be supplied, as it would in a future far more imminent than most Americans in 1915 could foresee, and the central state would not scruple to lay a levy on the spirit of the university, as well as on its faculties and young men. Full recognition of this came in 1918 when, on behalf of a country mobilized and gladiatorial, the Congress transformed every college male into a soldier, every college dormitory into a barracks, every college lawn into a training ground under the aegis of the Secretary of War. The Student Army Training Corps, like the agencies of propaganda filled with scholars, was decried as a folly and an aberration as soon as World War I closed. But at the outbreak of World War II the academic system was once more militarized, and this time the marriage of Mars and Minerva would not only be solemnized but preserved.

It is not very difficult to see why the authors of the 1915 statement on academic freedom ignored the macrocosm of society and concentrated on the smaller campus world. It was there that significant things could happen. A college or university was then no mere appendage of government, no mere component in a great machine. It was a unit of considerable completeness, an agency possessed of powers that were almost governmental in kind. It suggested a checkerboard view of power and a concept of academic freedom that was equally sectioned and discrete.

So much for the general bias of the theory. To account for its specific arguments one has to note another feature of the system: its capacity to generate within each unit an inordinate amount of status strain. This was the period when the academic profession came of age: when it came to think of itself as specialized, competent, and scientific; when it sought to act as mentor to society on a wide range of social issues; when it demanded the deference and the courtesy that befitted these pretensions and that role. It happened, however, that this was also the period when many academic trustees and administrators adopted a style of management that conceded little to these demands. Derived from the views and manners of prerogative-minded business managers, falling between an older authoritarianism with its familial emphasis and a yet-to-come bureaucratism with its codes and forms, the style struck many professors as both overweening and capricious, and in any case hostile to their status claims.

An example of the irritating potential of this new managerial psychology can be found in one of the earliest academic freedom cases investigated by the AAUP. In 1915 the Board of Trustees of the University of Pennsylvania dismissed the economist Scott Nearing on grounds they refused to disclose. (The evidence is all but conclusive that they took exception to his opinions, which were radical then, but not yet Marxist.) In explaining why he did not have to explain, George Wharton Pepper, a prominent trustee of the university, said: "If I am dissatisfied with my secretary, I suppose I would be within my rights in terminating his employment." Was, then, a professor simply a clerk? an amanuensis? The chancellor of Syracuse was willing to concede that he was more than that, that he dealt in some fashion with ideas. Still, this administrator did not believe that the creative function of the professor gave him leave to oppose the man who signed his check. The dismissal of Nearing, Chancellor Day believed, was entirely proper. "That is what would happen to an editorial writer of *The Tribune* if he were to disregard the things for which the paper stands...." Were, then, the trustees of a university, like the publishers of a newspaper, the formal proprietors of the property? The editors of the New York *Times,* in choosing not to go so far, offered their own enlightening treatise on academic relationships in America. As they saw it, the university belonged to the donors, who were its fount of wisdom and ideology *in saecula saeculorum;* the trustees were the agents of the donors, charged with the execution of that immortal claim. Professors? They were simply spoilsports, ever ready, under the academic freedom cover, to ask for privileges they never bought:

> Men who through toil and ability have got together enough money to endow universities or professors' chairs do not generally have it in mind that their money should be spent for the dissemination of the dogmas of Socialism or in the teaching of ingenuous youth how to live without work. Yet when Trustees conscientiously endeavor to carry out the purposes of the founder by taking proper measures to prevent misuse of the endowment, we always hear a loud howl about academic freedom.
>
> We see no reason why the upholders of academic freedom in this sense should not establish a university of their own. Let them provide the funds, erect the buildings, lay out the campus, and then make a requisition on the padded cells of Bedlam for their teaching staff. Nobody would interfere with the full freedom of professors; they could teach Socialism and shiftlessness until Doomsday without restraint.

Among the changes wrought by time has been the departure of this kind of liveliness from the editorial pages of the New York *Times.*

Cast in general terms, the report of the AAUP professors did not seem to stoop to rebuttal. Yet these Gothic business doctrines shaped the contours of its major themes. The norm of institutional neutrality was not just an ethicist's abstraction: it was a denial of the proprietary claims of trustees, donors, and their spokesmen. The widening of the zone of academic freedom was not simply a reflex of libertarianism: it was an effort to reduce the sphere in which philistine administrators could take action. And the notion that men were in conflict with their organizations—and that this conflict drew the battle lines of freedom—stemmed only in part from an individualistic ethos: it also expressed the viewpoint of a profession whose institutional existence offered too meager status gains. For all its transcendent qualities, the 1915 report was a tract developed for its times.

The times, I submit, have changed. Not everywhere, not in all respects. A small denominational college may still look as it looked in 1915. A major university may still be living off the precedents set long ago. Here and there a donor may still wish to establish an ideology in the course of establishing a schoolroom, or a trustee may still be tempted to utter the platitude of possession. But at the height where one loses particulars and gains synopsis one can see enormous transformations. Of these, one of the most important has been the flow of decisional power from authorities on the campus to those resident outside. Richer, larger, more complex than ever before, the typical modern institution of higher learning is less self-directive than ever before. It has become, to coin a word, "delocalized," with consequences we are just beginning to perceive.

Delocalization has not been a single process but a congeries of processes, all working in the same direction and achieving a common end. The engulfing of many universities by the central city, with the result that everything that they do in the way of land use becomes imbued with political implications and ensnarled in municipal law, is one delocalizing process. The growth of bureaucratized philanthropy as a principle source of academic innovation, the subordination of the judgment of admissions officers to legislative judgments concerning civil rights, the involvement of universities in social welfare and thus with clients it can serve but not control, may be considered others. And so too may the integration of public higher education, the assault on the principle of extraterritoriality, and the enlargement of federal influence due to federal sponsorship of research. These latter processes are so important, both in affecting the character of academic institutions and the viability of the academic freedom theory, that I should like to examine each in some detail.

In 1915 only two states attempted to coordinate the activities of their tax-supported institutions of higher learning. By 1965 only nine states let their state university, land-grant colleges, technical institutes, and teachers' colleges go their separate ways. The trend, moreover, has not only been toward greater coordination but also toward higher degrees of integration. By 1965 as many as fifteen states had given superordinate public bodies the power to alter and create new schools by plan. SUNY, the gigantic State University of New York, was established in 1949 to take charge of forty-six existing public institutions and to set up as many new ones as its over-all blueprint would prescribe. By current reckoning the California Master Plan brings seventy-six junior colleges, eighteen state colleges, and a nine-campus university under the sway of dovetailing central bodies. In the coordinated systems the power of central bodies may be limited to reviewing budgets and programs initiated by the institutions themselves. In the more integrated systems the off-campus boards of control may make decisions on capital investment and tuition levels, architectural design and new site locations, entrance requirements and degree capacities, while the on-campus boards and administrations may make decisions on how those decisions will be carried out. These vertical and horizontal combinations of plants in similar and diverse lines, these unequal allocations of power between the central office and the local branch, this division of territorial markets state by state, make the integrated academic organization and the modern business corporation seem very much alike, if not of kin. And these resemblances are not lost on the faculties they appoint. If we are employed by the educational duplicate of General Motors or United States Steel, some of them seem to be saying, let us be responsive to that reality: let us elect a single bargaining agent to match the collective strength of management; let us fight for our economic interests without the constraints of a service ethos; let us, if need be, strike. Localized institutions tended to generate professional resentment, but delocalized institutions seem to eviscerate professional élan.

The rationalization of public higher education proceeds from three demands that are made upon it: (1) that it accommodate vast enrollments; (2) that it stimulate economic enterprise; (3) that it accomplish both objectives at something less than crushing public cost. These very demands speak eloquently of the new importance that has come to be attached to this activity. So high is the putative correlation between income earned and degree awarded that a college education has become compulsory, not by the edict of law but by the mandate of ambition. So close is the symbiosis of productive industry on the knowledge industry, so glaring is the cheek-by-jowl abutment of technological parks and college greens, that the advertised presence of a campus has become, next to tax abatements, a primary lure to new investment. Private higher education has grown as a consequence of these connections, but public higher education has grown much faster, so that today it enrolls almost two-thirds of all academic students, and is much more heavily subsidized, receiving one hundred dollars in tax money for every thirty-five dollars its private competitors receive in gifts. With the change in the public-private balance, the old popular affection for the small-scale venturer has given way to a quest for tax economies, and the alleged efficiencies of central planning is urged successfully even in staid legislative halls. What had once been regarded as a mere propaedeutic enterprise has thus become, in the course of time, a key to the life chances of everyone, an object of urgent public policy, and a stimulant to the GNP. New layers of relevance have been added; but in the process the old attribute of localness has been stripped away.

The assault on extraterritoriality—the second delocalizing process—engages another set of forces, at work both in the private and public sectors, both on the campuses and beyond. On the campuses the assault is being mounted by a new generation of student radicals: white revolutionaries and Negro militants, advocates of more effective student power, persons lonely in their alienations or drawn into dissentient subcultures—the varied student cadres that distinguish the convulsive present from the prankish and catatonic past. Each group has its own visions and motivations, as can be seen from the instability of their alliances; and none is yet numerically dominant in any student body in the land. But they are increasingly becoming a powerful, pace-setting minority and they share, amid all their differences, a common animus against the discipline which their predecessors did not oppose. Different groups issue different challenges to that discipline. Advocates of student power dispute the validity of rules that are made for but not by the student client; theirs is a constitutional challenge aimed, as are all the challenges of emergent classes, at the habit and principle of exclusion. Partisans of the New Left break the rules to change the policies these rules facilitate; theirs is a tactical challenge aimed, as are all radical challenges, at the going morality of ends and means. At times these challenges overreach their mark. The breaking of certain rules may mean the disruption of the operations of the university, which may require the intercession of police forces and the use of violence on a massive scale. The end of this chain of consequences is a greater loss of internal authority than any may have anticipated or approved. The surrender of the administration to the harsh protectorship of policemen is often more costly to its authority than the precipitating student offense. On the other hand, only the most Sorelian of student radicals could delight in all aspects of this denouement: the substitution of military for civilian options, the traumatization of students by police attack, the devolution of a community based on shared assumptions into a community nakedly based on force. Of late, the politics of confrontation has found another way to exceed its immediate object. Students engaged in coercive protest have come to insist that amnesty be granted before they will agree to relent. For those who reject the legitimacy of the guardians and who wish to stay to do battle yet another day, this demand serves practical and symbolic purposes. But amnesty wrested from the institution may not always bring total forgiveness: violations involving trespass or vandalism may result in criminal arrests. Where the institution is the sole complainant, it may influence the disposition of these cases; but it may find it hard to convince the courts to dismiss the charges when it has surrendered the means to protect itself. The natural effect of amnesty, granted under duress, is thus to displace the disciplinary power from the universities to the civil courts. Whether courts or universities act more justly is a question one need not resolve. It is clear, however, that they do act differently, the one being more interested in behaviors, the other in underlying intentions; the one just beginning to grant academic freedom legal status, the other having long made this the value it cherishes above all. But the thrust of modern student politics is to give the temporal rather than the spiritual authority a legitimate judicial role.

Meanwhile, forces outside the university have been working to constrain academic discipline when it *is* applied. Starting in 1961, the federal courts have been deciding that the disciplinary actions of officials in publicly supported colleges and universities must adhere to the due process standards of the Fourteenth Amendment of the Constitution. Whether the officials of private institutions must adjust their conduct to these standards is not, at the moment, certain; but it is highly probable that they will one day be made to do so or suffer reversal in the courts. One may note that the cases setting the legal precedent involved the interests of Negro students who had been punished for participating in sit-ins by administrators of Negro colleges yielding to the pressures of Southern whites. Clearly the judicial concern for student rights was inspired by a judicial concern for civil rights and not by purely academic considerations. Here again, the college, in acquiring new social significance, has lost a measure of its old autonomy. But here one may be permitted the conclusion that, on balance, justice gained.

I come finally to the last delocalizing tendency: the growing involvement of the federal government with the affairs and fortunes of academe. This is perhaps not the order or the language that the most passionate critics of that involvement would prefer. But the virtue in saving it till last is that we may then perceive it not as something *sui generis* but as part of a broader development; and the virtue in using the word "delocalizing" when a more accusative vocabulary is at hand is that we can avoid the dubious imputation of Pentagon plotting, power elitism, establishment cooption, and the like. Nevertheless, after this dispassionate preface, I hasten to admit that I believe the issue now before us is of burning importance. The advent of a formidable central state—harnessed almost without limit for a world struggle apparently without end, richer than any other benefactor by virtue of the federal income tax resource, able to seek solutions to any social problem, if need be, by purchasing compliance with the cure—is a momentous event in the life of our universities. Such a behemoth, as it draws close, cannot help but siphon authority from other agencies. In part, but only in part, the speed and volume of the drain from the universities can be measured by the increase in its assistance. In 1964 federal contributions to higher learning totaled $1.5 billion. Though this came to only one-tenth of the total funds received, it constituted, because of its distribution, a large percentage of the incomes of the major places—83 per cent of Cal Tech's, 81 per cent of MIT's, 75 per cent of Princeton's. For home reference, it may be noted that Columbia, third among recipients, got $51,000,000, an intake that amounted to almost half of that year's operating budget, while the University of Illinois, then sixth in order, got $44,000,000, a smaller part of its total budget but a not inconsiderable sum. By 1966 the federal contribution had doubled and the federal share of total contributions had risen to approximately one-fifth. In that year the largesse was a little more evenly distributed, but the major institutions were even more glaringly beholden to the generosity of the central state.

It is in the "how" as well as in the "how much" that we locate the delocalizing pressure. During and after World War II, academic scientists high in government and governmental and military officials high on science hit on two devices for channeling federal funds to universities. One was the project grant or contract, which a faculty member negotiates with the granting agency with minimal involvement by his university; the other was the specialized research center, which the university operates for the agency, sometimes without the participation of any faculty member. These devices are supposed to confer a variety of social and scientific benefits. It is claimed that the distant granting agency, with its advisory panels of distinguished scientists, is more likely to rate applicants on their merits than are members of a department when they judge their own. It is claimed that the separation of federal subsidy from federal employment helps preserve individual research initiative, since an academic scientist is free, as a governmental scientist is not, to pursue the project of his own desire. And it is claimed that the funds allotted under these formulas make possible the purchase of scientific apparatus which would otherwise be lost to the academy in the expensive space and atomic age. It is tempting to investigate these claims, to ask whether personal, institutional, or regional loyalties never tincture the judgments of reviewing panels, whether certain kinds of extravagantly priced equipment—like accelerators with ever increasing BEVs —deserve the national priority they have been given, whether freedom of choice is not subtly constrained by the workings of the well-known principle that a man need not marry for money, he may simply seek out the company of wealthy women and marry one of them for love. But these are not the questions before us: what is pertinent is that these devices rob the university of autonomy, the one by making it a bystander in the fostering and reward of its members' talents, the other by making it a kind of subcontractor, dispensing someone else's cash to attain someone else's objectives. Here one might add a quantitative footnote: today, from two-thirds to three-quarters of all money expended on academic research comes from the federal giver through these circumventive routes.

"Washington," notes Clark Kerr, in his study of the "multiversity," the delocalized institution unsurpassed, "did not waste its money on the second-rate." Did it make what was first-rate even better? Looking at the institutional breeding places of the greatest scientific advances of the last two decades, Kerr concludes that the federal research effort did give existing excellences an added gloss. But on the evidence he himself musters, a more pessimistic conclusion might be formed. Taking what is given without question and doing what is asked for by the gift, the front-rank university tends to find itself rich but troubled, powerful in its impact on the nation but weak in the control of its own affairs. It falls prey to what Kerr refers to as "imbalances": the dominance of science over the humanities, the dominance of research over teaching, the dominance of graduate interests over undergraduate concerns. It takes on an ever increasing number of those whom Kerr refers to as "unfaculty": scholars who are added to the staff to assist externally aided projects. Set to the sponsored task but performing no other service to the institution, never eligible for tenure no matter how often contracts are renewed, this new academic breed lives at the periphery of the profession. Fifty years ago only a relatively small group of graduate students, serving as assistants to the senior faculty, was in as marginal a position. Since then, the ranks of this subaltern force have grown, to take care of the burden of instruction that the increased number of students has created and that a research-minded faculty will not assume. In the leading universities these two anomalous groups—the teacher who is still a student and the researcher who is not a teacher—make up a very large part of the total academic work force. With enrichment, then, has come a new diminishment: an increase in the number of appointees who are in but not of the university, sharing in its tasks but not its perquisites, existing under the predestinarian doctrine (so alien to professional doctrine) that good works can never assure election.

A full estimate of the losses incident to gains must include the acceptance of secrecy and deceit, not as adventitious vices but as part of the academic way of life. Federal support for military research must bear a part of the responsibility for the institutionalizing of shady tactics. The aim of military research is to secure time advantages against the enemy; often, to secure these time advantages, it is necessary to prevent premature disclosures; frequently, to prevent disclosures, it is necessary to test the loyalty of participants, limit access to facilities, guard the research records, or control what appears in print. With the Pentagon no less interested in quality than the National Science Foundation or the National Institutes of Health, it was inevitable that funds for the necrophilic sciences, as well as funds for the healing and heuristic arts, would flow to the better universities. But federal support for military research does not account for all the slyness and covertness that afflict modern academic life. Only a small part of federal support is avowedly military (in 1966, of the total sum supplied by the granting agencies, only 10 per cent went to academia from the Department of Defense). If the secretiveness of warrior organizations accounts for something, the enfeeblement of academic organizations accounts for more. A high susceptiveness to deception was built into the very flabbiness of the grant arrangement. Almost any agency out to promote an unpleasant mission can find a pretext for lodging it in the university, to acquire gilt by association. Federal undercover agents find it easier to carry on their impostures amid the para-academic members of a research project than amid the faculties at large. Above all, universities involved in the project system developed a trained incapacity to look suspiciously at their gift horses, if indeed they looked at all. Thus it happened at Michigan State University that a program for training policemen for Vietnam, set up by a mission-minded agency without close monitorship by the university, was infiltrated by agents of the CIA. The structure, if it did not require hugger-muggery, was certainly not well made to prevent it. And thus it happened that the same surreptitious body gave secret subsidies to a variety of academic enterprises, ranging from area study institutes to international conferences; once inserted, trickery by government became routine.

This is not to say that trickery by government does not exist on the campus in other forms. Modes of underhandedness have long been associated with law enforcement: viz., the policeman posing as a student, the student doubling as a policeman, the government employer asking teachers to snitch on their students and peers. Especially prominent in "Red scare" periods, these forms of deception are not uncommon in the current period, when drugs take precedence over dogmas as items on the list of search. But these tricks have the capacity to outrage professors in almost all institutions where they are practiced. The secret subsidies of the CIA, by contrast, seem to be a good deal less inflaming. For a decade or so they went undetected, though not without the collaboration of a good many professors and administrators in the know. When some of these were uncovered (largely by left-wing student muckrakers), they did cause a stir in certain faculties. Still, it is almost certain that the taint has not been removed from certain projects and that administrative and professional winking goes on. As late as 1964 Clark Kerr could maintain that the federal grant procedure was "fully within academic traditions." Since the CIA revelations, the academic mood has probably not been so complaisant. Yet it is doubtful that many members of the profession would think it wise to change the title of their book from *The Uses of the University* to *How the University Has Been Used.*

How to account for the difference in responses? Simply to say that one form of police penetration serves to enrich professors while the other may serve to chastise them puts the matter of self-interest much too crudely. It would be, I think, both more subtle and more accurate to say that no process of delocalization, unless it threatens the well-being of professors, is presumed to violate academic freedom; and that without a violation of academic freedom, no insult to the university causes broad alarm. In fact, by the tests which the inherited creed imposes, some of the trends I have spoken of seem to have strengthened academic freedom. Ideological dismissals have become rare to the point of being oddities in the larger delocalized institutions. This is all the more impressive because outspoken opposition to war in wartime, which had always been subject to academic penalties, has been allowed to flourish in these places. Furthermore, with very few verified exceptions, the governmental granting agencies have not discriminated against opponents of governmental policies. Not only in crimes, but also in crime prevention, the current period seems to improve upon the past. Tenure (for those eligible to receive it) is at least as safe in integrated public systems as in any other. Academic due process has, if anything, become more rigorous and more codified as the scattered *gemeinschafts* of before merge into centralized *gesellschafts.* Federal-grant universities, with their congeries of projects, are less likely to get domineering presidents (they are lucky to get presidents able and alert enough to keep track of all that is going on). Less privileged colleges and universities, hoping for federal assistance, are less likely to prescribe religious or other doctrines (this is one reason why certain Catholic institutions are moving toward lay boards of control and even toward the norm of neutrality). For renowned professors the new order is particularly comfortable and protective. If they have greater leverage in bargaining with their institutions, they may thank the federal grantor for adding to their other marketable assets the value of a movable money prize. The flow of perquisites from Washington dissolves their reliance on the local paymaster, while the tenure granted by alma mater prevents their subservience to the outside source. Status satisfactions only dreamed of may now in actuality be possessed. The autonomy and integrity of universities? These heavenly things on earth are not contained in this philosophy.

This is hardly the place to write an academic freedom theory that would meet this day's demands. All I can do is sketch out certain areas where changes in the reigning wisdom would do us good. I ask you to take this as a prolegomenon; a theoretical and practical formulation of the academic ethics we require must await another Lovejoy or Dewey, distilling salient ideas from new institutional experiences.

At the top of the list of credos ripe for change I would put the view that a crime against academic freedom is a crime against an academic person's rights. In relevant doctrine it may still be that; but it may also be an attack on academic integrity, sustained by the university as a whole. It should be the name we give to the intrusion of lock-and-key research into an ostensibly open enterprise.

Next I would part with the notion that curbs on administrative power answer all of academic freedom's needs. They answer only part of its needs; the other and equally essential instrument is effective academic government. It was well understood by the makers of our Constitution that freedom could be jeopardized by the weakness, as well as the tyranny, of officials.

In the quest for relevant doctrine, I would also take issue with the notion that the only respectable university is a politically neutral university. It may not be easy to reconceive this notion. The norm of institutional neutrality has rolled through our synapses so often we hardly ever challenge it with thought. Therein lies the problem: applied unthinkingly to every issue, it loses its value as a norm and becomes a recipe for paralysis. One illustration may make this clear. The Selective Service Administration recently decreed that college students would be deferred if they achieved a certain grade-ranking or passed a certain standardized test. In other words, instead of classifying by status (all college students), it classified by status and performance (only *good* college students), and fixed the criterion of judgment. To grasp the implications of this procedure one need only ask what the consequences would have been if the draft authorities had decided to defer not all women but only *good* women, not all husbands but only *good* husbands, not all workers in essential industries but only *good* workers in essential industries. In academic no less than in conjugal and economic matters, privacy and autonomy are threatened when virtue is not its own but the state's reward. The academy, however, took little corporate action to defend its corporate rights. Proposals for institutional resistance (say by not ranking students or sending in the grades) were usually defeated by the argument that such acts would by politically unneutral, signifying institutional opposition to the draft or the war in Vietnam. This ritualistic application of the neutrality principle resulted from a failure to distinguish between essentially political questions and essentially educational questions having political implications. A theory adequate for our times would have to emphasize that distinction. It would have to reserve the norm of institutional neutrality for questions of the former sort and for them alone. For questions of the latter sort, and I believe the class-rank issue falls squarely within this category, it would formulate a different norm—a norm of institutional regulation, under which things central to the academy could be dealt with by the academy and not passed to other powers by default. Some questions would fall on or near the borderlines and raise jurisdictional dilemmas. But many more would fall to one side or another once the theoretical line was drawn. Thus, whether the state should build an arsenal of secret weapons would plainly be a political question; on this, for reasons that were given long ago and have never lost their validity, the university should be mute. But whether classified research, under state support, should be permitted on the campus would plainly be an academic question; on this, for different reasons, the university should be heard. To assert a normative choice is to reject the radical view that the university must always be political or consent to the evils of society, and the traditionalist view that the university must always be neutral or succumb to the divisiveness of society. Neither argues potently that the university must be independent, and act or not act as its needs demand.

Even if theories were remade, many pressures to delocalize would continue. To ask that the academy come to grips with these is to ask it to formulate counter-policies in apparent conflict with its needs. Delocalization is in part a product of the growing importance of the university: no one could realistically suggest that it retreat to its older insignificance. Delocalization is in part an answer to the financial exigencies of the university: it would be difficult to demand an autonomy that required enormous dollar sacrifices. Moreover, certain delocalizing forces serve as a counter to the overreach of others: large universities in consolidated public systems may squeeze a measure of autonomy from the fact that they can draw on federal subsidies as well as on state appropriations. Nevertheless, some measure of localness can be restored in ways neither retreatist nor impoverishing. The breaking up of large public configurations into smaller subregional complexes might be a step in this direction. The use of collaborative techniques like the sharing of faculties among independent colleges might be another. The diversion of federal aid into student loans, on a scale large enough to let client fees bear the major burden of client costs; the increase in federal aid in the form of institutional lump-sum payments; the decrease in federal aid for big science under academic auspices (other auspices might handle it as well)—all might reinvigorate local power. The localist need not be contemptuous of the rationalizer or believe that he is living in a cost-free system. He need only insist that rationalizations be really rational and that, in the building and rebuilding of systems, costs of every kind be assayed.

5

Political Action, Faculty Autonomy, and Retrenchment: A Decade of Academic Freedom, 1970-1980[1]

Sheila Slaughter

Academic freedom is the intellectual climate established by faculty when they are able to control personnel policies via due process mechanisms and have the job security that comes with tenure. Academic due process is nothing more nor less than the elaboration of rules and regulations covering terms of employment. These range from specification of dates of notice for assistant professors' nonrenewal to procedures for hearing dismissal charges brought against full professors. Tenure confers permanence of office so long as unwritten and variable codes of political conduct are not violated and the employing institution's fiscal health remains sound. When faculty decision making on these personnel matters is enforced through grievance committees, hearing boards, and tenure review, academic freedom should obtain. Theoretically, the state of academic freedom at any given moment depends on the collective consciousness of the senior faculty.

This chapter will briefly review academic freedom's emergence in industrial America and then more fully examine developments in the past decade. Generally it is argued that the mechanisms of academic freedom—due process and tenure review—were not easily won and require continuous faculty effort for maintenance. At issue is professors' occupational autonomy. From 1915 forward conflict has most often centered around wresting a minimal amount of personnel decision-making power from unenlightened managements that prefer to treat faculty as "mere employees." This continuing struggle for occupational autonomy is powered by faculty's professional aspirations and is closely tied to the expansion and contraction of higher education. Professional status, not ideology, is most often at stake. Within this quest for occupational autonomy, ideological or political cases have their own cycle, coinciding with periods of extreme social unrest in the wider society. In these troubled times, protection of professors with unconventional or unpopular ideologies depends on having well-exercised due process mechanisms in place. In their absence, tenured and untenured professors are easily fired; in their presence, arbitrary dismissals are more difficult but still occasionally occur.

The Quest for Occupational Autonomy: Due Process and the AAUP

As the graduate university emerged in the last quarter of the nineteenth century, the American professoriate was unable to claim the same occupational autonomy as their European peers due to that peculiar institution of academic governance characteristic of the United States: lay control. Trustees and their administrative agents had and have formal legal authority over the university. This authority was demonstrated in the famous academic freedom cases of the 1880s and 1890s when political economists suspected of unsound views were dismissed: Carter Adams at Cornell, Bemis at Chicago, Commons at Syracuse, E.B. Andrews at Brown, Ross at Stanford. Only Ely at Wisconsin was reinstated after a hearing by the Board of Regents.[2]

These cases occurred at a critical juncture in American history, during the violent capital-labor conflicts that marked the transformation of laissez-faire into corporate capitalism. Economists and political economists were at the storm center, but faculty not holding avant-garde economic views fared little better. When questions concerning a professor's right to tenure of office irrespective of his economic views reached the courts, judges upheld the laissez-faire theories liberal economists were challenging. In case after case, the courts took the position that faculty and governing boards were equal parties to a contract, and if a faculty member could leave at his pleasure, so the board could fire at its pleasure. As with the laborer who needed the factory for his livelihood, the weaker position of the institutionally dependent professor vis-à-vis the board was ignored. What tenure existed depended on the good will of trustees and could be abrogated at any instant with unqualified judicial approval.[3]

Although the dismissals of the 1880s and 1890s exposed professors' precarious position, they also precipitated a still continuing public debate on academic freedom. Professors started to proselytize for it and presidents of major graduate universities also began to offer limited support. Key to professors' and sympathetic university managers' claims was the centrality of knowledge in a technological age. Professors saw themselves as experts providing necessary technical information for the smooth functioning of a complex society and argued that academic freedom was necessary to this knowledge production.[4] Enlightened university managers saw it as creating working conditions that would assure the generation of new knowledge critical to an industrial era. As Yale's President Arthur T. Hadley put it, the problem was to secure "the advantages of freedom without exposing ourselves to the worse dangers....[to] combine....the maximum of progress with the minimum of revolution."[5]

In the Progressive era faculty began to show they could contribute to the solution of technical and social problems. Ever growing numbers of Ph.D.'s began to serve government and the private sector as experts, demonstrating the utility of knowledge and thus building support for academic freedom.[6] However, in the second decade of the new century, economic recession and resurgence of violence between capital and labor revealed the limits of Progressivism. In response to widespread agitation over social and economic issues, a wave of repression swept over the country. Faculty as well as labor suffered. In 1913, violations of academic freedom made national headlines for the first time since 1900.[7]

Reluctant to lose the prestige they had gained through consulting outside the university and the increased occupational autonomy they had achieved within it, senior faculty at elite institutions in 1915 used the newly formed American Association of University Professors (AAUP) to present a "Declaration of Principles on Academic Freedom and Tenure." The Association made explicit the agreement senior faculty and enlightened trustees had tacitly worked under since the turn of the century: faculty would undertake the management of knowledge in return for academic freedom. In effect, faculty gained some occupational autonomy by assuming trustees' responsiblities for monitoring the social content of knowledge to ensure that its revolutionary potential was damped by a code of scholarship emphasizing deliberation, "long views into the future," and "a reasonable regard for the teaching of expereince."[8] The rights that came with this responsibility were limited: freedom to follow research where it led, to pursue advanced and controversial ideas with graduate students, to speak freely outside the university in areas of professional competence and with the decorum befitting a professor on general social and political issues. These rights were extended only to professors with long years of service and were enforced solely through their right to fire for cause. This definition of academic freedom was designed primarily to ensure that established professors giving scientific advice to government, foundations, and private sec tor organizations would not suffer reprisals.[9]

The 1915 Declaration of Principles was issued to guide employment relations between faculty and university managers and trustees. University officers at a handful of graduate centers engaged in generating knowledge for industrial society recognized its importance. However, most trustees did not, and the AAUP was forced to undertake their education. It began to publish didactic instances of infringements of professorial rights in the *Bulletin* and the 1915 Declaration became the first rather than the definitive document in a long series of policy statements. Taken together, these published investigations and policy statements were the beginning of an extralegal body of occupational case law focused on internal university due process. It would shape academic personnel policy and definitions of academic freedom into the 1980s.

The First World War, however, revealed the problems of protecting academic freedom when this was entrusted to senior faculty supported by sympathetic university managers. While most professors wholeheartedly embraced the war, some stood forth against it, exercising their rights as citizens. The AAUP did nothing to protect these dissidents, many of whom were fired.[10]

Although the AAUP failed to protect the academic freedom of anti-militarist professors, it worked closely on the war effort with associations of college and university managers: the Association of American Colleges, American Association of State Universities, American Association of Agricultural and Experiment Stations, and others. This cooperation with officials representing a wide spectrum of institutions prepared the way for a detailed accord with college and university managers after the war.[11] In 1924, working under the auspices of the war-generated American Council of Education, the AAUP gained managerial approval of a shortened form of the 1915 Declaration as well as a more explicit definition of due process mechanisms. Although the rights defined were no more extensive than in 1915, the AAUP hoped to make academic freedom more secure by reaching a formal agreement with officials from a variety of managerial associations.[12]

This hope was not fulfilled since the 1925 Conference Statement did not deal with the perplexing issue of civil liberties. Economic depression and social strife in the 1930s involved increasing numbers of professors in left politics and academic freedom cases that turned on ideological issues. A fair number of trustees and administrators at universities of all types supported academic freedom so long as controversy was confined to the classroom and academic journals but proved unwilling to allow professors to speak freely in the political arena, whether within their field of specialization or not. Civil liberties were at issue, not technical competence. The professors fired in political cases were rarely terminated for giving scientific advice to mainstream public or private agencies. Instead, they were fired when publicly championing unpopular or controversial social causes.[13]

The 1940 Statement of Principles, drawn up conjointly with the Association of American Colleges, was in large part an attempt to clarify professors' civil liberties. With regard to "extra-mural utterances" made in the course of exercising the political rights of a citizen, the professor no longer has the same latitude as other men and women. "His special position in the community imposes special obligations." While the professor should be "free from institutional censorship or discipline," he should nonetheless always keep in mind "that the public may judge his profession and his institution by his utterances. Hence, he should at all times be accurate, should exercise appropriate restraint, should show respect for the opinions of others, and should make every effort to indicate that he is not an institutional spokesman." Finally, professors are expected to lead exemplary lives since "moral turpitude" also constitutes grounds for dismissal.

In return, precise definition is given for the first time to the tenure process. After a probationary period of a maximum of seven years, professors, after peer review, should have permanent or continuous tenure of office that can be terminated only for "adequate cause." What adequate cause might be is not addressed, but the interpretation appended to the 1940 document specifically states that the exercise of a professor's political rights as a citizen might legitimately be considered sufficient.[14]

In essence, the 1940 Statement relieved the AAUP of any obligation to insist that professors be accorded the same rights as citizens in comparable positions in times of widespread social unrest. Civil liberties were exchanged for tenure. As a past president of the AAUP and law professor, William Van Alstyne, has pointed out:

> the trade-off that the AAUP appeared to have accepted with the Association of American Colleges in 1940 (namely, to cultivate public confidence in the profession by laying down a professionally taxing standard of institutional accountability for all utterances of a public character made by a member of the profession) is substantially more inhibiting of a faculty member's civil freedom of speech than any standard that government is constitutionally privileged to impose in respect to the personal politics or social utterances of other kinds of public employees.[15]

The 1940 Statement is of critical importance since it still stands as the AAUP's basic formulation of academic freedom and tenure.[16]

Because civil liberties were not defined as professional prerogatives in its accord with management, the AAUP took no action when World War II gave way to the Cold War and professors became the target of the House Un-American Activities Committee, were subjected to scrutiny by the Federal Loyalty Program, and made objects of surveillance by the National Security Act. In state and national heresy trials, professors were forced publicly to recant ideological sins committed a decade or more before.[17] According to the AAUP's own calculations, there were over seventy-five dismissals resulting from alleged participation in left or Communist Party politics between 1949 and 1955. However, the Association remained silent through them all. When it finally took positions (1956 and 1958) on the relation between professors' politics and national security, the AAUP was unclear as to whether Communist Party membership unfitted professors for the university and insisted on faculty disclosure of such affiliation to the employing institution, even though this meant loss of Fifth Amendment protection in inquiries outside the university.[18]

In the 1960s, social and economic conditions presented professors with an opportunity to recoup occupational autonomy lost during the McCarthy era. The rapid expansion of postsecondary education resulted in a shortage of Ph.D.'s, giving faculty some leverage with regard to civil liberties. This advantage was reinforced by strong social reform movements—civil rights crusades and the war on poverty—in the wider society. Individual professors and the AAUP began to combine litigation with the time-honored but too often ineffective means of publicity to safeguard professors' political rights. The narrow construction of academic freedom as protecting faculty acting exclusively in a professional capacity began to be expanded through defense of civil liberties on First Amendment grounds. Frequently using language and concepts developed through the AAUP's extralegal body of academic case law, the courts gradually incorporated academic freedom into legal canon. Currently, academic freedom is widely understood to confer civil as well as professional liberties. However, successful defense usually depends on discovery of procedural violations rather than any substantive definition of academic freedom, and the point at which liberty becomes license remains, as always, elusive.[19]

As the "due process" revolution continued in the 1970s, faculty sought further clarification of the broader construction of academic freedom and also brought suits that gave tenure some legal status under the Fourteenth Amendment.[20] In the tenure cases the courts recognized contract and property claims of already tenured faculty that make administrative demonstration of adequate cause necessary to terminate. However, the rights of the untenured remain uncertain, and adequate cause, like academic freedom, lacks substantive definition.[21]

Thus, in the United States, the mechanisms of academic freedom—due process and tenure—were slowly articulated through the AAUP's development of an extralegal body of case law, and, more recently, through the civil courts and union organization as well. In the main, recognition of academic freedom has involved a series of negotiations between the AAUP and organizations of managers over due process mechanisms. Faculty demanded occupational autonomy as a necessary condition for professional work and presidents of leading research universities and elite colleges were the first to grant due process and tenure. The governing boards and managers of state colleges and small private colleges began to recognize academic freedom when they sought university status during the expansion of post-secondary education after World War II, or when they were compelled by the courts or collective bargaining agreements.

However, in the currently contracting higher educational economy, managers are sometimes unwilling or unable to recognize due process and academic tenure. Moreover, neither managers nor the courts have ever agreed to unconditional freedoms with regard to professors' extramural utterances. Faculty continue to have a "particular obligation," as the AAUP put it in 1970, as representatives of the academy outside the university. The nature of this obligation continues to shift with the prevailing political climate, creating an unwritten and variable code used to judge professors' political activity. Thus, behavior often tolerated in the 1930s was anathema in the 1950s, and what was acceptable at the height of the student protest movement in the 1960s may be beyond the pale in the 1980s.

Academic freedom, then, is still an evolving concept, depending on professorial organization, judicial decisions, institutional procedure, and the collective consciousness of senior faculty at any given institution. Since academic freedom varies with historical circumstance, it can best be understood in terms of specific cases in a particular time period.

Academic Freedom Cases: 1970-1980

Since the AAUP is the only national organization that consistently reports academic freedom cases in rich detail and fairly standard format, the data presented are based on investigations made by Committee A and publicly reported in the Association's journal, supplemented by interviews with AAUP staff members.[22] There are, however, numerous problems in using AAUP data to assess the state of academic freedom. First, examination of complaints and cases handled in a five-year period (1975-1979) indicates that only a small percentage of cases ever become available for public scrutiny. A complaint is the registration by a professor of a suspected violation of academic freedom; a complaint becomes a case when the AAUP staff finds it merits further investigation. Forty-three percent of the 2135 complaints received were handled by the AAUP staff without ever achieving "case" status. Although 1312 (57 percent) became cases calling for further probing, only 23 cases (2 percent) were subject to full-dress investigation and public report by Committee A. Even if the 366 cases (27 percent) said to be successfully closed are omitted on the grounds that positive resolution does not result in publication, approximately 70 percent of the cases are unaccounted for.[23] Thus, the nature of complaints as well as the vast majority of cases, all indicators of the climate of academic freedom, remain unknown.

Second, the cases reported by Committee A reflect the AAUP's selection process. They are chosen for their importance in illuminating a pressing problem through setting precedent.[24] Although clarifying issues and procedures critical to the profession is laudable and central to the AAUP's self-definition, many unremarkable cases go unrecorded. Third, while the AAUP will investigate complaints lodged regardless of whether or not faculty belong to the Association, it rarely takes action unless aid is requested. Presumably, persons seeking such intervention must have some degree of conviction as to the justice of their case, the responsiveness of the academic system, and the effectiveness of the AAUP. The timorous, the deviant, and the cynical may never call attention to perceived violations of their academic freedom.[25] Fourth, as in the past many faculty may turn to organizations and institutions other than the AAUP—associations of learned disciplines, caucuses, conferences and support groups in their field, unions, the ACLU, the courts, political parties.

In sum, the AAUP is the only consistent, central, national data source for academic freedom cases, but it tells us little about the possible universe. There is no way of estimating the percent of complaints and cases handled by the Association compared to actual violations. However, the AAUP does serve clearing-house and consultant functions within the profession and is likely to be at least tangentially involved in well-publicized cases.[26] As AAUP Associate General Secretary Jordan Kurland says, "We have a monopoly on academic freedom even if we don't hold the copyright."[27] Thus, even though Association data is incomplete, analysis of those cases investigated by Committee A and reported in the AAUP's journal between 1970-1980 probably gives a fair indication of the overall pattern of academic freedom infringements.

Between 1970-1980, there were fifty-nine cases, each representing an institution.[28] In prestige terms, cases reported seem to come most often from higher education's middle ranks where fluctuations in faculty and student market make for volatile conditions. Thirty-two (or 62 percent) occurred in the public sector, with the majority at institutions rapidly and recently upgraded from normal school to university status. The twenty-three (38 percent) cases in the private sector took place largely at small, church-related colleges.

The concentration of cases in the middle ranks is probably best explained by the expansion and contraction of the postsecondary sector that brought national norms into conflict with local during a period of financial instability. Both state schools and private colleges profited from overproduction of Ph.D.'s in the 1970s and absorbed previously unobtainable cosmopolitan faculty members from nationally known universities. These new faculty may have combined arrogance with a consciousness of professional rights, creating conditions for confrontation. These quickly expanded and sometimes overextended institutions were also among the first to feel financial pressure when student enrollments peaked. Thus, they often faced retrenchment with young and belligerent faculties who expected a voice in decision-making.

Geographical distribution of cases also reflect these patterns in growth and decline, mitigated by tradition. The South, where the greatest growth in the past decade took place, had the same number of cases (eighteen or 31 percent) as the middle states, the area most beset by financial crisis. The Midwest had thirteen (22 percent), the West nine (15 percent) and New England, economically depressed but rich in academic heritage, had only one. The concentration of cases in the South may reflect conditions at institutions not yet socialized to national norms, while those in the middle states may point to financial pressures that cause these norms to be abandoned.

While no cases were reported at long-established universities with departments consistently ranked in the top ten, and few from community colleges, this lack of reported violations does not necessarily indicate their absence; it merely suggests they might be handled by means other than the AAUP. At the bottom, faculty located in community and state colleges may rely more on union organization and strict contractual obligation to protect their academic freedom. In the topmost tier, highly rated research universities might have more sophisticated administrators and colleagues might bring more subtle pressures. Most importantly, faculty at the top are able to move elsewhere, often without great loss of prestige. Thus, it is the vast middle, composed of faculty aspiring to attain or maintain the privileges of the most highly ranked universities, on the one hand, and of those too weak and divided about their professional status to organize, on the other hand, who bring cases reported by the AAUP.

As Table I indicates, the fifty-nine cases resulted in the firing of 1348 faculty members, and in eight having their pay docked. The number of faculty dismissed from each institution varied extremely. On the one hand, thirty cases concerned a single faculty member each; on the other, a single case involved the firing of 1000. The largest numbers are accounted for by financial exigency in New York state, but groups ranging from five to forty were fired in all the remaining categories with the exception of "other." Each case represents a violation of academic due process or academic freedom since all resulted in censure by the AAUP.

In cases involving large numbers of faculty, tenure status was often not reported. However, most of the 990 in the financial exigency column were fired from CUNY, where a seniority principle was used in making cutbacks. Thus, untenured faculty are probably a great deal more vulnerable than tenured when an institution faces financial crisis. In those cases where rank of fired faculty is known with certainty, tenured and untenured faculty are almost evenly matched overall. However, untenured professors are much

TABLE I

ACADEMIC FREEDOM CASES REPORTED BY AAUP 1970-1980

			MAJOR CAUSE, AS INDICATED BY AAUP REPORT						
Year	No. of Cases	No. Fired	Financial Exigency	Political Action	Policy Shift	Religious Action	Anti-Admini-stration	Other	ND
1970	9	20	0	10	0	0	10	0	0
1971	6	10	0	8	0	0	1	1	0
1972	4	4	0	4	0	0	0	0	0
1973	10	20*	1	15	2	0	1	0	1
1974	3	29	0	16	13	0	0	0	0
1975	6	82	0	0	33	40	9	0	0
1976	6	14	0	1	0	1	9	1	2
1977	4	1118	1116	0	0	0	1	1	0
1978	2	37	36	0	0	0	1	0	0
1979	5	12	1	1	0	0	2	1	7
1980	4	10	4	0	0	0	4	2	0
Totals	59	1356	1158 (85%)	55 (4%)	48 (4%)	41 (3%)	38 (3%)	6** (.5%)	10 (.5%)
Tenured		149	87	6	30	2	16	4	4
Un-tenured		151	81	35	18	0	2	2	6
No Answer		1046	990	14	0	39	20	0	0
	59	1356	1158	55	48	41	38	6	10

*8 docked pay, but not fired
**incompetence, personality, moral turpitude, etc.

more likely to be dismissed for political action than tenured professors, while the tenured are much more likely to be removed when acting against the administration or during a policy shift involving change of institutional mission. There are several possible explanations for these differences. First, and contrary to popular professional wisdom, young untenured professors, perhaps not as fully cognizant of the perils of academe as their well-socialized seniors, may speak and act more openly on political questions. Second, administrators and trustees may feel they face greater difficulties in removing tenured faculty on political grounds and thus tolerate more outspokenness. Third, the tenured may defend their role as guardians of professional prerogatives at the institutional level rather than in the wider political arena. Their concern with institutional politics is perhaps not misplaced since they are more likely to be dispensed with than young faculty when policy shifts call for new skills or credentials. Although risks may vary with age and status, tenure is not a firm guarantee against violations of academic freedom.

Of the fifty-nine reported cases, twenty were successfully closed and removed from the AAUP's censured list. Censure, inaugurated in 1932, is a warning to professors that the institution so listed does not subscribe to AAUP academic freedom and tenure policies. It is usually lifted when two conditions are met: rules and regulations are revised in accord with Association policy, and the faculty members fired are offered some sort of redress. Reinstatement is exceedingly unusual. Settlements are most often financial, with a year's salary as the standard. However, this can vary and when it does it is usually less rather than more. These twenty successfully resolved cases involved sixty-three faculty members. Many of the remaining 1293 are unlikely to receive redress since they are caught up in cases involving mass layoffs where such expectations are unrealistic.

Economic Causes: Policy Shifts and Financial Exigency

During the 1970s, managers at a wide array of postsecondary institutions recognized faculty's occupational autonomy by granting them control over due process mechanisms and tenure review. However, a depressed higher educational economy is eroding these gains. Financial exigency accounts for 85 percent of the faculty fired in the last decade, and policy shifts for 4 percent, for a total of 89 percent. This strikes at the heart of due process and tenure since reorganization and cutbacks are often defined by fiscal agent, administrators, and sometimes by faculty as a management problem thereby legitimating administrative rather than professional decision making about who should stay and who should go. Further, a climate of austerity is created throughout the American academic system, increasing administrative intervention with regard to credentials, class size, faculty load, and the general shape of academic programs, all areas previously reserved at least theoretically for faculty self-governance. Administrators sometimes appear to take advantage of the opportunity presented by fiscal crisis and austerity conditions to (1) upgrade or change institutional mission, and (2) reorganize along lines more profitable to management.

Firings during policy shifts usually occur when administrators and trustees decide to upgrade their institutions by taking advantage of a buyers' market. With jobs in short supply faculty previously not in reach are hired to replace faculty lacking Ph.D.'s or low in productivity, whether in terms of publications or F.T.E. (full-time equivalent) enrollments. In all but one case falling into the "policy shift" category, administrators at growing and ambitious state or private colleges and universities rid themselves of professors who had come to be considered marginal in view of the faculty available.[29] The Bloomfield College case provides an example. After a period of expansion, the administration claimed financial exigency on the basis of a slight drop in enrollments. The tenure system is abolished and eleven tenured and two untenured faculty, most with service preceding the expansion, were fired. Yet at the same time administrators and trustees were negotiating to build a larger campus on a new site and almost immediately engaged twelve new full-time faculty and twenty-four part-timers. The AAUP, elected collective bargaining agent during the fracas, brought suit. The New Jersey Superior Court reinstated both the dismissed faculty and the tenure system.[30] This unusually clear-cut decision may have discouraged upgrading at the expense of faculty with legitimate claims on an institution. No further attempts to take advantage of the buyers' market in this fashion were made in the second half of the decade.

CUNY starkly illustrates the problems created by higher education policies that promise equal access without making arrangements to foot the bill. Tuition-free enrollment in reputable public four-year colleges was designed to provide unprecedented opportunity for the nonwhite urban poor constituting the majority of the City's population. They seized it. After open enrollment the number of students in four-year institutions increased by 60 percent, in two-year schools by 100 percent. The number of faculty grew concomitantly. Expansion of the educational sector accounted for a large part of the City's swelling budget between 1970-1974. However, this commitment to social services diverted public funds from the support of basic economic redevelopment, and the City, near bankruptcy, drastically cut its spending. As an economically weak unit in a national system of recycling regions, the City was unable to keep its promise to the urban poor. In the austerity program that followed New York City's fiscal crisis, 1000 full-time faculty (and roughly 5000 part-time faculty not included in the figures in Table I) were fired with thirty-day notice in August, 1975.[31]

Financial exigency is a problem higher education has not faced since the Great Depression and neither administrators nor faculty are sure about how to retrench. CUNY and SUNY illustrate two different methods, each with its own problems for occupational autonomy and academic freedom. At the AFT-organized CUNY, a seniority principle was invoked. Indeed, no full-time tenured faculty were fired although ten faculty who technically did not receive tenure until September first were terminated. Cutbacks designed to protect those with seniority present several problems. First, the formula is mechanical and allows no room for faculty participation in long-term program planning. Second, talented young professors, high in energy and ideas, are lost. Third, the university is deprived of the contributions of women and minorities since they are concentrated disproportionately in the lower ranks.

SUNY, faced with a financial crisis of decidedly lesser proportions, tried a different method. General guidelines were provided by the state and each institution was asked to make cuts based on long-term plans. In some instances there was considerable faculty participation, in most very little. Lack of faculty participation was in large part due to the system's union's insistence that making cutbacks was a managerial function. Professorial participation was thought to give tacit approval and destroy faculty solidarity in resisting retrenchment.

Despite widespread faculty and union opposition, selective cutting occurred. Moreover, it gave administrators a chance to dismiss troublesome faculty and reorganize the general academic program on management terms. Thus, there are indications of violations of academic freedom in the SUNY system's procedures. An example is the case of a distinguished senior professor and outspoken critic of the administration. When his small program was abolished, he was not allowed to move to a related department where he regularly taught classes. Similarly, another troublesome professor in an Asian studies department found Chinese language, a specialty represented only by himself, designated a unit for retrenchment. He was fired and the rest of the department retained.

As disturbing as these violations is the faculty roster following retrenchment. The SUNY system had one hundred and four more faculty members in 1967-1977 than in 1975-1976, the year when cuts were made. Moreover, the system's average salary dropped from $19,180 to $18,750. Indeed, the AAUP has accused SUNY of using financial distress to reorganize the system at the expense of well-paid professors.[32]

Although the massive cutbacks at CUNY and SUNY represent retrenchment extremes, financial exigency continues to pose serious problems for academic due process and tenure. As the fiscal crisis of the state continues, many institutions are facing cutbacks. However, there is little shared agreement among faculty organizations about how to meet calls for retrenchment, beyond a general conviction that the tenured should be the last to go. The strongest unions resist participation on the grounds that retrenchment is a managerial function that should be uniformly resisted or guided by the seniority principle. The AAUP stresses participation at all levels: declaring a state of financial exigency, setting criteria for identifying those individuals or departments to be terminated, hearing grievances to assure fairness in criteria application.

However, neither unions nor the AAUP have any program that enables faculty to cope with the atmosphere of panic engendered by the possibility of financial exigency. Lack of coherent professorial policy on retrenchment at the institutional or national level seems to have demoralized faculty to the point where individual professors, whether or not members of organizations refusing or countenancing participation in planning for financial exigency, respond to state and managerial creation of a climate of austerity by investing inordinate effort in documenting their usefulness to the university. This often results in activity that mitigates against creative scholarship and teaching, destroys collegiality, and perhaps inadvertently shifts the delicate internal balance of university power into administrative hands. Such behavior seems to indicate a tacit recognition on the part of faculty that tenure no longer exists in practice.

Anti-Administrative Behavior: The Fight for Occupational Autonomy

Although financial exigency is undercutting occupational autonomy, the majority of postsecondary institutions in the 1970s at least recognized faculty claims about control of due process and tenure review. However, some faculty are still engaged in the struggle that began in 1915. The thirty-nine faculty members fired for anti-administrative behavior all engaged in some form of open criticism of their administrations, usually as part of a struggle for a modicum of occupational autonomy. Although not comprising a large percentage of cases, anti-administration dismissals occur more regularly than any others. Administrators, invariably backed by trustees, assert their sense of managerial privilege and retaliate against faculty demands, especially at new state colleges and universities, community colleges, and small private colleges. In only one of the thirteen cases did anything so radical as a demand for union organization precipitate dismissals. Most were what AAUP Associate General Secretary Kurland calls "mean little cases," where administrators casually rid themselves of troublesome faculty and appear affronted when called to task.[33]

The institutional charges made against faculty during investigation give an idea of the contempt in which their right to a voice in governance is held.[34] These ranged from "not fitting in with college philosophy," to "not playing on the team," and included several false claims of financial exigency. These anti-administration cases indicate that some administrators and trustees still see their colleges as private fiefdoms. Here faculty are regarded as "mere employees" and any challenge to the administration—as in the case where a professor protested unilateral administrative alteration of a faculty committee's work on tenure policy—is grounds for termination.[35] Running a college like a plant with a company union, where even AAUP membership must sometime be kept secret, may account for the sharp rise in collective bargaining in the past decade.[36] As AAUP Associate Secretary and Director of Collective Bargaining Geri Bledsoe put it, a union is often "the only way to curb a rogue president," and all encompassing contractual protection may be the best way to guarantee job security and academic freedom at institutions disregarding professional custom.[37]

Ideological Causes: Political and Religious Action

Although anti-administrative cases currently occur most frequently at institutions far from the academic mainstream, the achievement of occupational autonomy for these faculty members remains critical since the protection of professors with unconventional or unpopular ideologies depends on systemic recognition of and agreement on due process. The investigation, publicity, articulation of standards and due process as well as the litigation surrounding the cases discussed above all contribute to tradition, custom, and law that makes some degree of ideological freedom possible. Moreover, political cases are not confined to the bottom tier of the middle ranks but occur as well at institutions not far from the top: for example, UCLA, Ohio State, the Universities of Southern Illinois, Maryland, Arizona State. Despite efforts over a half century and more to clarify professors' political rights, the degree and manner of faculty participation in politics that trustees, administrators, and colleagues will tolerate is not yet firmly fixed and remains difficult to predict at specific institutions.

Clearly established procedures for academic due process and tenure are thus far the only means the professoriate has discovered to protect controversial and unpopular faculty, whether left, right, or simply deviant. And this protection is still desperately needed. If political cases are combined with religious cases to account for all dismissals on ideological grounds, they total 7 percent or almost twice the number of dismissals in any category other than financial exigency. Indeed, according to some calculations, between 1965-1975 professors were fired on overtly ideological grounds at a rate unmatched since the height of the McCarthy era.[38]

Those political cases reported seem to occur in a specific context. They are rooted in periods of social unrest, as was the case in the 1880s and 1890s, World War I, the 1930s, and the 1950s.[39] Most of the cases reported by the AAUP in the years 1970-1980 stemmed from events that took place between 1969-1971, even though they were often not published for one to three years later due to the sometimes lengthy process involved in exhausting internal university due process procedures and the time needed to complete an AAUP investigation. With one exception, faculty were not involved in events resulting in political cases after 1972. Thus, the political cases correspond to those turbulent years when order on campus was often maintained at gun point. Again, as in the past, all but one case involved professors exercising their civil liberties by engaging in overt political activity: making radical social commentary before public audiences, working with controversial organizations or causes, or participating in tension-fraught protests.

Teaching was seldom at issue. Indeed, only two cases touched on professors' classroom performance. Both involved extremely provocative behavior—professors' burning of flag and draft card—ending in immediate dismissal.[40] This relative lack of interference in the classroom is subject to several possible interpretations. First, professors may in the main follow established practice and scholarly format, confining themselves to their subject matter and presenting all sides of controversial materials equitably, thereby avoiding charges of indoctrination or abuse of their position. Second, faculty may vigorously uphold long recognized claims about the private and privileged nature of the exchange between professors and students. Thus, faculty who encountered undercover government agents or media representatives in their classrooms often effectively made student-backed complaints to their administrations.[41] Perhaps all members of the university community have a vested interest in sheltering the uncertain and unpredictable transactions between professor and students from the public eye. Third, the classroom may be difficult to monitor effectively. In any event, what professors tell their students rarely results in charges of ideological deviance. Violation of academic freedom in the classroom is probably much more likely to stem from state legislative attempts to mandate curricula and competencies than from any interference with the conduct of a specific class.

What stands out in these cases is the readiness with which repression was used to keep knowledge from leading to action. While official role did not always condition response to faculty activism and many persons formally connected with or interested in postsecondary education refused to condone repression, a fair number did not hesitate to use any means at hand for social control. Activist faculty were subject to pressure from colleagues and administrators, trustees and legislators, the media, and monitored secretly by local and national police forces. Indeed, those opposed to popular decision making and social change may understand better than academics the combustible potential of deviant ideas and spokespersons attached to legitimate institutions of learning.

Of course, not all cases involved this full phalanx of repression. Civil rights cases in particular offered faculty some latitude, especially if the action undertaken did not suggest radical restructuring of society. In these cases, most of which took place in the South, local elites were pitted against national and faculty could appeal to outside audiences and institutions for support.

The University of Mississippi provides a good example of the dynamics of repression in civil rights cases, illustrating both the intransigence of local authorities and the potential of alleviating repression through appeal to national norms. Following the Brown decision, Mississippi's Board of Trustees tried to combat support for integration through a variety of means: outside speaker bans, freezes on the salaries of faculty who litigated

over speaker censorship, rules that prevented faculty use of expertise on external projects that might further civil rights. When two Yale-educated law
professors announced their intention of continuing work on the OEO-
funded Northern Mississippi Legal Services Project despite university warnings, their contracts were not renewed. However, they were able to bring
successful suit against the university as well as initiate a joint investigation
on the part of the AAUP and the American Association of Law Schools.[42]

Although some professors at Mississippi were fired and others
economically penalized, their careers were not irreparably damaged. Institutions representing national norms offered some recourse to professors
able and unafraid to tap their resources. Ultimately, a federal appellate
court put the university on notice that its procedures would be reviewed until at least token compliance was reached. The dismissed professors found
other positions and received financial redress. However, not all professors
involved in civil rights cases—especially those who were regionally based
and not well connected or familiar with national support networks—were
able to solicit aid as effectively as the University of Mississippi faculty.

The penalties to academic career appear more enduring when exercise of
civil liberties involves a call for far-reaching social change. Professors participating in the violent rhetoric or action that were part of the student
movement sometimes found their academic careers ended. Angela Davis's
dismissal points to the increasingly radical tenor of the struggle for civil
rights and the consequences thereof. In this case, civil rights and student
movement concerns were bridged by the linking of minority and third world
peoples' issues with the U.S. presence in Vietnam through a radical cri-
tique of American society.

Davis, black, young, a woman, and a radical, ran afoul of the Regents in
her first semester at UCLA when it became widely known that she was a
member of the Communist Party. Using a 1949 law of dubious constitu-
tionality, the Regents suspended her from teaching. However, strong faculty protest accompanied by litigation resulted in rapid reinstatement. Yet
after this point she was always in the public eye. Faculty as well as students
attended her classes in large numbers and her outside activities in support of
the Soledad Brothers were extensively covered by the media. Davis drew a
careful line between her professional work and her extramural utterances,
but the public did not. Although it was uniformly agreed that she was a
competent, well-prepared instructor who did not use her classroom as a
platform for indoctrination, her outside speeches were uncompromisingly
revolutionary, well attended, and often scathingly critical of higher education. While she did not incite to specific, immediate acts of violence, thus
keeping within the limits of the law, she clearly advocated radical structural
change through extralegal means. Ultimately, the Regents charged her with
"lack of appropriate restraint," and when department, faculty hearing
committee, and administration did not find her guilty, the Regents fired her

anyway.[43]

In civil rights cases where legally sanctioned ameliorative reform was at issue there was a chance for relief from repression through appeal to national audiences and institutions with some power and authority. In cases where radical change is demanded, national publicity campaigns can be mounted, as they were in the Davis case, but the audience that responds is usually not incorporated in or connected with institutions that can legitimately and effectively intervene. For Davis, the Regents were the academic court of last resort and they refused to recognize the decisions faculty made through due process mechanisms. Moreover, they underlined the fact that they were well within their rights in doing so when they permanently rescinded authority previously delegated to faculty for personnel review. Faculty control of due process is still a privilege, not a right to be taken for granted.

Unlike Davis, most faculty fired in political cases were not celebrated radicals and many were not even well-known activists. However, they were severely disciplined when moved to take a moderate stand by extreme campus political polarization. The case of William Wickersham, who was fired from two higher educational institutions, illustrates this point. A committed pacifist, he did not try to "escape the responsibility of choice," but took a leave of absence from his post at the University of Missouri at Columbia in order to devote himself to peace work. In this he followed AAUP policy recommending that professors who see "an insoluble conflict between the claims of politics, social action, and conscience, on the one hand, and the claims and expectations of their students, colleagues and institutions on the other," either take leave or resign.[44] While on leave he served as a mediator between students and administrators during massive demonstrations following the Kent and Jackson State shootings and was a central figure in media accounts. Despite his acting consistently as a moderating force he was fired. Moreover, the position he then accepted at another college was withdrawn because the trustees at this small, private institution feared adverse reactions from possible donors and parents as a result of the media attention Wickersham had received.[45] Thus, media coverage portraying the professor as activist in dubious battle seems inimical to career even when that activism does not spring from a call for radical change.

Although Wickersham was the only professor fired at the University of Missouri, other faculty members who canceled classes at the height of the demonstrations had their salaries docked. This form of reprimand followed AAUP introduction of a new policy on sanctions. Up to this point, only dismissal proceedings required due process. In 1971, the AAUP called for full-scale hearings on the imposition of major sanctions and grievance procedures in the case of minor ones. These sanctions range from oral reprimands to suspension from service without prejudice for a stated period.[46] While incorporating sanctions less severe than dismissal in due process proceedings may prevent extreme solutions to problems created by infractions of rules, they also give administrators and trustees greater opportunity to legitimately monitor a wider range of faculty activities. Thus, in the 1970 Teaching Assistants' Association strike at University of Wisconsin, Madison, faculty were not brought to book for their support, while in the 1980 strike faculty who did not meet classes on campus were involved in proceedings that ended with over fifty professors threatened with having their salaries docked.[47]

The *Morris Starsky* case at Arizona State is the last arising from the agitation over the Vietnam war and reveals most fully the forces that can be mobilized against professors who are openly and consistently anti-establishment: the public, the media, Regents, conservative elites, and the FBI. Starsky was a "publicly acknowledged Marxist Socialist" committed to social action. He was active in antiwar demonstrations and labor disputes, served as faculty advisor to socialist and radical student groups, and was active in Socialist Party politics. He had received tenure almost automatically during the rapid expansion of Arizona State in the 1960s, but despite media outcry no one moved against him until the FBI took a hand in his affairs. FBI documents released in the course of a law suit brought by the Socialist Worker's Party revealed the Bureau, as part of its counter-intelligence program against the New Left (COINTELPRO), decided to use a highly placed contact influential in the state and with the board of Regents to push for Starsky's dismissal. When Starsky cancelled a class to speak at a Tucson rally ending in a disruptive demonstration, he opened himself to charges. Not content with moving the Board to bring proceedings, the FBI also tried to influence the faculty hearing committee's deliberations. It mounted a covert operation that included sending committee members anonymous letters charging him with threatening a fellow Socialist Party worker with bodily harm. The faculty committee as well as the administration, however, recommended that Starsky be retained, at which point the Regents intervened and fired him. Although he found a one-year appointment immediately after his dismissal, Starsky's reputation as a trouble maker has since prevented him from holding a full-time job.[48]

Most professors, however, are unlikely to identify themselves with controversial causes, and thus are not involved in academic freedom cases. Still, the attitude of the many toward the few caught up in controversy is critical since they must defend their colleagues' right to civil liberties. In the twenty-three political cases in the 1970s, there was no reported evidence of any faculty support in twelve, or approximately half. Administrators apparently acted without undue outside pressure and without due process to rid themselves of faculty they defined as risks to their institutions' well-being in terms of publicity, possible donors, parental or legislative wrath. There is no record of faculty protest over what was often heavy-handed or abrupt action.

However, in seven cases there was evidence of some faculty support for fired colleagues, and in four additional cases—UCLA, Ohio State, Southern Illinois University at Carbondale, and Arizona State—faculty hearing committees supported by administrators resisted forceful direction by lay boards as well as strong outside pressure to recommend that colleagues involved in political action be retained. In each of these four instances, Regents intervened and fired the professors in question regardless of the opinion of the faculty as a whole. In a fifth instance of strong support, faculty at Concordia Seminary struck when a colleague and the President were suspended. The President had championed the faculty member in question when he was charged with "false teaching" of religious doctrine. The forty striking faculty members were dismissed and established a university in exile.[49]

Although faculty, often supported by administrators, are beginning to defend professorial rights to civil liberties by defending colleagues accused of misusing them, lay trustees sometimes make such defense academic. This continued vulnerability of faculty is perhaps inevitable. Faculty associations and unions are reluctant to press too far in seeking substantive and procedural guarantees for fear they will lose more ground than they gain. For the most part, trustees are representatives of the established order with at best an interest in perfecting rather than changing this. To test the legality of lay control in the course of defending political activists may be to confirm it, weakening existing traditions of occupational autonomy. Thus, academic custom and tradition offer ambivalent protection to professors' exercising their civil liberties, and this tug of war between the house of intellect and the power and social preferences represented by lay boards is reflected in the law.[50] Yet, this lack of clarity puts professors at risk since "freedom of speech has a very special function in the case of those whose job it is to speak."[51]

However, radicalism in and of itself is not necessarily cause for dismissal. Political *action* was the issue in the 1970s. Academic Marxists who addressed their social criticism primarily to each other did not figure in academic freedom cases even as liberals were fired for activism. Ideas alien to the established order were tolerated so long as they did not move men and women to deeds. Civil liberty more than intellectual substance was at issue. However, as activism becomes a thing of the past ideas in and of themselves may become suspect. In 1978, in the last political case of the decade, Bertell Ollman was denied the chair of political science at the University of Maryland, apparently due in part to Regental and media opposition to his scholarly and entrepreneurial reputation as a Marxist.[52] Ollman, whose extracurricular activities seem limited to inventing the successful game *Class Struggle,* becomes a victim of ideological contest and is thus far the only professor to suffer reprisal without directly engaging in action.

Although research and teaching seldom seem to have precipitated dismissals resulting in nationally reported academic freedom cases in the 1970s, this does not mean that professors working in ideologically questionable scholarly paradigms all survived unscathed by avoiding action. Given the low number of tenured professors involved in political cases, many probationary faculty silently engaged in controversial research may have been quietly removed during tenure decisions. The structure of scholarship lends itself to removal of deviants at this point. First, tenure review is governed by senior faculty in part selected for their adherence to national academic norms that define extremism of any stripe as suspect.[53] Second, professors outside the intellectual mainstream have fewer publication outlets and those that are available are often regarded with disdain by established academics. Third, they may have difficulty attracting students, especially when market conditions make exploration of unworn paths a luxury. Finally, there is little chance of making a convincing case to the courts or the professoriate at large when collegial consensus defines the quality of their intellectual output as lacking. When practice matches theory and senior faculty are able to control fully the mechanisms of due process and tenure review, the climate of academic freedom may still not be conducive to professors working in unacceptable intellectual paradigms.

"Other" Cases and Women

Apparently few faculty see themselves as wrongly dismissed for incompetence. Only four of the cases in the category "other" stem from this cause. This could mean that faculty who are incompetent know it and leave the university, or that they are removed by their colleagues after annual reviews or during tenure proceedings. More likely, incompetence is hard to prove in a profession difficult to evaluate, and, with the increase in litigation, such charges are not made unless they can be backed. With peer review, such cases should not appear on the AAUP censured list at all and do so largely because they involve notable violations of due process.

Two women appear in the "other" category, one fired for an irreconcilable personality conflict with a colleague, another for "moral turpitude" in the only case of its kind in some years. "Moral turpitude" has always been a mysterious charge; in a permissive age, what degree of baseness or depravity brings dismissal? In the case in question, a woman made the mistake of living openly with a man other than her husband in faculty housing located next door to the President's residence. Her colleagues found her indiscreet but not guilty of moral turpitude since they were unable to agree among themselves about what this might be. However, the President was seemingly convinced that he knew and fired her anyway.[54]

Thirteen women were involved in those cases where gender is known.

There seems to be nothing remarkable in their distribution across categories, except that four of the five involved in political cases were black. What is remarkable is the lack of sex discrimination cases. Although the AAUP called for use of procedural standards in instances of sex discrimination that are similar to those used when violations of academic freedom are alleged in 1971, only two cases involving sex discrimination were brought and neither were sustained by Committee A investigations.[55]

AAUP Associate Secretary Lesley Francis sees the lack of reported sex discrimination cases as due to the AAUP's function and the problem of proof. The AAUP is primarily a mediatory agency and does not have the financial resources, personnel, or subpoena powers necessary to mobilize the evidence needed to prove discrimination. However, the AAUP has devised progressive guidelines for sex discrimination complaints and can mediate when a case is still in university due process channels. Further, its policy and *amicus* briefs can successfully support women in sex discrimination cases tried in the courts, as in *Kunda* v. *Muhlenberg College*.[56] What is not clear is whether or not the AAUP allocates an even-handed proportion of its admittedly thin resources to its female constituency.

When women turn to government agencies and the courts, the problem of proof persists. Individual complaints of sex discrimination in hiring, promotion, or tenure fall under Title VII and are investigated by the Equal Employment Opportunity Commission. The complainant's first step in a court review is to make a *prima facie* case of discrimination. Statistical evidence can be offered on this point but may not be sufficient to establish a claim of discriminatory treatment. Though the plaintiff is not technically required to prove intent, she must show that the employer had a discriminatory motive in making the disputed employment decision. If she succeeds in doing this, the employer need only articulate some legitimate, nondiscriminatory reason for the decision. The burden of proof again shifts to the plaintiff to show that the employer's reason is a "mere pretext." Even if statistical evidence of discrimination is impressive, court opinions show that faculty women have found it difficult to meet the levels of proof required.[57] Although there have been some victories, especially in class actions brought by the agencies themselves, the process is costly, time-consuming, and so nerve-wracking that many women may be discouraged from becoming central figures. However, the number of women who brave this process is not known since federal agencies do not publish consistent statistics.[58]

Sex discrimination complaints brought by faculty women have been notably unsuccessful due to the courts' consistent deferral to decisions made by faculty and administrators concerning qualifications for hiring, retention, tenure, and promotion. In general, faculty try to avoid court interference in these decisions, perhaps to protect their due process privileges. At the extreme, the recent *Blaubergs* case demonstrates a tenured professor's willingness to defend his autonomy in these matters even if it means jail. As with all aspects of academic freedom, peer review controlled by white, male senior faculty may create a climate in which they flourish but others do not.

Conclusion

In the last decade, efforts were made by faculty to codify the meaning of academic freedom through the courts, unions, and professional associations. Although the law, contracts, and personnel policies currently grant greater recognition of internal university due process and tenure by peer review than in any other era, these gains are made tenuous even as they are achieved. Some postsecondary institutions have abolished permanent tenure, financial exigency renders due process uncertain, the question of collective bargaining has been reopened with the Yeshiva decision, and, as the Ollman case indicates, espousing unorthodox ideologies still makes faculty suspect.

The undermining of the mechanisms thought to guarantee academic freedom stems in the main from events and circumstances external to the academy. Economic austerity and attendant rationalization of state systems have created a political and fiscal climate where a university's declaration of financial exigency and abrupt dismissal of tenured and untenured faculty is unremarkable. Indeed, the widespread pruning of academic programs may mean that tenure and due process have already ceased to exist as uniform practice. While these mechanisms may not be the best or only way to protect academic freedom, abandoning them under financial duress before alternatives have been tested may inhibit the free circulation of ideas. In the pruning process, removal of those with ideas defined as extraneous, unorthodox, or controversial might well pass unnoticed and unmourned.

Paradoxically, the Yeshiva decision acknowledges tenured faculty as managers at a point when tenure is insecure and many professors have come to view themselves as employees seeking due process and job security through collective bargaining. While the extent of the decision's application even in the private sector remains unclear, it raises the possibility that collective action may no longer be an easily accessible avenue for securing professional privileges.[59] More importantly, it serves as a reminder that faculty status, together with its rights and responsibilities, is still evolving.

Although there have been few political cases in recent years, this may be due more to faculty quiescence and the lack of social turmoil than to a general regard and tolerance for professors' exercise of civil liberties. While many institutions seem to have accepted national norms that allow ideological deviance, the number of cases early in the decade indicate that political action on the part of professors is still viewed askance by some administrators and that trustees are not averse to intervention even against a united faculty. With academe in a steady state and the economy in an unsteady condition, the limits of tolerance may soon be tested.

In sum, the mechanisms of academic freedom—due process and tenure review—were not easily won and still require continual effort for maintenance. Faculty depend on their institutions for employment but demand the occupational autonomy they see as necessary for creative work and productive scholarship. At present, as in the past, the academy's close links to the wider society make these professional privileges subject to economic conditions, judicial review, the prevailing political climate as well as the collective consciousness of the senior faculty.

Notes

1. I would like to thank Jordan Kurland, American Association of University Professors' (AAUP) Associate General Secretary and spirit of Committee A, for his careful reading of several versions of this manuscript. While his help has been invaluable, he should not be held responsible for my interpretation of cases and policy. I would also like to thank Ms. Patricia Hyer, graduate student, College of Education, Virginia Polytechnic Institute and State University for her help in preparing the section on women.

2. See Walter P. Metzger, "The German Contribution to the American Theory of Academic Freedom," *American Association of University Professors Bulletin* (hereafter *AAUPB*) 41 (Summer 1955):214-230, and Walter P. Metzger, *The Development of Academic Freedom in the United States* (New York: Columbia University Press, 1955). For another interpretation of these early cases see Mary O. Furner, *Advocacy and Objectivity: the Professionalization of Social Science, 1865-1905* (Lexington: University of Kentucky Press, 1975).

3. Matthew W. Finkin, "Toward a Law of Academic Status," *Buffalo Law Review* 22 (1972): 575-601, and Walter P. Metzger, "Academic Tenure in America: A Historical Essay," in *Academic Tenure,* Commission on Academic Tenure in Higher Education (San Francisco: Jossey-Bass, 1973): 93-159.

4. For a discussion of the emergence of the expert, see Edward T. Silva and Sheila Slaughter, "Prometheus Bound: The Limits of Social Science Professionalization in the Progressive Period," *Theory and Society* 9 (November 1980): 781-819.

5. Arthur Twining Hadley, "Academic Freedom in Theory and in Practice," *Atlantic Monthly* 91 (February 1903): 160. See also John S. Brubacher and Willis Rudy, *Higher Education in Transition: A History of American Colleges and Universities, 1636-1976* (New York: Harper and Row, 1976): 308-329. For a fuller account of the attitude of enlightened trustees, usually located at emerging research universities, see Burton J. Bledstein, *The Culture of Professionalism: The Middle Class and the Development of Higher Education in America* (New York: Norton, 1977).

6. For details of academic service to government see David Michael Grossman, "Professors and Public Service, 1885-1925: A Chapter in the Professionalization of Social Science" (Ph.D. diss., Washington University, 1973) and Sheila S. McVey, "Social Control of Social Research: The Development of the Social Scientist as Expert, 1875-1916" (Ph.D. diss., University of Wisconsin, Madison, 1975).

7. There were continued violations between the Ross case in 1900 and the Mecklin and Fisher cases in 1913, but for the most part these were not at newly emerging graduate centers and did not make the national news. See Howard Crosby Warren, "Academic Freedom," *Atlantic Monthly* 114 (November 1914): 689-699 for a partial listing.

8. "Report of the Committee on Academic Freedom and Tenure," reprinted from 1915 in *AAUPB* 40 (Spring 1954): 89-112.

9. For a fuller interpretation of this exchange see Sheila Slaughter, "The 'Danger Zone': Academic Freedom and Civil Liberties," *Annals of the American Academy of Political and Social Science* 448 (March 1980): 46-61.

10. Carol S. Gruber, *Mars and Minerva: World War I and the Uses of the Higher Learning* (Baton Rouge: Louisiana State University Press, 1975) and William Summerscales, *Affirmation and Dissent: Columbia's Response to the Crisis of World War I* (New York: Teacher's College Press, Columbia University, 1970).

11. See for example, "Emergency Council of Education," *AAUPB* 4 (April 1918): 4-6.

12. "American Council on Education: Conference on Academic Freedom and Tenure," *Bulletin of the AAUP* 11 (February 1925): 99-102. The ACE was and is an umbrella organization with a number of higher educational associations representing managers among its constituents. Although the Conference was held under ACE auspices and endorsed by a number of member organizations, negotiations over the document were in the main carried out by the AAUP and the Association of American Colleges. For an account of the AAUP's relation in ACE see Ralph E. Himstead, "The Association: Its Place in Higher Education," *AAUPB* 30 (Autumn 1944): 445-447.

13. Slaughter, " 'The Danger Zone,' " *Annals:* 46-61.

14. "The 1940 Statement of Principles on Academic Freedom and Tenure," in *Academic Freedom and Tenure: A Handbook of the AAUP*, ed. Louis Joughlin (Madison: University of Wisconsin Press, 1969).

15. William Van Alstyne, "The Specific Theory of Academic Freedom and the General Issue of Civil Liberties," in *The Concept of Academic Freedom*, ed. Edmund L. Pincoffs (Austin: University of Texas Press, 1975): 81-82.

16. Although the 1940 document serves as a sort of Bill of Rights for the profession, it has been subject to clarifying interpretations over time by the Association. The most recent was in 1970. See "Academic Freedom and Tenure. 1940 Statement of Principles and (1970) Interpretive Comments," *AAUP Policy Documents and Reports* (Washington, D.C.: AAUP, 1977): 1-4.

17. See Robert M. McIver, *Academic Freedom in Our Time* (New York: Columbia University Press, 1955); Robert Iverson, *The Communists and the Schools* (New York: Harcourt Brace, 1959); and Melvin Rader, *False Witness* (Seattle: University of Washington Press, 1979).

18. For a list of the cases between 1949-1955 see "Academic Freedom and Tenure in the Quest for National Security: Report of a Special Committee of the AAUP," in *The American Concept of Academic Freedom in Formation,* ed. W.P. Metzger (New York: Arno, 1977), irregular pagination: 61-107. For AAUP policy statements see "Academic Freedom and Tenure in the Quest for National Security: (1956) report of a Special Committee," in *Academic Freedom and Tenure: A Handbook:* ed. Joughlin, 47-56, and "A (1958) Statement of the Committee on Academic Freedom and Tenure Supplementary to the 1956 Report," also in Joughlin: 56-63. For the AAUP interpretation of its role in the McCarthy era, see "Report of the Self-Survey Committee of the AAUP," *AAUPB* 51 (May 1965): 103-109. It should be noted that while the AAUP's Committee A was inactive between 1949-1955, the Association dealt with a backlog of cases from this period, insisting on due process in light of its equivocal 1956 and 1958 policy statements.

19. See Finkin, "Toward a Law of Academic Status," and Metzger, "Academic Tenure in America: A Historical Essay." For the AAUP's role in litigation see "Record of the Council Meeting," *AAUPB* 59 (March 1973): 12-16, which reviews some of the legal suits brought with the aid of the AAUP's Academic Freedom Fund. The AAUP also has a Legal Defense Fund to finance litigation involving faculty members on issues other than academic freedom, but with broad application for academic employment. See "The 60th Annual Meeting," *AAUPB* 60 (June 1974): 139-144.

20. "Report of Committee A, 1976-1977," *AAUPB* 63 (April 1977): 137.

21. See for example William Van Alystne, "The Supreme Court Speaks to the Untenured: A Comment on the Board of Regents v. Roth and Perry v. Sinderman," *AAUPB* 58 (September 1972): 267-278.

22. Other organizations have reported on academic freedom, for example, the AFT and ACLU in the 1930s and the New University Conference in the 1960s, but their reports are

sporadic and lack detail. On this point see Lionel S. Lewis, *Scaling the Ivory Tower: Merit and its Limits in Academic Careers* (Baltimore: Johns Hopkins University Press, 1975): 148-149.

23. "Report of Committee A, 1978-1979," *AAUPB* 65 (September 1979): 296. For an explanation of the processing of complaints received by the AAUP see "Report of the Special Committee on Procedures for the Disposition of Complaints under the Principles of Academic Freedom and Tenure," *AAUPB* 51 (May 1965): 210-224.

24. Interview with Irving Spitzberg, Jr., General Secretary, AAUP, December 29, 1980.

25. On this point see Lewis, *Scaling the Ivory Tower:* 148.

26. Irving Spitzberg, Jr., General Secretary of the AAUP, estimates that the AAUP was contacted in at least 90 percent of the cases in the 1970s; interview, December 29, 1980. Jordan Kurland, Associate General Secretary, indicated by letter, February 23, 1981, that the contact number is roughly 50 percent.

27. Interview with Jordan Kurland, AAUP, December 29, 1980.

28. This and the following data are compiled from the academic freedom cases reported by the AAUP from 1970-1980.

29. The exception was a state college that shifted from a traditional to an experimental mission and back again, accompanied by great tension and twelve dismissals. The AAUP supported litigation with its Academic Freedom Defense Fund and a decision was made in the terminated professors' favor. See "Academic Freedom and Tenure: University of Science and Arts of Oklahoma (formerly Oklahoma College of the Liberal Arts)," *AAUPB* 61 (April 1975): 39-48.

30. "Academic Freedom and Tenure: Bloomfield College (New Jersey)," *AAUPB* 60 (March 1974): 50-66; see also "The Bloomfield College Case: the Decision of the New Jersey Superior Court," *AAUPB* 60 (September 1974): 320-330.

31. "Academic Freedom and Tenure: City University of New York: Mass Dismissals under Financial Exigency," *AAUPB* 63 (April 1977): 60-81. See also James O'Connor, *The Fiscal Crisis of the State* (New York: St. Martin's Press, 1973), and Eric Lichten, "The Development of Austerity: Fiscal Crisis in New York City," in *Power Structure Research,* ed. G. William Domhoff (Beverly Hills: Sage, 1980): 139-171.

32. "Academic Freedom and Tenure: the State University of New York," *AAUPB* 63 (April 1977): 237-260. For AAUP policy on financial exigency see "Termination of Faculty Appointments Because of Financial Exigency, Discontinuance of Program or Department, or Medical Reasons," *AAUPB* 61 (Winter 1975): 329-331.

33. Interview with Jordan Kurland, AAUP, December 29, 1980.

34. Institutions were not required by the AAUP to give reasons for the dismissal of untenured professors until 1972. Even after this was required, many institutions refused to provide information for fear they might be opening themselves to legal suit. See "Development of Association Policy," *AAUPB* 57 (June 1971): 202-205, for the debate that preceded this policy decision. For the problems this has created in AAUP investigations see William Van Alstyne, "Furnishing Reasons for a Decision Against Reappointment: Legal Considerations," *AAUPB* 62 (August 1976): 285-286.

35. "Academic Freedom and Tenure: Onondoga Community College (New York)," *AAUPB* 57 (June 1971): 167-174.

36. "Academic Freedom and Tenure: Blenn College (Texas)," *AAUPB* 62 (April 1975): 78-82. For the rise of collective bargaining in the 1970s see Joseph W. Garbarino, "Faculty Unionism: the First Ten Years," *Annals* 448 (March 1980): 74-85.

37. Interview with Geri Bledsoe, AAUP Associate Secretary for Collective Bargaining, December 29, 1980.

38. Robert Justin Goldstein, *Political Repression in Modern America, 1870 to the Present* (Cambridge, Mass.: Schenkman, 1978): 522-523.

39. Slaughter, "The 'Danger Zone' ": 46-61.

40. "Academic Freedom and Tenure: Indiana State University," *AAUPB* 56 (March 1970): 52-61; "Academic Freedom and Tenure: The Ohio State University," *AAUPB* 58 (September 1972): 306-321.

41. Although the AAUP condemned government and police interference in classrooms by resolution in the 1970s, it did not develop a policy position on domestic monitoring. However, it did debate the relation between universities and the CIA. See "Universities and the Intelligence Community," *AAUPB* 65 (February 1979): 15-26.

42. "Academic Freedom and Tenure: the University of Mississippi," *AAUPB* 56 (March 1970): 75-86.

43. "Academic Freedom and Tenure: the University of California at Los Angeles," *AAUPB* 57 (June 1971): 382-420. See also Bettina Aptheker, *The Morning Breaks: The Trial of Angela Davis* (New York: International, 1975).

44. "A Statement of the Association's Council: Freedom and Responsibility," *AAUPB* 56 (December 1970): 375-376.

45. "Academic Freedom and Tenure: University of Missouri, Columbia," *AAUPB* 59 (March 1973): 33-45; "Academic Freedom and Tenure: Columbia College (Missouri)," *AAUPB* 57 (June 1971): 513-517.

46. See "Report of the Joint Sub-Committee on Faculty Responsibility," *AAUPB* 57 (June 1971): 524-527.

47. This dispute is still in the process of settlement. After the penalty was known, the professors brought suit in federal district court, and it now appears that only those faculty who did not meet classes at all will have their pay docked while those who met their classes off campus to honor picket lines may not be docked.

48. "Academic Freedom and Tenure: Arizona State University," *AAUPB* 61 (December 1975): 55-69, supplemented by an interview with Jordan Kurland. After a one-year appointment at San Diego State, Starsky accepted a position as associate professor and chair of the philosophy department at California State University, Dominguez Hills. But his appointment was cancelled before he assumed his duties due to the President's discovery of the circumstances under which he left Arizona State. Although Starsky received $20,000 from California as redress for the cancelled contract, he never won recompense from Arizona even though two courts affirmed his First and Fourteenth Amendment rights had been violated. On his attorney's advice he had accepted 60 percent of a year's salary for a terminal sabbatical on leaving Arizona State and the courts held this technically constituted redress. However, the AAUP has continued to press for a settlement and negotiations with Arizona State are continuing.

49. "Academic Freedom and Tenure: Concordia Seminary (Missouri)," *AAUPB* 61 (April 1975): 49-59.

50. For clarification of the AAUP's 1940 position on political action see "A Statement of the Association's Council: The Question of Institutional Neutrality," *AAUPB* 55 (Winter 1969): 448; "Academic Freedom and Tenure. 1940 Statement of Principles and (1970) Interpretative Comments," *AAUP Policy Documents and Reports* (Washington, D.C.: AAUP, 1977): 1-4, and "A Statement of the Association's Council: Freedom and Responsibility," *AAUPB* 56 (December 1970): 375-376.

51. Fritz Machlup, "On Some Misconceptions Concerning Academic Freedom," *AAUPB* 41 (Winter 1955): 75-86.

52. "Academic Freedom and Tenure: University of Maryland," *Academe* 65 (May 1979): 213-227. Although the AAUP put Maryland on the censured list, there was internal disagreement. See "Report of Committee A, 1978-1979," *AAUPB* 65 (September 1979): 293-303, and "Developments Relating to Censure by the Association," *AAUPB* 66 (May 1980): 223-224.

53. Most senior faculty would have received their primary socialization during the McCarthy era (1950-1960). For a notion of the ideological mind set in this period see Paul L. Lazarsfeld and Wagner Thielens, Jr., *The Academic Mind: Social Scientists in Times of Crisis* (Glencoe: Free Press, 1958).

54. "Academic Freedom and Tenure: Lynchberg College (Virginia)," *AAUPB* 65 (December 1979): 598-505.

55. "Report of the Council," *AAUPB* 58 (June 1972): 160-163.

56. Telephone interview with Lesley Lee Francis, Associate Secretary, AAUP, January 22, 1981. For AAUP discrimination guidelines see "On Processing Complaints of Discrimination on the Bias of Sex," *AAUPB* 63 (August 1977): 231-236; see also "News: Kunda Decision Affirmed," *AAUPB* 66 (May 1980): 172.

57. *A Program for Renewed Partnership: A Report of the Sloan Commission on Government and Higher Education* (Cambridge: Ballinger, 1980); Bruce A. Nelson and Richard W. Ward, "Burdens of Proof Under Employment Discrimination Legislation," *Journal of College and University Law* 4 (1979-1980): 301-316.

58. B. Haber, "Why Not the Best and the Brightest? Equal Opportunity vs. Academic Freedom," *Forum* 19 (January 1981): 19-25.

59. "The Yeshiva Decision," *AAUPB* 66 (May 1980): 188-197.

6

Happenings on the Way to the 1980s
Verne A. Stadtman

Nothing survives the passing of years without change, and, just as very hard rocks yield their shape and size to nature's elements, colleges and universities, however steeped they may be in tradition, also change to accommodate forces of history and social developments. It makes sense, therefore, to take stock occasionally and find out how colleges and universities are different now than they were the last time we looked at them systematically. By doing so, we may be able to anticipate the shape of higher education in the years ahead. At the very least, we may learn something about the changes students, faculty members, and administrators must take into consideration as they plan their futures.

Higher Education in 1969

The characterizing feature of American higher education in 1969 was the crescendo of student activism, dissent, and disruption that had started early

Reprinted with permission from Verne A. Stadtman, *Academic Adaptations* (San Francisco: Jossey-Bass, 1980).

in the 1960s and at the end of that decade approached the peak of its volume and intensity. Martin Luther King, Jr., was murdered in 1968, and, across the country, in their shock, guilt, and indignation, students protested and demonstrated on behalf of efforts to improve the lot of black students on college campuses. The war in Vietnam, the presence of military training programs on campuses, university involvement in defense-related research, and a rash of maverick political, social, and campus issues troubled students and brought them into conflict with campus and civil authorities.[1] By the end of 1969, the fatalities at Kent State and Jackson State that climaxed this era of student unrest were only five months away.

On many campuses political action was interpreted as evidence of student dissatisfaction with educational programs and institutional governance. Students began to talk about these things themselves, and colleges and universities began to look seriously at curricular adjustments and alternatives and to expand the role of students in campus decision making.

But the resulting reform was more than a sop to student power. It was also an accommodation to a greater diversity of students than colleges had known before. Open doors that made colleges and universities more hospitable to members of minority races and to young people who had been educationally disadvantaged in their pre-college years brought not only more students but more exceptions to campus standards and regulations. Differences among students became important, and programs designed for homogeneous student bodies had to be adjusted. Openness to new kinds of students, therefore, engendered receptiveness to new instructional technologies and curricular change.

Some of the programmatic reforms of American colleges and universities in 1969 were designed to save money or generate income. David Henry, a university president at that time, explained that financial difficulties began to appear in 1968. Except for a relatively few institutions that remained small throughout the 1950s and 1960s as a matter of policy, colleges and universities had been growing rapidly since the end of World War II. By 1969 the whole higher education enterprise was not only bigger, it was also more costly. And money became harder to get. More specifically, Henry said:

> The unexpected acceleration in the general inflation rate magnified costs, and dollars bought less. Federal resources that had gone to institutional income declined as a proportion of educational expenditures; unsettled economic conditions affected income from endowment and gifts; and tuition income could not be significantly increased without diminishing returns or incurring political opposition or both. What increases there were in public appropriations were often earmarked for community colleges or programs in the health sciences, including medicine. Capital expenditures followed the same course.[2]

Hodgkinson found that funding was the number one concern of virtually all college presidents in 1968-69.[3] For college presidents today who are inclined to say, "It was ever thus," it should be pointed out that for many presidents in 1968-69 the experience of hard times was new.

Second to funding, the problem of most concern to college presidents was growth. "Almost every questionnaire mentioned the word—more students, more faculty, more facilities."[4] How quaint that notion seems in 1979! But it was not based on wishful thinking. The first report of the Carnegie Commission on Higher Education came out in December 1968 and explained the matter this way: "Today's enrollment is almost 6 million students on a full-time equivalent (FTE) basis. More than one-half of this growth took place in the decade from 1958 to 1967. Estimates indicate that enrollment will pass 8 million by 1976, and this figure may well rise to 9 million if Carnegie Commission or other proposals are adopted to remove financial barriers for students from low-income families."[5] The Commission's estimate was a little optimistic but close to the mark (actual enrollment in 1976 was 7.8 million). Of more significance is the fact that it was consistent with the general expectations of the time.

That the end of the Vietnam war would result in decreased enrollment by males who found going to college an honorable alternative to involuntary military service was not anticipated, and the public perception that college attendance was not the reliable kind of insurance against unemployment or underemployment it had historically been had not yet dawned. To the extent anyone knew about them, low birthrates in the 1960s, which would result in fewer college students in the 1980s, were a matter for interesting speculation. *Growth was the present reality,* and presidents were accountable to their trustees, their faculties and students, their state governments, their alumni, and the public for how they led their institutions' adjustments to it.

The growth in the 1960s was accommodated by extensive college building and expansion. Colleges and universities spent $21.5 billion for buildings and improvements during the decade. The National Center for Education Statistics reports that 702 new institutions were established between 1960 and 1969.[6] Of these, 534 (3 out of 4) were public institutions. That statistic says a great deal about the economic condition of state governments in the 1960s. Some of them had built up considerable reserves during World War II; they also participated in the general prosperity of the country. They had the fiscal capacity needed to expand higher education. More importantly, such expansion seemed to be supported by the general public.

Part of the public confidence derived from the widely presumed success of colleges and universities in their roles as cultivators of higher culture and trainers of manpower and leadership for the productive pursuits of the nation. It also derived from the respect of the public for the nation's scientific achievements during and after World War II. These achievements were closely linked to the intellectual and physical resources devoted to science at American universities.

The universities' role in the scientific achievements of the nation generated more than public support. It also contributed to the maturation of what Jencks and Riesman called *The Academic Revolution*.[7] Fundamentally, this revolution involved the gradual assumption of more authority on university and college campuses by members of the academic profession. For most practical purposes, the faculty already had control of the methods of instruction; the curriculum; admission of students; and the hiring, retention, and promotion of their colleagues. Now they set the standards for student performance and also for the award of the Ph.D., and thus for access to their own profession. College and university presidents normally begin their careers in the academic ranks and, increasingly, are appointed to their jobs with the explicit approval of the faculty they are selected to lead. Through their academic disciplines and their professional and scholarly associations, the faculty maintain standards for academic research. Independently, they choose their own research projects and cultivate outside sources of support. The public's support of scientific activities after the war tended to increase the authority and independence of faculty members and contributed to the success of the academic revolution, which may have peaked in 1969.

To summarize, then, the major contextual factors that affected higher education when Hodgkinson studied it for his work were campus dissent and disruption related to both social and campus issues; an opening of the campuses to different types of students than had been admitted before; accommodations to individual differences among students through innovations in programs and instructional technologies; greater concern for the rising costs of operating increasingly expensive institutions; anticipation of continued enrollment growth for the ensuing decade; reasonably strong public confidence in higher education; and the acceptance of extensive authority in college and university affairs by the academic profession.[8]

The Intervening Years

In comparing the contexts in which colleges and universities operated in 1969 with those that prevail in 1979, one gets the impression that old problems are never really solved—they just get renamed and redefined. One reason for this impression is that, although colleges and universities tend to follow the leader in their responses to challenges and opportunities, they do not do so in concert, except perhaps as members of consortia or multicampus systems. Each approaches problems in its own way and on its own schedule. Some institutions solve a problem; others accommodate it; still others founder on it. The result is that the problems that confront all institutions of higher education are in evidence for a long time. They linger in some places long after others have responded to them successfully. Eventually, solved or not, they simply change form.

A good example of this phenomenon is provided by the fiscal concerns of colleges and universities. As we have seen, in 1969 the problems usually were defined in terms of the increased costs of operating expanded institutions and systems just when inflation was depreciating available revenues. In the 1970s, matters got worse as inflation continued, but the country experienced a recession as well. Then, in 1976 the financial prospects of colleges and universities began to look brighter as the recession ended. Some state treasuries were again accumulating reserves, but, before the outlook for more state support could really brighten, a taxpayers' revolt, first in California, but soon in other states, forced governments to reduce spending and turned the "bright" switch for college and university funding prospects to "dim." By 1978, then, "financing" was still the number one problem of leaders of higher education. In the Carnegie Council's surveys of that year, about one-third of the presidents of public colleges and universities and more than one-half of the presidents of private institutions give financial problems that ranking. The public's frugal mood has obvious consequences for all institutions. For public colleges and universities, appropriations are smaller, and fewer new projects are funded. Private colleges that hoped for new state support see such prospects growing more remote.

Another dimension for the financial difficulties of some colleges and universities involves a loss of revenue from tuition and other student fees as enrollments decline. Thus, financing problems overlapped a second-ranked concern that will be increasingly prominent in the 1980s.

The concern for growth that characterized higher education in 1969 is now converted into a concern for excess capacity. A few institutions that resisted growth or were unable to accommodate it in the 1960s and 1970s approach the 1980s without the burden of large investments in buildings and equipment to amortize and without commitments to faculty members for whom there are no students. But even these few institutions may face difficulties in the 1980s if they have to compete for students with lower-priced, program-rich, neighboring institutions.

The irony is that enrollments have, in fact, grown. Between 1970 and 1978, enrollments increased by 2.7 million FTE students—an increase of 46 percent. The increase alone is greater than the total higher education enrollment in most other countries of the world. But it does not represent an unlimited market for educational services. Often overlooked by college planners is the fact that the increase is divided among 3,100 institutions, many of which were not built or not operating at full capacity in 1969. Moreover, the large numbers hide the fact that substantial numbers of students are now more than twenty-two years old and attend classes only part-time; many students now alternate college attendance with periods of a term or more devoted to work, travel, or leisure; and many students now do not complete their work toward a degree after they enroll. To add to the problem, the rate of enrollment growth has already been slowed down by such factors as the termination of compulsory military service for young men who are not enrolled in college and the widely accepted belief that a college education is no longer a guarantee of desirable employment.

The relationship of education to work careers was underscored in the 1970s by Sidney Marland who, as U.S. Commissioner of Education, became a strong and articulate advocate of career education. Some of the impact of this movement was rhetorical because higher education has always been utilized in preparing for careers, even when it was not highly specialized. The historical significance of the career education movement of the 1970s is that it tended to legitimate and even elevate the status of educational programs that concentrated on skills needed in specific occupations. By suggesting that such programs were not only appropriate but desirable in institutions of higher learning, the movement encouraged institutions to expand their offerings and acquire the physical capabilities that made it possible for them to attract different kinds of students than they had reached in the past.

The consequences of these efforts to seek out new types of students are now quite clear:

1. Students have been diverted from liberal arts programs into vocational, preprofessional, and professional programs. In 1977 the Carnegie Foundation for the Advancement of Teaching reported that the percentage of undergraduates majoring in the "professions" (a category that includes vocational and occupational programs) increased from 38 to 58 between 1969 and 1976. During the same period, the percentage of undergraduate majors fell from 9 to 5 in the humanities; from 18 to 12 in the social sciences; and from 12 to 11 in the sciences.

2. Many liberal arts colleges have added one or more professional departments or schools to their programs. The most frequent new additions are in business, but new programs in engineering, nursing, and other health-related fields are also common. At these institutions, education programs have shrunk because of the decreasing job market for teachers. The net result, however, seems to be that more and more liberal arts colleges are becoming comprehensive institutions.

3. The distinction between specialized vocational and technical schools and the occupationally oriented programs of more "academic" institutions is becoming blurred.

4. Some colleges are under pressure to offer higher-level degrees (typically the master's) for short-term, specialized programs in occupational fields than those offered for four years of liberal arts education.

5. Colleges across the country are experimenting with new curricula, new calendars, and new instructional technologies in attempts to match the learning needs of the new types of students. The 1970s has been a decade of innovation, partly to improve learning for all students and partly to serve new clienteles better.

6. The faculty requirements for the new programs differ considerably from those of offerings for full-time students in traditional courses. Part-time instructors are often preferred, and they are likely to be drawn from the pool of available practitioners employed by business and industry in the nearby community rather than from college and university graduate schools. Unfortunately, this further erodes the already diminished job opportunities for new Ph.D.'s looking for teaching positions in colleges and universities.

The extent to which faculty, generally, influence the course of higher education in the coming decades may be determined by the successes or failures of faculty unionism. In 1969, the faculty of the City University of New York chose a bargaining agent and, by so doing, brought national attention to efforts to unionize the academic profession. These efforts initially were most successful in public community colleges but gradually spread to other public institutions in which faculty members felt left out of institutional decision making—even when the decisions that were made affected their working conditions and livelihood. By 1976 faculty members had unionized about 430 colleges and universities.[9] Wherever it exists, collective bargaining introduces a new element into the governance procedures of colleges.

In some cases faculty unionism increases the likelihood of the involvement of state government in institutional affairs. Wherever collective bargaining has forced final decisions to levels beyond the institution itself, it strengthens a tendency in that direction that has been apparent since the 1960s. For many public colleges and universities, the locus of ultimate governing authority has shifted from the trustees and administrators of individual institutions to statewide coordinating agencies. Regulations at both the state and federal level accompany public funding for institutions. College and university presidents and their key administrative associates find that a great deal of time is spent adjusting institutional policies to the demands of government agencies. Administrative skills become more important than intellectual leadership and educational statesmanship. The burden of governmental reporting and compliance is felt by public and private institutions alike and has vastly increased in the 1970s with the expansion of student aid programs, the enforcement of affirmative action policies that govern student admissions and staff hiring, and regulations that impose minimum health and safety standards on institutions.

Although the authority of university and college presidents is eroded to some extent by these governmental intrusions, it may be stronger internally. One reason is that the president and his fellow administrators are, in fact, the principal interpreters and enforcers of all of the new governmental regulations and controls at the institutional level. Another is that, in times of fiscal stringency, the interests of all units in an institution are best served by centralized, rather than diffused, authority. Few presidents can survive periods such as those that higher education has been going through in the past decade without the authority to plan, coordinate, consolidate, and eliminate programs, and to divert funds to the departments and divisions that most need them. By and large, the governing boards of American colleges and universities have given presidents that authority and supported them when they exercised it.

After the student protests of the 1960s, many observers expected students to play a larger role in institutional governance than they had in the past. At least nominally, students now do have formal representation on important administrative and academic committees on many campuses. On a few campuses that were visited by members of the Carnegie Council staff, students were regarded as at least equal in power to the faculty. But my impression is that most of this power is exercised by students informally as consumers of education, rather than as part of the formal machinery of institutional governance.

Shifts of power and authority, changed levels and sources of funding, reduced enrollments, efforts to reach new clienteles, pressures to expand career education (often at the expense of liberal arts), shortages of jobs for new Ph.D.'s, the continued growth of collective bargaining, and the increasing influence of state and federal governments—all of these changes occurred within higher education in the 1970s.

External Developments

Colleges and universities are never isolated from the major events and trends of the times in which they exist, and many of their internal changes are responses to the swirl of the world around them. Five events in the 1970s should be highlighted because they significantly altered the context in which colleges and universities operate.

1. The Twenty-Sixth Amendment to the Constitution, ratified in 1971, lowered the voting age and made 98 percent of the national college student body eligible to vote. As a special interest electorate, students are not as yet fully organized, although there are efforts to enlist their votes on education-related issues and lobbies claiming to represent their views in state and national capitals. Organized or not, however, students can no longer be ignored as interested parties in the develop-

ment of public as well as campus educational policy.

2. The arrest of five men who broke into the offices of the Democratic National headquarters in the Watergate complex in Washington, D.C., in 1972 touched off a series of political scandals that reached the highest offices of the land and resulted in the resignation of Richard M. Nixon from the presidency in 1974.

   Watergate raised questions about the integrity of all social institutions and inspired government officials and agencies to become increasingly sensitive to criticism, more protective of their credibility, and more insistent upon the accountability of all who benefit from their support. At another level, Watergate made the general public less confident of the morality of its leaders, and this concern translated into increased interest in the capabilities of colleges and universities (from which leadership is presumed to come) to provide ethical and moral education. Part of the recent and continuing effort to strengthen general education and liberal learning in the college curriculum responds to this concern.

3. One feature of American compulsory military service, which ended in 1973, was that exemptions were extended to college students. When the draft ended, the artificial demand for higher learning created by exemption ceased. The termination of the draft explains a significant portion of the decrease in enrollments, particularly as it is evident among white males, in the 1970s. Another effect of the end of the draft is that campus-centered dissent from unpopular national military and foreign policies has abated.

4. The most serious depression to hit the country since World War II occurred in 1974-75. Coupled with continuing inflation, it posed severe problems for institutions forced to pay larger bills with smaller revenues. Increased fuel costs in 1975 were particularly burdensome to colleges and universities in regions with cold winters. The costs of attending college were beyond the reach of many young people, and student enrollments in private institutions dropped noticeably during these years. During the depression, unemployment reached 9.2 percent, and stories about Ph.D.'s driving taxis and college graduates washing dishes or working on assembly lines were told and retold in college dormitories, dining commons, and placement centers. These challenges to long-standing beliefs about the economic returns of education, popularized by books like *Education and Jobs: The Great Training Robbery*[10] and *The Case Against College*[11] cast public doubt on presumptions of an inevitable link between success and the college degree. Many colleges attempted to restore the faith by strengthening programs that offered occupational and professional training, and the strength of the liberal arts in college curricula was eroded somewhat as a con-

sequence. It was widely expected that increasingly gloomy employment prospects for graduates would keep thousands of young people out of college entirely.

5. The federal government, for most of the post-World War II era, was a strong partner of American universities in the development and support of scientific research. But the federal government's share of support of research activities in colleges and universities began to decline after 1966, when it reached 73.6 percent of the total until 1977, when it was 67 percent. Although the nation's 133 doctorate-granting institutions were most directly affected by these reductions, all colleges ultimately felt the consequences in the form of a slowdown in knowledge production and the curtailment of opportunities to apprentice prospective college teachers in major research activities in academic settings.

The realities and consequences of all these trends—internal and external to campus—have affected different types of institutions in different ways. The record of their adaptations to the forces at work on the events of the 1980s is the burden of the chapters that follow.

Notes

1. David Riesman and Verne Stadtman, eds., *Academic Transformation* (New York: McGraw-Hill, 1973).

2. David D. Henry, *Challenges Past, Challenges Present: An Analysis of American Higher Education Since 1930* (San Francisco: Jossey-Bass, 1975), p. 135.

3. Harold Hodgkinson, *Institutions in Transition* (New York: McGraw-Hill, 1971), p. 24.

4. Ibid., p. 25.

5. Carnegie Commission on Higher Education, *Quality and Equality: New Levels of Federal Responsibility for Higher Education* (New York: McGraw-Hill, 1968), p. 5.

6. National Center for Educational Statistics, *Digest of Education Statistics, 1977-78* (Washington, D.C.: U.S. Government Printing Office, 1978), p. xlii.

7. Christopher Jencks and David Riesman, *The Academic Revolution* (Garden City, N.Y.: Doubleday, 1968).

8. Harold Hodgkinson, *Institutions in Transition*.

9. J.W. Garbarino, "State Experience in Collective Bargaining," in Carnegie Council on Policy Studies in Higher Education, *Bargaining in Public Higher Education* (San Francisco, Jossey-Bass, 1977), p. 30.

10. I. Berg, *Education and Jobs: The Great Training Robbery* (New York: Praeger, 1970).

11. C. Bird, *The Case Against College* (New York: McKay, 1975).

7

Current and Emerging Issues Facing American Higher Education
Clark Kerr and Marian Gade

There have always been problems for higher education and for American society. Crisis and change have been the rule, not the exception. Even during what now looks like the "Golden Age" of the late 1950s and 1960s, the period of the greatest expansion higher education has ever seen, administrators were under current strain and pressure to meet the challenges that growth brought.

Even before the Golden Age, problems were nothing new. From the beginning of the colonial era through most of the nineteenth century, the struggle was for survival, as the record of colleges founded and failed indicates. Then new universities arose to meet the needs of an industrializing society, a task that occupied the builders of post-Civil War institutions. World War I brought threats to stability that were not entirely allayed by the time the Great Depression hit. World War II saw the beginning of the university-government partnership in research, but reduced enrollments as potential students became soldiers instead. In the late 1940s the GI Bill flooded colleges and universities with students and pressed them to provide new programs, counseling and placement services, and to change administrative mechanisms at an unprecedented rate.[1]

Higher education met all these challenges and many more. It has responded to events in the political and social world, such as wars and depressions, as well as crises of confidence and internal dissension, as during the Vietnam War and the concurrent student movement of the late 1960s and early 1970s.

It is less certain that American higher education can meet the challenges posed by current and emerging issues facing it, although past successes augur well.

1. Changing composition *and* changing numbers of students

Until now the trend has been one of almost constant growth; sometimes slow and steady and with minor fluctuations, as during the first two centuries when the average growth rate was less than 250 students per year. Enrollments rose from about 10 students in 1638 (all at Harvard) to 50,000 in 1870. Sometimes growth was very rapid, as from 1870 to 1890, and from 1960 to 1970, when higher education enrollments in each instance doubled.

Because of declining fertility rates beginning after 1960, the number of young people in the age group from 18 to 24 years, those who make up the traditional college-going age cohort, will drop about 23 percent between 1978 and 1993. The issue before higher education institutions and planners is, what effect will the falling numbers in the group have upon enrollments? What are appropriate responses?

Estimates of the impact of an age-cohort decline upon enrollments vary widely. Enrollments might drop the same amount, about 23 percent, as the group declines. Some observers forecast a much greater enrollment decline, as the economic returns to investment in a college education fall, so that a smaller proportion of even the traditional college attenders choose to pursue postsecondary education. Some people expect there to be an actual increase in student numbers, in spite of a declining traditional group from whom to draw students, as persons who have not in the past participated in higher education continue to attend in greater numbers—members of minority groups, foreign students, older persons, and women, for example —and as institutions increase retention rates.[2]

It is necessary, therefore, to take a careful look at the composition of the potential college applicant pool, and not just at overall numbers.

Differential fertility rates among racial and ethnic groups, along with immigration, mean that blacks and Hispanics are enlarging their share of the traditional age cohort. In the past, high school graduation rates and college attendance rates have been lower in these groups than in the white or Asian populations. Blacks and Hispanics have increased their graduation and attendance rates in recent years, however. If they continue to attend college at rates approaching those of the white population, there could be a considerable offsetting effect to the age-cohort decline. (See Table 1.)

TABLE I
Participation of women and minority groups in higher education

Women	1960[a]	1979[b]
Percent of undergraduate enrollment	38.0	51.3
Percent of graduate enrollment	29.0	47.0

Racial and ethnic groups

	Black %	Hispanic %	Asian & others %	White %	All races %
Percent of total U.S. population, 1979[c]	11.5	5.6	1.9	86.4	*
High school completion rates[d]	64	54	n.a.	80	75
Percent of 1978 higher education enrollment[e]	9.4	3.7	5.0	81.9	100
Percent of 18-24 year olds enrolled in college, 1979[f]	19.8	16.6	n.a.	25.6	25

*Totals add to more than 100 percent because persons of Hispanic origin are also counted among other races.

[a] U.S. National Center for Education Statistics, *Projections of Education Statistics to 1975-76* (Washington, D.C.: U.S. Government Printing Office, 1966), Tables 11 and 12.

[b] U.S. National Center for Education Statistics, *Opening Fall Enrollment 1979* (Washington, D.C., unpublished data, 1980).

[c] U.S. Bureau of Census, *Current Population Reports,* Series P-20, No. 350, "Population Characteristics" (Washington, D.C.: U.S. Government Printing Office, May 1980), Table 15.

[d] Carnegie Council on Policy Studies in Higher Education, *Three Thousand Futures* (San Francisco: Jossey-Bass, 1980), p. 43.

[e] U.S. National Center for Education Statistics, *The Condition of Education, 1980 Edition* (Washington, D.C.: U.S. Government Printing Office, 1980), Table 3.5.

[f] U.S. Bureau of the Census, *Current Population Reports,* Series P-20, No. 355, "School Enrollment—Social and Economic Characteristics of Students: October 1979 (Advance Report)" (Washington, D.C.: U.S. Government Printing Office, August 1980).

The college-going propensities of women, too, have changed rapidly. Traditionally less likely to attend college than males, by the late 1970s they constituted over half of undergraduate students in the U.S.

Persons older than the 18-24 age cohort are also attending college in increasing numbers. In 1979, 36 percent of the students were 25 years or older. Almost two-thirds of the students in the over-35 age group are women.

Older students tend to be enrolled only part-time, and these nontraditional groups also are heavily concentrated in certain kinds of institutions, mainly in community colleges and comprehensive colleges instead of in four-year liberal arts colleges or research institutions. Both changing numbers and the changing composition of the college attending group will affect different institutions and different segments of the higher education universe in different ways.

The challenges to institutions set by changing demographic factors are to maintain or raise quality of education while seeking new clienteles; to remain flexible without losing a sense of identity and mission; and to avoid unfair competitive practices that would destroy public confidence in higher education or make it less possible to retain the capacity to serve the larger numbers of students that are expected again after the mid-1990s.

2. Quality in college *and* in high school

As the needs of our technological society become increasingly complex, so too will its need for highly trained and personally competent individuals, able to manage their own lives wisely, to perform productively in the labor force, and to participate effectively in the affairs of the nation and the world. At the same time, there will be fewer young persons available to meet these needs. More disturbing, there is evidence that they may be less, rather than more, prepared than in the past, as levels of developed aptitudes (as measured by standardized tests) of young people continue to fall.

The proportion of the labor force in jobs classified as technical, managerial, and professional has risen from 10 to 25 percent (1900 to 1980) and is likely to keep on rising. Job requirements within these occupations intensify as technology becomes more complex and as systems of control become more complicated. Coping skills[3] become more important as society becomes more bureaucratized. People must learn to be discriminating consumers, to invest prudently, to preserve their health, to fill out forms and keep accounts, and to cultivate other skills necessary to survival in an industrialized world. Quality of life will increasingly be measured in ways that require use of mental and artistic skills.[4]

The decline in the number of persons in the next generation, of course, means that the number of people with high innate talent will drop by the same 23 percent that the age cohort decreases. In addition, test scores of developed ability of students leaving high school and headed for college have declined on the order of 5 to 10 percent since their high point in the early 1960s. (See Table 2.) About half the decline can be attributed to the larger number of persons taking the tests, many of them from groups in the society that have not in the past participated in higher education; but test scores have dropped for all groups.[5]

Scores on standardized tests for college graduates have behaved in more erratic ways, but scores on the Graduate Record Examination, the test that most closely corresponds to the Scholastic Aptitude Test for college entrance, have also dropped in most fields. The proportion of test-takers scoring in the "high ability" group dropped from about 19 to 13 percent between 1966 and 1979. Scores for students in some scientific fields, such as physics, have risen, but in some of the social sciences and humanities, average scores have declined as much as 20 percent. Relatively steady average scores for students taking admissions tests for entrance to law, medical, and graduate business and management schools suggest that the better students may be moving into these professions and away from graduate education that would prepare them to teach coming generations of students in high schools and colleges.

TABLE 2
Median scores on standardized tests, 1965-1980

Academic year ending	SAT[1] [a] Verbal	SAT[1] [a] Math	GRE Verbal	GRE Math	GMAT[2] [a]	LSAT[a]	MCAT Verbal	MCAT Math
1966	471	496	520	528	485	511		
1967	467	495	519	528	486	514	524	557
1968	466	494	520	527	485	516	525	560
1969	462	491	515	524	484	516	529	568
1970	460	488	503	516	478	518	517	566
1971	454	487	497	512	472	519	519	564
1972	450	482	493	508	466	521	517	557
1973	443	481	499	513	463	522	513	559
1974	440	478	495	510	461	527	522	561
1975	437	473	493	508	461	520	511	568
1976	429	470	492	510	460	525	523	569
1977	429	471	490	514	460	528	b	b
1978	429	469	484	518	461	533		
1979	426	466	476	517	462	n.a.		
1980	423	467	474	522	462	n.a.		
% change 1966-1980	-10.2	-5.8	-8.8	-1.1	-4.7 (no change since 1974)	+2.7	-0-	+2.2

SAT = Scholastic Aptitude Test
GRE = Graduate Record Examination
GMAT = Graduate Management Admissions Test
LSAT = Law School Admission Test
MCAT = Medical College Admission Test

(1) All candidates. High school seniors only scores do not differ significantly.
(2) Based on 3-year rolling average for period ending in indicated year.

a For all cases attending test administrations during a testing year. Thus, an individual may be counted more than once if he/she was tested more than once in a given year.

b The MCAT and its scoring method were changed in 1977 so that subsequent test results are not comparable to 1976 and earlier, but scores on the new test have not changed significantly since its first administration in 1977.

SOURCE: For SAT, GRE, GMAT, Educational Testing Service, Princeton, New Jersey; and for LSAT and MCAT, U.S. National Center for Education Statistics, *The Condition of Education, 1977 Edition* (Washington, D.C.: U.S. Government Printing Office, 1977), vol. 3, pt. 1, Table 5.04.

On the whole, it appears that test scores out of college have dropped to some extent, but the decline has been no greater, and probably less, than that out of high school. The "value added" by college has stayed the same or increased.

The issue for society, and for higher educaton, is to increase quality to meet increased needs, to close the "quality gap."

Efforts will also be concentrated on reducing the "talent loss." Young people in the top quartile of academic ability, but from families with lower incomes, are still less likely to attend college than are equally talented students from higher income families. One 1980 study showed a 10 to 15 percent difference in college attendance intentions among students in the high ability quartile from families with incomes under $20,000 a year as against those with incomes over $25,000.[6] Financial aid policies at institutional, state, and national levels, as well as recruitment and admissions policies, will need to be reviewed for their potential contribution to reducing the talent loss.

Efforts to retain students in high school for longer periods (i.e., reducing drop-out rates, now 23 percent overall); to increase high school graduation rates, especially among groups that now fall below the national average; to reduce voluntary absenteeism; and to increase the amount of time actually spent in education and training during the school year will all come under scrutiny as states and local school districts try to raise the quality of secondary school graduates and reduce the loss of talent. Colleges and universities will be expected to assist in these efforts, both through direct partnership with secondary schools, as in the case of court-ordered linkages between universities in the Boston area and public high schools, as well as through the traditional task of training teachers and administrators for the public schools. How colleges can maintain and increase their own quality, while contributing to higher quality secondary education, will be a major issue in the 1980s.

3. Serving *all* of youth

Just as colleges and universities are becoming resources for the improvement of secondary schools, they are also being asked to serve a larger proportion of the postsecondary population. In 1978, 38 percent of the nation's youth aged 16 to 21 years were enrolled in school or college. Another 41 percent were employed; 6 percent were unemployed; and almost 6 percent were neither in school nor in the labor force nor in the armed forces nor homemakers. They had opted out of society. At present, there is no institution in the society responsible for looking after the welfare of youth as a whole, linking strategies to reduce teenage unemployment (which runs over 50 percent for some groups such as black male high school drop-outs) with strategies to create easier transitions from the world of school or college to the world of work. It is likely that educational systems will be asked to take a larger role in developing programs to serve all the youth in an area, not just those who enroll in classes.

The community colleges, which have proven successful in their outreach programs and in establishing cooperative arrangements with industry, businesses, high schools, and other community groups, will be in the forefront of this movement. One proposal calls for community colleges to take "a residual responsibility for youth."[7] They would be available to advise youth on academic and empoyment opportunities, to offer job preparation and placement, to refer young people to other community services such as medical and legal advice, and to make referrals to apprenticeship programs and government-subsidized programs such as CETA (the Comprehensive Employment and Training Act).

Whether this proposal is adopted or not, involvement of colleges and universities with the needs of a larger segment of the postsecondary age group is likely to increase. This is partly because the "youth problem" will not go away of its own accord, even with fuller employment, and postsecondary educational institutions have shown more success in educating and training young people than have some other institutions. It is partly, too, because the possibility of declining postsecondary enrollments will create incentives for colleges and universities to widen their base of recruitment and the range of services they offer.

4. Meeting the new competition: Sectors II, III, and IV

Although the universe of some three thousand nonprofit colleges and universities, both public and private, is the one that generally comes to mind when we speak of postsecondary education (this is Sector I), there are other institutional forms that are rapidly expanding their educational functions.

The for-profit, or proprietary segment, Sector II, has existed almost as long as Sector I and may account for 5 percent as many full-time equivalent enrollments as Sector I.

Sector III includes educational and training programs offered by organizations such as corporations, trade unions, and the military, whose basic functions are noneducational. Some estimates place the number of persons enrolled and the resources expended in Sector III as higher than those in Sector I, or over 12 million persons each year.[8] A more modest estimate is that, on a full-time equivalent basis, Sector III includes perhaps 10 percent as many enrollments as Sector I.

Although the "technological revolution" in education has been predicted for a number of years, recent developments in video discs, low-cost computers, and TV satellites indicate that Sector IV, electronic education, may be on the verge of substantial expansion.

Beyond all this lies what might be called Sector V, on-the-job informal training, where perhaps up to 50 percent of all skills actually used in employment are learned.

As it is perceived that the schools and colleges in Sector I are unable to meet all the complex needs of the labor market, or to supply all the education people want for personal fulfillment, the other sectors will continue to grow and to offer competition for students, for funding, and for programs. Public policy makers will have to address questions such as how to provide possible "consumer protection" for users of educational products coming from organizations that fall outside Sector I accreditation procedures, and how to provide freedom of choice for students receiving financial aid while at the same time assuring that public funds are wisely spent.

Educational policy makers in Sector I will come face-to-face with the dilemma of how to meet competition from the other Sectors and to serve new needs, while maintaining institutional integrity and a sense of academic mission.

5. Still the "Home of Science"?

The flow of young scholars into scientific positions in universities is likely to slow greatly in the next decade. This is not so much because of declining enrollments, which will fall little, if at all, in the research universities, but because of low faculty turnover. The large numbers of faculty members who were hired in the 1960s and early 1970s will not be ready to retire until the 1990s or later, and few new positions will be added. Many potential young scientists will be discouraged from getting a Ph.D. degree at all, or they will look to government or industry for jobs. American society could be seriously weakened in its ability to meet competition from abroad and to respond to new scientific opportunities if some action is not taken to encourage young scientists to enter teaching and research careers and to preserve the university as "the home of science."[9]

The United States, unlike many other nations, concentrates basic scientific research in its colleges and universities. These institutions spend over half of all basic research funds in the nation, about $3.2 billion in 1978, most of which came from the federal government.

Federal funds for basic research dropped in constant dollars from 1968 to 1975, mainly because of decreased spending in defense and space programs. Funding increased in every subsequent year, growing 24 percent in constant dollars between 1975 and 1979. Within the total allocated to research by the federal government, basic research constituted an estimated 40 percent in 1980 compared to 35 percent in 1975, indicating a recognition on the part of the federal government of its continuing primary responsibility for maintaining the nation's basic research capacity.

Within the universities, on the other hand, there has been a shift away from basic and towards applied research. (See Table 3.) Basic research spending in universities and colleges increased 20 percent in constant dollars during the decade of the 1970s; applied research spending increased 74 percent. The question arises whether universities, the principal home of basic research, ought to be shifting resources away from this activity.

TABLE 3
Academic Research and Development Expenditures by Colleges and Universities

	Basic research	Applied research
1968	77%	19%
1978	69	26

SOURCE: U.S. National Science Foundation, *National Patterns of Science and Technology Resources, 1980,* (NSF 80-308) (Washington, D.C.: U.S. Government Printing Office, 1980), p. 7.

The distribution of funds is another issue that arises with respect to federal funding of scientific research in universities. In 1978, the 100 leading universities, in terms of receipt of federal funds for research and development, received over 80 percent of all such funds, a proportion that held steady during the 1970s.[10] This pattern results from decisions made during World War II, and followed since, that research funds should go to institutions that have the best scientists and the greatest possibility of extending the frontiers of scientific investigation. Arguments are likely to continue between those who advocate distributing federal research funds only on the basis of excellence, and those who want a wider, more egalitarian system based on geography or some other criterion.

Questions about allocations of funds among fields, among and within institutions, and about the methods used to make allocations will become even more pressing than in the past as public budgets level off and as university funds from nonfederal sources decrease along with enrollments. As long as totals available were rapidly expanding, as in the two decades after World War II, few hard decisions were necessary. Now the temptation to shift more funds into applied or development fields in hopes of a quick "payoff" will have to be weighed against the need to support science as a cultural activity in its own right, against the need to ensure a supply of young scientists in the coming decades, and against the ultimate payoff to society of pursuing scientific research in directions dictated by the nature of the disciplines themselves.

Some universities have found themselves involved in clashes with agencies of the federal government over the management and accounting procedures used in connection with research grants and contracts. There has also been increasing federal regulation of the actual content of research, as in the case of federal guidelines prohibiting certain kinds of experiments in "gene-splicing" or "genetic engineering," and in regulation of research methods in experiments using human subjects. The government-university partnership in scientific research appears to be a permanent one, but no longer one in which the federal partner supplies the funds and the university partner takes them, no strings attached. New rules for the partnership will need to be negotiated.

6. Plan or market?

One of the important changes that has taken place in American higher education in the past half-century is the shift in both financing and enrollments from the private to the public sector. In 1930, public sources supplied 42 percent of all current income for higher education institutions, and in 1977, the public share was over 63 percent. Private sources of funding dropped correspondingly from 58 to 37 percent. The public share of enrollments, too, has increased. In 1950 students were evenly divided between public and private institutions, but by 1976 the public share had increased to 78 percent of headcount enrollments, and this during a period of greatly increased numbers overall.

Public concern with coordinating and planning for higher education went along with growth of the public sector and increased public financial commitments. In 1980, only one state lacked a mechanism for coordination of all higher education within the state, including the private sector; forty years earlier, only one state had such a mechanism.

Coordinating bodies, which came into existence to plan for orderly growth, will find it harder to plan for decline, where decisions involve taking away resources, reducing personnel, consolidating or eliminating programs, and possibly closing campuses. There are few general rules that can be offered in this period, as there will be tremendous variations in circumstances over which planners have little or no control, and plans will have to be adjusted to them.

Some regions and states, and even parts of states, will continue to grow. The Sunbelt states of the southwest may never notice that the age group has declined in numbers. Some categories of institutions, such as community colleges, will experience increased growth while other types, such as some small liberal arts colleges, will be struggling for their existence. Some programs will continue to grow and others to decline, as market forces move students into some fields and out of others. For example, the proportion of students with professional school majors rose by over 50 percent in the first half of the 1970s, while social science and humanities majors decreased by 50 percent; masters degree programs are the fastest growing segment of higher education.

Both market and plan will continue to affect higher education, as students "vote with their feet," taking their interests, and their financial aid packages, to institutions of their own choosing.

Planning has accomplished several things that will help provide guidance in a period of decline. First, many states have clearly defined and differentiated the functions of different segments of higher education, as in the early decision by California to establish a tripartite system consisting of a multicampus university, a system of state colleges and universities, and a community college sector, each with somewhat different functions, financing and staffing formulas, and admissions standards.

Second, there has by now been considerable experience with developing budgetary formulas for the support of higher education. (See Section 8 of this chapter.) Third, most states, over forty of them, have established some form of support for the private sector. These decisions were easier to make during a period of growth, but they will help mitigate the chances of cut-throat competition among institutions and sectors for resources and students during a period of decline.

A central decision will be about how much to rely on the market and how much on planning. There are several arguments, however, for placing more reliance on the market during a period of decline. First, plans are based on political reality, and politically it is almost impossible to reduce drastically or close out a campus or program. The impersonal forces of the student market can accomplish reduction a little at a time, and in a manner that carries legitimacy. Second, planned reductions bring greater state intrusion into the private lives of academic institutions than do planned increases. Increased resources enable participants to do what they want to do, while planned reductions involve coercion by the state. They will bring on protests and claims that academic freedom has been infringed. Again, the slower, more impersonal actions of the student market may be more effective. Third, people react differently to planning than to market forces. Faculty and other staff may respond to planned decline with confrontation, as through collective bargaining, but a reduction in student demand may, on the other hand, bring a response to improve the attractiveness of programs.

A major role for planners could be to utilize the market forces constructively. For example, students will need good information on costs and programs at alternative institutions. The plan may need to place enrollment ceilings on some programs, or assist in shifting faculty and students from one institution or program to another. There should be a plan for dealing with closings or mergers of institutions in both the public and private sectors.

And above all, the plan should provide a set of positive goals for higher education, beyond holding on to past gains. With fewer new students to provide for, attention can be turned to providing the best possible education for those within the system, to meeting the needs of the state and its students.

7. Preserving the private sector

The United States and Japan are the only industrial nations in the world that rely on private institutions to supply a substantial part of their higher education. Much of the diversity and flexibility of the American system—its ability to respond quickly to changing numbers of students, changing fields of interests, changing clienteles—stem from the existence of a large private sector. All of the institutions with religious affiliations, and almost all single-sex institutions, fall in the private sector.

Private colleges and universities constitute the majority of all higher education institutions in the U.S. (1,659 private and 1,472 public institutions reported enrollment figures to the National Center for Education Statistics in 1978), but they enroll only 22 percent of all (headcount) students. This compares with 50 percent of the students in 1950, 41 percent in 1969, and about 25 percent in 1970.

Absolute numbers of students at private institutions have been increasing even while the private share has dropped. Headcount enrollment went up by two-thirds between 1960 and 1978, and during the decade of the 1970s, FTE (full-time equivalent) enrollment increased by 16 percent at private institutions, compared to a 24 percent increase at all institutions. It is only in comparison with the public sector's tremendous growth during the same period that the private sector has lost.

Yet there are strains and pressures on private institutions that jeopardize their future, or at least the future of some of them. Private colleges that closed during the decade of the 1970s outnumbered new institutions by almost two to one, and by more than three to one if specialized institutions, mainly religious seminaries, are omitted. Some private colleges merged with other institutions, either public or private; a few were taken over by the public sector. Most of the colleges that closed were very small (under five hundred students), were church-related, and were coeducational. Private two-year colleges were particularly vulnerable; one-fifth of those in existence in 1970 were closed eight years later.

The private research, comprehensive, and highly selective liberal arts colleges appear highly resilient, but, while they are less vulnerable than the two-year institutions and the less selective liberal arts colleges, they, too, will encounter difficulties. In the first place the overall age-cohort decline may hit private liberal arts colleges harder than public colleges. The former have tended to enroll heavily from the traditional age group, offer fewer opportunities for part-time study or for non-traditional scheduling, and are often too small to mount new programs to attract new clienteles without a major change in institutional mission.

Second, private colleges are caught in a cost squeeze to a greater extent than are many public institutions. Tuition and fees at private institutions have provided about half of their total income for the past half-century (and are a higher proportion, over two-thirds, of their unrestricted educational and general revenue), and private gifts have remained steady at about 15 percent of income. Funds generated by endowments, however, have plummeted, from almost one-third of private institutional income in 1930 to less than 10 percent in the late 1970s. Tuition can only be changed once a year, and then at the risk of pricing some potential students out of the market. Inflation, a fact of life for the foreseeable future, raises costs and eats away at the value of endowments. Events outside the realm of higher education, such as the OPEC oil crisis of 1973, raise costs unexpectedly. And in most areas, public education is available at a much lower out-of-pocket cost to the consumers, the students, and their families. Public and private tuitions have risen, in recent years, in about the same percentage terms, but since private tuitions started from a much higher base, the dollar difference between tuition at public and private institutions, the "tuition gap," has become larger.

Private institutions can themselves do much to preserve their existence and their quality, but public policy must also be carefully designed to preserve the balance of the system by supporting private higher education institutions, while at the same time making sure they remain independent. Federal financial aid policies that distribute funds to higher education institutions as tuition provide financial support with little interference or control. In addition, federal funds for research, including for physical plant and research libraries, make no distinctions between public and private universities. In fiscal year 1978, about 43 percent of federal R&D funds to universities and colleges went to private institutions.

A survey in 1975-76 showed that most of the states, about forty of them, had some kind of program to provide state support to private institutions, largely in the form of financial aid to students attending those colleges. About one-fifth of state aid took the form of general institutional grants on a formula basis, and about the same amount was spent for specific educational programs, institutions, or purposes.[11] The total state support per FTE student was found to be about 11 percent of state support for students in public institutions. The Carnegie Council, in the study cited above, concluded that a state subsidy amounting to not more than half the educational subsidy to students in public institutions would be a reasonable maximum to provide support for private institutions while preserving their freedom from state control.

8. New financial formulas for rising marginal cost curves

Public as well as private colleges are financially threatened by declining enrollments. Most public institutions are funded on a formula that takes full-time equivalent (FTE) enrollment as its basis. As a result, when more students enroll, the institution receives more money from the state. Well over half of funding for public institutions comes from state sources. Federal sources provide about 16 percent, and local and private sources, including tuition, roughly a quarter. When enrollments decline, less state money is provided. Most states now have more sophisticated formulas that take into account a number of factors besides sheer numbers of students, but no matter what form the formula takes, a number of problems arise when formulas devised during a period of growth are applied to decline.

The basic problem arises because of the difference between "average cost" and "marginal cost" per student. If all the expenses of an institution are added up and the total divided by the number of FTE students, the result is average cost per student. A considerable portion of that cost, however, is fixed and does not vary directly with the number of students. Maintenance of the physical plant, and many administrative costs, some minimum of counseling services, for example, are ongoing regardless of the number of students, within broad limits. More students can be accommodated without increasing them, so that the marginal cost of adding one more student will be less than the average cost per student. A lecture course can accommodate 35 students as easily as 30. If a college is funded on an average cost basis, it will get more money for each new student than it costs to serve that student, and it was exactly that "profit," or difference between average and marginal cost, that allowed much of the improvement of programs that took place during the boom years of the 1960s.

On the other hand, if an institution loses funds equal to the average cost per student as enrollment declines, contraction is very rapid. Fixed costs continue at the same level while numbers and support drop. Some factors that are related to enrollments, such as numbers of faculty, may be difficult to cut back in the short term because of the need to staff most programs on at least a minimum basis, contractual or tenure agreements with faculty, and for other reasons.

In response to such problems, some states have tried to cushion public institutions against budgetary cutbacks due to small variations in enrollment and are experimenting with formulas that will smooth out long-term decline. For example, in the University of California system, only enrollment changes greater than 2 percent of the previous year's enrollment trigger budgetary increases or decreases. Several states have adopted measures of workload that take into account headcount (as well as FTE) enrollment, square feet of building space, projected rates of inflation, and other factors. Other states have adopted a formula relating average and marginal costs, so that some fixed percentage of average cost, rather than the full amount, is deducted for enrollment losses. In a study by John Millett for the Ohio Board of Regents, it was estimated that only one-fourth to one-third of the average cost could be considered to be variable; the remainder is fixed or only semivariable.[12]

Another approach is to adopt different funding formulas for various levels and types of instruction. Upper division and graduate instruction carry larger costs than does lower division instruction; teaching in a laboratory setting is more expensive than are large lecture sections. Such differentiation can reduce the temptation for institutions to eliminate programs that have high average costs as an immediate response to budget cuts. That decision should be made on educational and not purely financial grounds, and sensitive formulas can help ensure good educational decision making.

As states review financing formulas, they also have to take into account what their educational priorities are. Some programs and institutions need special protection because they are essential at some minimum level, such as research. Protection of persons hired under affirmative action programs, who otherwise, as last hired might be first fired, is considered high priority in many states. Education of the handicapped, remedial, and continuing education, are other examples of programs where special categorical funding (rather than an enrollment based formula) has been adopted.

Protection of innovative instructional programs may be a priority as they are likely to be one of the first areas to be cut back under an average cost formula. Some states require institutions to hold some fixed percentage of their enrollment-generated income in a discretionary or priority fund to meet innovative or special needs.[13]

After a five-year period of planning and pilot studies, the State of Tennessee and its Higher Education Commission instituted, in the 1979 budget cycle, a method for making an additional allocation of up to 2 percent of an institution's educational and general funds on the basis of performance criteria. This addition to the basic enrollment-driven formula rewards institutions that are willing to set goals congruent with their academic mission, and to conduct evaluations to appraise how well they meet those goals. It is designed so that institutions compete against standards appropriate for institutions with their mission, and not directly against one another. Financial incentives are used to reward quality improvement, and not just those institutions that start, for instance, with better students.[14]

All of these state studies and experiments are aimed at maintaining the mission and integrity of their educational and research programs on a short-term basis. A longer term decline in enrollments of 25 percent or more would entail not only cushions to soften year-to-year changes, and categorical funding for priority programs, but examination of the roles and functions of whole programs and institutions, keeping in mind that, at the end of the period of retrenchment in the mid-1990s, we may again be traveling back up the marginal cost curve. Different formulas may well need to be developed for periods of contraction and for times of expansion.

9. The survival of faculty morale after the Golden Age

Faculty morale in the late 1970s was considerably lower than the buoyant optimism of the 1960s. The reasons why faculty are concerned about the future, and why policy makers need to be concerned, center around faculty compensation, the role of faculty in governance, and declining labor market demand.

Faculty compensation (salaries plus fringe benefits) increased 41.2 percent in constant dollars during the 1960s, but in the 1970s the rate of advance first slackened, then stopped, and finally reversed itself. By 1978-79, real faculty salaries were over 10 percent below what they had been a decade earlier, because of inflation and lessened bargaining power as faculty hiring decreased. Not only has faculty compensation failed to keep up with the cost of living, it has also failed to keep pace with compensation in the rest of the economy. Faculty salaries are considerably higher than those earned by the average American worker but are lower than those received by business executives, federal government executives, and others with comparable qualifications.

As enrollments decline, and financial pressures on institutions mount, it is likely that cost-of-living increases for faculty will not keep pace with inflation so that faculty will fall farther behind in the coming years.

Collective bargaining agreements between faculty unions and institutional or system administrators are one response to falling real salaries, but they also represent a banding together for protection of job security in an era of decline. However, unionization has not proceeded nearly so rapidly as many expected from the original spurt in the late 1960s and early 1970s. By mid-1979, about one out of every six colleges and universities was organized, four-fifths of them in the public sector, and three-fifths of them two-year campuses. About 32 percent of full-time faculty were covered by collective bargaining agreements.

Collective bargaining in the private sector was dealt a severe blow by the U.S. Supreme Court decision early in 1980 that the faculty members at Yeshiva University in New York City were, in effect, the managers of the institution and that their "professional interests—as applied to governance at a university like Yeshiva—cannot be separated from those of the institution."[15] Governing bodies of some other private universities and colleges subsequently refused to bargain with representatives of faculty unions, and there are likely to be a number of drawn-out legal battles before clear guidelines emerge with respect to faculty bargaining rights. One interesting result of the *Yeshiva* decision may be a strengthening of collegial mechanisms of governance, such as faculty senates, as administrators try to increase faculty involvement in governance so that courts will, as in the *Yeshiva* case, rule that they are too involved in management to have separate interests that could be represented through collective bargaining agents.

The academic labor market in many fields has suffered drastic declines, with net additions to faculty ranks falling from about 20,000 per year at the peak to zero in the late 1970s. The prospective decline in enrollments means continued low rates of new hires for at least the next decade, and lowered rates of mobility for faculty wishing to change institutions.

Another result of the collapse of the labor market for faculty members is the large bulge of faculty in the age range between about 34 and 48 years, those hired during the unprecedented growth years of the 1960s. These persons, mainly white males, have low mortality rates, are too young for retirement until the 1990s, and are heavily tenured in—over 80 percent of faculty members at some institutions have the job security afforded by tenure. Prospects for young Ph.D. recipients looking for teaching jobs in colleges and universities are very poor; students face in their classrooms a faculty increasingly distant in age from themselves; more women and minorities are qualifying for nonexistent faculty positions; and the researchers and teachers of the 1990s and the years thereafter, when present faculty will retire and more may be needed to teach in new fields and to deal with a new bulge of students, are not coming up through the ranks.

10. Dealing with uncertainty

All of these issues have a high probability of being important in the next ten to twenty years. But the one thing we can be certain about is that there will be a number of other issues, equally important, that we do not now recognize. The signs pointing to them may be there now. We have missed or ignored warnings of impending crises in the past. Allan Cartter noted as early as 1965 that we were turning out more Ph.D.'s than the academic labor market could absorb,[16] but few noticed his warnings. The turndown in the fertility rate that resulted in the smaller age cohort coming into college now began in the early 1960s, but was not noticed until a few years later.

Some other issues with tremendous impact upon higher education could not have been foreseen, such as wars or the world political crises that led to high fuel costs. We will continue to have uncertainty that stems from actions of others outside the control of higher education institutions. Policies that increase the intake of young persons into the military or other forms of national service could have a great impact on higher education enrollments. Changes in the nation's economic climate, such as high unemployment, could affect enrollments as young people prolong their educational careers in times of job scarcity. Student movements tend to run in cycles, and there is bound to be another wave of student protest sooner or later, although we cannot now tell what the specific issues will be.

The rate at which these uncertain events occur is likely to increase. The more uncertainty there is in society, the more uncertainties there are for higher education.

11. Renovation of the role of leadership

Academic administrators have made huge adjustments to changing circumstances in the past several decades. Issues such as those discussed here, as well as those we cannot now anticipate, require ever more effective leadership of higher education as it is tied more closely to society and suffers the shocks that rock the rest of the nation.

But several things have happened to make the position of leadership of a college or university less tenable than in former times. It is easier, and more satisfying, to be the leader of an expanding institution than of a declining one. The "management of decline"[17] requires making decisions that satisfy no one. Increasing regulation from outside, from state boards and legislatures, and from federal agencies, makes it harder to exercise effective leadership. As power to make decisions affecting persons or groups within institutions moves farther and farther away from those affected, the roles of managers and accountants expand, and the role of leadership decreases, becomes diffused. The irony is that responsibility for what goes on in the institution is also more diffused with the introduction of the spirit and mechanisms of "participatory democracy." The push for ever more centralization and accountability results in no one being accountable. The president of a major state university recently said, "When no one is in charge, no one is fully accountable. I could once say decisively, 'the buck stops here.' Now it never stops." He went on to say, "If an occasional administrator abuses...discretion, it makes more sense to replace the administrator than to remove the discretion."[18]

Leaders who can exercise discretion, adjust rapidly to new developments, handle the sudden crisis, will be more, not less, important in the higher education of the future.

Notes

1. David Henry, *Challenges Past, Challenges Present: An Analysis of American Higher Education Since 1930* (San Francisco: Jossey-Bass, 1975).
2. In 1974, Howard R. Bowen stated that "A doubling of college attendance is not beyond possibility." *Educational Record* 55 (Summer 1974), p. 150. In the same year Joseph Froomkin suggested, in the most pessimistic of three scenarios he presented for the year 1985 and beyond, that college enrollments might decline as much as 50 percent from the 1974 level *Changing Credential Objectives of Students in Post-Secondary Education* (Washington, D.C.: U.S. Department of Health, Education, and Welfare, Contract #0574257, 1974). In its final report, the Carnegie Council on Policy Studies in Higher Education projected an enrollment

decline in the range of 5 to 15 percent from 1978 to 1997. *Three Thousand Futures: The Next Twenty Years for Higher Education* (San Francisco: Jossey-Bass, 1980), p. 34. For alternative strategies to increase enrollment by as much as 3.5 percent between 1980 and 1990, see Carol Frances, *College Enrollment Trends: Testing the Conventional Wisdom Against the Facts* (Washington, D.C.: American Council on Education, 1980).

3. See chapter 3, "Coping," in Stephen K. Bailey, *The Purposes of Education* (Bloomington, Ind.: Phi Delta Kappa Educational Foundation, 1976).

4. For evidence that higher education is correlated with more prudent financial behavior, better care of one's health, and other skills, see F. Thomas Juster, ed., *Education, Income and Human Behavior* (New York: McGraw-Hill, 1975). Also see Howard R. Bowen, *Investment in Learning: The Individual and Social Value of American Higher Education* (San Francisco: Jossey-Bass, 1977). For a summary of these issues, see Charlotte Alhadeff and Margaret S. Gordon, "Supplement E: Higher Education and Human Performance," in Carnegie Council on Policy Studies in Higher Education, *Three Thousand Futures: The Next Twenty Years for Higher Education* (San Francisco: Jossey-Bass, 1980).

5. Advisory Panel on the Scholastic Aptitude Test Score Decline, *On Further Examination* (New York: College Entrance Examination Board, 1977).

6. The study is "High School and Beyond," a study of students in 1015 high schools throughout the U.S. carried out for the National Center for Education Statistics by the National Opinion Research Center.

7. Carnegie Council on Policy Studies in Higher Education, *Giving Youth a Better Chance: Options for Education, Work, and Service* (San Francisco: Jossey-Bass, 1979), p. 25.

8. Estimates range from $10 billion to $100 billion a year for education and training for as many as 16 million workers. Beverly T. Watkins, "Post-Compulsory Education by U.S. Companies May Be a $10 Billion Business," *Chronicle of Higher Education* 21 (22 September 1980), p. 7.

9. Dael Wolfle, *The Home of Science: The Role of the University* (New York: McGraw-Hill, 1972).

10. Previous figures in this section are from NSF 80-308 (see source for Table 3). This figure is from U.S. National Science Foundation, *Federal Support to Universities, Colleges, and Selected Nonprofit Institutions, Fiscal Year 1978,* NSF 80-312 (Washington, D.C.: U.S. Government Printing Office, 1980), p. 6.

11. Carnegie Council on Policy Studies in Higher Education, *The States and Private Higher Education: Problems and Policies in a New Era* (San Francisco: Jossey-Bass, 1977), p. 32.

12. Ohio Board of Regents, *A Strategic Approach to the Maintenance of Institutional Financial Stability and Flexibility in the Face of Enrollment Instability or Decline* (Washington, D.C.: Academy for Educational Development, 1979), p. 132.

13. This survey of state experiments with budgetary formulas is indebted to the work of the California Postsecondary Education Commission, "State Budget Formulas for Declining Enrollments in California's Public Segments of Postsecondary Education" (Sacramento, February 1980).

14. E. Grady Bogue, *Allocation of State Funds on a Performance Criterion: The Report of—The Performance Funding Project—of the Tennessee Higher Education Commission* (Nashville, 1980).

15. *NLRB* v. *Yeshiva University,* 48 U.S.L.W. at 4179.

16. Allan M. Cartter, "A New Look at the Supply of College Teachers," *Educational Record* 46 (Summer 1965), pp. 267-77; and "The Supply and Demand of College Teachers," *Journal of Human Resources* 1 (Summer 1966), pp. 22-38.

17. Kenneth E. Boulding, "The Management of Decline," *AGB Reports* (September/October 1975), pp. 4-9.

18. Harold H. Enarson, "Quality and Accountability: Are We Destroying What We Want to Preserve?" *Change* 12 (October 1980), p. 9, 10.

Part 2
External Forces

8

State Governments
John D. Millett

The commentary issued by the Carnegie Foundation for the Advancement of Teaching in 1976 entitled *The States and Higher Education* bore the subtitle: "A Proud Past and a Vital Future."[1] The record of state governments in planning and support of higher education in the years from 1950 to 1980 was indeed a record of which to be proud. The fifty state governments, in different ways and in different magnitudes, responded remarkably to the social expectations for expanded instructional programs, expanded enrollments, expanded geographical access, and expanded economic access. This expansion was expensive, and here too state governments did their part to improve and advance the economic status of higher education in the United States.

It must be kept in mind that in the American federal system of government it is the states and not the federal government that plan, locate, and support colleges and universities as institutions of higher education. To be sure, the federal government has established various military academies and other specialized professional schools of the armed forces; and in its capacity as the state legislature for the District of Columbia has chartered private colleges and universities in that area and has recently established the consolidated land-grant institution known as the University of the District of

133

Columbia. The federal government's role in higher education has become particularly essential in the support of research at the leading research universities and in the support of financial assistance to students. The role of institution building, however, has been a function of state government. And the private colleges and universities that comprise the independent sector of higher education have been chartered by state governments under provisions of state law.

In its final report entitled *Three Thousand Futures,* published in 1980, the Carnegie Council on Policy Studies in Higher Education listed nine "very consequential" decisions affecting the performance of higher education in the years between 1950 and 1980.[2] These nine important decisions were identified as follows:

1. The move toward open access, particularly through the expansion of community colleges;
2. The continued concentration of basic science research in the leading universities;
3. The shift of teachers colleges to comprehensive universities;
4. The introduction of vast new student aid programs at the federal level;
5. The introduction of affirmative action for minorities and women;
6. The predominantly ad hoc response to the student movement, "containing it and channeling it rather than confronting it or embracing it";
7. The clarification and preservation of differentiation of functions among different types of institutions;
8. The perpetuation of the private colleges in general and of predominantly black colleges in particular;
9. The continuation of a system of higher education with major reliance on state support and control.

Of these nine decisions, it is factually correct to assert that at least six were decisions made primarily by state governments, including the negative decision by most state governments to permit colleges and universities to respond individually to the student movement rather than for state governments to intervene and respond as state governments. The federal government was dominant in student financial aid and in affirmative action. In its research support the federal government tended to follow the initiative of state governments in building up leading research universities in the public sector. Certainly the federal government was far more ambivalent than state governments in seeking to preserve the predominantly black colleges and universities.

The record of state governments in higher education planning and support is worth reviewing as a reminder of the vitality of the federal system in America.

The Proud Past

In 1950 there were 2.3 million students enrolled in institutions of higher education in the United States, of whom 1.2 million were enrolled in public institutions. In 1980 total enrollment had reached 12.1 million students, and 9.4 million of these students were enrolled in the public sector. Thus, while the independent sector of higher education was expanding from 1.1 million students to 2.7 million students (or 145 percent) in this thirty-year period, the public sector was expanding some 680 percent, or almost 8 times.

As of 1948-49 the Commission on Financing Higher Education enumerated 547 public institutions, of which 64 were classified as universities, 37 as liberal arts colleges, 200 as separate professional schools, and 246 as two-year colleges.[3] As of 1976 the Carnegie Council on Policy Studies in Higher Education counted 1,466 public institutions, 119 were classified as doctoral-granting universities, 354 as comprehensive universities, 14 as liberal arts colleges, 70 as separate professional schools, and 909 as two-year colleges.

In 1950 the public institutions of higher education had a total income of 1.2 billion dollars, of which some 445 million dollars were provided by state governments. As of 1980-81, it was estimated that public institutions of higher education had total income of around 50 billion dollars, with around 20 billion dollars provided by state governments. To be sure, inflation in the American economy meant that 20 billion dollars in 1980-81 was equivalent to only about 7 billion dollars in terms of 1950 dollars. Even so, while the enrollment in public institutions was expanding nearly eight times, state governmental support of higher education increased nearly sixteen times.

The objectives of state government planning for higher education from 1950 to 1980 were several: (1) to ensure for all high school graduates who wished to enroll access in some institution and in the appropriate program of instruction; (2) to expand the opportunity for youth and adults to enroll in major urban areas; (3) to expand particularly programs in technical education, in various needed professional fields of study, and at the graduate level; and to maintain or develop outstanding research capabilities at selected universities. These objectives were related to certain particular social expectations, notably the expanding demand for educated talent in the American labor market, the encouragement of economic growth within a state, and the advancement of social mobility.

The remarkable economic development of the United States in the decade of the 1960s undergirded and emphasized the objectives of state higher education planning and the social expectations placed upon higher education. The social and economic environment of the 1970s was quite different from that of the 1960s. The rate of economic growth slowed down; surpluses rather than shortages of educated talent appeared in the labor market; the rate of inflation became especially troublesome, in part because of the oil embargo of the Arab nations and the rapid increase of energy costs after 1973; and relatively high rates of unemployment persisted throughout the decade. As a result, public attitudes toward higher education in general and toward state-supported higher education more particularly were different at the end of the 1970s from what they had been in the 1950s and 1960s.

By 1980 state governments had begun to identify major areas of public policy concern in relation to higher education. These major areas of concern may be summarized under four headings:

1. The mission and performance of public institutions of higher education.
2. The future of the independent sector.
3. The cost of higher education institutions and programs.
4. The accountability of the public sector of higher education.

It is important to examine each of these concerns in turn.

Mission and Performance

A first concern is one of program scope and of program quality for the various public colleges and universities authorized by law and financially supported by each state government. With nearly 1500 different public colleges and universities in the United States, there is an average of 30 public institutions in each state. In fact, the range is from 3 campuses in Rhode Island to 134 in California. As of 1976, there were 92 public institutions of higher education in Texas, 84 in New York, 73 in North Carolina, 62 in Pennsylvania, 61 in Ohio, and 61 in Illinois.

There was a time before World War II when a four-tiered structure of institutional types existed in many states: an original (or flagship) state university, a college or university of agriculture and mechanical arts, several teachers colleges, and various local junior colleges. Some states also had one or more separate professional schools, usually of medicine. This structure underwent substantial change after 1945 under the impact of rising enrollments and enlarged social expectations. Colleges of agriculture and mechanical arts became research universities. Teachers colleges became comprehensive state universities. Junior colleges gave way to community colleges, technical colleges, and area vocational/technical schools or colleges. The separate professional schools included thirty-two public medical centers, eight schools of engineering and technology, five schools of art or music, and twenty-one other specialized schools.

By 1980 state governments were beginning to ask questions and even to express doubts about the utility and the cost of this new structure of state doctoral-granting universities, comprehensive universities, and two-year institutions offering the associate degree. Were all of these institutions necessary in order to provide needed higher education services? Were all of the instructional programs of these institutions needed, and especially programs in teacher education and Ph.D. programs designed to produce higher education faculty members? What differentiation might appropriately be made between the mission of each of these various kinds of public institutions of higher education? If a reasonable differentiation of mission was not possible, then were consolidations, mergers, and even eliminations in order?

To be sure, this state concern was prompted in large part by projections of enrollment decline in the decade of the 1980s. Enrollments had continued to expand in the 1970s, reaching an all-time peak in 1980. But adequate demographic warnings had been issued early in the 1970s of a prospective decline nationwide of some 25 percent in the number of 18- to 21-year-olds between 1982 and 1990. In some states the decline in the number of young people of the traditional college age would be relatively small; in other states the number would be large. Some state universities began to experience enrollment loss during the 1970s. State governments began to ask how state universities would respond to a decrease in student enrollment.

A second set of questions of concern to state chief executives and legislators had to do with the quality of instructional performance by state universities and two-year institutions. As enrollments expanded, as an even larger proportion of high school graduates sought admission to two-year institutions and to state universities, and as open access became the prevailing practice in public higher education, administrators began to point out that the open door quickly became a revolving door unless developmental or remedial instruction was added to the programs of the institution. The development of learning skills, of communication skills, and of mathematical skills was necessary for many of the "new" students, especially students from inner-city schools. The provision of developmental instruction was not only a new dimension of student service but also a new program cost for public institutions. State government officials then began to ask why should higher education institutions have to spend money to make up for the deficiencies that apparently existed in secondary education.

Beyond this particular question were other questions about the quality of instructional performance in public institutions of higher education. The accommodation of student activism in the 1960s was said to have led to the modification of degree requirements and to grade inflation. Personnel managers of corporations reported that college graduates could not read and follow instructions, or write effectively and grammatically. Some degree recipients did poorly on state professional licensure examinations, and other graduates were said to be poorly prepared for professional practice. It was sometimes asserted that standards were being watered down or even abandoned in various degree programs.

Yet in some instances the insistence upon qualitative standards of admission by certain state universities was criticized as erecting barriers to higher education admission, as reducing access for minorities, and even as denying opportunity for some students to obtain the benefit of higher education in a prestigious state university. Where qualitative standards of access were observed, state universities could not be certain that these standards would be approved and supported by state government officials.

Still another issue arose about the location of major research activities and about certain degree programs such as those in law, medicine, nursing, engineering, and the physical and biological sciences. In general, these programs tended to be high-cost programs. In general, these programs tended to be located in the "flagship" state universities, with some expansion in the state universities that had originally been colleges of agriculture and mechanical arts. Of the fifty states, the flagship state university and the second state university were located in the largest city of the state in only six instances. The state universities in the nineteenth century had purposefully been located away from the distractions and the temptations of large cities, or of cities destined to become large industrial and commercial centers.

As new state university branches or as new state universities were established in these cities after World War II, and as representation in state legislatures finally reflected the realities of population, these urban institutions desired the full complement of graduate and professional programs already available in the older state universities. Legislators reinforced this desire, seeking to advance the individual aspirations of their constituents and the economic welfare of the cities they represented.

The result of all these conflicting concerns was to make the rationalization of institutional mission in terms of assigned instructional programs, research and public service emphasis, qualitative standards, enrollment size, open or selective access, residential or urban orientation, and racial characteristics a veritable nightmare of state-government decision making. The problems were clearly evident. The solution was obscure, at least a solution satisfactory to different urban, faculty, student, and other interests. State governments as of 1980 wanted, indeed demanded, a solution. But state governments were scarcely ready to accept any proposed solution.

The Independent Sector

As state-sponsored universities and colleges were expanded in number and enrollment during the 1960s, it became increasingly evident that the independent sector of so-called "private" colleges and universities was beginning to feel the pressure of competition. In the 1970s this competition became increasingly troublesome as some private institutions went out of existence, as others were merged, and as the tuition charges of private institutions were continually increased under the impact of inflation and other cost demands.

The question of the welfare of the independent sector of higher education presents troublesome philosophical, governmental, and practical issues to resolve. If the social structure of the United States is founded upon a pattern of pluralistic groupings of people who live and function separately, and if the governmental structure of the United States is founded upon a principle of a limited authority over the lives and activities of individuals and groups, how important is the existence of an independent sector to the perpetuation and progress of social pluralism and liberal government? This question is not simple to answer, but many persons would argue that the disappearance of an independent sector of higher education would substantially reduce the prospects of social pluralism and liberal democracy in this country.

Several state governments in the 1960s and early 1970s commissioned study groups to inquire into the desirable relationship between government and private colleges and universities. In general, these studies urged increased concern in state planning for the welfare of the independent sector, as well as state financial assistance for those students enrolling in private institutions. National private studies were undertaken also to call attention to the precarious status of the independent sector. All these reports presented cogent arguments for public attention to the survival of the independent sector.

The primary proposition in favor of such public attention is the importance of an alternative to public higher education. This alternative provides a separate opportunity for quality, innovation, and integrity in higher education. This alternative also presents standards of performance to serve as a guiding light for public higher education and as a protection against political interference that might do damage to the quality and integrity of public higher education.

Beyond these considerations is a highly practical one. If the independent sector were to disappear, then the public sector would presumably have to absorb its enrollment at increased cost to state governments. There is a financial advantage to state governments in providing some assistance to the independent sector at less cost than full absorption of its enrollment.

A governmental problem in providing assistance to the independent sector is the matter of the First Amendment to the federal Constitution and a similar provision in state government constitutions. The First Amendment states clearly: "Congress shall make no law respecting an establishment of religion...;" and the Fourteenth Amendment has been interpreted as imposing a similar restriction upon all state governments. About two-thirds of the some 1600 private institutions of higher education in the United States as of 1976 had some kind of affiliation with a church denomination. Oftentimes the affiliation was tenuous, and church-related colleges and universities could not discriminate in admissions or employment on the basis of religion and continue to receive public funds for themselves or their students. The United States Supreme Court has been disposed to look upon the religious affiliation of colleges and universities, other than theological seminaries, as somewhat remote and not in the same relationship as parochial schools or as laws mandating religious observance in public schools.

The competition of the public sector with the independent sector of higher education is of two kinds: (1) a competition in the pricing of tuition to students; and (2) a competition in the location of public institutions in urban areas. A major element of state government policy in the support of public institutions has been to fix a relatively low tuition or instructional charge to students. Thus as much as two-thirds of the average instructional costs of students might be provided by state appropriations, and only one-third or even less of the cost might be charged to students. In the independent sector a rule of thumb has been to charge students a tuition equal to around 80 percent of average cost and to seek 20 percent of average cost from philanthropic support. There have been considerable variations around these "standards" at different public and private colleges. As the costs of higher education increased in the years after 1950, the "gap" between public and private tuitions tended to increase in dollar amounts. As of 1980 it was not uncommon to find some state universities charging $1,000-a-year tuition to in-state students, while better known private colleges and universities were charging $5,000-a-year tuition.

State governments responded in several ways to criticisms from the independent sector that it had become an endangered species. One response was to undertake a direct subsidy to independent institutions, as in Pennsylvania, New York, and Illinois. Another response was to develop student financial assistance programs that often provided more tuition assistance to students in private colleges and universities than in public institutions. A third response was to restrict the enrollment size and program offerings of state universities in urban areas. In 1979 the State of Florida adopted a tuition voucher plan offering every Florida student $1,000 toward the cost of tuition if the student enrolled in a private college or university.

In its 1977 report on the states and private higher education the Carnegie Council on Policy Studies in Higher Education set forth a number of recommendations.[4] The Council declared it was in the public interest that the private sector should be preserved and strengthened. It urged state governments to develop long-range policies for private higher education and proposed that financial aid to students should be "the primary vehicle" for the channeling of state funds to private institutions. Need-based tuition grants should be the "mainstay" of state programs of student aid, the

Council asserted. In addition, "where appropriate," the Council recommended contracts with private institutions for educational services, categorical grants for some programs such as library activities, and construction and equipment "awards." The Council recognized the need for some private institutions to merge with other institutions, and for some private institutions to be taken over by public universities. The Council insisted that state aid should not reach such a level as to make private institutions more public than private and should not be given in such ways and in such amounts "as to cause significant disadvantage to public institutions." Decisions concerning the expansion of public institutions should take into account the effect such expansion would have upon private higher education, and private institutions should be "fully represented" in all state coordinating mechanisms.

State Support

In the financial support of public higher education in the United States, the instruction of students is largely financed by state governments. Even though two-thirds to three-quarters of all separately budgeted research activity at public universities is financed by the federal government, it is the state governments that have provided the basic resources of personnel, facilities, and general support that make state research universities possible. Even though student financial assistance is largely financed by the federal government, it is the state governments that have provided the institutions where students enroll. And while the federal government has made grants for some public service programs, again it is the state governments that have largely provided the personnel and facilities for agricultural extension, educational broadcasting, teaching hospitals, and other programs. As a consequence, it is the financial ability and disposition of state governments that determine the quality and scope of public higher education in the United States.

The story of state support of higher education is quite different state by state. Just as the structure of higher education institutions differs from one state to another, so also does the record of financial support. Some states have been relatively generous in their appropriations from tax funds, while other states have been less so. The states that have been relatively generous in their appropriations tend to insist upon relatively modest tuition charges to students; the states that have been less generous tend to be states where the tuition charges to students are relatively high. State governments have tended to view their expectations from, and their commitment to, public higher education differently. In general, state government support of higher education tends to correlate closely with the economic condition of the state. States with mature or declining economies are likely to find the support of their institutions of higher education burdensome, while states with developing or expanding economies find higher education support less burdensome.

The condition of the general economy throughout the nation affects the tax revenues of state governments and further affects the disposition to provide appropriations. State tax systems that rely heavily upon sales taxes rather than upon progressive income taxes find their revenues especially sensitive to fluctuations in consumer spending. Inflation has also had a heavy impact upon state financing. Moreover, the higher education system of a state necessarily finds itself in competition for the state tax dollar with other demands: the subventions to local elementary-secondary school districts, public welfare, mental health programs, and the expense of penal institutions.

Data published annually in the *Chronicle of Higher Education* present a vivid record of the variations that exist in state government support of higher education. The data published under date of October 14, 1980, indicate the record of appropriations state by state for the fiscal year 1980-81. The average state government appropriation in support of higher education was just above $95 per capita. There was one state (Alaska) where the appropriation was above $200 per capita. There was one state (Wyoming) where the appropriation was nearly $157 per capita. There were twenty states where the appropriations per capita ranged between $100 and $150. There were another twenty-two states where the appropriation per capita was under $90.

Another basis of comparison has been state appropriations per $1,000 of personal income. The average for all fifty states in 1980-81 was an appropriation of just under $11 for every $1,000 of personal income. By this measure, the ten most generous states in the appropriation support of higher education were Alaska, Mississippi, South Carolina, Utah, Alabama, Hawaii, North Carolina, Wyoming, New Mexico, and North Dakota. The ten states with the least appropriation per $1,000 of personal income (in ascending order) were New Hampshire, New Jersey, Massachusetts, Pennsylvania, Ohio, Connecticut, Maine, Nevada, Vermont, and Illinois.

A notable effort at providing comparative data about the fifty states has been undertaken by Dr. Kent Halstead of the National Institute of Education. In a study published in 1978 Halstead ranked the fifty states on the basis of tax capacity and tax effort. Tax effort represented the actual record of a state and its local subdivisions in raising revenue as measured by the national average of $643 per person in the year 1975. Tax capacity represented the amount of revenue that might be raised if a state levied taxes at the rate of the national average. Halstead analyzed data on sales and gross receipts taxes, license fees, income taxes (individual and corporate), general property taxes, death and gift taxes, and severance taxes state by state. Tax capacity represented the potential tax return if a state levied these taxes at the rate of the average tax prevailing in the United States.

The concepts of tax capacity and tax effort are important to state government higher education planners as measures of the individual state performance in raising tax revenues. Some state governments levy tax rates upon their taxable resources at rates higher than the national average. Other states levy tax rates lower than the national average. The state governments whose tax efforts exceed the criterion of tax capacity have decided that their needs for various state and local government services are considerable and have been willing to levy the taxes required to render the desired level of service. The state governments whose tax efforts were less than the calculation of their tax capacity (thirty-five such states) have decided that their needs for state and local government services were less than the calculation of their tax capacity. In these states higher education planners might plead for increased appropriations based upon the circumstance that tax rates were less than the national average.

The comparison of tax capacity and tax effort involves gross data about tax receipts. Insofar as public higher education is concerned, the more important factor is the proportion of tax receipts spent for public higher education. This relationship is shown in Table 1. For the fifty states together, the appropriations per capita were 10 percent of the per capita tax revenues in 1976. The highest proportions occurred in Alabama, Alaska, South Carolina, Wyoming, and Utah; the lowest proportions occurred in Connecticut, Massachusetts, New Hampshire, New Jersey, Pennsylvania, and Vermont.

A more elaborate study of comparisons in state government support of higher education was prepared by Marilyn McCoy of the National Center for Higher Education Management Systems and Kent Halstead and published in 1979.[5] The McCoy and Halstead study presented data state by state as of 1976 on public enrollments, state and local finances, institutional revenues (by major types of institutions), and institutional expenditures (by major types). The McCoy and Halstead study indicated the kind of information in detail that is required if any meaningful comparisons are to be made among the states about their differences in the support of public higher education. Unfortunately, such data are not available on a current basis.

Yet another extensive set of comparative data was published in November 1980 by the Education Commission of the States, with the joint sponsorship of the National Center for Higher Education Management Systems and the State Higher Education Executive Officers Association.[6] In this report the data were for the year 1977-78. The expectation was that such data would be published annually. This report included information about state structures of higher education, state populations, state and local expenditures for

TABLE 1

Per Capita Tax Revenues and Per Capita Appropriations
for Higher Education by States, 1976

	Per Capita Tax Revenues	Per Capita Appropriations	Percent
Alabama	$395	$61	15
Alaska	770	130	17
Arkansas	397	46	11
Arizona	651	89	14
California	851	102	12
Colorado	617	66	11
Connecticut	690	40	6
Delaware	673	67	10
Florida	496	50	10
Georgia	493	45	9
Hawaii	838	94	11
Idaho	517	75	14
Illinois	712	58	8
Indiana	578	50	9
Iowa	631	69	11
Kansas	588	71	12
Kentucky	465	56	12
Louisiana	545	48	9
Maine	562	40	7
Maryland	680	57	8
Massachusetts	792	36	4
Michigan	681	63	9
Minnesota	727	59	8
Mississippi	434	59	14
Missouri	512	47	9
Montana	604	55	9
Nebraska	567	71	13
Nevada	678	62	9
New Hampshire	501	31	6
New Jersey	708	41	6
New Mexico	528	60	11
New York	994	69	7
North Carolina	473	61	13
North Dakota	596	74	12
Ohio	525	37	8
Oklahoma	466	46	10
Oregon	623	80	13
Pennsylvania	582	37	6
Rhode Island	635	52	8
South Carolina	429	64	15
South Dakota	523	47	9
Tennessee	429	42	10
Texas	492	66	13
Utah	500	73	15
Vermont	656	36	5
Virginia	526	50	9
Washington	646	83	13
West Virginia	490	46	9
Wisconsin	717	86	12
Wyoming	687	103	15
Average	$643	$61	10

SOURCE: Marilyn McCoy and D. Kent Halstead, *Higher Education Financing in the Fifty States,* p. 29.

higher education, institutional revenues, institutional expenditures, faculty salaries and faculty tenure, enrollment, and charges to students. This ECS report may well become the standard reference material on state support of higher education.

Apart from indicators of the willingness of state governments, and others, to provide financial support to public institutions of higher education, and apart from comparisons of expenditures for instruction, student aid, research, public service, and institutional overhead, one other factor in public support must be mentioned. This factor is the distribution of state appropriation support among the varied public institutions within a particular state. About one-half of the states utilize some kind of a formula that distributes appropriations by enrollment at various levels (associate, baccalaureate, master's, doctoral, first professional, and medical) and in various fields of study (general education, technical education, arts and sciences, and professional). Some of these formulas are quite elaborate and others are relatively simple.

In a time when enrollments were increasing, formulas based upon average cost per student were generally employed. With enrollment loss beginning to occur in some public institutions and threatening other institutions, efforts have been made in various states to define costs in terms of fixed, semivariable, and variable components. These efforts tended to be in an early stage of development as of 1980.

Public institutions of higher education generally believe that they are underfunded by state governments, underappreciated by the public, and misunderstood in terms of the different outputs they produce and the different circumstances in which they operate. Chief executives, budget analysts, legislators, and legislative staffs tend to believe that public institutions of higher education are poorly managed, misuse available resources, conceal or misstate information about their operations, and overvalue the economic utility of their products. Faculty collective bargaining has been resorted to in some states in order to improve faculty salaries and to standardize faculty personnel practices including work load. But such faculty collective bargaining has accomplished little in improving the political climate of state government-institutional relationships. It is the improvement of this climate that is the major challenge of state government support of public higher education.

Accountability

In general, the term "accountability" as a process of social and institutional behavior means demonstration that the benefits from an organizational endeavor are worth the costs. Unfortunately, benefit/cost analysis is anything but an exact science. The benefits of so many organized endeavors are intangible, not lending themselves to precise quantitative measurement. What is the social benefit obtained because an individual is not permitted to starve to death, because an individual is not permitted to die of disease, or because an individual is not permitted to live without an education? Most Americans accept the proposition that there is a social benefit in each of these cases, but few if any Americans are prepared to place a particular value upon such efforts.

In public higher education there is an increasing social expectation on the part of state government officials that state colleges and universities will be able to demonstrate the benefit/cost relationship in instruction, research, public service, and student aid. The costs are known within reasonable limits. The benefits are as much a matter of judgment as they are of quantitative enumeration: students instructed by levels and programs, degrees awarded, research projects undertaken, hospital patients cared for, clinics visited by individuals, farm demonstration projects conducted, hours of public broadcasting provided, persons enrolled in short courses, students assisted in meeting enrollment expenses. All these activities can be counted in various ways. But what social benefit is derived from them? Is that social benefit worth the cost?

There are also the questions to be answered that we have outlined already: questions about institutional mission and performance, questions about the state role in relation to the private sector of higher education, questions about the appropriate level of public financial support for state colleges and universities. The concept of accountability dictates that state colleges and universities must be able to answer these questions as well as questions about benefit/cost. In practice, different institutions provide different answers; different groups provide different answers. The research state university has one set of answers and the comprehensive, urban-oriented state university has another set of answers. Governing boards and administrators have their answers; faculty members have almost as many answers as there are faculty members, and students have a variety of answers as well.

Increasingly, state government officials have been asking themselves yet another question: is there an organizational arrangement that will contribute to providing a clear and comprehensive answer to all these basic problems confronting higher education? Is there an organizational solution to complicated issues? Since the social enterprises of America are conducted in large part by organized entities, surely there is some kind of organizational response that will advance the realization of accountability in public higher education.

The organizational structure of state colleges and universities was initially patterned according to four primary influences: (1) the colonial importation of the idea of a board of trustees as a governing board for universities;

(2) the state board of education as a governing board for normal schools and then of teachers colleges; (3) the local school board as a governing board for public junior colleges; and (4) the state university governing board as the governing board for newly established "branches." Without reviewing these arrangements in any detail we may note two important factors: the concept of the governing board as the insulation between campus and state government, and the concept of multi-campus governance as public universities, colleges, and branches grew in number, size, and scope.

For the most part, the governing boards of state universities, however designated (regents, trustees, curators), were appointed by governors for lengthy and overlapping terms and were approved by state senates. In a few instances these boards were elected by the state legislature, or even by the state voters. The governing boards were expected to protect the state university from state politics and tended to exercise authority that was vested for most state government activities in state executives, the legislature, and the judiciary. Governing boards appointed presidents, faculty members, and principal officers and fixed their salaries. Governing boards formulated their own standards of faculty and student behavior, authorized degree and support programs, and received income from other than state sources. In many instances the state university was a body politic and corporate, in effect a governmental corporation.

As state governments created normal schools and then state teachers colleges, the state board of education usually served as the governing board. As these teachers colleges became comprehensive state universities after 1945, many state legislatures created new governing boards for them but tended to prefer a multi-campus governing board rather than a single governing board for these changing institutions.

As state universities, first in the 1920s and then particularly after 1945, established branches in various large cities, the existing governing board retained governing authority over these new institutions. An outstanding illustration of this trend was the development of the University of California from a two-campus system in Berkeley and Davis into a nine-campus system.

The multi-campus system, which has been studied by Lee and Bowen, created a precedent for a statewide multi-campus system embracing all senior colleges and universities in the state.[7] Governors and legislatures were attracted to this organizational arrangement in the expectation that a single governing board would have the authority to plan higher education needs on a statewide basis, would rationalize different missions for different kinds of institutions, would reduce or eliminate competition for programs and funds among institutions, and would distribute available funds equitably among all institutions.

The principal alternative structure to a statewide multi-campus system was the establishment of a state board of higher education with planning and coordinating authority. As state institutions of higher education grew in enrollment size, expanded their programs in various professional and graduate fields, developed branches in various locations, and requested ever larger appropriations from state government, state executives and legislatures sought some organizational device to stand between the institutions and the state government. Where a single state multi-campus structure was not politically feasible, state governments turned to the arrangement of a state board of higher education.

These state boards of higher education had no power of government over an individual state university or over a multi-campus state university system. In some instances the state board of higher education had only an advisory role: to study state needs for higher education services and to advise the governor and the legislature about desirable legislative action affecting the programs, location, structure, and financing of higher education activities in the state. In other instances the state board of higher education was vested with both a regulatory and an advisory role. Such boards might control the undertaking of any degree programs by state universities and might control the establishment of any new branch campuses. The state board might also review the budget requests of state universities and recommended appropriation needs. In addition, these boards also prepared state master plans and made legislative recommendations to the governor and legislature.

The problem of state government organization for higher education was first studied in some detail by Lyman A. Glenny in a book published in 1959.[8] Glenny found two primary explanations for the existence of the problem: the multiplication of state universities and the increased costs of public higher education. In evaluating the relative merits of statewide governing boards versus statewide planning and coordinating boards, Glenny declared that both had been inadequate in long-range planning, that governing boards had the greater success in allocating programs among state universities, that governing boards appeared to be more aggressive in pushing their budget recommendations with governors and legislatures, and that state university autonomy was greater under the coordinating arrangement.

A second extensive study of statewide coordination of higher education was undertaken by Robert O. Berdahl and published in 1971.[9] Berdahl concluded that by 1970 there was a "basic and inescapable need for the coordinating function to be performed at the state level." But he was unwilling to make a specific choice between a statewide governing board and a state higher education planning and coordinating board, saying that this choice was a matter for each state to decide for itself and that there were advantages and disadvantages in each arrangement.

Berdahl developed a classification scheme for types of state agencies as of 1970 and allocated each of the fifty states to this scheme. He also included data about the year when the agency was first created and about the membership of the agency board. There have been several changes in the coordinating structure of each state since 1970. Employing the same classification as that set forth by Berdahl, I would assign the states as follows as of the end of 1980:

TABLE 2

Statewide Coordination of Higher Education, 1980

	Berdahl Number
I. No State Agency - 1	2
Wyoming	
II. Voluntary Association - 0	2
III. Coordinating Board	
A. Advisory Agencies - 8	13
California	
Delaware	
Michigan	
Minnesota	
Nebraska	
Pennsylvania	
Vermont	
Washington	
B. Regulatory Power - 19	11
Alabama	
Arkansas	
Colorado	
Connecticut	
Illinois	
Indiana	
Kentucky	
Louisiana	
Maryland	
Missouri	
New Jersey	
New Mexico	
New York	
Ohio	
Oklahoma	
South Carolina	
Tennessee	
Texas	
Virginia	
IV. Consolidated Governing Board - 22	19
Alaska	
Arizona	
Florida	
Georgia	
Hawaii	
Idaho	
Iowa	
Kansas	
Maine	
Massachusetts	
Mississippi	
Montana	

Nevada
New Hampshire
North Carolina
North Dakota
Oregon
Rhode Island
South Dakota
Utah
West Virginia
Wisconsin

It should also be noted that in at least four states with a statewide governing board, the legislature has deemed it desirable to set up also a state higher education planning board. This action has been taken because the statewide governing board had no jurisdiction over community colleges and area vocational/technical schools and because a statewide governing board could not be expected to give adequate attention to the needs of the independent sector of higher education within the state.

In the years between 1967 and 1980 both the Carnegie Commission on Higher Education and the Carnegie Council on Policy Studies in Higher Education devoted some attention to the problem of state government organization. The published reports included *The Capitol and the Campus* (1971),[10] *Governance of Higher Education* (1973),[11] *The States and Higher Education* (1976),[12] and *Three Thousand Futures* (1980).[13] These reports expressed concern about an apparent increase in the dominance of governors over higher education in several states, the "development of heavy-handed regulatory councils over higher education," and the loss of institutional autonomy. At the same time the reports acknowledged that the autonomy of institutions of higher education neither could be nor should be "complete."

In its 1973 report on governance the Carnegie Commission attempted to formulate a balance between "public control" and "institutional independence" for state institutions of higher education. This formulation is set forth in Table 3. Although the Carnegie report did not specify how the public control was to be organized and exercised, the general scheme appears to me to be quite reasonable and to provide a useful guideline for state government actions.

At the same time, I find in the various Carnegie studies and reports a certain degree of bias against the state board of higher education as an organizational arrangement. To some extent this bias may reflect the continuing hostility of state university presidents toward such boards. In general, university presidents appear to get along fairly well with statewide governing boards, even when such boards have a chancellor as chief executive officer rather than an executive director as a coordinator. State boards of higher education are considered to be agents of state government rather than agents of the state universities.

In 1977 the Alfred P. Sloan Foundation established the Sloan Commis-

TABLE 3
Proposed Pattern for Distribution of Authority

Public Control	Institutional Independence
GOVERNANCE	
Basic responsibility for law enforcement	Right to refuse oaths not required for all
Right to insist on political neutrality of institutions of higher education	citizens in similar circumstances
Duty to appoint trustees of public institutions	Right to independent trustees; no *ex officio* trustees with subsequent budget authority
Right to reports and accountability on matter of public interest	
Duty of courts to hear cases alleging denial of general rights of a citizen and of unfair procedures	
FINANCIAL AND BUSINESS AFFAIRS	
Appropriations of public funds on basis of general formulas that refect quantity and quality of output	Assignment of all funds to specific reasons
Post audit, rather than preaudit, of expenditures, of purchases, of personnel actions	Freedom to make expenditures within budget, to make purchases, and to take personnel action subject only to post-audit
Examination of effective use of resources on a post-audit basis	
Standards for accounting practices and post audit of them.	
General level of salaries	Determination of specific salaries
Appropriation of public funds for building on basis of general formulas for building requirements	Design of buildings and assignment of space
ACADEMIC AND INTELLECTUAL AFFAIRS	
General Policies on Student Admissions: Number of places Equality of access Academic level of general ability among types of institutions General distribution of students by level of division	Selection of individual students
Policies for equal access to employment for women and minority groups	Academic policies for, and actual selection and promotion of, faculty members
Policies on differentiation of functions among systems of higher education and on specialization by major fields of endeavor among institutions	Approval of individual courses and course content
No right to expect secret research or service from members of institutions of higher education; and no right to prior review before publication of research results; but right to patents where appropriate.	Policies on and administration of research and service activities

TABLE 3
(continued)
PROPOSED PATTERN FOR DISTRIBUTION OF AUTHORITY

	Determination of grades and issuance of individual degrees
	Selection of academic and administrative leadership
Enforcement of the national Bill of Rights	Policies on academic freedom
Policies on size and rate of growth of campuses	Policies on size and rate of growth of departments and schools and colleges within budgetary limitations
Establishment of new campuses and other major new endeavors, such as a medical school, and definition of scope	Academic programs for new campus and other major new endeavors within general authorization
Encouragement of innovation through inquiry, recommendation, allocation of special funds, application of general budget formulas, starting new institutions	Development of and detailed planning for innovation

SOURCE: Carnegie Commission on Higher Education, *Governance of Higher Education,* April 1973, pp. 25-27.

sion on Government and Higher Education to study the question of changing relationships between governments and colleges and universities.[14] Although most of the report published in 1980 was concerned with federal government concerns, one chapter was devoted to state governments. The suggestions for improvement in state university-state government relationships did little to advance the general discussion of institutional accountability in a changing political environment.

State governments and state higher education as of the end of 1980 were still struggling to find the organizational as well as the policy lines of action appropriate to the changing circumstances of the 1980s. The political climate had changed from one concerned with the demands of economic growth and population expansion in the college-age cohort to one concerned with the demands of economic recession, inflation, and population decline. If relationships were troublesome in the "golden age," how much more troublesome these relationships might become in a time of retrenchment.

The Carnegie Council in its final report, *Three Thousand Futures,* expressed the fear that changing circumstances might lead state governments to place the public systems of higher education under increased state control. The Council declared that such actions would do great harm to state higher education. It was acknowledged that some closings and mergers might be desirable. The Council urged that contraction be determined primarily upon the basis of student enrollment, letting student choice decide what programs and institutions to curtail. At the same time the Carnegie Council recommended that state governments should maintain their current level of per capita funding of higher education in constant dollars, should utilize flexible funding formulas, should provide support for private higher education, and should avoid excessive regulation of higher education.

What has often been overlooked, however, has been the differential economic outlook for various states. The 1980 census showed for the first time a majority of people in the United States living in the South and West. The economies of the Northeast and Middle West had been hard hit by underinvestment in the renewal and expansion of industrial plants and by foreign competition in steel, automobiles, electronics, clothing, and other durable goods. Unless public higher education in the economically disadvantaged states could develop a new relationship to the reindustrialization of these states, the prospects for improved relationships in the accountability of state higher education were dim.

General Observations

The basic issue of organizational structure still unresolved as of 1980 was the question of statewide governing boards for state universities as against a state board of higher education as the device for ensuring the accountability of public higher education. And there was a possibility that neither arrangement would be considered useful as the decade of the 1980s unfolded.

In my own studies and experience, I have found that the statewide multi-campus governing board can be an effective agency for defining university missions, for expanding and contracting academic programs, and for allocating available resources on an equitable basis among institutions. There is no guarantee that a multi-campus governing board will accomplish these goals but the potential authority is present to do so. I have known statewide governing boards that handled these tasks poorly because of various political pressures that the board could not repel or compromise.

My principal concern with the statewide governing board simply is that such a board must necessarily advocate the interests of the institutions it governs and cannot take a statewide point of view. Such a governing board usually gives little if any attention to the needs and concerns of community colleges and other two-year institutions and to the needs and concerns of the independent sector of higher education.

The state board of higher education is organizationally better suited to prepare a master plan for higher education embracing a definition of state needs, an inventory of available resources (public and private), and an allocation of missions in meeting state needs. The state board of higher education can be a fair-minded arbitrator about programs and budget needs among competing institutions. But state boards of higher education must rely upon governors and legislators for political support and influence. These boards have no constituencies of administrative colleagues, faculty members, students, and alumni. They continue to be the object of attack by presidents and governing boards of state universities.

It is quite evident that state boards of higher education do tend to give special attention to the point of view of particular governors and of legislative leaders. The staffs of these boards, although often including individuals with some kind of academic experience and background, tend to be persons who understand the political process and seek to accommodate it in various ways. It has been said that the staffs of state boards of higher education behave like bureaucrats, while the staffs of governing boards and university presidents behave like academics.

Governors and legislative leaders may be dissatisfied with the performance of state boards of higher education because these boards have too little authority over governing boards and individual institutions. Chief executives and legislators would like to have as many political conflicts as possible settled at a level lower than their own. They want state boards of higher education to "order" governing boards, presidents, and faculties to take particular actions. They would rather have a state board do the ordering than a state law. And when state boards of higher education point out that they have no power to do any such ordering, then governors and legislators began to look with some longing upon the device of a statewide governing board.

The complication is that while the statewide governing board may have the power to order certain desired types of action, no governor or legislature can be sure that the statewide governing board will do so. In fact, there is considerable evidence to indicate that they have not done so. The most cordial recent relationship to exist recently in any state between a statewide governing board and the political leadership of a state has been evident in North Carolina, and that cordial relationship has been based upon the threat of a common enemy, the federal government.

What is the desirable relationship between a state board of higher education and the governor and legislature? Two or three states have experimented with the device of an executive department of education, with a state board of education and a state board of higher education "reporting" to a politically appointed secretary or commissioner of education. The arrangement does not appear to have been notably successful. As budget staffs in the governor's office and in the legislature have expanded in recent years, there have been complaints that these staffs duplicate the work of the staff of a board of higher education. And the criticism has been justified. Unless the governor's staff and the legislature's staff work closely and cooperatively with the staff of the state board of higher education, there is duplication of activity and new burdens for state universities to bear.

Some observers seem to believe that the preferable organizational relationship in the long run will be for the governor's staff to absorb the staff of the state board of higher education and then for higher education to be structured under one or more multi-campus systems. How far any such arrangement is likely to go, the events of the 1980s will have to determine.

The situation seems fairly clear. A clarification of institutional missions must be undertaken. Output and support programs of individual institutions must be reviewed in terms of cost and the possible economies of consolidation, merger, and elimination. The quality of academic performance within state institutions of higher education must in some fashion be preserved and even advanced. The future of the independent sector of higher education must be carefully monitored and even assisted. The financial support of public higher education must meet the needs of enrollment and program objectives.

Up to 1980 it had been generally assumed in various states that the appropriate policy actions or recommendations on these issues would be forthcoming from either statewide governing boards or state boards of higher education. Both organizational arrangements implied a certain degree of insulation or protection for state universities from the political processes of state government. The possibility that political attitudes and political lobbying might result in political favoritism for certain universities, certain locations, certain programs, and certain individuals was thereby blunted.

But if neither the statewide governing board nor the state board of higher education could satisfy governors and legislatures, yet another possibility existed. Indeed, to some extent this possibility was already becoming a reality in some states as of 1980. This alternative was the development of staff organizations for legislatures that would become not just reviewers of higher education policy and funding. This new bureaucracy could be expected to mirror the political concerns of governors and legislators rather than the educational concerns of the state universities.

The consequence of such development could be a loss of that arms-length relationship between state universities and state governments essential to the fulfillment of the basic purposes of higher education involving student instruction, research, creative activity, educational justice, and constructive criticism of individual and social performance. Public higher education had greatly to expand in order to meet enlarged social expectations. But that expansion was accomplished without a loss of political autonomy.

The issue of the 1980s accordingly is whether or not higher education adjustment can be accomplished without a loss of political autonomy. The answer will lie in the processes whereby state universities and state governments undertake to define and resolve the issues outlined herein. A failure to resolve substantive issues on a basis of mutual accommodation may well lead to some further organizational changes not in the best interests of either public higher education or society.

156 Higher Education in American Society

Notes

1. Carnegie Council on Policy Studies in Higher Education, *Three Thousand Futures* (San Francisco: Jossey-Bass, 1980).
2. Ibid.
3. John D. Millett, *Financing Higher Education in the United States* (New York: Columbia University Press, 1952).
4. Carnegie Council on Policy Studies in Higher Education, *The States and Private Higher Education* (San Francisco: Jossey-Bass, 1977).
5. Marilyn McCoy and D. Kent Halstead, *Higher Education Financing in the Fifty States: Interstate Comparisons Fiscal Year 1976* (Washington, D.C.: U.S. Government Printing Office, 1979).
6. Education Commission of the States, *Challenge: Coordination and Governance in the '80s* (Denver: Education Commission of the States, 1980).
7. Eugene C. Lee and Frank M. Bowen, *The Multicampus University: A Study of Academic Governance* (New York: McGraw-Hill, 1971).
8. Lyman A. Glenny, *Autonomy of Public Colleges* (New York: McGraw-Hill, 1959).
9. Robert O. Berdahl, *Statewide Coordination of Higher Education* (Washington, D.C.: American Council on Education, 1971).
10. Carnegie Commission on Higher Education, *The Capitol and the Campus* (New York: McGraw-Hill, 1971).
11. Carnegie Commission on Higher Education, *Governance of Higher Education* (New York: McGraw-Hill, 1973).
12. Carnegie Council on Policy Studies in Higher Education, *The States and Private Higher Education*.
13. Carnegie Council on Policy Studies in Higher Education, *Three Thousand Futures*.
14. Sloan Commission on Government and Higher Education, *A Program for Renewed Partnership* (Cambridge, Mass.: Ballinger, 1980).

9

The Federal Government and Postsecondary Education
Aims C. McGuinness, Jr.

Introduction

The American academic community has long had a basic distrust of government involvement. The community has been quick to raise the specter of a fundamental violation of academic freedom and other sacrosanct values at any attempt by government to set conditions and means of accountability for use of public funds in colleges and universities.

Yet, government has played a steadily increasing role in support of higher education, a role spurred on to a large degree with the encouragement of members of academia. A strong case could be made that many of the major innovations in higher education have come, not from within the academic community, but from the stimulus of government action. The federal government, in particular, has been the catalyst for development of the nation's public higher education system, the massive expansion of the basic and applied research capacity of colleges and universities, and the commitment of higher education to equal access and opportunity.

The objective of this chapter is to provide a brief overview of the federal involvement in postsecondary education. The particular interest is in the

nature of past, present, and future federal activities that impinge upon the
independence and autonomy of institutions. Included are:

- a brief elaboration on the scope of the federal role;
- an introduction to key elements of the federal policy process;
- a review of the evolution of the federal role up through the 1960s;
- an examination of the federal role in the decade of the 1970s;
- a review of the Education Amendments of 1980 and identification
  of some of the issues likely to face institutions in their relations with
  the federal government in the next decade.

Scope of the Federal Role in Postsecondary Education

Any discussion of the federal government and postsecondary education
must begin with several common understandings:

- there is not a monolithic system of higher education in the nation,
  but an array of institutions and programs, each with different purposes, traditions, students or clientele, and sources of financing;
- there is no deliberate, unitary "policy" of the federal government
  toward postsecondary education, but an unbelievably complex set
  of policies and programs (some aimed at educational objectives,
  but many not) that affect postsecondary education either directly or
  indirectly;
- the complex interaction between postsecondary education and the
  federal government takes place not in isolation from, but in integral
  relationship to, the multiple political, economic, and societal forces
  affecting the nation as a whole and all social institutions.

These assumptions may seem obvious; yet individuals within postsecondary education, whether they be college presidents, students, faculty
members, student aid administrators, or policy analysts, inevitably experience relationships with federal policies from relatively narrow perspectives. In fact, the literature on federal policy and higher or postsecondary
education is replete with discussions from a particular viewpoint: that of
major research institutions or of private higher education, as examples.
Each observer feels a different part of the elephant, yet few gain a sense of
the total beast.

The scope of the role of the federal government in postsecondary education is graphically illustrated by the following points made in the agenda for the 97th Congress prepared by the American Council on Education (ACE), the major overall association for colleges and universities on the federal scene.

- The higher education community is large and diverse: a $55 billion sector employing over 600,000 instructional and research staff and 1.3 million administrative and support personnel in some 3,000 institutions—large, small, public, independent, two-year, four-year, and graduate—enrolling more than 11 million students and serving millions more citizens in public service programs.

- Public colleges and universities rely on state and local funds for more than half their resources; independent institutions receive over half of their resources from tuition and private contributions. Nevertheless, the federal government contributes approximately 20 percent of total operating expenditures for higher education.

- Student aid is the primary means of federal support, totaling $10 billion ($6 billion in grants and loans from Education Department programs, $4 billion in educational benefits under social security and veterans programs). Federally supported research and development from a variety of agencies accounts for another $5.3 billion; categorical programs and training in the health professions account for about $900 million.

- In addition to priority concerns regarding funding for student assistance and for research and categorical programs, higher education's concerns range across the entire spectrum of national policy issues before the committees of Congress: broad problems of the economy, tax policy, human resources, research, energy; specific issues such as regulatory reform, postal rates, privacy; and administration of grants and contracts.

- The concerns of higher education span the jurisdiction of twenty-eight House and Senate committees.[1]

As a further indication of the breadth and complexity of the federal activities in postsecondary education, the Congressional Research Service conducted a study in 1975 that found 439 separately authorized programs touching on colleges and universities. Only a small percentage of these were under the jurisdiction of the congressional committees directly responsible for postsecondary education (the Higher Education Act). Many of the programs were small and a few had never been funded.[2]

Historically, and according to the U.S. Constitution, education is a state and local responsibility. Nevertheless, as suggested by the ACE agenda, the federal government not only contributes about a fifth of the financial support for postsecondary education, but also has a far-ranging regulatory and policy effect even beyond what this funding share implies.

In broadly stated terms, the federal role in postsecondary education is focused on:

- assisting in overcoming barriers, such as income, race, and sex, to equal educational opportunity;

- supporting the generation of fundamental knowledge and the conduct of research and development related to major issues of national concern;

- insuring that nationwide manpower needs in health, science, and other critical fields are met;

- supporting innovation and improvement in postsecondary education, and dissemination of the results of research and demonstration efforts.[3]

Precise figures on total federal expenditures for postsecondary education are difficult to come by. An analysis prepared by the Office of Management and Budget (OMB) in 1978 identified outlays primarily for educational purposes at the higher education level of $4.6 billion for fiscal year 1977. To this OMB added federal outlays for higher education for other purposes (veterans readjustment, health professions training, etc.) of $4.4 billion for total federal outlays in fiscal year 1977 of approximately $9 billion. Not included in these figures were outlays for a category of "adult and continuing education" totaling $1.3 billion and "other" federal programs. It can reasonably be assumed that a major portion of these funds also went to postsecondary education institutions.[4]

Finn developed an estimate, based largely on the OMB 1978 analysis, of federal expenditures of $13.852 billion in fiscal year 1977, including $2.1 billion in tax expenditures. Finn's estimate included $2.7 billion for research and development conducted in colleges and universities.[5]

The Congressional Budget Office (CBO), in an analysis of options for federal assistance for postsecondary education in fiscal year 1979, identified four major sources of federal aid:

- the Office of Education (now the Department of Education), which administers the postsecondary education programs authorized by the Higher Education Act (the major student assistance programs and several small institutional assistance programs);

- other agencies that provide educational benefits, such as the Veterans' Readjustment Benefits and social security student benefits;

- tax expenditures that provide assistance in the form of reduced tax liabilities;
- science-funding agencies that provide resources to higher education institutions.[6]

The 1978 CBO analysis reported for fiscal year 1978 direct and indirect expenditures for postsecondary education (excluding research support) of $9.9 billion. Seventy-five percent of those dollars were directed toward the purpose of providing equality of educational opportunity (primarily through student assistance), more than 15 percent was directed toward easing the financial burden of higher education to the population in general, and approximately 10 percent was focused on programs designed to assure a strong and diverse system of higher education.[7]

Looking only at the programs within the jurisdiction of the Department of Education (the major student and institutional assistance programs), federal outlays have increased dramatically since the 1978 CBO analysis. Outlays for the subfunction of "higher education" increased from $3.5 billion in fiscal year 1978 to a projected $6.5 billion for fiscal year 1981.[8]

In general, then, while the precise figures are not available, federal outlays for postsecondary education, including tax expenditures and other elements identified by Finn in 1978, will clearly approach $20 billion in fiscal year 1982.

Federal Policy Process

Before a review is made of the evolution of the federal role in postsecondary education, brief mention should be made of the major elements and steps in the formal process by which federal policies develop.

In general, the federal policies affecting postsecondary education (other than those arising from court actions) stem from the following:

- *"Authorizing" statutes,* which set forth the purposes of a program and how it is to be carried out, and "authorize," usually for a limited number of years, the appropriation of funds for the program. The Higher Education Act of 1965 is the principal authorizing statute affecting postsecondary education. Authorizing statutes are handled by authorizing committees of the Congress. In the case of the Higher Education Act, these are the House Education and Labor Committee and the Senate Labor and Human Resources Committee.

- *Budget resolutions,* including the First Budget Resolution, usually adopted by Congress by May 15 of each year, setting the targets for appropriations for major functions within the budget; the Second Budget Resolution, adopted by September 30 or near the end of each congressional session, setting the ceilings for spending in the coming fiscal year; and Reconciliation Resolutions adjusting both authorizing and appropriations provisions to conform to the ceilings set in the Second Budget Resolution. Budget resolutions are initiated by action of the House and Senate Budget Committees.

- *Appropriations statutes* and legislation to approve or disapprove recisions and deferrals of appropriations, which set forth the exact dollar amounts to be spent in a given fiscal year for "authorized" programs. In other words, funds cannot be spent for most of the programs authorized by the Higher Education Act until they are appropriated through action initiated by the House and Senate Appropriations Committees.

- *Executive orders* issued by the president, such as those setting forth the requirements for affirmative action.

- *Regulations* issued by the executive branch and published in the *Federal Register.* These are of at least three general types:

  a. Regulations to implement a specific authorizing statute, such as the Higher Education Act;
  b. "Circulars" or regulations governing the general operation of government programs (fiscal accountability, etc.), such as the Office of Management and Budget (OMB) Circular A-21 governing accountability requirements for federal contract and grant recipients;
  c. Regulations implementing general statutory requirements or actions of courts, such as those implementing provisions of the Civil Rights Act of 1964, or the Occupational Safety and Health Act (OSHA).

Another point that would help one not familiar with the federal policy process is that, with a few major exceptions, the process follows an established pattern. For example:

- The major authorizing statutes, such as the Higher Education Act, authorize programs for three to five years. Toward the end of the authorized period, the programs undergo a thorough review by the appropriate authorizing committees of the House and Senate, a process that usually extends over one to two years. The programs are then "reauthorized" before they expire. Hence, the Higher

Education Act of 1965 has been reauthorized four times: in 1968, 1972, 1976, and 1980. This and other statutes have, of course, been amended from time to time in the periods between reauthorizations.

- The annual budget and appropriations process follows a schedule set by the Congressional Budget and Control Act of 1974 (P.L. 93-344), which established the House and Senate Budget Committees, the Congressional Budget Office (CBO), and reasserted the congressional role in the federal budget process. Points in the schedule include:
  - The President submits his budget to the Congress fifteen days after the Congress convenes.
  - By May 15, the First Budget Resolution should have been adopted and authorizing legislation should have been reported from committee.
  - By September 15 (but in practice later) the appropriations committee should have completed their work and the Second Budget Resolution should have been adopted.

The activities of the Washington-based higher education "community" —the major associations, representatives of individual institutions or groups of institutions, state representatives, and the multiplicity of other higher education interest groups—are generally organized in relationship to the cycles and schedules of the reauthorization, budget, and appropriations processes. Every three to five years, attention is focused on reauthorization of the Higher Education Act, a process that usually extends over two or more years (beginning with broad policy debate and analysis, and then concluding with intense activity surrounding congressional action on a bill). The budget and appropriations processes, of course, require ongoing attention throughout each year.

The arena of federal regulation is *not* keyed to a particular schedule or pattern, except, of course, in the period directly following enactment of major changes in authorizing legislation. In recent years, the Washington-based community has had to devote an increasing portion of its effort to monitoring regulatory actions of the Office of Management and Budget, the Veterans' Administration, the Office of Civil Rights within the Education Department, and the multitude of other noneducation agencies that might affect higher education. As is suggested later in the chapter, this trend has complicated the picture for individual institutions as they seek to maintain their independence in the face of federal actions.

Historical Perspective

The current federal role in postsecondary education evolved over a 200-year period beginning with the earliest years of the nation. Initial involvement developed slowly and usually for reasons other than a deliberate federal action to assist higher education. In fact, the pattern through the history of the federal role in higher education has been that "education" has been seen as a means to achieve some other worthy federal objective: national defense, the quest for knowledge to address concerns about health, energy, space exploration, etc., or major drives to achieve equity among all segments of the nation's population.

The evolution of the federal role in the period prior to the early 1970s can reasonably by divided into two periods: the late 1700s until the late 1950s (the National Defense Education Act of 1958); and the period up to the enactment of the Education Amendments of 1972.

1787 to the Late 1950s

A proposal to establish a national university was considered but rejected by the Constitutional Convention, and in the late 1700s and early 1800s, similar proposals were rejected by a Congress firmly opposed to the establishment of a national system of education.[9]

The first involvement of the federal government in support of higher education came through in the form of land grants, initially through the provisions of the ordinance authorizing sale of lands to the Ohio Company in the Northwest Territory in 1787, and then, on a more extensive basis through the provisions of the Morrill Land-Grant Act of 1862.

The Morrill Act of 1862, frequently cited as the beginning point of a significant federal role in higher education, provided, through distribution of federal lands and land script for the endowment, support, and maintenance of at least one college in each state, for the teaching of subjects related to agriculture and the mechanic arts. The Act is also important as the origin of the federal system of grants-in-aid for specific categorical purposes with basic accountability and annual reporting requirements.

The second Morrill Act, passed in 1890, extended federal assistance to states for instructional purposes in land-grant colleges. The concept of federal assistance to states for specific areas was extended in subsequent years through amendments to the Land-Grant Acts and through the Hatch Act of 1887 (agricultural experiment stations), the Smith-Lever Act of 1914 (university extension-agricultural research and home economics), and the Smith-Hughes Act of 1917 (vocational education, including college training for vocational education teachers).

World War II stimulated the most dramatic increase in the involvement of the federal government in higher education, first through the massive increase in federal investment in research and development associated with the war effort, and second, with the programs to assist the nation to adjust to the postwar period.

The Service Man's Readjustment Act of 1944 (the G.I. Bill), intended to assist servicemen to adjust to civilian life and to avoid a glutted labor market as millions of soldiers were demobilized, provided assistance to veterans for tuition, books, and living expenses to begin or continue their education. Within a short time after the end of the war enrollments in higher education institutions had increased fourfold, leading to serious shortages in faculty and facilities.

As indicated, the world war required a massive increase in federal support for military-related research and development, much of which was conducted in colleges and universities. Recognizing the need for continued federal support for research, but with a need to shift from a major emphasis on military purposes, the Congress enacted legislation in 1950 establishing the National Science Foundation.

By 1960, the federal government was spending three-quarters of a billion dollars on research at higher education institutions, and providing two-thirds of all higher education's research funding, to the extent that this had become the major source of involvement of the federal government in support of higher education.[10]

In general, however, the federal government's involvement in higher education up to the late 1950s was consciously limited to the support of specific programs aimed at narrowly defined areas of federal concern. Proposals for a broader federal role in support of higher education were consistently rejected, frequently in the heat of debates regarding race and religion.

1958 to 1972

The enactment of the National Defense Education Act of 1958 (NDEA) (P.L. 85-865) is frequently cited as the key breakthrough for a massive expansion in the federal role in education. The launching of Sputnik by the Soviet Union in 1957 served as a catalyst for a variety of forces concerned about the condition of American education and the shortage of trained scientists and teachers. The connection with "national defense" served to overcome the long-standing objections to an increased federal role in education and continued the pattern of enactment of federal laws affecting education for essentially noneducation purposes.

In addition to provisions for grants to states for elementary and secondary level purposes, NDEA authorized the U.S. Commissioner of Education to make capital contributions to student loan funds at institutions of higher education. Priority was to be given to students intending to teach and to those with ability in science, mathematics, engineering, and modern foreign languages. Loans were forgiven for those who actually went into teaching following graduation. NDEA also authorized 4,400 three-year graduate fellowships, with preference for those going into teaching.

Following NDEA, the next major advance in the federal role in post-secondary education came with the enactment of the Higher Education Facilities Act of 1963 (HEFA) (P.L. 88-204). For the first time, the Congress enacted a program that was directly aimed at educational purposes without the benefit of another national purpose, such as national defense, as the vehicle. HEFA provided for grants and loans to institutions of higher education, both public and private, for construction of academic facilities. The programs of grants for undergraduate academic facilities were made through the states, while the other programs of grants for graduate facilities and for loans were made directly by the federal government to institutions.

In 1965, the Congress enacted the Higher Education Act (HEA) (P.L. 89-329). This act, which serves as the foundation for the major federal programs of aid to postsecondary education, moved far beyond the NDEA by establishing for the first time a federal program of scholarships to students, the Educational Opportunity Grant program. Other student assistance programs in HEA included a revised and extended version of the National Defense Student Loan Program (NDSL), a new program of guarantees and interest subsidies for loans (the Guaranteed Loan Program), and a work-study program transferred from the Economic Opportunity Act of 1964. HEA also included provisions authorizing federal grants for community service and continuing education, college libraries, developing institutions, teacher education, and undergraduate instructional equipment.

The Higher Education Act and the Higher Education Facilities Act were not the only major pieces of legislation enacted in the mid-1960s with far-reaching implications for the federal role in postsecondary education. Perhaps of greatest significance is the Civil Rights Act of 1964, especially Title VI that prohibits discrimination on the ground of race, color, religion, sex, or national origin, by recipients of federal assistance.

After the surge of social legislation associated with the "War on Poverty" in the mid-1960s, the climate affecting public attitudes toward support of postsecondary education changed dramatically: the disillusion-ment regarding the effectiveness of public programs following the inner-city riots, deepening involvement in the Vietnam War, severe campus unrest, and growing financial difficulties of colleges and universities resulting from the massive enrollment increases of the previous decade. A president was also elected with a concept of the federal role in domestic affairs far more limited than that of his predecessor. It was this changed climate that pro-vided the backdrop for the process leading to the Education Amendments of 1972.

The Education Amendments of 1972 and the Decade of the 1970s

Education Amendments of 1972

The Education Amendments of 1972 (P.L. 92-318), signed into law in June 1972, were hailed at the time as the most significant changes in federal policy toward higher education since the Morrill Land-Grant Act of 1862. In retrospect, the 1972 Amendments marked a turning point in the federal role in postsecondary education and ushered in a period of major increases in funding, especially for student assistance.[11]

Enactment of the 1972 Amendments culminated about four years of debate about the appropriate mechanisms for delivering federal aid to higher education. In simple terms, the choice was between federal grants directly to institutions, on one hand, and federal grants to students, on the other. Faced with severe fiscal pressures following a decade of unprecedented expansion, colleges and universities (as represented through their Washington-based associations) argued strongly for a program of general institutional aid. It was suggested that this could be added to the existing programs of aid to students authorized by the Higher Education Act (Educational Opportunity Grants, College Work Study, and loans). In contrast, the Carnegie Commission and several prestigious economists argued that the most effective approach to federal aid to higher education was aid to students.[12]

The case for general institutional aid was essentially rejected by the Congress. The final version of the 1972 Amendments established a major new program of grants to students, the Basic Educational Opportunity Grant Program (BEOG), now known as "Pell Grants" after the sponsor of the original proposal, Senator Claiborne Pell, then chairman of the Senate Education Subcommittee. The student aid programs of the existing Higher Education Act were retained in slightly modified form. In partial response to the institutional concerns, a complicated program of institutional aid was established but in the form of cost of education allowances that would follow student assistance. Although authorized, this program has never been funded.

A key element of the new BEOG program was that grants were to be made directly by the federal government to students on the basis of a federally established family contribution schedule. Under the previous federal student aid programs, the federal government allocated funds to colleges and universities and the funds were granted to students on the basis of a determination of need and other criteria appropriate to the program and other circumstances. This indirect approach was maintained by the 1972 Amendments for the programs other than the BEOG program. Under the BEOG program, as originally enacted in 1972, a student was entitled to a basic grant of $1,400 minus the expected family contribution (set forth in a federally established table).

Other important provisions enacted through the 1972 Amendments included:

- A new program of incentives to states to establish need-based student aid programs, the State Student Incentive Grant Program (SSIG), was authorized.

- Eligibility for federal student assistance was extended to students attending proprietary institutions.

- The National Institute of Education (NIE) and the Fund for Improvement of Postsecondary Education (FIPSE) were established.

- States desiring to participate in newly authorized programs of grants for comprehensive statewide planning and for occupational education and community colleges were required to establish "broadly and equitably representative" state commissions, called "1202 commissions."

One of the most far-reaching changes made by the 1972 Amendments was to extend the concept of the audience for federal policy from the relatively narrow field of collegiate higher education institutions to the full range of institutions and programs encompassed in the term "postsecondary education." In addition to the broadened eligibility under the student aid programs, the 1972 Amendments required participation of a full range of institutional representatives in federally assisted planning by the 1202 commissions. This had the effect of opening up the planning process in a number of states to both private nonprofit and proprietary institutions.[13]

Education Amendments of 1976

Although changes were made in federal higher education programs authorized by the Higher Education Act in the Education Amendments of 1976 (P.L. 94-482), the basic goals of federal policy were not significantly altered from those implied by the 1972 Amendments:

- to promote equality of educational opportunity, by helping to remove economic and social barriers to access to postsecondary education, to encourage those who otherwise might not continue their schooling to attend college;

- to reduce the burden of college costs on families with students who would likely continue their education without government assistance (primarily through the loan programs and tax provisions);

- to assure a strong system of higher education through the provisions encouraging choice among institutions in the student aid programs and through selected programs of direct grants to institutions.[14]

The 1976 Amendments made several changes of a somewhat technical nature in the federal student assistance programs (increasing the maximum grant under the BEOG program and modifying the Guaranteed Loan Program to give states increased incentives to establish state loan programs). A major debate occurred during congressional action on the amendments regarding the effects of the student assistance provisions on students' choice of independent, private institutions. The move to modify these provisions was not successful, leaving the issue to emerge again three years later. The Amendments included a new program for Lifelong Learning in Title I of the Higher Education Act.[15]

Beyond the questions related to reauthorization of the Higher Education Act, much of the attention during the 1976 Amendments was given to revisions in the Vocational Education Act that were included in the same omnibus bill. From the perspectives of postsecondary education, the principal issues in the Vocational Education Act reauthorization concerned the proportion of the state grants allocated for postsecondary education (the minimum had been 15 percent, yet in a number of states, the percentage was found to be lower than this), and the provisions for statewide planning and governance of vocational education.

Middle Income Student Assistance Act

The Middle Income Student Assistance Act (MISAA) emerged from the heated debate through much of 1978 regarding alternative approaches to reducing the financial burden of higher education costs for middle-income families. The most direct stimulus for enactment of the legislation was the proposal for tuition tax credits, a proposal that advanced in slightly different forms through both the Senate Finance Committee and the House Ways and Means Committee. The high probability that a tuition tax credit bill would eventually pass before the end of the Ninety-fifth Congress led the Carter Administration to propose a major alternative focused on broadening the eligibility for middle-income students under existing student assistance programs coupled with major increases in funding. In an effort to head off tax credits, both the House Committee on Education and Labor and the Senate Committee on Human Resources reported bills expanding existing programs in the direction of assisting middle-income families.[16]

In the closing hours of the Ninety-fifth Congress, an effort to develop a compromise between House- and Senate-passed tax credit bills failed, while final agreement on a compromise Middle Income Student Assistance Act (MISAA) was reached. In its final form, MISAA modified the BEOG Program to extend the number of middle-income students who would be eligible, modified the authorization levels for the other student assistance programs, and in a move that would have major long-term cost implications, removed the income ceiling for eligibility for interest subsidies under the Guaranteed Student Loan program.

At the end of the decade of the 1970s, then, the federal role in postsecondary education, especially as reflected in the major student assistance programs authorized by the Higher Education Act of 1965, had broadened considerably. From a spending level of only $250 million in fiscal year 1965, federal spending for student assistance increased 20-fold, to more than $5.2 billion in 1980.

At the same time, significant social, economic, demographic, and educational changes were at work that would have an impact in the short term on congressional consideration of the 1980 amendments to the Higher Education Act and, in the long term, on the scope and character of the federal government's role in postsecondary education.[17]

Other Concerns Raised in the 1970s about the Federal Role

The period from the enactment of the Education Amendments of 1972 through to the enactment of the Middle Income Student Assistance Act in 1978 could be characterized as a time more for refinement of existing policies, for improving the coordination of management of existing policies than for fundamental reassessment of the goals established reflected in the 1972 legislation.

Several efforts were made during the period to improve the *management of student financial aid*. Issues addressed included:

- updating, refining, and coordinating various systems for determining student financial need, including the development of a "uniform methodology" as a national standard for all systems;

- efforts to simplify the application process for the various federal programs and for state programs, including use of a common form or systems of gathering information from multiple sources to meet the eligibility determination needs of several programs;

- examination of issues in coordination of federal and state student assistance policies and administration;

- efforts to clarify the purposes and interrelationships among the different federal programs (Basic Educational Opportunity Grants, Supplemental Education Opportunity Grants, State Student Incentive Grant Program, College Work Study, National Direct Student Loans, and Guaranteed Student Loans).[18]

Also of growing concern during this period (and of continuing concern today) was the *effect of regulatory actions* of multiple federal agencies on postsecondary education. In fact, as reflected in the ACE agenda for the Ninety-seventh Congress, the 1970s saw a virtual explosion in the number of federal agencies and committees of the Congress engaged in activities with some potential for substantial additional costs (without federal compensation) or simply inconvenience for institutions. Of even greater concern are federal actions that threaten essential values such as academic freedom.

In a discussion of the "regulatory swamp," Finn identifies three "modes" of federal regulation affecting higher education: allocation of federal funds; use of funds; and social regulation.[19] By allocating funds for certain purposes, the federal government "bribes" institutions to undertake activities that they would not have undertaken with their own resources. A small categorical program for Lifelong Learning, for example, might encourage a college department to apply for a grant. The problem arises when the funding ceases. The institution is faced with either dropping the program or picking up the funding from other sources. The multiplicity of small federal grant programs can stimulate a variety of campus-level grant-seeking efforts that, if funded or when funding stops, can have a disruptive, fragmenting effect on institutions.

The attachment of extensive conditions on the use of funds also creates a major regulatory burden for all recipients of federal funds. The conditions relate not only to the specific program under which funds are reviewed, but also to the broad requirements of cross-cutting mandates such as those in A-21, an Office of Management and Budget circular setting accountability requirements for federal contractors and grant recipients. Social regulations are the most far-reaching of any of the federal regulatory actions affecting colleges and universities, and for that matter, all federal fund recipients. The most well known are the various affirmative action and equal opportunity mandates stemming from the Civil Rights Act of 1964, Presidential Executive Orders, and Title IX of the Education Amendments of 1972.

In a study of federal regulation conducted by the Office of Management and Budget, fifty-nine cross-cutting "National Policy and Administrative Requirements" from nineteen agencies aimed at socio-economic policy objectives were identified. These were grouped according to ten categories: nondiscrimination; environmental protection; protection and advancement of the economy; health, welfare, and safety; minority participation; labor standards; public employee standards; general administrative requirements; administrative and fiscal requirements for recipients of federal funds; and freedom of information requirements. Most of these requirements apply to colleges and universities.[20]

What is particularly difficult for the academic community is that there is often agreement with the objectives of the regulations, especially the "social" regulations. Nevertheless, there is strong reaction to the *means* chosen for implementation and to the frequent insensitivity to the costs and other consequences for colleges and universities. And as suggested earlier, there is no single target toward which the community can address its concerns because the regulations come from throughout the government and often from agencies whose day-to-day concerns are far afield from higher education. Only a small percentage of the regulations, and even fewer of the "social" regulations, are within the jurisdiction of the Education Department.[21]

Issues in the 1980s

The Education Amendments of 1980

In 1979, just a short time after enactment of the Middle Income Student Assistance Act (MISAA), the Congress began work on the reauthorization of the Higher Education Act for the fourth time. The House passed its version of the reauthorization in late 1979, but Senate action did not come until mid-1980.[22] Final passage came just before the congressional recess for the November elections. For a time, enactment was in doubt, as the Senate, at the urging of the Senate Budget Committee, rejected the first House-Senate conference agreement. The Budget Committee argued convincingly that the conference agreement failed to curb the costs of the loan programs (especially the Guaranteed Student Loan Program). A second conference agreement made several concessions and cleared the way for final enactment. The 1980 Amendments (P.L. 96-374) were signed into law on October 3, 1980.[23]

The Amendments extended most of the provisions of the Higher Education Act through fiscal year 1985 without substantial modification. Among the more extensive changes were the following:

- consolidation of several small, related programs (education information centers, comprehensive statewide planning and continuing education, and community service) in a revised Title I, Part B, Education Outreach;

- replacement of the former 1202 state commission requirement with a simplified state agreement necessary for state participation in the revised Title I, the State Student Incentive Grant Program and the undergraduate facilities grant program;

- most importantly, extending the eligibility under the student grant programs to a wider income range, and extension of the loan programs (with changes in loan limits and other provisions).

Even as final action on the 1980 Amendments was being taken, it was clear that several of the issues debated through the reauthorization process would arise again soon after the Ninety-seventh Congress convened. Gladieux analyzes the situation as follows:

> In 1980 Congress cannot fairly be accused of doing too little for higher education. The question is whether by trying to do *too much* the most recent legislation may blunt the effectiveness of federal efforts to equalize educational opportunity, the overriding object of federal higher education policy for more than a decade. There is a real danger that federal benefits will draft increasingly toward the relatively well-off at the expense of the poor and the neediest.[24]

Gladieux continues by outlining the problem:

> Escalation in the loan program began when Congress passed the Middle Income Student Assistance Act in 1978....
>
> Before 1978 only students from families under $25,000 income were eligible for fully subsidized loans. MISAA removed the income limitation....
>
> No one fully anticipated the explosion in student borrowing that was to follow. Pre-MISAA, about one million students borrowed under the Guaranteed Student Loan Program; more than 2.5 million are currently borrowing and the number is growing. Total volume of Guaranteed Student Loans, less than $2 billion in fiscal year 1978, jumped to $3 billion in 1979 and will probably reach over $5 billion in 1980. The total could be as high as $7.8 billion in 1981....
>
> And as lending has shot up, so have federal expenses associated with the program—interest subsidies (the interest paid by the government while the borrower is in school), special allowances to the banks, and default claims. These costs totalled less than $500 million in fiscal year 1978. They came to an estimated $1.6 billion in 1980—more than tripling in two years. The price tag could be $2 billion in 1981—almost as much as the BEOG program provides in need-tested grants.[25]

As indicated earlier, the final passage of the 1980 Amendments was threatened by demands that the loan programs be modified to curb long-term costs. Gladieux points out, however, that despite last-minute changes, the amendments did not really address the problem in an effective way.

In contrast to the student grant programs (Pell Grants, SEOG, etc.), which must be funded through the annual budget and appropriations process, the costs of the Guaranteed Student Loan Program *must* be funded much as an entitlement. The effect of the dramatic increases in GSL costs is likely to be that funding for the student grant programs will be reduced in the budget and appropriations process.

In terms of implications for the overall role of the federal government in postsecondary education, a failure to curb the costs of the loan programs, programs that tend to benefit middle- to upper-income families whose children are likely to attend college even without federal aid, could mean a diminished federal role in aiding students from low-income families who might not attend without such aid.

As the Ninety-seventh Congress convenes, proposals to modify the student loan programs are assured. The Carter Administration's final budget made several legislative proposals in this direction, and there is every indication that the Reagan Administration intends to do the same.

Future Issues of Concern to Postsecondary Education

The foregoing discussion has focused primarily on the reauthorization of the Higher Education Act, but other issues, only tangentially related to the Higher Education Act, should be of concern to colleges and universities in the years immediately ahead. The following are examples of such issues:

1. *Budget constraints.* Every indication suggests that the coming decade will see a leveling off, if not a significant decrease, in federal funding for programs that involve colleges and universities. Also of central importance, as suggested by the foregoing discussion of the Education Amendments of 1980, the congressional budget process will lead to more thorough examination of both authorization and appropriations actions than ever before. In contrast to the Education Amendments of 1972, the Middle Income Student Assistance Act and other major advances in the past decade, it is unlikely that significant new programs will be enacted in the foreseeable future.[26]

The implication of this situation is that the focus for government action for funding of postsecondary education will shift to the state level. With the fiscal status of states varying dramatically across the nation, and the trend toward enactment of state tax and expenditure limitations, it is not clear that the state level will be a more likely source of additional funding for higher education than the federal government. Especially in areas such as graduate education, research and science, the need to develop a state-level political awareness of the needs of colleges and universities will be stronger than ever before.

Breneman and Nelson suggest that "the most significant question regarding federal policy for higher education in the 1980s is whether the federal government should attempt to influence the outcome of the coming struggle for enrollments and resources, or remain officially neutral and above the fray."[27] Given the situation as just reviewed, it would seem unlikely that the federal government will attempt to play a direct role, although one should expect a major move to alter the student assistance policies to favor one type of institution or another, and to enact a tuition tax-credit program for the postsecondary education level. If changes are made, however, they will inevitably by accomplished through reallocation of existing funding levels rather than through substantial additional funding.

2. *Regulations.* The new administration and many of the members of the Ninety-seventh Congress were elected with a strong mandate to reduce the burden of federal regulations, and it is reasonable to assume that efforts in this respect will address some of the concerns of colleges and universities. Yet two aspects of the problem should be of particular concern to academia:

   a. While there is clearly an interest in reducing the burden of regulations, there is also an equally serious concern for reducing fraud and abuse, and for achieving maximum efficiency in the use of public funds. These pressures may lead to an increase in the regulatory activities associated with *fiscal accountability,* an area of major concern for the academic community in the past few years.
   b. There is no single focal point in the federal bureacracy where the impact of federal regulatory actions on colleges and universities is monitored. The Department of Education administers only a small number of the federal programs affecting postsecondary education. The academic community should not look to the federal bureacracy to solve its problems in this regard (and there are also good reasons why one should not look to a bureacratic solution anyway).

One of the most critical issues in the late 1970s concerned the role of voluntary accreditation in the process for determining eligibility of institutions for federal assistance. Since the Korean War G.I. Bill, certain federal laws have called upon the Commissioner of Education (and now, the Secretary of Education) to publish a list of accrediting agencies acceptable for determining the quality of institutions. For a long time, this seemed to be an excellent way for the federal government to be assured of quality without itself becoming involved in a sacrosanct area of academia.

Yet in recent years, serious questions have been raised about the effectiveness of this approach for meeting the federal government's needs, especially for determining the fiscal soundness of institutional policies and procedures. As the government has moved to establish more stringent criteria for approval of accrediting agencies, questions have been raised by the academic and accrediting communities about federal intrusion into a private voluntary process. During the reauthorization of the Higher Education Act in 1979, proposals were made to eliminate or severely curtail the role of accreditation in the institutional eligibility process. The proposals would have relied more heavily on state licensure and quality determination processes and on direct federal actions on fiscal accountability points. For varying reasons, these ideas were less-than-enthusiastically received in the academic community.

No changes were made in the previous provisions by the Education Amendments of 1980, although the direct federal role in assuring fiscal accountability was strengthened. The issue will most assuredly arise again in the Ninety-seventh Congress. One of the questions will be whether the current "tripartite" system involving accrediting agencies, the states and the federal government will stand the test of the need for more stringent accountability systems. In the long run, it will be up to the academic community itself to develop and maintain a system for monitoring and marshaling political reaction to federal regulatory actions.

3. *Support for basic research.* Even with an increased focus at the state level for funding of postsecondary education, the federal government will remain the principal source of support for basic research. In a period of severe fiscal constraints and with an interest in some corners for more immediate payout and application of research results, the task of maintaining the research support levels of the late 1970s may be especially difficult. The projected low rate of turnover of faculty members in the sciences and other key fields and the resulting shortage of faculty positions for young researchers will complicate the picture. It remains to be seen whether the public will recognize the extremely serious implications for the nation of a weakening of the basic research effort and the nation's long-term scientific capacity. In the past, this recognition has come about only in a national emergency or in response to an event such as Sputnik. Building political support for federal action in this area may be the academic community's greatest challenge in the next few years.

4. *Increased specialization in federal relations.* As the provisions of federal laws affecting higher education become more and more complicated (the student aid provisions, for example) there is a tendency for the representation of the views of higher education to be made primarily by experts, in most instances specialists within the administration at the campus, system, or state level. This is entirely reasonable and important if postsecondary education is to have an influence in much of the legislative or regulatory process. There is a danger, experienced by higher education for some time in its relations with the federal government in the contracts and grants process, that the multiplicity of relatively technical relationships between institutions and government will even further undermine the functioning of colleges and universities as integrated academic communities, or as a whole.

As suggested earlier, the solution to this problem will not come through some reorganization of the federal bureaucracy. Monitoring systems can be encouraged at the level of the White House or elsewhere within the bureaucracy, but the most effective monitoring must come from the academic community itself. The extent of the problem in the next decade will demand:

- increased commitment of "generalists" from the academic community (presidents, chancellors, members of boards of trustees) to take active, personal leadership in the political process, not only through national associations but also directly at the state and federal level (again, dependence upon technicians alone will not do the job);

- continuing the efforts of recent years to strengthen the capacity of the Washington-based higher education associations, especially the presidential associations, to monitor federal developments and to express the views of the community as a whole in an effective, coherent manner.

Conclusion

The intent of this chapter has been to provide an overview of the scope and evolution of the federal role in postsecondary education. While many within academe may claim that federal activities are encroaching upon previously sacrosanct areas, there is also broad acknowledgement that the federal government has contributed significantly to other valued objectives: the enhancement of graduate education and the research capacity of institutions, and the advancement of equal educational opportunity, as examples. In this respect, it is helpful to recall Honey's point in his 1977 report, *Federal Leadership for a More Effective Partnership in Postsecondary Education,* that

> A basic difficulty affecting the institutional relationship to the partnership with...the federal government...is academia's deep-seated concern over federal domination of postsecondary education....
> While there may be some federal policy or program thrusts that were ill-conceived in design, implementation and effect, there are also many others which are proving to be progressive and beneficial. It is important that institutions recognize their responsibility to participate in the political process and to respond to citizens needs emerging from that process.[28]

Colleges and universities must approach the question of the appropriate role of the federal government in postsecondary education with a recognition of the extent to which federal policies in this one field are interwoven with virtually every other major federal policy arena. In no respect is the academic community exempt from the obligation to gain broad understanding within American society of its needs as a condition for obtaining support in the political process.

178   Higher Education in American Society

Notes

1. American Council on Education, "A Higher Education Agenda for the 97th Congress" (revised draft, December 18, 1980 [processed]), pp. 1-3.
2. Robert C. Andringa, "The View from the Hall," *Federalism at the Crossroads* (Washington, D.C.: Institute for Educational Leadership, 1977), p. 73.
3. For an unusually comprehensive statement of the federal interest in postsecondary education see John C. Honey and Terry W. Hartle, *Federal-State-Institutional Relations in Postsecondary Education* (Syracuse, N.Y.: Syracuse University Research Corporation, 1975), pp. 46-49.
4. U.S. Executive Office of the President, *Special Analysis: Budget of the United States Government, Fiscal Year 1979*, Table J-6, p. 221.
5. Chester E. Finn, Jr., *Scholars, Dollars, and Bureaucrats* (Washington, D.C.: Brookings Institution, 1978), pp. 10-11.
6. U.S. Congress, Congressional Budget Office, *Federal Assistance for Postsecondary Education: Options for Fiscal Year 1979*, May 1978, p. 12.
7. Ibid.
8. U.S. Executive Office of the President, Office of Management and Budget, *The United States Budget in Brief: Fiscal Year 1982*, Table 4, "Budget Outlays by Function and Subfunction, 1972-1984," p. 82.
9. For information on the federal role in higher education in the nineteenth century, see George Rainsford, *Congress and Higher Education in the Nineteenth Century* (Knoxville: University of Tennessee Press, 1972). For information on federal policy up to 1960, see Alice M. Rivlin, *The Federal Role in Financing Higher Education* (Washington, D.C.: Brookings Institution, 1961). Other helpful accounts of the evolution of the federal role are presented in Honey and Hartle, *Federal-State-Institutional Relations*, pp. 6-28; and Finn, *Scholars, Dollars and Bureaucrats*, pp. 4-8.
10. Rivlin, *Federal Role in Financing*, p. 24.
11. For extensive examination of the policy process leading to the Education Amendments of 1972 see: Lawrence E. Gladieux and Thomas R. Wolanin, *Congress and the Colleges: The National Politics of Higher Education* (Lexington, Mass.: D.C. Heath, 1976), and Chester E. Finn, Jr., *Education and the Presidency* (Lexington, Mass.: D.C. Heath, 1977). For key reports from which policy options included in the 1972 Amendments were drawn see: Carnegie Commission on Higher Education, *Quality and Equality: New Levels of Federal Responsibility for Higher Education* (New York: McGraw-Hill Book Company, 1968); U.S. Department of Health, Education, and Welfare, *Report on Higher Education*, the "Newman Report" (Washington, D.C.: U.S. Government Printing Office, 1971); and U.S Department of Health, Education, and Welfare, *Toward a Long-Range Plan for Federal Financial Support for Higher Education*, the "Rivlin Report" (Washington, D.C.: U.S. Government Printing Office, 1969).
12. See Carnegie (1968) and Rivlin Report (1969).
13. Aims C. McGuinness, Jr., "Intergovernmental Relations in Postsecondary Education: The Case of the 1202 Commissions," (Ph.D. diss., Syracuse University Graduate School, December 1979).
14. U.S. Congress, Congressional Budget Office, *Federal Assistance for Postsecondary Education: Options for Fiscal Year 1979* (Washington, D.C.: Government Printing Office, May 1978), pp. 1-3.
15. For recommendations contributing to the debate on amendments to the Higher Education Act in 1976 see: Carnegie Council on Policy Studies in Higher Education, *The Federal Role in Postsecondary Education: Unfinished Business, 1975-1980* (San Francisco: Jossey-Bass, 1975), and Consortium on Financing Higher Education, "Federal Student Assistance: A Review of Title IV of the Higher Education Act" (Hanover, N.H.: COFHE, April 1975) (processed). See Lawrence E. Gladieux and Thomas R. Wolanin, "Federal Politics," in *Public Policy and Private Higher Education*, ed. David W. Breneman and Chester E. Finn, Jr. (Washington, D.C.: Brookings Institution, 1978), pp. 197-230, for analysis of the political process leading to the 1976 amendments to the Higher Education Act.
16. Congressional Budget Office (1978), pp. 32-36.

17. U.S. Congress, Congressional Budget Office, *Federal Student Assistance: Issues and Options,* Budget Issue Paper for Fiscal Year 1981 (Washington, D.C.: Government Printing Office, 1980), pp. 1-15.

18. See National Task Force on Student Financial Aid Problems, *Final Report,* "Keppel Task Force" (Washington, D.C.: National Association of Student Financial Aid Administrators, 1975); and U.S. Department of Health, Education, and Welfare, Student Assistance Study Group, *Recommendations for Improved Management of Federal Student Aid Programs,* Report to the Secretary (Washington, D.C.: U.S. Government Printing Office, 1977).

19. Finn, *Scholars, Dollars, and Bureacrats,* p. 142-144.

20. U.S. Congress, Senate Committee on Governmental Affairs, *Federal Assistance Reform Act of 1980,* Report No. 96-972, 96th Cong., 2nd. Sess., pp. 26-29.

21. For further discussion of federal regulation and higher education see: Carol Frances and Sharon L. Coldren, *The Costs of Implementing Federally Mandated Social Programs at Colleges and Universities* (Washington, D.C.: American Council on Education, 1976); Louis W. Bender, *Federal Regulation and Higher Education* (Washington, D.C.: American Association for Higher Education, 1977), ERIC/Higher Education Research Report No. 1; and Sloan Commission on Government and Higher Education, *A Program for Renewed Partnership* (Cambridge, Mass.: Ballinger Publishing Company, 1980).

22. See Congressional Budget Office (1980) for an analysis of the various policy alternatives and the House and Senate bills.

23. For a review and analysis of the 1980 Amendments see the College Board, "Report from Washington on the 1980 Amendments to the Higher Education Act," Washington, D.C, October 1980.

24. Lawrence E. Gladieux, "What Has Congress Wrought?" *Change* (October 1980), p. 26.

25. Ibid., pp. 26-28.

26. David W. Breneman and Susan C. Nelson, "Education and Training," The Brookings Institution, *Setting National Priorities: Agenda for the 1980s,* ed. Joseph A. Pechman (Washington, D.C.: Brookings Institution, 1980), pp. 242-245.

27. Ibid., p. 242.

28. John C. Honey and Donna Clark, *Federal Leadership for a More Effective Partnership in Postsecondary Education* (Syracuse, N.Y.: Syracuse University Research Corporation, May 1977), pp. xii-xiii.

10

The Courts
Walter C. Hobbs

It is fashionable among academics today to decry the alleged increased involvement of the courts in higher education's affairs. The traditional deference, it is said, long paid by courts to decisions made by academic experts, has been replaced by a judicial activism that not only inhibits the autonomy of the academy but, worse yet, jeopardizes academic freedom that is autonomy's chief justification.

The view is widespread. But is it valid? This chapter will summarize the complaints, review the countercriticisms, examine the doctrine of "academic abstention" (judicial deference to academic expertise), describe the functions of the courts, and discuss the impact of judge-made law on three core academic concerns.

We shall conclude the chapter by taking the (minority) view that to the very slight extent judicial deference to academe has lately been eroded, the consequence has been a modest limitation on institutional autonomy in favor of a major reinforcement of the legal bases of academic freedom. In that outcome, higher education—not to be confused with colleges and universities, let alone with academic administrators only—has the better end of the bargain. Both individuals within the academic enterprise and the enterprise per se have been and are today the beneficiaries of a strong judicial bias toward academic liberty, a bias that operates generally to limit incursions by others, including the courts, on the autonomy of the academics, but that refuses even to academics the liberty to infringe academic liberty.

Complaint: The Courts Intrude Too Much

In an eloquent and lengthy passage we only excerpt here, Fishbein speaks for many an academic who is persuaded the courts have hobbled academic administration by heaping inappropriate and dysfunctional procedural requirements on the everyday activity of college and university personnel:

> [T]he due process requirements that the courts have imposed upon public universities have had an unfortunate consequence, namely, that today students and faculty alike appear to have a legal cause of action no matter how minor the dispute. Almost every [administrative decision] is thus escalated to the level of a constitutional issue, and there is commonly a race to the door of the federal courthouse by every dissatisfied party....In other words, everything becomes a federal case. As a result, ...relationships between students and administrators, between students and faculty and between faculty and administrators become increasingly adversarial....This is an appalling development....It is regrettable that so many aspects of life at public universities have been remolded in a legalistic, highly procedural fashion. It means, of course, that the administrator in the public university must undertake his or her daily tasks in the company of a lawyer.[1]

Six years earlier, O'Neil reviewed challenges posed to campus autonomy by various elements of government including the courts and offered the following comment concerning the costs incurred by colleges and universities by reason of court activity:

> Judicial intervention...poses a significant threat, as witness the...suits brought against campus administrators and governing boards as a result of campus disorder. All but one of the cases [O'Neil had described] were ultimately dismissed—but not without considerable costs in legal fees, time and energy, and a virtually certain chilling effect upon future administrative behavior.[2]

More recently, the Sloan Commission on Government and Higher Education worried about not only the inhibition of effective academic management born of caution in the face of the likelihood of litigation, but also the changes that litigation itself produces in interpersonal relations:

> The Commission views the reliance on litigation as counterproductive since it reinforces adversary relations....The adversarial cast of the trial process fos-

ters tensions that may continue for years, tensions inimical to [academic productivity].[3]

In sum, say the complainants, the willingness of the courts to review and, at times, to reform the decisions made within academe is inflicting on colleges and universities costs both direct and indirect. Resources of time and money that would ordinarily go to support teaching, scholarship, and the ancillary services on which these central activities depend are being diverted instead to lawyers' and court stenographers' fees and the various other expenses incurred when defending against a lawsuit. Institutional personnel, moreover, become skittish about exercising their creative judgement, preferring rather to "play it safe" than to run the risk of legal challenge to themselves and to their institution. Most seriously of all, the collegiality that is the warp and woof of the academic fabric is brought to the tearing point by the adversarial character of the litigation encouraged by the judicial willingness to be involved in academic disputes.

On the face of things, the complaints are at least plausible. Lawsuits are indeed expensive; anyone who has been involved in litigation will do—or refrain from doing—almost anything to avoid getting to court again, and the character of the dispute process before the bench forever changes relationships among former friends.

Response: The Complaints Are Overdrawn

Edwards sharply disagrees both with the particulars of the complaints and with the thread of the argument.[4] His response addresses each element of the complaint, and he appends a countercomplaint of his own:

a. *Monetary costs*—Quoting the U.S. Supreme Court in *Cannon* v. *University of Chicago* (441 U.S. 677 [1979]) and implicitly generalizing to all of academe, Edwards recites *Cannon:*

Although victims of discrimination on the basis of race, religion or national origin have had private Title VI [of the Civil Rights Act of 1964] remedies available at least since 1965,...[the university has] not come forward with any demonstration that Title VI litigation has been so costly or voluminous that either the academic community or the courts have been unduly burdened.[5]

The Court's observation is consistent also with the Sloan Commission's findings concerning the cost to academe of the regulatory process: in a study prepared expressly for the Commission, Kershaw found that (in Edward's words) "many of the institutions surveyed viewed the monetary costs of dealing with the Federal Government as a bargain."[6] From other reports as well, Edwards concludes "that the financial benefit derived from governmental assistance outweighs the financial costs of regulation."[7]

b. *Nonmonetary costs*—The fear that academic administrators and/or faculty will be coerced by judge-made law (not to be confused with legislation) to reach and implement decisions that dilute academic quality plainly irritates Edwards. Statutory law might have produced such effects, for

> There is nothing in...national policy...to support the exemption of [college and university] employees—primarily teachers—from [coverage by the Civil Rights Acts]. Discrimination against minorities and women in the field of education is as pervasive as discrimination in any other area of employment. (House of Representatives Rep. No. 238, 92d Congress, 2d Sess. [1971].)[8]

But the courts have not seen fit to give force to that congressional intent. As the U.S. Circuit Court of Appeals for the Second Circuit has put it (*Powell* v. *Syracuse University,* 580 F.2d 1150 [1978]):

> [M]any courts have accepted the broad proposition that courts should exercise minimal scrutiny of college and university employment practices....This anti-interventionist policy has rendered universities virtually immune to charges of employment bias, at least when that bias is not expressed overtly.[9]

If there is any substance to the oft-heard claim that the judicial presence hangs like Damocles' sword over the wary decision-maker in academe, that person need only peek up to see that the sword swings for, not against, the institution and its administrators. It is the plaintiff, usually female or minority, not the defendant college, who stands to learn from the litigation: "faculty status is not won in the courtroom."[10]

c. *The death of collegiality*—The short answer here is that neither litigation nor the courts themselves kill collegiality; they only constitute the evidence of a death already transpired. One can not prevent conflict by choking off its channels,[11] for conflict will find a path to follow or, like lava, create its own. Nevertheless, whatever academics may do to one another in their internecine warfare, Edwards notes that the courts—unfairly the putative culprits here—abstemiously avoid to the extent possible playing any role in wrecking collegiality. As a matter of law, indeed, spoken by the U.S Supreme Court, "traditions of collegiality [demand] that principles developed for use [elsewhere] cannot be 'imposed blindly on the academic world.' "[12]

d. *A countercomplaint*— Edwards appreciates the frustration that academics feel who have long perceived themselves as immune to judicial prescription and proscription and are now experiencing the reality of judicial power. But not only does he contend that that power is sparsely used and its effects greatly exaggerated when scrutinized against hard data, he goes on as well to suggest that in given matters the courts ought to do more than they do—not more expansively, certainly not more harshly, but simply more pointedly in response to appeals for redress of academe's injustices. Under current law, public institutions can dismiss an untenured faculty member for false and damaging reasons without affording him/her opportunity of rebuttal, simply by not themselves making public the basis of dismissal. But what will the person do when asked by the next employer why he/she left the college? Similarly, a person who believes that he/she has been discriminated against for promotion by reason of race or gender must show that the institution's stated reasons for nonpromotion (e.g., poor teaching performance, inadequate research) are pretext, rather than being able to throw on the institution the burden of demonstrating they used legally permissible grounds. The imbalance of advantage in such instances, where the individual must make the entire case while the institution may simply stand pat, says little to Edwards on behalf of the judicial system's sensitivity to fairness in the resolution of academic dispute.

Judicial Deference: The Doctrine of "Academic Abstention"

Fundamental to the foregoing debate is the question whether courts should, can, and/or do refrain in given circumstances from exercising their considerable powers, yielding to others who enjoy expertise in the matter at hand the final substantive determination of the issue. Courts do refuse, for example, to reach a judgment whether a surgical procedure used by a physician was the best approach that might have been taken to a plaintiff-patient's malady. Neither will courts decide questions of scholarly competence, such as whether a given researcher's experiment was well designed or a given teacher's syllabus was sound.

The vocabulary of law refers to the principle of judicial deference to academic expertise as "the doctrine of academic abstention." It is not a novelty in the law, for courts traditionally have in fact deferred to expertise in all esoteric areas: such deference is the bedrock, for example, on which rests the judicial review of administrative agency actions such as the promulgation of pure food standards.[13] But it is important to distinguish judicial deference to the expertise of others from the exercise of judicial power in matters well within the courts' undoubted competence, e.g., the question whether an institution has complied with standards duly promulgated by a government agency. Whether the standards should have been imposed on academe was a question for the legislative branch to decide; whether the standards are substantively valid is a question for the agency (and ultimately the legislature) to decide, so long as no arbitrariness can be shown in their actions; but whether the college or university has in fact complied with the standards is a question no court need avoid.

The simple reality that a court will not substitute its own judgment in an esoteric matter for the judgment of a trained professional such as a physician or an educator, or for the judgment of an agency established by a legislature, does not mean there is nothing else for courts to decide. Courts are especially sensitive to the *procedural* care that experts show to those they affect. The student whose grade was a disappointment will seek in vain for a court to raise it, but if arbitrariness can be shown in the evaluation *process* that led to the grade the student will find in the court a champion quick to require the academic professionals to behave fairly. Judicial deference, in other words, does not mean complete judicial abstinence.

Neither does deference rest on a legal doctrine of institutional autonomy. To date at least, there is no such doctrine. Judicial deference to any party at all, academic or other, is a function of the court's self-acknowledged incapacity to address esoteric concerns, not of some imagined legal monopoly of the experts in that area. Where a court is precluded by law from addressing a matter, e.g., "has the Rev. Dr. Smith, theologian of a given denomination, embraced a heresy?" there the court is not exhibiting deference: it is legally powerless to act (in this illustrative instance by the First Amendment's "wall" between church and state). But courts *can* constitutionally evaluate a student's work and order that his/her grade be changed. They simply don't—not because colleges and universities are legally autonomous, but because courts understand the wisdom of leaving professional judgments to professionals.

Judicial deference is most commonly confused with the court's jurisdiction of a case. In the federal jurisprudence of the United States (and in the vast majority of the states), courts sit to decide cases and controversies. They are not at liberty to refuse to decide cases properly brought before them, nor are they empowered to solicit or compel parties to seek redress from them. To the extent there was a detectable period in history when little or no academic dispute was decided by the courts, it is not because courts were refusing to decide such cases in deference to academic expertise; it is rather because academics were not bringing their quarrels before the bar. Likewise, any increase in the incidence of academic litigation tells us little about judicial activism; chiefly it tells us that academics are becoming more litigious.

The incidence of academic litigation has clearly increased over the past decade and a half since the mid-1960s. But as is elaborated in the last section of this chapter, with one instructive exception there has been no perceptible decline of judicial deference to academic expertise, the conventional wisdom in many quarters to the contrary notwithstanding. Courts have made clear that public universities, under the requirements of the U.S. constitution's Fourteenth Amendment, which covers all public entities, must provide procedural safeguards to students about to be suspended or expelled for misconduct, and to tenured faculty about to be discharged. But the courts have maintained deferential silence concerning the criteria on which such dismissals are decided, inquiring only into the character of the procedures by which a person may be deprived of a significant interest—which hardly bespeaks an unsophisticated meddler intruding on the domain of the academic professionals.

The sole exception to the general practice of judicial deference to academic expertise, the archetypical instance in which the courts have unhesitantly substituted their own judgment for the positions taken by colleges and universities, has arisen when in the name of institutional autonomy constitutionally impermissible limits have been placed on the exercise of academic freedom by faculty and students. In such cases, the doctrine of "academic abstention" has been ignored, judicial deference has been eschewed, and the courts have landed foursquare on the side of academic freedom against institutional autonomy.

The Functions of Courts

Government in the United States finds its theoretical underpinnings in the twin principles that (1) sovereignty lies in the people, not in a monarch or other ruling body, and (2) an effective system of "checks and balances" protects the people against abuse of power by the government that they create. As to the latter principle, government comprises three branches—the legislature, the executive, and the judiciary—each of which enjoys primacy within its own sphere of responsibility, but the exercise of the power of each is limited by the counterpart powers of the other branches. Legislatures declare social policy and enact statutes to implement it; the executive, however, may veto the enactments or may implement them less vigorously than the legislature contemplated. The courts may invalidate the legislation either for its unconstitutional character or for its impermissible application in given instances. Legislatures may override vetoes, and they typically have opportunity to review prospective judicial appointees nominated by the executive, preventing the coming to the bench of those they deem unfit.

All these safeguards and more are rooted in the constitutions of the federal government and of the several states. The federal government is one of limited jurisdiction: only such matters as are enumerated in its constitution fall within its power, all others being retained by the states or the sovereign people. But within that limited scope, the constitution and laws of the United States are "the supreme law of the land," binding on all judges in every state regardless of state law (Article VI, Constitution of the United States). By contrast, the governments of the several states are governments of general jurisdiction and, save for matters included in the federal power and therefore covered by the aforementioned "supremacy clause," state governments may authoritatively address any topic of interest.

When in 1787 the Continental Congress submitted the proposed federal constitution to the states for ratification, it was understood that several matters too controversial for initial inclusion would be taken up immediately upon formation of the new government. The Congress of the United States was convened in March 1789, and by December 1791 the first ten amendments to the Constitution, often called the Bill of Rights,[14] had been adopted. But in the first test of the amendments' power to protect a citizen against the action of state government, the U.S. Supreme Court held they are not applicable at the state level.[15]

Following the War Between the States, the Thirteenth Amendment was adopted rendering slavery unconstitutional, together with the Fourteenth Amendment requiring evenhandedness in the treatment of all persons within the reach of state power: "No state shall...deprive any person of life, liberty or property without due process of law; nor deny to any person within its jurisdiction equal protection of the law."

The Fourteenth Amendment's provisions, fashioned in the aftermath of emancipation, were designed to secure to former slaves legal rights long enjoyed only by free persons, and initially the U.S. Supreme Court insisted upon maintaining that focus.[16] In later years, however, the doctrines of due process and equal protection were interpreted literally to include *"any* person" regardless of race or former condition of servitude, regardless even whether he/she were a citizen of the United States. Moreover, beginning in the 1930s and continuing through the 1960s, the Court incorporated—piecemeal and never completely, but substantially nonetheless—many of the protections of the Bill of Rights against abuse of power by state government as well as by the federal, by interpreting the term "liberty" (in "No state shall deprive any person of liberty...without due process of law") to include many of the liberties guaranteed by the first ten amendments.

Two fundamental implications for academic law derive from the foregoing review. One concerns the respective boundaries of federal vis-a-vis state jurisdiction in academic matters, and the other concerns the relative limits imposed by the federal Constitution on governmental vis-a-vis independent (on "public" as distinguished from "private") higher education.

Education is nowhere mentioned in the federal Constitution. By reason, therefore, of the principle (made explicit in the Tenth Amendment) that all matters not enumerated in the federal Constitution are reserved to the states and/or to the people, the federal government is without power to address educational matters per se. To reach education—which, of course, it does—the government must address itself to aspects of education constitutionally within its power, e.g., by funding various programs within education under the provision of the preamble to the Constitution that government is to "promote the general welfare"; or by prohibiting school authorities from infringing a person's First Amendment right of free expression; or by requiring educational management to engage in collective bargaining with employees in order that labor disputes not impede commerce among the states (Article I, Section 8, Constitution of the United States).

The jurisdictions of the two court systems—federal and state—mirror the enumerated constitutional powers, but with important qualifications. As courts of general jurisdiction, state courts enjoy wide latitude in what issues they are legally authorized to decide, whereas federal courts are limited to hearing disputes involving some federal issue. A zoning dispute, for example, over the legality of operating a college pub on a given street corner may go only to a state court, but a dispute over whether a person has been discriminatorily refused employment in that pub in violation of the equal protection clause may go to either a state or a federal court. State courts, that is, may hear disputes grounded in federal claims; but they may not decide those disputes on the basis of state law if it is inconsistent with the federal. The federal courts, on the other hand, may not entertain any suits between residents of the same state quarreling over a matter devoid of any element of federal law, e.g., again, a zoning ordinance.

Most litigants prefer to take federally based claims to a federal court for disposition, especially when the federal law runs counter to the mores of the locality. Consequently, as the momentum of the civil rights movements of the 1950s and 1960s built to a crescendo in the late '60s and early '70s, the pattern of primarily state court activity in academic litigation gave way to chiefly federal activity instead, leading many an observer to conclude the federal courts were activist. As indicated above, however, courts sit to hear cases, and hear them they must. Activity, therefore, i.e., the relative incidence of cases that come before a bench, is a function primarily of social forces over which the courts exercise negligible control. Activism, on the other hand, i.e., the forsaking of the traditional judicial deference to academic expertise in favor of the courts' own judgments, has yet to be demonstrated. We shall return to the question more fully below.

The second implication for higher education of the "separation of powers" principle in American government concerns the legal distinctions drawn between the public and private sectors of academe when they come before the courts. In chapter 2 of this volume, Duryea discusses the role of the celebrated *Dartmouth College* case in refashioning the concept of institutional autonomy in American higher education. The divorce of state control of colleges and universities from their creation by the state via the chartering process gave rise, on the one hand, to institutions governed by independent boards of private citizens and (later), on the other hand, to institutions governed by boards of state officials acting under authority either of statute or of the state constitution.

Private institutions can not be reached by the Bill of Rights or the due process or equal protection clauses, because such institutions are neither part of the federal government nor part of a state's, the only entities addressed by those constitutional provisions. If one wishes to draw a private college or university within the prescriptions and proscriptions of those constitutional demands, the task must be accomplished by building bridges from the state to the institution by means of the doctrine of "state action." One of two tests will suffice: if a state has so pervasively insinuated itself into the activities of the institution that, for all practical purposes, the state and the college are interdependent partners, then the college—though formally private by reason of its charter and the composition of its governing board—will be deemed a public institution for purposes of constitutional analysis; the University of Pittsburgh is a case in point.[17] Or if an institution acts on behalf of the state to secure the latter's interests, then in whatever matter it so serves it too will be deemed for constitutional purposes a public institution; the colleges under contract to New York State, such as Cornell University's College of Agriculture and Life Sciences, and Alfred University's College of Ceramics, are cases in point: these institutions are "public," though sister colleges within the university are not.

Absent evidence of "state action," however, the private institution is free of constitutional constraints. But that is not to say it is at liberty to be a law unto itself. It means only that the legal grounds of any challenge to the college's actions must be found elsewhere than in the Bill of Rights or in due process or equal protection. The most common two such grounds are the law of contract and the statutes, rules, and regulations enforced by government administrative agencies. Together they comprise the basic arsenal of the litigant who seeks to vindicate his/her rights as a "consumer" of higher education.[18] Separately they constitute the primary legal wherewithal of the litigant who seeks redress for losses sustained when an institution fails, say, to honor the terms of his/her employment contract, or when the institution discriminatorily refuses to promote the person on grounds of gender. However, if the success rate of such suits is indicative of the power of these weapons, the legal arsenal is full of BB guns and noisemakers.[19]

The Impact of the Courts on Academe

To this point in the discussion, we have persistently gainsaid the prevalent view that judicial activism has placed institutional autonomy in check, both directly by the substitution of the judgment of the court for academic expertise, and indirectly by the chilling effect it has had on the exercise of administrative discretion. It is time for demonstration instead of assertion.

Several core interests of academe have been brought before the bench sufficiently to provide a clear statement of where and why, if at all, courts are willing to second-guess academics: the admission and retention of students;

the appointment, promotion, and dismissal of faculty; and the freedom of faculty and students to inquire into and advance whatever points of view they wish.

Students. Cases now speak the law of (a) standards of admission; (b) discipline for misconduct; and (c) bases of academic dismissal. None of them impinge upon the power of institutions to establish effective criteria in any of the three areas of student affairs.

a. In private institutions, "a State through its courts does not have the authority to interfere with the power of [the] school to make rules concerning the admission of students."[20] In public colleges and universities, no particular admissions standards have ever been judicially required, and only two—race and physical condition—have even been considered. As to race, it is a permissible but not mandatory criterion,[21] and as to physical ability or disability, "[n]othing in the language or history of [the Rehabilitation Act of 1973] reflects an intention to limit the freedom of an educational institution to require reasonable physical qualifications for admission."[22]

b. Students in public institutions may not be suspended or expelled for misconduct without opportunity to hear the charges placed against them, to defend themselves against those charges before an impartial tribunal, and to purchase a written record of the proceedings.[23] No substantive standards of the validity of such charges beyond "reasonableness" have been required. Nor is such "due process" required when lesser penalties are inflicted. No student in any private institution is afforded any such protection except the requirement of reasonableness, unless the institution chooses to extend it.

It is commonly presumed in academic circles that the doctrine of *in loco parentis,* i.e., the institution stands "in the place of the parent" with respect to the student, is dead. As a practical matter, the presumption is probably sound; *in loco parentis* is dead at many, if not most, colleges and universities. But it was the institutions, not the courts, that sounded its death knell. No reported opinion by a court of any jurisdiction has yet repudiated the legal vitality of the doctrine.[24] Nor is it implicitly overruled by the requirement of minimal due process in cases of suspension or expulsion for misconduct any more than a true parent's legal power over a child is dissolved simply because in most jurisdictions parents are no longer immune to suit by their children for conduct that visits a legal injury on the minor.

c. If the procedural requirements in disciplinary action are minimal, they are virtually nil in cases of academic termination. In *Horowitz,*[25] the landmark case in the matter, the U.S. Supreme Court held that "the significant difference between the failure of a student to meet academic standards and the violation by a student of valid rules of conduct...calls for *far less* stringent procedural requirements in the case of academic dismissal" (emphasis added). "Far less" stringency than is required in disciplinary actions is tantamount to astringency.

In addition and more important to the issue of institutional autonomy, the Court continued:

> [W]e decline to ignore the historic judgment of educators [and] to further enlarge the judicial presence in the academic community....We recognize... that a hearing may be "useless or even harmful in finding out the truth as to scholarship."
>
> "Judicial interposition in the operation of the public school system of the Nation raises problems requiring care and restraint."...Courts are particularly ill-equipped to evaluate academic performance. The factors discussed [earlier] with respect to procedural due process...warn against any such judicial intrusion into academic decision-making.

In short, the challenges brought in the last decade to institutional policy and practice toward students may have made for greater activity in the courts, but the courts themselves have not used the opportunity thus provided them to become more activist in their treatment of academic issues. Their sole imposition was procedural only, limited narrowly to instances of disciplinary suspension or expulsion, and avoiding admissions and academic evaluations questions virtually completely. Nor were they any more rigorous procedurally than to require that a charged party who could be suspended or expelled have opportunity to know and rebut if he/she can the charges on which the discipline is laid, and to secure at the individual's own expense a written record of the proceedings. Institutional autonomy is hardly threatened by such judicial involvement in academic dispute. A reasonable person might even think it strengthened.

Faculty. The power of courts to impose criteria alien to the academic profession on the faculty appointment/retention function is probably more unsettling to academe than the counterpart judicial power in student admission/retention. But academics have no more reason to date to fear intrusion by the judiciary at this level than has been experienced in student affairs. No court has ever required any institution to hire a given candidate for a faculty position. Moreover, (a) nonrenewal of term contracts by an institution can be decided with impunity, for no reasons whatever need be provided; (b) in any controversy whether unlawful discrimination prevented one's promotion, the burden of proof rests with the plaintiff faculty member, not with the defendant institution; and (c) faculty in private institutions who participate extensively in university governance are precluded from compelling the administration to negotiate a collective bargaining agreement with their union.

   a. The law of faculty termination in public institutions (contract law controls the issue in private colleges and universities) was enunciated by the U.S. Supreme Court in two companion cases handed down in 1972, *Roth*[26] and *Sindermann.*[27] No untenured faculty member need be provided a hearing at which to contest his/her nonrenewal of contract unless (i) there are grounds on which to believe the nonrenewal may be in impermissible reprisal for his/her exercise of a constitutionally protected right such as public criticism of the university administration; or (ii) the reasons for nonrenewal are defamatory or would otherwise injure his/her reputation such that employment elsewhere is prevented. Defamation and/or the staining of one's reputation, however, must be public to trigger a hearing. If the institution refrains from publicizing such grounds of the nonrenewal, no opportunity to rebut the reasons need be provided.[28]

As to impermissible reprisals for the exercise of constitutionally protected freedoms such as expression or association, institutional administrators responsible for such unconstitutional behavior who knew or should have known the unlawful character of their action can be held personally liable in money damages to the plaintiff.[29] It is here that some critics contend that judicial awards of such damages have a chilling effect on other administrators' willingness to exercise their judgment in whether to renew an incompetent but outspoken faculty member's contract. The argument is not compelling. The penalty is for behavior that not even the most rabid advocate of absolute institutional autonomy can justify, namely, the deliberate or exceedingly careless infringement of another person's right of expression. The penalty does not apply when the actual grounds of renewal are the candidate's professional performance, but only when the administrator has infringed the individual's rights. That will never trouble the truthful decision-maker.

When the faculty member about to be dismissed is tenured, then in the public university he/she must be provided a hearing, if requested, "where he could be informed of the grounds for his nonretention and challenge their sufficiency."[30] But the Court imposes no definition of "sufficiency" on the university; the standards to be met for retention still are formulated by academics to whom the Court pays judicial deference. And when the grounds for dismissal of the tenured faculty member are not his/her professional performance or other personal characteristic but rather the financial exigency of the institution, no procedural protection is afforded: it is "peculiarly within the province of the [college] administration to determine which teachers should be released, and which should be retained....[I]t is not the province of the court to interfere and substitute its judgment for that of the administrative body."[31]

b. Much of the concern over judicial intrusion into the faculty employment process focuses on the courts' interpretations of the "affirmative action" requirements of the Civil Rights Acts of 1866, 1871, and 1964, as enforced by the regulatory process. *Sweeney*[32] suggests the concern is probably misplaced (from candidate to institution) and at least unnecessary. There the U.S. Supreme Court held the aggrieved candidate must first establish a plausible showing that he/she was denied promotion on grounds of gender or race, following which the institution need only "articulate some legitimate, nondiscriminatory reason for the employee's rejection" (hardly an insuperable barrier to overcome). That done, the burden returns to the plaintiff to show that the institution's alleged reasons are sham, a mere pretext to disguise the true and discriminatory reasons, an almost impossible task.

The institution, of course, has control of the essential information in the matter—minutes of committee meetings, memoranda, personnel who participated in the decision process, resources with which to store and retrieve the data—but the Court has nonetheless seen fit to allocate the significant burden in the case to the individual. Under ordinary procedures in litigation, a plaintiff may conceivably secure much of the information necessary to his/her argument through pretrial "discovery." In Georgia, however, a professor who had participated in committee deliberations concerning one such case refused to disclose his vote and his reasons therefor, claiming it was his academic freedom to remain silent (a novel twist on the concept). The court disagreed, found him in contempt, fined him one hundred dollars a day for thirty days in an unsuccessful effort to loosen his tongue, then jailed him for ninety days more. Academic critics of the court suggest that in the interest of the preservation of the integrity of institutional processes (i.e., autonomy) alternatives to such extreme measures ought first have been exhausted: not all members of the professoriate are likely to display such heroic obstinacy as this gentleman. Only once it becomes clear that unarguable injustice will flow from a rigid adherence to the principle of institutional autonomy should that principle be judicially breached for the higher good. By such a time, however, the institution itself should have cast its fortunes with justice over secrecy. At this writing, the issue has been taken on appeal from the trial court to the appellate level.

c. The faculty of Yeshiva University in New York City formed a union and sought through the regulatory processes of the National Labor Relations Board to compel a reticent Board of Trustees to negotiate a labor agreement with the union. The trustees insisted that Yeshiva faculty are "managerial employees" excluded from the coverage of the National Labor Relations Act, and the U.S. Supreme Court concurred.[33] Of greater general importance to higher education than the Court's interpretation of what actually takes place at Yeshiva University is their stated view (quoted earlier in this chapter) that "traditions of collegiality [between faculty and administrators] continue to play a significant role at many universities [and therefore] principles developed for use [elsewhere] *cannot be 'imposed blindly on the academic world'* " (emphasis added). Courts, that is, may not treat academe as but one more enterprise; instead, says the Supreme Court, they must accommodate higher education's distinctive traditions of collegiality in their resolution of academic disputes.

On point of faculty, then, we see no greater evidence of judicial activism than was exhibited in respect of students. Tenured faculty in public institutions are owed a hearing, if requested, at which to challenge the sufficiency of the grounds on which they are about to be terminated (other than financial exigency; no protections are afforded in such cases). The Court does not, however, delimit the character of permissible grounds. That substantive determination is left to academe. And where it is plausible that the basis of one's nonrenewal/nonpromotion is impermissible by reason of statute, e.g., discrimination on grounds of gender, the burden rests nonetheless with the challenger to make the case, not with the institution to show they have acted lawfully. As to collegiality, the tradition so evident in the historic faculty role in institutional governance may not be sacrificed to principles of labor relations developed in other sectors of the economy. In such data as these, one finds no showing of judicial impairment of institutional autonomy.

Academic freedom. At last the critics hit pay dirt. The courts do quite blatantly intrude on autonomy in the matter of academic freedom. The difficulty, however, is of course that they do so in defense of the value that academe professes to cherish above all others. Several cases make the point, but two will suffice here.

The constitutional foundation of academic freedom is in the First Amendment's provisions that Congress (and now the states) "shall make no law...abridging the freedom of speech or of the press; or the right of the people peaceably to assemble." In a loyalty oath case that reached the U.S. Supreme Court in 1967, the Court held:

> Our Nation is deeply committed to safeguarding academic freedom, which is of transcendent value to all of us and not merely to the teachers concerned. That freedom is therefore a *special* concern of the First Amendment, which does not tolerate laws that cast a pall of orthodoxy over the classroom (emphasis added).[34]

Quoting from an earlier case,[35] the Court continued:

> The essentiality of freedom in the community of American universities is almost self-evident....Scholarship cannot flourish in an atmosphere of suspicion and distrust. Teachers and students must always remain free to inquire, to study and to evaluate, to gain new maturity and understanding; otherwise, our civilization will stagnate and die.

One can hardly conceive a more potent, more authoritative affirmation of the legal vitality of academe's *raison d'être.* But in nourishing academic freedom thus, the Court knowingly and deliberately intruded upon the autonomy of the governing authorities in a state university who had required a loyalty oath of the faculty.

Later the Court similarly intruded upon the autonomy of a particular institution, this time to safeguard the academic freedom of a group of students.[36] The students had been denied official recognition by a state college as a local chapter of Students for a Democratic Society (SDS), on grounds that their professed independence from the politically radical and often disruptive national organization was doubtful, and SDS philosophy was antithetical to college policy. Consistent with established case law, the Court held that even if the group were not independent of the national SDS, their association with an unpopular organization would not be a legally valid basis on which their First Amendment rights of expression and association may be denied. Only action or specific intent to engage in or to further unlawful action—not the advocacy of ideas, no matter how repugnant—may be proscribed. And the burden falls upon the college to demonstrate a legal basis of any refusal to extend official recognition, not upon the student group to show they are entitled to enjoy their First Amendment freedoms.

Three quotes from the several opinions in the case provide glimpses into the justices' views of institutional autonomy and the role of the judiciary. From the majority opinion:

> [W]here state-operated educational institutions are involved, this Court has long recognized "the need for affirming the comprehensive authority of the States and of school officials, consistent with fundamental constitutional safeguards, to prescribe and control conduct in the schools." ...Yet, the precedents of this Court leave no room for the view that because of the acknowledged need for order, First Amendment freedoms should apply with less force on college campuses than in the community at large.

From the concurring opinion of a justice who had also joined the majority opinion:

> It is within...the academic community that problems such as these should be resolved. The courts, state or federal, should be a last resort....[But] in spite of the wisdom of the [trial] court in sending [this] case back to the college, the issue...was not adequately addressed in the [college's] hearing.

And from the concurrence of another such justice who had also joined the majority opinion:

> [T]he fact that [this case] had to come here for ultimate resolution indicates the sickness of our academic world, measured by First Amendment standards.

Strong stuff! The U.S. Supreme Court's preference is that higher education conform its behavior on its own initiative to the fundamental constitutional principles that sustain its claim to academic freedom. But if academe elects not to do so, the Court will unabashedly exercise its considerable power to require conformance, no matter what unfettered authority a given party might otherwise enjoy.

Conclusion

There is no evidence to suggest that courts today are more *activist* than were their counterparts of an earlier day. To be sure, they are undeniably more *active* in the adjudication of academic dispute. But that is not because courts are exercising an invalid "roving commission" to go about setting wrongs right. They are hearing more cases today because more are being brought to them. Especially are plaintiffs appealing to the federal judiciary for relief from various alleged harms, as the statutory and regulatory fallout of the civil rights movement continues to stimulate litigation in academic matters as well as elsewhere.

Activity, however, is not to be confused with activism. Today's courts, though busier in academic concerns than were their predecessors, are no more likely than were their forebears to substitute their own judgments for judgments reached by experts within academe. To the contrary, despite the anguished cries of more than a few academics, deference to institutional determinations is still the rule. The doctrine of "academic abstention" is as robust as ever. Where the courts might plausibly be considered "activist" (especially if one has a high tolerance for hyperbole) is in the vindication of constitutional rights—especially the First Amendment freedoms of expression and association—of academic plaintiffs. But to the very minor extent that that activism has infringed upon institutional autonomy, the loss is heavily outweighed by the strength it has brought to the legal bases of academic freedom.

We recognize that one might reasonably contend the legislatures and regulatory agencies of government have gone "too far" in their invasion by statute and promulgated rule of institutional self-determination. That is not, however, an issue discussed in this chapter, nor is it one on which we here take a position. Courts, in any event, are not to be lumped willy-nilly together with the other branches of government. For better or for worse they have become increasingly involved in academic dispute, but consistently they have maintained a very sensitive deference to academic judgment.

198   Higher Education in American Society

Notes

1. Estelle A. Fishbein, "The Academic Industry—A Dangerous Premise," in *Government Regulation of Higher Education,* Walter C. Hobbs, ed. (Cambridge, Mass.: Ballinger, 1978), pp. 57-58.
2. Robert M. O'Neil, *The Courts, Government and Higher Education* (New York: Committee for Economic Development, 1972), p. 10.
3. The Sloan Commission on Government and Higher Education, *A Program for Renewed Partnership* (Cambridge, Mass.: Ballinger, 1980), pp. 10, 55.
4. Harry T. Edwards, *Higher Education and the Unholy Crusade Against Governmental Regulation* (Cambridge, Mass.: Harvard University Institute for Educational Management, 1980).
5. Ibid., p. 39.
6. Ibid., p. 17.
7. Ibid., p. 20. Perhaps, retorts the critic. But when I must raise $10,000 to render reports that none of my $100,000 categorical grant may be used to prepare, or to improve physical facilities for which I receive no grant, then it's costing me money I don't have and must generate to comply with government regulation.
8. Ibid., p. 20.
9. Ibid., p. 29.
10. Sloan Report, *Program for Renewed Partnership,* p. 61.
11. Walter C. Hobbs, "The 'Defective Pressure-Cooker' Syndrome: Dispute Process in the University," *Journal of Higher Education* 45 (November 1974).
12. National Labor Relations Board v. Yeshiva University, 444 U.S. 672 (1980).
13. Walter C. Hobbs, "The Theory of Government Regulation," in *Government Regulation,* pp. 4-5.
14. The rights are actually enumerated in the first eight amendments.
15. Barron v. Mayor and City Council of Baltimore, 8 L. Ed. 672 (1833).
16. The Slaughterhouse Cases, 16 Wall. 36 (1873).
17. Braden v. University of Pittsburgh, 552 F.2d 948 (1977).
18. Joan S. Stark, ed., *Promoting Consumer Protection for Students* (San Francisco: Jossey-Bass, 1976).
19. Edwards, *Higher Education and the Unholy Crusade,* p. 19.
20. Steinberg v. Chicago Medical School, 354 N.E.2d 586 (1976).
21. Regents of the University of California v. Bakke, 438 U.S. 265 (1978).
22. Southeastern Community College v. Davis, 442 U.S. 397 (1979).
23. Dixon v. Alabama State Board of Education, 294 F.2d 150 (1961); Esteban v. Central Missouri State College 277 F.Supp. 649 (1967), afmd., 415 F.2d 1077 (1969).
24. Richard C. Conrath, *"In Loco Parentis:* Recent Developments," (Ph.D. diss., Kent State University, 1976).
25. Board of Curators of the University of Missouri v. Horowitz, 435 U.S. 78 (1978).
26. Board of Regents v. Roth, 408 U.S. 564 (1972).
27. Perry v. Sindermann, 408 U.S. 593 (1972).
28. Bishop v. Woods, 426 U.S. 341 (1976).
29. Wood v. Strickland, 420 U.S. 308 (1975).
30. *Sindermann case.*
31. Levitt v. Board of Trustees of Nebraska State Colleges, 376 F.Supp. 945 (1974).
32. Board of Trustees of Keene State College v. Sweeney, 439 U.S. 24 (1978).
33. *Yeshiva case.*
34. Keyishian v. Board of Regents of the University of the State of New York, 385 U.S. 589 (1967).
35. Sweezy v. New Hampshire, 354 U.S. 234 (1957).
36. Healy v. James, 408 U.S. 169 (1972).

11

Private Constituencies and Their Impact on Higher Education

Fred F. Harcleroad

Postsecondary institutions have opened and endured in the United States for thirty-five decades. All except those established very recently have been modified over the years and changed greatly in response to pressures from external forces. Particularly in the last century and a half, literally thousands of diverse institutions have opened their doors, only to close when they were no longer needed by (1) sufficient students, or (2) by the public and private constituencies that originally founded and supported them. Those in existence today are the survivors, the institutions that adapted to the needs of their constituencies. Even Harvard closed for what would have been its second year (in 1639-1640) after Nathaniel Eaton, its first head, was dismissed for cruelty to students and stealing much of the college funds. After being closed for the year government officials determined that the Massachusetts Bay Colony still needed a college to train ministers and advance learning. A new president, Henry Dunster, reopened the college in 1640, and by changing regularly, and sometimes dramatically, it has remained in operation ever since. Two small examples illustrate this impact. As Massachusetts grew and secularized, ministerial training at Harvard was only one function, so it was placed in a separate divinity school. Also, by the late 1700s required instruction in Hebrew was replaced by student choice, a beginning of our current elective system.

The varied set of external forces affecting postsecondary education in the United States has grown out of our relatively unique, three-sector system of providing goods and services for both "collective consumption" and "private" use. First, the *voluntary enterprise sector*, composed of over six million independent nonprofit organizations, often has initiated efforts to provide such things as schools, hospitals, bridges, libraries, environmental controls, and public parks. They are protected by constitutional rights to peaceful assembly, to free speech, and to petition for redress of grievances. These formidable protections plus their record of useful service led to their being nontaxable, with contributions to them being tax free. Second, the *public enterprise group*, composed of all local, state, and federal governments, administers the laws that hold our society together. Third, the *private enterprise sector*, composed of profit-seeking business and commerce, provides much of the excess wealth needed to support the other two sectors. This pluralistic and diverse set of organizations implements very well the basic ideas behind our federated republic.

Our constitution provides for detailed separation of powers at the federal level between the presidency, the Congress, and the judiciary. The Tenth Amendment establishes the states as governments with "general" powers and delegates "limited" powers to the federal government. "Education" is not a "delegated" power and, therefore, is reserved to the states, where their constitutions often treated it almost as a fourth branch of government. In addition, the Tenth Amendment reserves "general" powers to citizens who operate through their own voluntary organizations, their state governments, or state-authorized private enterprise. Consequently, only a few higher education institutions are creations of the federal government (mostly military institutions, to provide for the common defense), but over 99 percent are creations of states, voluntary organizations, or profit-seeking business.

External groups, associations, and agencies from all three sectors impact on the many varied types of institutions of postsecondary education. This very diverse group of organizations includes everything from athletic conferences and alumni associations to employer associations and unions (or organized faculty groups that function as unions). Of course, the corporate boards that administer all of the private colleges, universities, and institutes authorized to operate in the respective states belong in this group. Their power to determine institutional policies is clear and well known. However, many other voluntary associations can, and do, have significant effects on specific institutions or units of the institutions. To illustrate their potential, these five selected types of organizations will be described in some detail to indicate their backgrounds, development, and possible areas of impact on institutional autonomy and academic freedom. They are:

1. Private foundations;

2. Institutionally based associations;
3. Voluntary accrediting associations;
4. Voluntary consortia;
5. Regional compacts.

Private Foundations

The first beginnings of private foundations in the U.S. took place over two centuries ago. As a precursor, Benjamin Franklin led in the establishment in Philadelphia of a number of voluntary sector organizations, including the American Philosophical Society in 1743, an association with many foundation characteristics. In 1800 the Magdalen Society of Philadelphia, possibly the first private foundation in the United States, was established as a perpetual trust to assist "unhappy females who had been seduced from the paths of virtue." In the 1890s and early 1900s the Carnegie foundations, followed shortly by the Rockefeller foundations, set a pattern that continues to this day. These foundations established a high standard of operations and valuable service. Few academics realize that their current TIAA pensions were developed and are presently administered by a foundation resulting from Andrew Carnegie's feeling of public service responsibility. Decades before it became legal to tax incomes and before such "contributions" became tax deductible, he gave several million dollars to set up the first pension fund for college teachers.

Today, private foundations vary greatly in form, purpose, size, function, and constituency. Some are corporate in nature, many are trusts, and some are only associations. Many of them can affect postsecondary institutions through their choice of areas to support. They can be classified into five types as follows: (1) community foundations, often city wide and based on a variety of bequests or gifts (local postsecondary institutions, often, can count on some limited support from such foundations for locally related projects); (2) family or personal foundations, often with very limited purposes; (3) special purpose foundations (including such varied examples as the Harvard Glee Club, and a fund set up to provide every girl at Bryn Mawr with one baked potato at each meal); (4) company foundations, established to channel corporate giving through one main source; and (5) general foundations or general research foundations (including many of the large, well-known foundations such as Ford, Kellogg, Johnson, Lilly, and Carnegie, plus recent additions such as Murdock, MacArthur, and Hewlett). Over 90 percent of private foundation grant funds to higher education come from such general purpose foundations. A number of sources report that higher education receives between 35 and 40 percent of the total giving by foundations. The actual number of grant-making foundations probably approximates 28-30,000. They provide significant help to higher education institutions, and by their choice of the areas they will finance they entice supposedly autonomous colleges to do things they might not do otherwise. Institutional change continues to be a prime goal of foundations as it has been for most of the past century. Thus, although their grants provide a relatively small proportion of the total financing of institutions, they have had significant effects on program development and even on operations. Important support has been provided for such critical activities as the upgrading of medical education, the development of honors programs, and the international exchange of students. Grants from foundations have been instrumental in the establishment of new academic fields such as microbiology and anthropology and the redirection of the fields of business and the education of teachers. Significant support has been provided particularly for the increasing opportunities for minority students' attendance at both undergraduate and graduate levels, and especially in professional fields. Complaints that the private foundations limit their significant funding efforts to "establishment" activities fail to recognize the many critical social changes in which private foundations have led the way. Often, foundation funds have encouraged colleges and universities to take forefront positions in some social causes.

It is important to stress, however, that private foundations affect institutional freedom only if the institutions voluntarily accept the funds for the purposes prescribed by the foundation. Redirection of programs, and even private institutional goals, is possible and has occurred on occasion. Nevertheless, the private foundation model has been so successful that government has adopted it in forming and funding such agencies as the National Science Foundation, the Fund for the Improvement of Postsecondary Education, and the National Endowments for the Arts and for the Humanities. Clearly, private foundations have been and undoubtedly will continue to be important external forces affecting postsecondary education.

Institutionally Based Associations

Voluntary membership organizations of this type are almost infinite in possible numbers. Although formed by officials from institutions for their own purposes, the associations often end up having either indirect or direct effects on the institutions themselves. Several large and quite powerful associations represent many of the institutions. The American Council on Education, probably the major policy advocate for postsecondary education at the national level, plays a critical coordinative role as an umbrella-type organization composed of a wide spectrum of institutions. Seven other major national institutional organizations include (1) the Association of

American Colleges, (2) the American Association of Community and Junior Colleges, (3) the American Association of State Colleges and Universities, (4) the Association of American Universities, (5) the Council For the Advancement of Small Colleges, (6) the National Association of Independent Colleges and Universities, and (7) the National Association of State Universities and Land-Grant Colleges. These organizations represent most of the public and private, nonprofit postsecondary institutions of the United States, with some institutions belonging to two or three of them. A recent study of the effectiveness of these diverse organizations, as judged by their presidents and by selected national observers, attested to their importance with regard to federal policies and budgets related to higher education.[1] All are based in Washington and, in general, were considered important in representing differing interests of the varied groups of institutions. A majority of the study respondents favored the current, pluralistic system of organizations but with stronger coordination and a more united front on key issues affecting postsecondary education in all departments of government and related congressional committees. The strength of these national associations will continue to grow along with taxes, the federal budget, and federal purchase of selected services from their member institutions. Even though most of the postsecondary institutions are state chartered and many basically are state funded, the increasing power of the federal tax system will make such national associations even more necessary.

Many specialized voluntary membership associations contribute in diverse ways to the development and operations of functional areas within institutions. For example, both the American College Testing Program and the College Entrance Examination Board (its service bureau, the Educational Testing Service, is not a membership organization) provide extensive information resources to their member institutions and program areas. These data are vital for counseling and guidance purposes, admissions of students, student financial aid programs, and related activities. In addition, different administrative functions (such as graduate schools, registrars, institutional research units, and business offices) have their own extremely useful representative associations. Likewise, most different academic fields and their constantly increasing subdivisions or spin-offs have set up specialized groups. Prime examples are engineering and the allied health professions, both with dozens of separate associations. Many of these academic organizations affect institutions and their program planning in very direct ways. In particular, the associations that set up extensive detailed criteria for membership in the association often influence very directly the allocation of resources. Of the several thousand membership organizations* in this category, sixty to seventy of them, from architecture to veterinary medicine, probably exert the greatest influence since those

---

*See Gale's *Encyclopedia of Associations* for a comprehensive list that includes many from higher education.

programs or academic units admitted to membership are considered "accredited." The following section will provide more detail on this group.

A small sampling of these varied types of organizations will illustrate their services and emphasize their significance. Very brief and highly condensed, they show in a limited way their potential impact.

1. *The American Council on Education* includes separate institutions and other associations, with approximately 1500 members. It serves as a key coordinating entity for development of major policy positions, especially in regard to federal legislation and regulatory agency activity. Through its Office of Educational Credit and Credentials it prepares and distributes such important guidebooks as the *Guide to the Evaluation of Educational Experiences in the Armed Services.* This guide is updated periodically and serves as a "bible" for most registrars' offices. Another comparable ACE publication is *The National Guide to Credit Recommendations for Non-Collegiate Courses.* The extensive overall service and publications program includes reports from the policy analysis service and many special studies on current critical issues in higher education.

2. *The National Association of College and University Business Officers* plays a critical role in all institutional administrative areas. For example, *College and University Business Administration,* which it compiles, updates and publishes, provides the national standards for public accounting in higher education. It conducts extensive surveys on administrative practices and needs, and an active nationwide workshop and seminar program. NACUBO leads in analysis of many other related areas. A critical instance was its central role in establishing the agreement for royalty payments to be paid by colleges and universities for their use of copyrighted music.

3. *The Council for the Advancement of Small Colleges* began in 1955, formed by a group of presidents of small independent colleges. This voluntary, member-directed association now has close to three hundred members and a significant, comprehensive program of services. Before joining the Council some member institutions operated without planned budgets, accreditation, or fund-raising programs and with only limited accounting records. During its early years many CASC institutions took advantage of its workshops, seminars, handbooks, and consultants and earned regional accreditation. CASC has secured many millions of dollars to operate programs for its constituency. Many of its special services are supported by useful publications such as its *Handbook for College Administration.* It has a modular Planning and Data System for colleges at various stages of data collection and usage and a related consulting service. Special efforts for the 1980s center on an executive development program for presidents and their spouses,

faculty development programs that include "alternate" career programs, and a continuing federal funds service. Recent publications include a *Federal Affairs Handbook* and *A Marketing Approach to Student Recruitment.*

4. *The American Association of State Colleges and Universities* represents three hundred and forty-two public four-year colleges and universities, over 60 percent of the total, plus thirty-three coordinating or governing boards for these institutions. Since its beginnings two decades ago the association has been a leading stimulator of all facets of international education. Its many presidential missions to such countries as Egypt, Israel, Greece, Poland, The Peoples Republic of China, Cuba, Argentina, Taiwan, Malaysia, and Mexico have fostered continuing educational exchange and on-campus programs. It has taken national leadership in developing cooperative, interassociation and interinstitutional programs and networks such as the Servicemembers Opportunity Colleges (with many AASCU institutions involved), the Urban College and University Network, and the Academic Collective Bargaining Information Service. Its Office of Federal Programs monitors current funding programs and priorities and has been instrumental in increasing AASCU institutions' participation in this ever-increasing source of funds. Its Office of Governmental Relations analyzes pending legislation, develops policy analysis papers, prepares testimony on major national issues, and monitors state developments affecting public higher education. The Office of Program Development assists institutions in various areas of current program development. Recent important areas of assistance have been allied health professions, environmental manpower needs, urban affairs, and public services. Its Research Center for Planned Change works actively with over two hundred and fifty of its member institutions and their chief academic officers, emphasizing future planning, academic program evaluation systems, faculty exchanges between institutions, and innovative educational ideas for new clientele. An extensive seminar, conference, and publication program supports this extensive alignment of institutional services. Overall, the association has had a profound effect on these institutions and their graduates, over one-fourth of those earning baccalaureate degrees and one-third of those earning masters degrees in the United States.

These vignettes from a few associations illustrate the significance and impact of this type of voluntary association. Each of them contribute in varied ways to the diverse needs of their member institutions, or to the program units within them. However, since these organizations continue to be the creatures of their founding members, their efforts do not seem to have noticeable effects on institutional autonomy or academic freedom. Quite the contrary, they seem to be buffering agencies that assist in this regard.

Voluntary Accrediting Associations

The voluntary membership organizations in this critical and important group did not exist a century ago. However, by that time the problems and confusion that led to their establishment had started to surface. Five key factors contributed to the turbulent state of affairs in the period from 1870-1910: (1) the final breakdown of the fixed, classical curriculum and broad expansion of the elective system; (2) new academic fields were being developed and legitimized (such as psychology, education, sociology, and American literature); (3) new, diverse types of institutions were being organized to meet developing social needs (such as teachers colleges, junior colleges, land-grant colleges, research universities, and specialized professional schools); (4) both secondary and postsecondary education were expanding and overlapping, leading to a basic question, "What is a college?"; and (5) there was a lack of commonly accepted standards for admission to college and for completing a college degree.[2]

To work on some of these problems the University of Michigan as early as 1871 sent out faculty members to inspect high schools and admitted graduates of the acceptable and approved high schools on the basis of their diploma. Shortly thereafter pressures developed for regional approaches to these problems, in order to facilitate uniform college entrance requirements.

In keeping with accepted American practice and custom groups of educators banded together in various regions to organize private, voluntary membership groups for this purpose. In New England, for example, it was a group of secondary schoolmasters who took the initiative. In the southern states it was Chancellor Kirkland and the faculty of Vanderbilt University. Six regional associations have developed throughout the United States starting with (1) the New England Association of Schools and Colleges in 1885. It was followed (2) in 1887, by the Middle States Association of Colleges and Schools; (3) in 1895, by the Southern Association of Colleges and Schools; (4) in 1895, by the North Central Association of Colleges and Schools; (5) in 1917, by the Northwest Association of Schools and Colleges; and (6) in 1923, by the Western Association of Schools and Colleges. Criteria and requirements for institutional membership (which now serve as the basis for institutions being considered "accredited") were formally established by these six associations at different times: (1) in 1910, by North Central, with the first list of accredited colleges in 1913; (2) in 1919, by Southern; (3) and (4) in 1921, by Northwest and Middle States; (5) in 1949, by Western; and (6) in 1954, by New England. Thus, at the same time that the federal government instituted regulatory commissions to control similar problems (the Interstate Commerce Commission, 1887, the Federal Trade Commission, 1914, and the Federal Power Commission, 1920) these non-governmental, voluntary membership groups sprang up to provide yard-sticks for student achievement and institutional operations.

Regional groups dealt in the main with colleges rather than with specialized professional schools or programs. The North Central Association finally determined to admit normal schools and teachers colleges, but on a separate list of acceptable institutions. Practitioners and faculty in professional associations gradually set up their own membership associations. These groups established criteria for approving schools and based on these criteria made lists of "accredited" schools and program units. In some cases, only individuals with degrees from an "approved" school could join the professional association. Later, some membership groups made the approved program unit or school a basis for association membership. In any case the specialized academic program and its operational unit had to meet exacting criteria, externally imposed, to acquire and retain standing in the field.

The first of the specialized or programmatic discipline-oriented associations was the American Medical Association in 1847. However, approving processes for medical schools did not start until the early 1900s. In 1905-7 the Council on Medical Education of the AMA led a movement for rating of medical schools. The first ratings in 1905 were a list based on the percentages of failures on licensing examinations by students from each school. This was followed in 1906-7 by a more sophisticated system based on ten specific areas to be examined and inspections of each school. Of 160 schools inspected, classified, and listed, 32 were in Class C, "unapproved," 46 were in Class B, on "probation," and 82 were in Class A, "approved." The Council on Medical Education was attacked vigorously for this listing and approving activity. The recently established Carnegie Foundation for the Advancement of Teaching (1905) provided funds for Abraham Flexner and N.P. Colwell to make their famous study (1908-1910) of the 155 schools still in existence. Obviously, five already had closed. By 1915, only 95 medical schools remained, a 40 percent reduction, and they were again classified by the AMA Council on Medical Education, with 66 approved, 17 on probation, and 12 still listed as unapproved. This voluntary effort led to the ultimate in accountability, the merger and closing of 65 existing medical schools. In the process medical education was changed drastically, and the remaining schools completely revised and changed their curricula—a process still continuing to this day. This provides an excellent example of the work of an external voluntary professional association, with financial support from a private foundation, that took the initiative and acted on its own to protect the public interest. Thus, in some cases intrusions into "autonomy" can have beneficial results.

The success of the AMA did not go unnoticed. The National Home Study council started in 1926 to do for correspondence education what the AMA after seventy years had done in medical education. Between 1914-1935 many other professional disciplinary and service associations were started in the fields of business, dentistry, law, library science, music, engineering, forestry, and dietetics plus the medically related fields of podiatry, pharmacy, veterinary medicine, optometry, and nurse anesthesia. From 1935-1948 new associations starting up included architecture, art, bible schools, chemistry, journalism, and theology, plus four more medically related fields, medical technology, medical records, occupational therapy, and physical therapy. Between 1948 and 1975 the number of specialized associations continued to expand rapidly, for programs from social service to graduate psychology and from construction education to funeral direction. Medical care subspecialties also proliferated, particularly in the allied health field, which included over twenty-five separate groups.

All of these external professional associations affect institutional operations very directly, including curricular patterns, faculty, degrees offered, teaching methods, support staff patterns, and capital outlay decisions. In many cases priorities in internal judgments result from the outside pressures. Local resource allocations, thus, often are heavily influenced by accreditation reports. For example, the law library, a chemistry or engineering laboratory, and teaching loads in business or social work may have been judged substandard by these external private constituents. If teaching loads in English or history also are heavy or physics laboratories inadequate will they get the same attention and treatment as specialized program areas with outside pressures? In such cases these association memberships are not really "voluntary," if the institution is placed on probation or no longer an "accredited" member, and sanctions are actually applied. Often, students will withdraw or not consider attending a professional school or college that is not accredited. States often limit professional licenses to practice in a field to graduates of accredited schools. Federal agencies may not allow students from unaccredited institutions to obtain scholarships, loans, or work-study funds. The leverage of a voluntary association in such cases becomes tremendous, and the pressure for accredited status can be extremely powerful.

Presidents of some of the larger institutions, starting in 1924, have attempted to limit the effects of accrediting associations and the number of these independent organizations with which they would work. Through some of the institutionally based associations described in the previous section they established limited sanctions and attempted to restrict the number of accrediting associations to which they would pay dues and allow on-campus site visits. These efforts to limit association membership and accreditation failed repeatedly to stem the tide. Shortly after World War II, in

1949, a group of university presidents finally organized the National Commission on Accrediting, a separate voluntary membership association of their own. It was designed to cut down the demands and influence of existing external associations and to delay or stop the development of new ones. The numbers of new ones dropped for a few years but pressures of new, developing disciplines on campus soon led to the many new organizations of this type since the 1950s.

In 1949, the regional associations also felt the need for a new cooperative association and set up what became the Federation of Regional Accrediting Commissions. In 1975 the two organizations, FRACHE and NCA, agreed to merge and they became major factors in the founding of the new Council on Postsecondary Accreditation. COPA also included four national groups accrediting specialized institutions, plus seven major, institutionally based associations. They in turn endorsed COPA as the central, leading voluntary association for the establishment of policies and procedures in postsecondary accreditation. By 1980 COPA had recognized fifty-two accrediting associations that met its standards. These associations "approve" or "accredit" approximately 4,000 different institutions of all types and kinds, varying by level (undergraduate, nondegree, or graduate), by form of governance (private/profit seeking, private/tax exempt, or public/tax supported), and by curricular emphasis (professional, liberal arts/general education, or vocational). In addition COPA and the separate accrediting associations increasingly are pressured for recognition of educational programs offered by government agencies, businesses, church groups and unions.

The six current goals of COPA are to:
1. foster educational excellence by developing criteria and guidelines for assessing educational effectiveness;
2. encourage improvement through continuous self-study and planning;
3. provide assurance of clearly defined and appropriate objectives and conditions under which they can be achieved;
4. provide counsel and aid to established and developing programs and institutions;
5. encourage educational diversity;
6. protect institutions' educational effectiveness and academic freedom.

The relationship of voluntary accrediting associations to the state and federal governments also is a major factor in current considerations of academic freedom, institutional autonomy, and institutional accountability. The states, of course, charter most of the institutions, and by so doing establish their missions, general purposes, and degree levels offered. However, the states also license individuals to practice most vocations and professions. In many fields the licensing of individuals is based on graduation from "accredited" programs. Thus, a form of sanctions has developed and membership in the involved, specialized, professional associations, supposedly voluntary, becomes almost obligatory. In the federal area, "listing" of institutions by federal government agencies had little or no effect prior to World War II. However, the entrance of the federal government into the funding of higher education on a massive basis since World War II has drastically changed the overall uses of accreditation. Reported abuses of the Servicemen's Readjustment Act of 1944 (G.I. Bill) led to a series of congressional hearings, which led in turn to major additions related to accreditation in Public Law 550, the Veterans Readjustment Act of 1952. Section 253 of that law empowered the Commissioner of Education to publish a list of accrediting agencies and associations that could be relied upon to assess the quality of training offered by educational institutions. State approving agencies then used the resulting actions of such accrediting associations or agencies as a basis for approval of the courses specifically accredited.

Extensive legal arguments about the resulting powers of the Department of Education still continue. However, greater institutional dependence of "eligibility" for funding is now based on membership in much less voluntary accrediting associations. The courts normally have ruled that accreditation by accrediting associations is not quasi-governmental action. Nevertheless, there has grown up an important new concept called the "triad." The triad involves delicate relationships between the federal government and eligibility for funding, the state government and its responsibilities for establishing or chartering institutions and credentialing through certification or licensure, and voluntary membership associations that require accreditation for membership.

Thus, these voluntary associations have come to represent a major form of private constituency with direct impact on internal institution activities. The possible multiple sanctions from state licensing of graduates, loss of eligibility for funds from federal agencies, and problems caused by peer approval or disapproval enhance the importance of these sometimes overlooked educational organizations.

Voluntary Consortia[3]

Formal arrangements for voluntary consortia based on interinstitutional cooperation among and between postsecondary institutions have been in operation for over half a century. The Claremont Colleges (California) started in 1925 with Pomona College and the Claremont University Center and were joined by Scripps College in 1926. The Atlanta University Center (Georgia), sometimes called the "Affiliation," started shortly thereafter in

1929, including Morehouse College, Spelman College, and Atlanta University. Over the decades both of these groups have added additional institutions to their cooperative arrangements and proven that voluntary consortia can be valuable for long periods of time. Some early examples from 1927-29 illustrate the reality of the cooperation between Morehouse and Spelman. In those years several faculty were jointly appointed to both faculties. Upper division students could cross-register and take courses offered by the other college. Also, they operated a joint summer school with Atlanta University. In 1932, a new library was built and the three libraries consolidated into a joint library serving all of the institutions. Thus, although they remained separate institutions they sacrificed some autonomy to extend the academic offerings and services available to their students.[4]

In the years since these early beginnings, hundreds of institutions have developed informal and increasingly formal arrangements for interinstitutional cooperation. In 1966, a national survey conducted by the United States Office of Education determined that there were 1017 consortiums operating in the United States and that the evidence indicated that a number of consortiums were not reported. The list included all types of consortia, from simple bilateral arrangements dealing with a single area of service to large complex consortia performing many services and contributing in many areas of education.[5] In 1967, the staff of the Kansas City Regional Council For Higher Education, a leading consortium, published the first directory of consortia, with a list of 31 having these exacting criteria: (1) it is a voluntary formal organization; (2) it has three or more member institutions, (3) it has multi-academic programs, (4) it is administered by at least one full-time professional, and (5) it has a required annual contribution or other tangible membership support. Twelve years later the 1979 Consortium Directory listed 126 general-purpose consortia with "at least six to eight separate services or programs; several administer as many as 30 or 40 different activities over a one year period."[6] Well over 1,000 institutions are involved in these consortia alone. Thus, today consortia represent a major development in American higher education and a significant factor in current planning and development of institutions.

The big push for the development of consortia in the 1950s, 1960s, and 1970s was based on the need to maximize the use of resources to meet the challenge of increasing enrollments, expanding research efforts, and increasing demands on the higher education community for additional services. The demands of the 1980s and 1990s appear to be just the opposite. The demands for efficiency in the use of the plant, facilities, and the faculty again require interinstitutional arrangements in order to make optimum use of facilities that are available. For both state-supported colleges and universities and for private independent institutions, there appears to be a continuing need for more cooperation among various types of educational institutions, including shared used of facilities and joint programs.

The need for this type of organization in the 1980s and later is well illustrated by the development of a number of statewide efforts to establish official, but voluntary, regional councils. States such as New York, Pennsylvania, and California have established regional councils for planning and interinstitutional communication between interested institutions, both public and private. In these cases regionalism revolves more around the planning of available curricular programs, rather than the extensive operational cooperation in most consortia. However, the interest in states in this method of operation, and the inclusion of both private and public institutions on a voluntary basis, represents a major and somewhat comparable departure. As another method of bringing about cooperative effort between both types of institutions, it has valuable implications for the future of all consortia. If the proposed regional councils could be expanded to include the many diverse activities of existing consortia, they could contribute greatly to demands for efficiency and effectiveness.

The importance of voluntary consortia to concerns regarding institutional autonomy becomes evident with the enumeration of their varied activities. An extensive study of twenty-nine consortia by the Academy of Educational Development divided their activities into seven major areas: (1) administrative and business services, (2) enrollment and admissions, (3) academic programs, (4) libraries, (5) student services, (6) faculty and (7) community services. In each of these areas, they found significant and extensive cooperative efforts that had been carried on by many institutions in several consortia.[7] Also, they found that consortia were geographically widespread with programs in all seven of the categories.

Advocates of consortia activity normally stress the educational advantages that accrue from their programs. Voluntary consortia have proven to be an ideal planning vehicle for joint programming of public and private colleges and universities or private colleges acting alone. In fact, a recent restudy of McGrath's fifty private-colleges' sample found that:

> Interinstitutional cooperative arrangements served as a method of providing new educational programs and as a method of retaining old programs for the least expense. Cooperative efforts were found to provide expanded capabilities while requiring a minimum of resources in faculty, facilities, and money. Cooperation was a management method which provided opportunities for students to participate in high cost programs through the use of shared resources.[8]

How very significant financial savings also are often obtained undoubtedly will become more important. In some cases, existing programs have been able to continue without cutbacks, due to economies based on consortium arrangements. In others, actual savings accrue that can be used to meet growth costs in other areas. A few selected examples illustrate their fiscal and planning importance.[9]

- Cross-registration provided derived value of instruction to several groups of institutions in 1977-1979—including Atlanta University Center, $1,518,000; and Five Colleges, Inc., $1,889,000 (in Amherst, Massachusetts).

- Cooperative academic programs save significant sums at, for example, the Claremont Colleges, Inc. where three colleges operated a joint science department with joint faculty and joint use of a single science laboratory complex.

- The Washington Metropolitan Area Consortium of Universities, in 1978, combined their purchases of liquid helium and liquid nitrogen through the physics department of Georgetown University and reported a saving of $500,000 from their total research budgets for that period.

- The Union of Independent Colleges of Art (nine institutions in the Kansas City area) made a preliminary study of the cost effectiveness in their joint admissions program alone. Direct cash benefits to each institution were found to be more than $62,986 each, with each college paying fees of only $8,256 per college. A joint film center saved $124,460.

- The Hudson-Mohawk Association of Colleges and Universities (with fifteen members) shared information on fuel oil prices. Three of the members in 1972 reported reduced costs by $20,000 in one year by using this data in their bargaining with suppliers. In February, 1978 they reported savings of over $50,000 during the summer of 1977 on fuel oil, paper and other office supplies. A cooperative surplus sale raised $12,450.

- The Worcester, Massachusetts, Consortium combined their oil purchases and the single supplier cut 10 percent to get the entire bid. The consortium members (including both public and private, two-year and four-year institutions) saved $30,000.

These examples of savings are representative of the actual financial savings possible through joint institutional planning.

Liberal arts colleges led the way for several decades in the establishment of consortia, and Patterson found in 1970 that approximately 75 percent of member colleges were private, nonprofit institutions. However, by 1975, 40 percent were public.[10] Recent federal and state support of cooperative ventures of this type have increased consortia in numbers and membership. For example, the Illinois Higher Education Cooperative Act of 1972 provided some state support for voluntary combinations of private and public institutions, including some from out of state, that applied for funds on a competitive basis. The Quad-Cities Graduate Center in Rock Island, Illinois, administered by Augustana College, combined the offerings of ten public and private colleges and universities in Iowa and Illinois to provide graduate degree programs to several thousand graduate students. Funding is provided by both states and the result is a major, free-standing graduate school drawing strength from its ten members. Several other states such as California, Connecticut, Massachusetts, Minnesota, Ohio, Pennsylvania, and Texas have used the consortium approach for specific, sometimes limited purposes. This trend toward public financing of consortia, thus, becomes another key factor to consider in future institutional planning, along with limited efforts to promote regional, intrastate planning.

In the past, consortia have been developed to provide for interinstitutional needs both in times of growth and in times of decline. They are uniquely capable of handling mutual problems of public and private institutions, and thus, provide a powerful deterrent to further governmental incursions into private and sometimes public institutional operation. At various levels of formality, consortia currently are being used by significant numbers of institutions of all types to adjust to changing curricular and funding necessities. As governmental controls continue to increase and to affect institutional autonomy and academic freedom, voluntary consortia provide another way to plan independently for future operations and program development.

Regional Compacts

Regional compacts, although they are nonprofit, private organizations, are quasi-governmental. Groups of states created them, provide their basic funding, and contract for services through them. Still, they operate much like private organizations and receive considerable funding from other sources, including private foundations. Some of their studies, seminars, workshops, and policy studies affect very directly the institutions in their regions.

Soon after World War II three regional interstate compacts developed to meet postsecondary education needs that crossed state lines. Originally they concentrated on student exchange programs for the medical education field; however, in the past 25 to 30 years their areas of service and influence have expanded considerably. Although established, funded, and supported basically by state governors and legislatures, their indirect effects on institutional programs and operations can be very, very significant. Listed in order of establishment, they are:

1. Southern Regional Education Board (1948)

2. Western Interstate Commission for Higher Education (1951)
3. New England Board of Higher Education (1955)

These three compacts cover thirty-three states, leaving out the midwest, New York, Pennsylvania, and Delaware. Efforts are underway to establish one in fifteen states of the midwest. Between 1978 and 1980 the Minnesota, South Dakota, North Dakota, and Ohio legislatures approved its establishment. In order to begin operations, six states had to adopt the plan. If established, it would provide for interstate student exchanges at in-state tuition rates, cooperative programs in vocational and higher education, and an area-wide approach to gathering and reporting information needed for educational planning.

The Southern Regional Education Board includes key governors, legislators, and other key figures, some from higher education, from fourteen states, Alabama, Arkansas, Florida, Georgia, Kentucky, Louisiana, Maryland, Mississippi, North Carolina, South Carolina, Tennessee, Texas, Virginia, and West Virginia. In its thirty years of operation, it has played a major part in the development of such important areas as equal opportunity for all students in higher education and expanded graduate and professional education. Its research and information program has been vital in state and institutional planning. Its regular legislative work conferences, planned by its Legislative Advisory Council, have been very influential in setting policy and funding directions in the region.

The Western Interstate Compact for Higher Education now has members from thirteen states, Alaska, Arizona, California, Colorado, Hawaii, Idaho, Montana, Nevada, New Mexico, Oregon, Utah, Washington, and Wyoming. It was planned originally (1) to pool educational resources, (2) to help the states plan jointly for the preparation of specialized skilled manpower, and (3) to avoid, where feasible, the duplication of expensive facilities. The student exchange program in the fields of medicine, dentistry, veterinary medicine, and later in dental hygiene, nursing, mental health, and other specialized fields, has been a major effort. Regional conferences on critical topics, annual legislative workshops, and extensive research studies and publications also are regularly carried on by WICHE. One of its developments, the program in higher education management and information systems, created so much demand for participation in the other thirty-seven states that it was "spun-off" to become the National Center for Higher Education Management Systems. WICHEN, its special Council for Nursing education, has operated continuously since 1957 and has been a key research, consultation, and planning source for the development of degree programs in the field of nursing. In 1978, an extensive study of future needs for nurses and differing types of nursing services was completed. These findings are important for academic decision making related to nursing programs in most of the western states.

Two recent studies were of critical importance to institutional academic planning in the region. One was a study of needs for optometry education, in which there are only three schools in the thirteen states, and projected shortages of optometrists in twelve of the states. Second, WICHE had a two-year grant from the Carnegie Corporation of New York during 1978-1980 to study the expansion of regional cooperation in graduate and professional education. Its purpose was to encourage sharing of graduate resources through establishment of an information system about such programs. Decision-makers were provided with a stream of data based on a regional perspective. Two major planning issues were addressed:

1. Do western-state graduate students have adequate access based on current interstate mobility? and

2. Can lower tuitions for out-of-state students be justified by improved resource sharing of graduate facilities?

With decreasing graduate enrollments and a need for programs to assure a reasonable flow of young doctorates into both academic service and newer, expanded areas needing doctoral graduates, this latter study was an important one and provided considerable guidance on needed academic decisions related to graduate professional programs.

The New England Board of Higher Education serves six states, Connecticut, Maine, Massachusetts, New Hampshire, Rhode Island, and Vermont. It administers such programs as (1) the regional student exchange program, (2) the New England Council on Higher Education for Nursing, (3) a library information network, and (4) an academic science information center. A major study of the past few years was the analysis of need and recommended location of a school of veterinary medicine, a very controversial topic.

Clearly, regional interstate compacts provide critical research data and have considerable impact on academic program decision making. In some cases their findings directly affect the location of an academic program at a particular institution or the source and size of the student body for an existing program. Expansion or contraction of an expensive program often is a critical planning decision. In areas such as this an external regional compact can greatly affect an individual college or university. Since regional compacts provide a unique blending of legislators, governors, officials of executive agencies, and key officials from institutions of higher education, these organizations will continue to fill a vital communication link in interstate planning.

Conclusion

During the first two centuries of American higher education's existence religious tenets and basic social agreements resulted in a relatively fixed, classically oriented program of studies. However, as the society began to open up, to industrialize and expand, it demanded greater change in its colleges. When this was slow to occur new institutions met these needs and many existing ones closed. Normal schools, engineering schools, military academies, and universities were copied from Europe and adapted to American needs between the 1830s and 1900. However, even these were not sufficient to meet democracy's needs. New types of institutions were developed, unique or almost unique to America. The land-grant colleges of 1862 and 1890, the junior colleges of the early 1900s, the comprehensive state colleges of the 1930s-1960s and the post-world war community colleges all represent essentially new types of institutions. Private constituency groups often pressured state or local governments to establish them. In some cases private constituency groups pressured Congress into funding some of them, including both the 1862 land-grant colleges, and particularly the 1890 land-grant colleges. The critical point, again, is that in the United States new institutions replace existing ones that do not change.

Private constituencies such as the five types detailed here can and do have significant impact on institutional autonomy and academic freedom. Much of this impact is positive, supportive, and welcome. However, those that provide funds can affect institutional trends and direction by determining what types of academic program or research efforts to support. For example, in the late 1960s and early 1970s significant financial support from Carnegie strongly influenced most of the twenty-five institutions that offer the Doctor of Arts degree for prospective college teachers. Ford support for learning by television led many institutions to test this method of delivery of learning materials. As federal and state funds tighten up even more in the years ahead, funds from alternate sources will become even more attractive. Acceptance of grants moves institutions in the direction dictated by fund sources, and faculties are well advised to consider this possibility as the "crunch" of the 1980s and 1990s becomes greater in more and more institutions.

Finally, the very real benefits provided to institutions by private organizations have been stressed previously. Many membership organizations, of course, have been created to provide such anticipated benefits. In some cases these have been greater than anyone could have foreseen. Probably the most dramatic examples have come from private accrediting associations in relation to state political efforts to limit seriously the autonomy and academic freedom of their own public institutions. In 1938, the North Central Association dropped North Dakota Agricultural College from membership because of undue political interference. The U.S. Court of Appeals upheld the action of NCA and the state government basically backed away from its prior method of political interference in internal institutional affairs. In the post-World War II period, likewise, sanctions of the Southern Association basically stopped on-campus speaker-ban legislation in North Carolina and, after 1954, contributed strongly to the development of open campuses in other states in its region.

Private organizations related in some way to postsecondary education clearly continue the great tradition of direct action by voluntary citizen associations in America. Increasingly, they stand in the middle between control-oriented federal and state agencies and both private and public institutions. Governments, literally, have abandoned the "self-denying ordinance" that in recent decades kept the "state" at a distance from the essence of many of its institutions. The nurturance of supportive and helpful private constituencies, therefore, becomes even more critical in the final decades of the twentieth century.

Notes

1. Joseph Cosand, et al., *Higher Education's National Institutional Membership Associations* (Ann Arbor, Mich.: Center for the Study of Higher Education, University of Michigan, 1980).

2. Fred Harcleroad, *Accreditation: History, Process and Problems* (Washington, D.C.: American Association for Higher Education, 1981).

3. Some of the sections on voluntary consortia and regional compacts are adapted from Fred Harcleroad, "Effects of Regional Agencies and Voluntary Associations," in *Improving Academic Management,* Paul Jedamus and Marvin Peterson, eds. (San Francisco: Jossey-Bass, 1980), chapter. 6.

4. Florence M. Read, *The Story of Spelman College* (Princeton, N.J.: Princeton University Press, 1953), pp. 217-9, 235, 247.

5. Raymond S. Moore, *Consortiums in American Higher Education, 1965-66* (Washington, D.C.: U.S. Government Printing Office, 1968).

6. Lewis Patterson, *Survival Through Interdependence* (Washington, D.C.: American Association for Higher Education, 1980).

7. Barry Schwenkmeyer and Mary Ellen Goodman, *Putting Cooperation To Work* (Washington, D.C.: Academy for Educational Development, 1972).

8. George Lepchenske and Fred Harcleroad, *Are Liberal Arts Colleges Professional Schools? A Restudy* (Tucson, Ariz.: Center for the Study of Higher Education, University of Arizona, 1978), p. 17.

9. Lewis Patterson, *Survival Through Independence,* pp. 28-30.

10. Lewis Patterson, "Evolving Patterns of Cooperation," *ERIC Higher Education Research Currents* (June 1975), p. 1.

Part 3
The Academic Community

12

Stark Realities:
The Academic Profession in the 1980s[1]
Philip G. Altbach

This essay has a simple theme: the American professoriate has emerged from a period of unprecedented growth and increased status into much less favorable circumstances. It is the purpose of this essay to describe the background and analyze current realities and future prospects. The present is made all the more difficult by the period of affluence and power that preceded it. The professoriate is beset on all sides and finds itself unable to defend its hard-won gains. Declines in enrollments, decreased mobility for academics, demands for fiscal and often for programmatic accountability from government and other authorities, and inflation are all part of the crisis. The prognosis for the future does not hold out much cause for optimism since these trends seem fairly long term in nature. That most academics do not as yet realize the scope of the crisis does not make it any less serious. At present, most academics—with the dramatic exception of younger scholars who are unable to find academic jobs or who cling tenuously to any kind of position—have been insulated from the grim realities of "reduction, reallocation and retrenchment."[2]

Yet, the academic profession is at the very heart of the academic enterprise. Without it, colleges and universities cannot function. Excellence depends on the professoriate. All of the other academic structures that have

been so intricately built up in the past several decades—student affairs offices, administrative hierarchies, and even statewide coordinating boards—
theoretically function to make the central tasks of the faculty—teaching and
research—more effective. The centrality of the role of the professoriate is
often forgotten in the bureaucratized university, and if it is possible to
reassert this centrality, it may be possible to keep at least a portion of the
gains of the recent past and to maintain a long tradition of academic power.

The American academic profession, it must be remembered, is large and
diverse. In 1969, there were 546,000 persons employed in full- or part-time
teaching positions in American colleges and universities. By 1980, the
number increased to 830,000. Only thirty years ago, the academic profession was largely white, male, and Protestant. It has grown increasingly
diverse, with major gains having been made by Catholics and Jews. The
middle-class domination of the profession has weakened somewhat and
women constitute nearly a quarter of the total.[3] Blacks now constitute 4 percent of the profession.[4] Academe is also divided by discipline, type of institution, orientation, and other factors. If anything, it is more difficult to
define, mobilize, or characterize now than at any time in its history.

Precisely because the professoriate finds itself at the center of an increasingly complex institutional nexus, it is subject to pressures from many directions. Increasingly complicated accounting procedures measure professorial
"productivity" but as yet have been unable to consider the basic issue—that
of the educational outcomes of teaching. A deteriorating academic job
market has raised standards for tenure and promotion at the same time that
outlets for scholarly communication, at least in book form, have somewhat
declined. Student "consumerism" in the 1970s and demands for "social
relevance" in the 1960s have disrupted the traditional curriculum and the
professoriate has yet to put the curricular pieces back together. Because the
bulk of the expenditures of any academic institution consists of staff
salaries, the working habits, remuneration, and other aspects of the professoriate have been subjected to increased scrutiny. Legislators demand accountability, administrators seek to create order out of what has traditionally been a disorderly yet creative institution, students make often contradictory demands, and the conditions for academic promotion and
mobility have become less favorable. These are a part of the crisis of the
professoriate.

The academic profession, despite these problems, retains considerable
power over academic institutions and is still a power in its own right.
Disunited, dispirited, and in disarray, the professoriate remains central not
only to the academic function but to the structures of the bureaucratized
university. The curriculum remains basically in the hands of the faculty,
despite some half-hearted efforts to involve students in the 1960s and some
governmental interference. Government involvement has become an increasingly serious issue at all levels in academe. Federal agencies influence

curriculum through grants and awards. State agencies engage in program review and approval and in some ways traditional faculty control has been significantly eroded.

The processes of academic promotion and hiring remain in professorial hands despite "tenure quotas" and bureaucratization strengthened by unions in some institutions. Faculty governance, especially in the established and research-oriented colleges and universities, remains a force to be reckoned with. The department, the basic building block of most academic institutions, remains in the hands of the faculty.

Yet academics have been particularly ineffective in articulating their centrality. Entrenched power, a complicated governance structure, and the weight of tradition have helped to protect academic power in a difficult period. But the professoriate itself has not articulated its own ethos.[5] The rise of academic unions has certainly made a contribution in terms of salaries but has created an adversarial relationship in some institutions.[6] The unions, with the partial exception of the American Association of University Professors, have not defended and articulated the professorial role.[7]

This essay, then, sees the American professoriate in an ambivalent role. Beset from all sides, the faculty nevertheless retains prestige, considerable authority, and a central if often unrecognized role. Academics themselves, insulated to some degree from harsh realities by layers of administration, do not in many cases recognize the nature of the dilemma.[8] If the crisis is to be profitably considered, it must first be placed in context and then analyzed.

The Historical Context

The academic profession has been conditioned by a complex historical development. As E.D. Duryea points out, universities have a long historical tradition and the academic profession, to a considerable degree, is the repository of this tradition.[9] However imperfectly, the professoriate retains a vision of a long historical development. The glories of the medieval universities, of Oxford and Cambridge, and the rise of the German universities are all part of this tradition. The traditions of the academic profession developed slowly.[10] The medieval origins were instrumental for the recognition of the self-governing nature of the professorial community and infused a certain amount of autonomy into the operation of universities. Much later, the reforms in German higher education in the nineteenth century greatly increased the power and prestige of the professoriate, while at the same time linking both the universities and the profession to the state. Professors were civil servants and the universities were expected to contribute to the development of Germany as a modern industrial state. Research, for the first time, became a key element in the role of the universities.[11] The role and status of the academic profession at Oxford and Cambridge in England also had an impact on the American professoriate, since the early American colleges were patterned on British models.[12]

These models, plus academic realities in the United States, helped to shape the academic profession in the United States. For our purposes, the most crucial period of development begins with the rise of the land-grant colleges and of the innovative private universities around the turn of the twentieth century.[13] Several aspects of the development of the modern American university are of crucial importance for the growth of the academic profession. The commitment of the university to public service and to "relevance" meant that academics were, of necessity, involved to some extent with societal issues, with applied aspects of scholarship, and with training for the emerging professions and for skilled occupations involving technology. Following the German lead, the innovative private universities (Chicago, Hopkins, Cornell, and Stanford, soon to be followed by the great state institutions such as Michigan, California, and Wisconsin) emphasized research and graduate training. The doctorate became a requirement for entry into at least the upper reaches of the profession. The prestige of elite universities gradually came to dominate the academic system and the ethos of research, graduate training, and professionalism permeated much of American academe. As these norms and values gradually permeated the American academic enterprise, they have become widespread and form the base of professional values in the 1980s.

The hallmark of the post-World War Two period has been massive growth in higher education. As noted earlier, faculty numbers tripled in a little more than twenty years. Student enrollments grew just as dramatically, with many institutions adding graduate programs. While the dramatic growth of the first three postwar decades has ended, the implications of this growth remain quite important for the academic profession.

It is fair to say that expansion characterized higher education in almost every respect. Growth became the norm, and departments, academic institutions, and individuals based their plans on continued growth. Part of the problem in adjusting to the current period of diminished resources and little growth is the very fact that the previous period was one of unusual expansion. Indeed, it can be argued that the period of postwar growth was the abnormal period and the current situation is more "normal."[14] The legacy of the period of expansion is thus significant.

Expansion has shaped the vision of the academic profession. The postwar period saw unprecedented growth, but it also introduced other changes. The basic fact was a "sellers' market" in which individual academics were able to sell their services at a premium. In almost every field there was a shortage of qualified teachers and researchers.[15] Average academic salaries improved dramatically and the American academic moved from a state of semipenury into the increasingly affluent middle class.[16] The image of Mr. Chips was replaced by the jet-set professor. As universities, and particularly those prestigious graduate-oriented institutions leading the "academic procession," were increasingly involved in research, they had greater access to funds for research.[17] The space program, rapid advances in technology, and a fear in 1958 that the United States was "falling behind" in education all contributed to greater spending by the federal government for higher education. Expansion in enrollments meant that the states invested more in higher education and that the private institutions also prospered.

Academics benefitted substantially from this situation. Those obtaining their doctorates found ready employment, with different institutions often bidding for their services. Rapid career advancement could be expected. Mobility was easy, and an individual faculty member could easily move if dissatisfied with his or her institution. This contributed to diminished institutional loyalty and concern. In order to retain faculty, colleges and universities lowered teaching loads and the average time spent in the classroom declined during this period. Both salaries and fringe benefits increased. Access to research funds from external sources increased substantially, not only in the sciences but also in the social sciences and, to some extent, in the humanities. This development also made academics less dependent on their institutions and gave them an independent source of funds. Those few academics with substantial access to external funds were able to build institutes, centers, and in general to develop "empires" within their institutions.

Rapid expansion also meant unprecedented growth in the profession itself, and this has had lasting implications. An abnormally large cohort of young academics entered professorial ranks in the 1960s. With the end of the period of growth, this large cohort has, in effect, inhibited entry to new entrants and has created a "bulge" of tenured faculty members who will not retire for perhaps twenty years. Many of this cohort participated in the campus turmoil of the 1960s and were affected by it. And many graduated from universities of lesser prestige and may not have been fully socialized into the traditional academic norms and values.

This extraordinarily large academic generation is now causing a variety of problems related to its size, training, and experiences. This generation now dominates the American system. It was socialized at a time when academic conditions were improving, professorial mobility was great, and when rapid advancement was the norm. These expectations were dashed with the changing circumstances of the 1970s, with the result that morale is low and adjustment has been difficult.[18] The size, shape, and opinions of this generation will dominate the profession for another decade or more and is one of the most important legacies of the period of expansion.

A final influence of the recent past is the turmoil of the 1960s. A number of elements converged in the turbulent sixties to produce an unprecedented crisis in American higher education. The university, once peripheral to the society, became a key social institution. It was called on to help solve such social problems as access to education and mobility, and academic experts could be found at the frontier of most every social problem. It is not surprising, therefore, that higher education became involved in the most traumatic crises of that period—the Vietnam war and the civil rights struggle. The antiwar movement emerged from the campuses and was most powerful there.[19]

But the campus crisis went deeper than the antiwar movement, although that was the major stimulant. A new generation of students (and some would argue faculty as well), to an extent unsocialized into the norms of higher education and from a more diverse social-class group, has entered higher education. The faculty, which had turned its attention from undergraduate teaching to research and advanced instruction, allowed the undergraduate curriculum to fall into disarray. Overcrowded facilities were common. And the overwhelming malaise caused by the war, racial unrest, and related social problems produced a powerful combination of discontent.[20] The crisis brought unprecedented, and highly critical, public attention to higher education. The faculty, unable to deal constructively with the crisis and feeling itself under attack from students, the public, and the authorities, was quickly demoralized. Faculty governance structures proved unequal to the task and administrators tried, often without much success, to deal with the crisis. It is fair to say that the crisis of the 1960s left the professoriate demoralized and with a sharply diminished public image. The legacy of this period, in many ways, has been a powerful and generally negative influence on the campus.

The history of the very recent past and the impact of twentieth-century trends have been key influences on the development of the academic profession and have shaped its size, attitudes, training, and orientations. In a sense, American higher education is now reaping the fruits of a complicated but highly eventful series of developments at a time when resources are limited and there is little leeway for maneuver.

The Sociological Context

While this is not an essay on the sociology of complex organizations, it is important to locate the professoriate in its institutional and societal contexts.[21] Academics are at the same time professionals and employees of large bureaucratic organizations. They are certified by obtaining the doctorate and have a self-image that is close to that of independent professionals. Unlike such professionals as physicians and lawyers, academics work in complex organizations—colleges and universities—and are subject to many bureaucratic constraints. The rules and regulations of academic institutions, from stipulations concerning teaching loads to policies concerning the granting of tenure, govern the working lives of the professoriate. Despite the existence, in many institutions, of the infrastructures of collegial self-government, academics in many cases feel increasingly alienated from their institutions. Indeed, with the constraints of the 1980s, this alienation is bound to increase. One of the dilemmas of the coming period is to reconcile traditional ideas of autonomy with the demands of bureaucratic controls.

Academics continue to have considerable autonomy over their basic working conditions. The classroom remains virtually sacrosanct and beyond bureaucratic controls. Except at academic institutions at the low end of the status hierarchy, professors have considerable control over the use of their time outside of the classroom. They choose their own research topics to a considerable degree and, until recently, had considerable geographical mobility. This sense of autonomy, built up carefully over the past half-century and linked to the historical traditions of the profession, has been an important part of the self-image of the profession, especially for the top half of the academic hierarchy.

As colleges and universities have become increasingly bureaucratized and as demands for "accountability" have extended to professorial lives, this sense of autonomy has come under pressure. For one thing, the trend that decreased the average teaching load for academics, evident through the 1960s, has been halted. In addition, administrators, under pressure from governing boards and governmental authorities, have tried to subject academic life to more bureaucratic procedures. Student demands during the 1960s for "relevance" and for better teaching also spurred efforts to "regulate" the professoriate. Without question, there is now considerable tension between the norm (some would say myth) of professional autonomy and a self-image of independence and pressures for accountability and to conform to "rules." There is little doubt that the academic profession will be subjected to increased rules in the coming period as the pressure for financial survival is intensified.

The basic organizational reality of the professoriate engenders a certain amount of ambivalence. Academics, unlike the *privatdozent* of the traditional German university, do not depend directly on student fees for their survival.[22] They are employed by institutions and, in the case of the public colleges and universities, are only quite indirectly dependent for their promotion, professional status, or income on their direct role—teaching. Basic judgments on such crucial matters as promotion and tenure and, at least traditionally, on salary increments, have been more related to research and publication than to teaching (at least in the universities) and such decisions are generally made by academic peers. Yet, important academic decisions are reviewed by a bewildering assortment of committees, administrators, and ultimately by governing boards. Increasingly, these levels of legal authority are becoming more important as arbiters of academic decision making. The ambivalance has always been present,but it was muted during the period of the rise of professorial power. At present, what might be seen as the inherent contradictions in the academic role are becoming more apparent.

Professorial myths—of collegial decision making, individual autonomy, and of the disinterested pursuit of knowledge—have come increasingly into conflict with the realities of complex organizational structures and bureaucracies. While many of the fondest dreams of the profession came close to reality during period of postwar growth, some have argued that increasingly close links to external funding agencies diminished autonomy through the selective granting of research funds.[23] The tension between self-perception and the historical tradition of autonomy on the one hand and the realities of work in a complex organization, particularly in a period of considerable stress, on the other is one of the important conflicts faced by the academic profession.

The American academic system is enmeshed in a series of complex hierarchies. These hierarchies, framed by discipline, institution, rank, and speciality, help to determine working conditions, prestige, and in many ways one's orientation to the profession. As David Riesman pointed out two decades ago, American academe is a "meandering procession" dominated by the prestigious graduate schools and ebbing downward through other universities, four-year colleges, and finally to the community college system.[24] Most of this procession attempts to follow the norms, and the fads, of the prestigious graduate institutions. Prestige is defined by how close an institution, or an individual professor, comes to the norm of publication and research, of participation in the "cosmopolitan" role of links to a national profession rather than to "local" institutional norms.[25] While some segments of the academic system, such as the community colleges, have few links to the prestigious "national" universities, the system as a whole is characterized by adherence, at least in form, to national norms. Even in periods of fiscal constraint, the hold of the traditional academic models remains very strong indeed. Within institutions, academics are also enmeshed in a hierarchical system, with the crucial differences between tenured and untenured staff a key to the hierarchy. Disciplines are also ranked into hierarchies, with the traditional academic specialties in the arts and sciences along with medicine, and, to some extent, law. Other applied fields, such as education, agriculture, and others are considerably lower on the scale. These hierarchies are very much a part of the realities of the academic profession.

Just as the realities of postwar expansion shaped academic organizations by reducing teaching loads, increasing the prestige of the professoriate, and, in many institutions, expanding the power of the profession over working conditions, internal governance, and the direction of higher education, altered circumstances will inevitably change the organizational and sociological aspects of academic life in ways that will affect the professoriate. For example, there has been a noticeable rise in administrative authority as the professoriate has lost some of its bargaining position. Colleges and universities have increasingly turned to part-time faculty as a means of maintaining institutional flexibility and avoiding granting tenure. As academic institutions adjust to a period of declining resources, there will be subtle organizational shifts that will inevitably work against the perquisites of the academic profession. Universities, as organizations, adjust to changing realities and these adjustments will work against the professoriate.

The Realities of the 1980s

There is little question but that the American professoriate is in a period of difficulty, and that prospects for the immediate future do not seem especially favorable. Yet, the profession retains many of its hard-won gains and the basic configuration of American higher education is unlikely to change dramatically. It is the purpose of this section to describe some of the realities of the current period, with particular stress on the relationship of the academic profession to the internal dynamic of colleges and universities and the impact of the broader society.[26]

Demographic changes and the decline of community

The professoriate has not only expanded in recent years, but it has substantially altered its composition. Without question, the "age bulge," which has been discussed earlier, is a reality of coming decades.[27] Fewer retirements, little mobility, and, as a consequence, growing dissatisfaction may be the hallmarks of this generation of academics.[28] Not only is the academic labor market very limited to entrants (creating severe problems for new doctoral-degree holders and preventing a younger generation of scholars from developing) but current faculty members find their prospects for mobility severely limited. In recent years, an academic dissatisfied with his or her circumstances could often find another position. At least there was a myth of ready mobility. This provided a safety valve for both individuals and institutions. Will academics limited in their options become, in Gouldner's terms, "locals" and concern themselves less with professional and "cosmopolitan" matters?[29] Fewer entry-level positions inevitably mean declines in graduate student enrollments, particularly in fields that largely depend on the academic employment market. According to some demographic projections, there will be another shortage of trained doctorates sometime toward the end of this century, causing different but nonetheless serious strains on the profession and on postsecondary institutions.[30] Complicated demographic pressures are a serious cause for concern.

Not only has the profession expanded, but it has changed in its composition. The largely white Protestant configuration of American academics has yielded to an influx of minorities and women. Jews and Catholics entered the profession in larger numbers than ever before following World War II.[31] More recently, and in part in response to the civil rights movement, the women's movement, and affirmative action pressures, the numbers of racial minorities and women have also increased. These developments have changed the nature of the profession. No longer is there a generally held consensus about the values and norms of the profession. There is more diversity and sometimes dispute among academics. Resistance, particularly to affirmative action, has been widespread, and it has been heightened by the deteriorating job market.[32] Differences in attitudes and orientations are evident among academics of different ages, institutions, and disciplines. Social scientists tend to be more liberal than those in professional schools. Those in high-prestige institutions are more liberal than those lower on the academic pecking order. Commitments to teaching and research vary. Women tend to have slightly different orientations toward the profession than men.[33] Variations within the profession have made a common viewpoint difficult, if not impossible.

Sheer size has also made community more difficult. As institutions have grown to include well over 1,000 academic staff and have substituted elected senates and other governance arrangements for the traditional general faculty meeting, a sense of community has become more difficult. Even academic departments in larger American universities can number up to fifty teaching staff. Committees have become ubiquitous and the sense of participation in the academic enterprise has declined. The bureaucratization discussed earlier has also contributed to this decline in a sense of community. This has been paralleled at the national level, where at one time the American Association of University Professors spoke for a relatively united profession. Now, the AAUP is challenged by such organizations as the American Federation of Teachers and the National Education Association, as well as a range of large and articulate groups representing the various academic disciplines.

Tenure and unions

The rise of the academic union movement is a direct reflection of the pressures on the academic profession. As the professoriate has seen its economic status eroded (after more than a decade of substantial gains in "real income," academic salaries began to decline in terms of actual purchasing power in the early 1970s), professional prerogatives threatened by bureaucratization and, in general, perquisites and autonomy less secure, sections of the profession turned to unions as a means of protecting status and advantages. It is fair to say that the American professoriate has turned to unionization reluctantly, and despite present difficulties, academic unions remain quite rare in the prestigious institutions. The number of campuses represented by academic unions was 682 in 1980. Of this number 254 were four-year institutions. This constituted about 17.8 percent of the 3,055 academic institutions in the United States. If community colleges are excluded, only 10.8 percent are unionized. Further, none of the members of the prestigious Association of American Universities was unionized. Thus, while academic unions tend to be concentrated in the middle and lower tiers of the system, the union movement has been one of the major responses to deteriorating conditions and uncertainties experienced by the profession. The growth of the academic union movement has slowed in the past few years, probably as a response to the realization that unions have been unable to solve the basic problems of the profession. The recent Supreme Court decision in the *Yeshiva* case, which makes unionization at private institutions quite difficult, will further inhibit the expansion of the movement. Despite recent setbacks, academic unions are a lasting and important part of the contemporary postsecondary education scene. Their rise has been directly related to the problems experienced by the academic profession in the past decade.

Unions were, in the early period, quite effective in raising salaries, but they have been less successful in protecting professional concerns. The worries of many academics have turned from purely economic issues to matters of protecting job security, tenure, and the like. To date, academic unions have been only marginally successful in such matters. Neither the rhetoric of the American Association of University Professors nor the trade-union tactics of the American Federation of Teachers has kept academic institutions, and sometimes legislatures, from raising teaching loads and in general contributing to a deterioration in academic life-styles.

Tenure has been very much related to the rise of the union movement and with efforts to maintain job security.[34] Originally intended to protect the academic freedom of individual academics, the tenure system has grown to represent the key means of promoting academics and then granting them permanent employment. The tenure system has come under attack from a number of quarters. It has become more difficult for an assistant professor to attain tenure (and usually promotion to associate professor) as standards have been raised. The system, which at one time protected junior staff by indicating a maximum number of years that one could remain in a lower academic rank, now places immense pressure on assistant professors to meet promotion criteria within six years. In addition, a growing number of institutions have instituted tenure quotas in an effort to maintain a balance between the various academic ranks. This places additional pressures on junior staff.

Retrenchment—the firing of academic staff without regard to tenure—has been one of the major fears of academics.[35] Institutions, under increasing pressure from declining enrollments, fiscal cutbacks, and changing student interests, have tried to cut costs and to reallocate academic resources to meet a changing market. Academic institutions have engaged in retrenchment only after careful consideration and, so far, rather infrequently. But there has been some retrenchment, and in a number of institutions, cuts have been made without regard to tenure, seniority, or other traditional protectors of job security. Institutions have eliminated departments or programs with relative impunity.[36] The courts have generally ruled that colleges and universities have the right to engage in this kind of reallocation of resources or response to fiscal crisis without regard to the protection of tenure but have demanded a careful definition of fiscal exigency. Thus, the traditional protection of the tenure system for permanent academic appointment has been severely vitiatiated by the problems of the 1970s and 1980s, and academics are beginning to realize that they have, in fact, relatively few legal protections for their job security.

There is no doubt that the intertwined issues of the growth of academic unions, the protection of traditional tenure and the related concept of academic freedom, and the general decline in the status and standards of academic life will have an impact. Some have raised the question that if it is possible for administrators or governing boards to fire professors for fiscal exigency, can the financial issue be used to make firings for other reasons? The issues are complex and, without question, place additional strains on the academic profession. What was once a profession with considerable job security has become much less secure in terms of employment. While most academics at present have few fears of losing their jobs, there is little doubt that the realities of the 1980s will bring a consciousness of insecurity more to the profession.

Accountability and autonomy

Academics have traditionally had a high degree of autonomy, particularly in their classrooms and research, and only minimal accountability. While most academics are only dimly aware of it, the thrust toward accountability has begun to affect their professional lives. It is likely that this trend will intensify. Institutions, often impelled in the case of public universities by state budget offices, require an increasingly large amount of data concerning faculty work, research productivity, the expenditure of funds for ancillary support, and other aspects of academic life. What is more, criteria for student-faculty ratios, levels of financial support for different types of postsecondary education and for productivity of academic staff have been established. The new sources of data permit fiscal authorities to monitor closely how institutions meet established criteria and adjustments in financial allocations are then quickly implemented. Most of these aspects of accountability are only indirectly perceived by most academics, but they nonetheless have a considerable impact on the operation of universities and colleges, since resources are allocated on the basis of formulas that are measured through the new means of accountability.

If autonomy is the opposite side of the accountability coin, then one would expect academic autonomy to have significantly declined. But, at least on the surface, this has not as yet happened in the United States. Basic academic decisions remain in the hands of departments for the most part, and individual faculty members, despite some pressure and a few changes, have not felt basic change in this area. Most academics retain most of the sense of autonomy that has characterized the past several decades, although many are beginning to worry. Yet, some change is evident, particularly in the less prestigious sector of postsecondary education. There have been pressures on academics in low-enrollment fields to participate in retraining programs. Pressure to have a minimum number of students in class has increased in many institutions. Academic planning, traditionally far removed from the individual professor and seldom impinging on one's academic career, has become somewhat more of a reality as institutions seek to streamline their operation and worry more about enrollments. Yet, basic individual autonomy remains fairly strong.

Academic freedom

Compared to the 1950s, American higher education enjoys a fairly high degree of academic freedom. There have been few public pressures aimed at ensuring political or intellectual conformity from professors and the concept of academic freedom seems to be fairly well entrenched. Even during the politically volatile period of the Vietnam war, few questioned the rights of academics to speak out on the war or related political issues.[37] There is little evidence that retrenchment, tenure quotas, and the like have been used in any substantial way for political motives. There have been few calls, from government officials or the public, for "loyalty" from the campus. Thus, it would seem, at least for the present, that the multiple crisis of the "steady state" have not substantially impinged on the academic freedom of the professoriate.

Students

The two basic elements of the academic equation are students and faculty. Students have greatly affected the current status of the academic profession. Increases in student numbers during the 1950s and 1960s were, of course, the major cause for change at that period. Recently, declines in enrollments at some institutions and changes in the configuration of student interest in many colleges and universities have greatly affected the academic profession. During the 1960s, the student activist movement had several impacts on the professoriate. For the first time, militant students attacked the university and the academic profession, and this demoralized many academics. Demands for relevance in the curriculum, for political consciousness and participation by professors, and for "participation" in governance all related to the profession. Despite considerable pressure, campus unrest, and demonstrations, the lasting impact of the student movement on the American university has been minimal.[38] Yet, the effect on the morale of the faculty can hardly be overestimated. Many academics felt guilty about their lack of involvement and lost confidence in the traditional curriculum. Administrative handling of student protest polarized and disoriented the faculty.

In the late 1970s, student interests and concerns changed, but their impact on the academic profession continues.[39] Changing student interests and concern with vocational rather than social relevance have meant a substantial shift in student academic interests. While students have not been interested in activist or ideological politics, they have been concerned with environmental issues, and with matters directly concerning their own special interests. The academic profession has regained some of its self-confidence, and the current interest at many institutions in the reform of the undergraduate curriculum is an indication of this trend among academics.

Students have a direct and indirect impact on academics. Student interests and attitudes affect the classroom and enrollments in different fields of study. Student opinions of the faculty affect morale and orientations. And a highly political atmosphere on campus, as existed during the 1960s, engendered a sympathetic reaction among some academics and concern among most.

Conclusion

The portrait presented in this essay is not a very optimistic one. The academic profession has been under considerable pressure but it is basically intact. Some of the gains made during the postwar period of expression have been lost but such losses are probably inevitable in view of the changed circumstances, the deterioration in the employment market, and economic problems for higher education. Further, comparisons with the period of unprecedented expansion during the 1950s and 1960s heighten the sense of crisis since this was an era of unprecedented and abnormal growth that benefitted the academic profession.

The professoriate stands at the center of any academic institution and in a way is insulated from direct interaction with the many of higher education's external constituencies. Academics do not generally deal with trustees, legislatures, or parents. Their concerns are with their own teaching and research, and with their direct academic surroundings, such as the department. Yet, these constituencies have a major effect on the careers and conditions of the academic profession.

- A decline in federal research expenditures has made research funds in many fields very difficult to obtain.

- Financial difficulties for scholarly publishers have reduced the opportunities for book publishing, thereby placing added stress on younger scholars who are faced with ever higher qualifications for tenure and promotion.

- Students have turned to vocational interests and their curricular choices have caused strains in such fields as business, engineering, and pre-medicine and have severely curtailed enrollments in foreign languages and the social sciences.

- Demands for accountability for expenditures from governmental authorities and elsewhere have inevitably extended to measuring faculty productivity in various ways.

- Fiscal problems combined with stable or even declining enrollments in many academic institutions have caused major financial problems for higher education, affecting the faculty in reduced travel budgets, sometimes higher teaching loads, and salary increases that have not kept pace with inflation.

- In a climate of increased accountability, academic administrators have gained increasing power over their institutions and, inevitably, over the lives of the professoriate.

- A decline in public esteem for higher education, triggered first by the unrest of the 1960s and enhanced by widespread questioning of the academic benefits of a college degree, has caused additional strees for academics and has contributed to financial exigencies.

- The academic employment market permits relatively few younger scholars to enter the profession and promises to reduce further salaries and limit mobility for those currently in the profession.

Given all of these stresses and the variety of forces, within and outside of the colleges and universities, combining to weaken the status of the academic profession, it is surprising that the basic working conditions of American academics have remained relatively stable. The basic structure of postsecondary education remains virtually unchanged despite many pressures for reform. Academic freedom, despite some challenges, remains largely intact. Despite criticisms of the tenure system, and its increasingly weak legal basis, most tenured academics can have a reasonable assurance of lifetime employment. Academics retain basic control over the curriculum, generally control their academic departments, and have a reasonable influence on institutional governance. Thus, despite serious problems, the profession remains intact as it enters the 1980s. The future does not hold promise of much improvement, but if the academic profession can maintain its self-confidence and a vision of quality and the academic role, it has a good chance to maintain itself in a period of considerable difficulty.

Without question, the "glory days" of the postwar period will not reappear in the near future. A combinaton of circumstances including demographic changes, increasingly conservative policy makers at both the state and federal levels who do not see education as a high priority, a decline in the public esteem given to higher education, and less stress on research as a national priority directly affects colleges and universities and the professoriate. How, then, can academics face the challenges of the coming period?

At one level, the academic profession needs to effectively represent its interests to external constituencies. Most academic unions have taken on the tactics and rhetoric of traditional trade unions and tend not to work with university representatives in an effort to convince the public of the value of higher education and of the key role and importance of the profession. Curiously, only the American Association of University Professors has effectively retained a professional image, and it has lost some of its membership. At the same time, unions do have a role in attempting to protect the hard-won prerogatives of the profession. Academic unions, a relatively new phenomenon, have not fully developed an articulate approach to issues of academic governance, representation of the faculty, and a public stance helpful to higher education. The unions are a powerful new force in higher education. If they can effectively represent the professoriate to the various external constituencies, they can play a powerful role.

The profession mostly reacted to the challenges of the postwar period. It was glad to accept more responsibilities, move into research, and take money from external agencies. It dropped much of its responsibility to students (at least in the universities) as research came to dominate the academic scene. The curriculum lost its coherence in the rush toward specialization. Now, it is necessary to develop a central thrust to the academic enterprise and to restore a sense of mission. The current "general education" movement may be a move in this direction. It is always more difficult to induce change as a result of conscious planning and concern than it is to react to external circumstance. But the present period demands that the profession examine closely its mission and role.

Notes

1. I am indebted to Lionel Lewis, Robert Berdahl, and S. Gopinathan for their comments on an earlier draft of this essay. For further discussion of these themes, see Philip G. Altbach, "The Crisis of the Professoriate," *Annals of the American Academy of Political and Social Science* 448 (March 1980), pp. 1-14.

2. Kenneth P. Mortimer and Michael I. Tierney, *The Three R's of the Eighties: Reduction, Reallocation and Retrenchment* (Washington, D.C.: American Association for Higher Education, 1979).

3. It is significant that, despite affirmative action programs, the proportion of women in the academic profession has not increased markedly in the past half-century.

4. See Verne A. Stadtman, *Academic Adaptations* (San Francisco: Jossey-Bass, 1980), pp. 46-74 for an overview of the academic profession.

5. Edward Shils, "The Academic Ethos Under Strain," *Minerva* 13 (Spring 1975), pp. 1-37.

6. Robert Birnbaum, "Unionization and Faculty Compensation: Part II," *Educational Record* 57 (Spring 1976), p. 116-118.

7. See E.D. Duryea and R.S. Fisk, eds., *Faculty Unions and Collective Bargaining* (San Francisco: Jossey-Bass, 1973) and E.C. Ladd, Jr. and S.M. Lipset, *Professors, Unions and American Higher Education* (Berkeley, Calif.: Carnegie Commission on Higher Education, 1973).

8. E.C. Ladd Jr., and S.M. Lipset, *The Divided Academy: Professors and Politics* (New York: McGraw-Hill, 1975).

9. E.D. Duryea, "The University and the State: A Historical Overview," in this volume, pp. 13-34.

10. See A.B. Cobban, *The Medieval Universities* (London: Methuen, 1975), pp. 196-217.

11. Joseph Ben-David and Awraham Zloczwer, "Universities and Academic Systems in Modern Societies," *European Journal of Sociology* 3, no. 1 (1962), pp. 45-84.

12. Frederick Rudolph, *The American College and University: A History* (New York: Vintage, 1965).

13. For a comprehensive view of the development of the modern American university, see Laurence R. Veysey, *The Emergence of the American University* (Chicago: University of Chicago Press, 1965).

14. This theme is developed at greater length in David Henry, *Challenges Past, Challenges Present* (San Francisco: Jossey-Bass, 1975).

15. The academic job market of this period is captured well in Theodore Caplow and Reece McGee, *The Academic Marketplace* (New York: Basic Books, 1958).

16. See Logan Wilson, *American Academics, Then and Now* (New York: Oxford University Press, 1979).

17. Jacques Barzun, in a chapter entitled "Scholars in Orbit," has some biting comments on jet-set faculty. See Jacques Barzun, *The American University* (New York: Harper and Row, 1968).

18. See Landon Y. Jones, *Great Expectations: America and the Baby Boom Generation* (New York: Coward, McCann and Geoghean, 1980) for a general discussion of the impact of the baby boom of the post-World War Two period.

19. The turmoil of the 1960s is covered well in S.M. Lipset, *Rebellion in the University* (Chicago: University of Chicago Press, 1976) and in Michael W. Miles, *The Radical Probe* (New York: Atheneum, 1971). Faculty activism is discussed in Edward E. Ericson, Jr., *Radicals in the University* (Stanford, Calif.: Hoover Institution Press, 1975).

20. See David Riesman and Verne Stadtman, eds., *Academic Transformation: Seventeen Institutions Under Pressure* (New York: McGraw-Hill, 1973).

21. For a broader discussion of these themes, see Talcott Parsons and Gerald M. Platt, *The American University* (Cambridge, Mass.: Harvard University Press, 1973).

22. In the traditional German universities, the rank of *privatdozent* was given to academics who were paid directly by their students. If few students attended lectures, income was very limited. In a sense, the increasing numbers of part-time teachers in American higher

education are perhaps linked to this marginal academic role. See Alexander Busch, "The Vicissitudes of the Privatdozent," *Minerva* 1 (Spring 1963), pp. 319-341.

23. Robert Nisbet has argued in *The Degradation of the Academic Dogma* (New York: Basic Books, 1971), that academe has suffered greatly because it gave up its basic orientation toward disinterested teaching and scholarship in order to gain the advantages of government and foundation largesse. Autonomy, he argues, was lost at that point. For a somewhat similar argument from a different point of view, see Edward T. Silva and Sheila Slaughter, "Prometheus Bound: The Limits of Social Science Professionalization in the Progressive Period," *Theory and Society* 9 (1980), pp. 781-819.

24. David Riesman, "The Academic Procession," in D. Riesman, *Constraint and Variety in American Education* (Garden City, N.Y.: Doubleday, 1958), pp. 25-65.

25. Alvin Gouldner, "Cosmopolitans and Locals: Toward an Analysis of Latent Social Roles, I and II," *Administrative Science Quarterly* 2 (December 1957 and March 1958), pp. 281-303 and 445-467.

26. For an overview, see Carol Herrnstadt Shulman, *Old Expectations, New Realities: The Academic Profession Revisited* (Washington, D.C.: American Association for Higher Education, 1979).

27. See Landon Y Jones, *Great Expectations.*

28. At least at one major university, there has been an influx of professors entering law school. The meaning of this development is unclear, but it might well signal a dissatisfaction with academe.

29. Alvin Gouldner, "Cosmopolitans and Locals."

30. The data on this topic is mixed and, given the accuracy of previous projections, subject to considerable question.

31. Stephen Steinberg, *The Academic Melting Pot: Catholics and Jews in American Higher Education* (New York: McGraw-Hill, 1974).

32. E.C. Ladd, Jr. and S.M. Lipset, *The Divided Academy,* discuss the variations in opinions and values of the academic profession.

33. See Oliver Fulton, "Rewards and Fairness: Academic Women in the United States," in *Teachers and Students,* Martin Trow, ed. (New York: McGraw-Hill, 1975), pp. 199-248. See also Bonnie Cook Freeman, "Faculty Women in the American University: Up the Down Staircase," *Higher Education* 6 (May 1977), pp. 165-188.

34. Bardwell Smith, ed., *The Tenure Debate* (San Francisco: Jossey-Bass, 1973).

35. See Marjorie C. Mix, *Tenure and Termination in Financial Exigency* (Washington, D.C.: American Association for Higher Education, 1978).

36. Kenneth P. Mortimer and Michael Tierney, *Three R's of the Eighties.*

37. The record, of course, is not entirely spotless. The firing of Bruce Franklin at Stanford University, for example, was a case in which both the political views—and the political actions—of a faculty member were called into question. A number of junior faculty were not given tenure during this period because of their antiwar activism as well. See Joseph Fashing and Steven F. Deutsch, *Academics in Retreat* (Albuquerque, N.M.: University of New Mexico Press, 1971).

38. Alexander W. Astin, et al., *The Power of Protest* (San Francisco: Jossey-Bass, 1975).

39. For a discussion of the current student scene, see Arthur Levine, *When Dreams and Heroes Die* (San Francisco: Jossey-Bass, 1980). See also Arthur Levine, "The College Student: A Changing Constituency," in this volume, pp. 239-251.

13

The College Student:
A Changing Constituency
Arthur Levine

Today's college students are different from the students who attended our universities only a little over a decade ago. First of all, there are more of them. Their number has increased from a little under 8 million in 1969 to 11.7 million currently, a rise of 42 percent.[1]

Second, their enrollment patterns have changed. Many more students than in the past are attending school part-time, in excess of 40 percent today. The majority of undergraduates work in addition to going to college. Two out of every five are enrolled in nighttime classes. And transfer and drop-out rates have risen appreciably. In short, current students are more mobile, less tied to a single institution, and college is a less central part of their lives.[2]

Third, the composition of the student body has changed. High-achieving young people from wealthier families with better educated parents are, as in the 1960s, most likely to attend college. However, increases have been registered in the proportion of students from traditionally underrepresented minority groups—blacks, women, the handicapped, and adults twenty-five years of age and over, among others.[3] Today's students are, as a result, more diverse in needs and more diverse in desires than their predecessors.

Fourth and finally, student character has changed. When student personnel administrators from nearly 600 colleges and universities were given a list of 52 words and phrases and asked to describe how students on their campuses had changed since 1969-70, they said that today's students were more career-oriented, better groomed, more concerned with material success, more concerned with self, and more practical.[4] Today's undergraduates want slightly different things out of life than the generation of the sixties and, as a consequence, they are demanding somewhat different things of college.

These changes are important. Their ramifications extend not only to the campus, but to the publics of higher education as well.

The Politics of a Changing Constituency

Today's college students are politically estranged. The majority came of age in the period in which Lyndon Johnson's dream of a "Great Society" died and Richard Nixon's nightmare of Watergate came to life. They witnessed the assassinations of national leaders and youth heroes, the burning of our cities, the fighting of an unpopular war in Asia, the revelation of illegal deeds by government agencies, the resignation of a president and vice-president for criminal acts, persistent economic woes, and continuing international crises. When today's students are asked what social or historical events most influenced their thinking, they answer Watergate and Vietnam.

There is a sense among today's undergraduates that things are falling apart, that there is nothing left to hold onto. This year's entering freshmen believe that all social institutions from large corporations to the church are at least somewhat immoral or dishonest.[5] To escape this horror, students, like much of the rest of the country, are turning inward. For many, the one remaining refuge is "me." If one were trying to characterize the politics of the current college generation on and off campus, "the politics of me" would appear to be an accurate description.

Other, more traditional political perspectives are fading. Between 1969 and 1979, the percentage of freshmen who considered it essential or very important to keep up with political affairs dropped from 51 percent to 38 percent. Student commitment to radical politics has diminished. Undergraduates are more moderate today. Relative to 1969, fewer students classify themselves as left of center or right of center. Most locate themselves exactly in the middle.

On off-campus issues, this shift has been translated into more traditionally conservative stances. Today, more students are likely to advocate the death penalty, less coddling of criminals, alternatives to busing, and increased concern for majority rights. Exactly the opposite has happened with respect to campus issues. On these topics, students are apt to oppose censorship of student publications, bans on extremist speakers, institutional regulation of student behavior, and compulsory public service for students.[6]

There is no conflict in these positions. On the campus issues, student opinions reflect an increasing interest in protecting their rights, just as on external issues they show a lower tolerance for those who might infringe upon their rights. A case in point is affirmative action, particularly in regard to preferential treatment for the disadvantaged in college admissions. Concern with racism on campus is down; fewer students believe special rules should govern minority programs. Fewer undergraduates today are likely to favor the administration of black studies programs by blacks, the relaxation of admission standards for minority undergraduates, and the reduction of hiring standards for minority faculty. Four out of five want exactly the same standards .of evaluation employed for themselves and for academically disadvantaged students admitted to college with lower test scores and grades under one affirmative action program or another.[7] This is the one campus issue on which students are now less traditionally liberal than in the sixties. The rationale for the change is that preferential admissions are injurious to majority students, reducing their likelihood of being admitted to a selective college and making it more difficult for them to gain admission to highly rated professional schools in medicine, law, or business. When this issue went to the U.S. Supreme Court in the case of *Bakke* vs. *Regents of the University of California*, the majority of the nine University of California campus newspapers, including the Berkeley paper, printed editorials favoring the Bakke or anti-affirmative action position. This raised eyebrows all over the country. It should not have. It's simply a reflection of the "politics of me."

Political Attitudes and Activity

Today there are more college students than steel workers, coal miners, automobile workers, needle workers, and farmers combined.[8] This makes students not only one of the larger interest groups, but also one of the potentially strongest voting blocks in the country. Passage of the Twenty-sixth Amendment to the U.S. Constitution in 1971 enfranchised nearly half of America's college students aged eighteen to twenty, who previously lacked the vote. This right has now been extended to state and local elections in at least forty-four states.

Prior to the change, particularly in the aftermath of the Eugene McCarthy presidential campaign in 1968, which had been propelled by an army of college student volunteers, there was speculation that eighteen-year-old suffrage would radically alter the face of national politics. This has not happened.

Part of the reason is that the vote was extended to all eighteen-year-olds, not just to the third attending institutions of higher education. Consequently, even though a majority of college students (53 percent) gave their votes to Jimmy Carter in 1976, the majority of eighteen-year-olds cast ballots for Gerald Ford.[9] There is enormous diversity among young people, and that diversity is more powerful in politics than any shared youth culture.

Diversity is a reality among college students as well. Campuses vary widely in political orientation. While 76 percent of the students at the University of California, Santa Cruz voted for Carter, 86 percent of the students at Brigham Young voted for Ford. Even within a single college, there are extreme differences between subgroups. For instance, at Berkeley only 28 percent of all students voted for Ford, but a majority of fraternity members favored him. When taken in aggregate, though, it is fair to say that student voters are somewhat left of the country and that there is a general tendency for them to support more liberal candidates and issues.[10]

College students favor the Democratic party over the Republican party about two to one, but the number of independents—people choosing no party affiliation—is growing. In contrast to other young people, who have the lowest voter registration rate (44 percent) of any age group in the country, college students register and vote in proportions comparable to the general population. This means, though, that at least 40 percent of the nation's college students, numbering some four million people, sat out the 1976 presidential election.[11]

The impact of the college students' vote has not been felt nationally, but it has been at the local level. Student enrollment exceeds the incumbents' margin of victory in ninety-one U.S. Congressional districts in thirty-three states.[12] One can only guess how many local- or state-elected positions students may control. According to college administrators, more political candidates than ever before are coming to campus to ask students for their votes. In fact, some student leaders complain that during election time "the place is crawling with candidates." It is this phenomenon that gives newly emerging student lobbies much of their strength with state legislators. It explains why these groups compile and publish individual legislator profiles, regularly engage in voter registration drives, and work so hard to overturn state barriers to student registration. And it also makes clear why at least two state student lobbies can confidently claim that they have legislators who will introduce any bill they draft.

Campus interviews reveal, however, that the student vote may be soft. Most students believe that they should vote and that voting probably makes some difference. Yet a substantial minority view their enfranchisement as a chore—a civic obligation or "hassle" they would feel guilty about neglecting. For these young people, voting has become ritualistic, and they have become marginal voters. Many are alienated from politics and share a sense that rhetoric, advertising, duplicity, and politics as usual are invincible.

This alienation does not mix well with voting motivated largely by recollections of civic lessons learned long ago. It seems in the future that one or the other will give way.

From Ideological Politics to Interest Group Advocacy

Hand in hand with these changes in off-campus politics has come a decline in ideological politics of all types—left, right, and center. Students for a Democratic Society (SDS), the best known and most visible of the 1960s campus groups, is gone. Less well-known leftist organizations, such as the Spartacus League, Young People's Socialist League, and the Communist Party, though still alive, are found on fewer campuses. This is also true of such conservative groups as Young Americans for Freedom and the John Birch Society. More traditional and mainstream political associations have also lost ground, most notably the college branches of the Democratic and Republican parties, which have a shadowy presence on the nation's campuses and come alive, if at all, only during election periods.[13]

These groups are being replaced, at a fast pace, by a very different style of political organization, one that is more compatible with the current student mood. These are self-interest or me-oriented groups, concerned with protecting or improving the lot of a single class of people, be they blacks, women, Hispanics, gays, or Native Americans. Some of the groups are old and familiar, others are new, but they all appear to be growing.

Student government officials and campus newspaper editors at twenty-six colleges describe these groups, particularly the oldest of them—black student associations—as among the most powerful or influential organizations at their schools. Only student government is mentioned more frequently. And remarkably, student newspapers and fraternities and sororities are cited less often.

Self-interest groups tend to be closed in character. Whites, for example, know little about black student associations and men are ignorant about the workings of women's groups. Self-interest groups are small in size, with a core membership generally numbering less than a score and seldom exceeding fifty on campuses of any size. Like ideological political groups, self-interest associations are fragile and subject to phoenixlike appearances and disappearances with changes in leadership. Mitosis or splitting is also a problem, with the spirit of me-ism encouraging the formation of smaller and smaller groups. The University of Oregon, for example, has six or seven women's groups. At another institution, black women have split from the black student's association, and the science majors have left the black women's group to form a black women scientists' club.

The activities of self-interest groups are of four principal types—service, political action, education and consciousness raising, and entertainment. By way of illustration, the service activities of women's groups at twenty-six schools in which they were examined are extensive, ranging from counseling, medical assistance, and rape prevention to neighborhood support groups, daycare, and tutoring. Their on- and off-campus political activities run the gamut from litigation, lobbying, and support for political candidates to plain, old-fashioned demonstrations and righteous indignation in support of such causes as daycare, the equal rights amendment, jobs, and women's recruitment. Consciousness raising, education, and entertainment overlapped, but included such tried-and-true activities as lectures, films, concerts, and school newspaper articles, as well as such novel approaches as coffee houses and women's days or weeks.

Program quality and success depend very much on the leadership, membership, and political persuasion of the individual groups, but by and large the self-interest groups have been much more visible and well financed than their size would seem to warrant. Though quite a few women's groups are inactive, student government officials and newspaper editors praise many for their political sophistication and easy access to institutional administrators. Some are described as moribund or only "a place to go and gripe," while others are credited with substantive accomplishments, such as making a campus more aware of sexism, forcing an institution to upgrade affirmative action, stopping a fraternity pornographic film festival and wet T-shirt contest, and getting an on-campus nurse practitioner hired.

Continuation of Student Protest

Gone is the din of the preceding decade's student unrest, and the relative quiet of today has inspired a wave of nostalgia pieces about the activists of yesteryear and a sheaf of obituaries and explanations for the death of student protest. But reports of its demise are premature.

It is true that, relative to the 1960s, the number and intensity of student protests have decreased. Officials at three out of every four institutions that were able to compare activity in 1969 and 1978 reported a decline. The proportion of students participating in demonstrations has also fallen, from 28 percent in 1969 to 19 percent in 1976.[14]

However, the fact that in 1976 one out of five undergraduates had taken part in a demonstration is certainly tangible proof that student unrest is far from dead.

The fact of the matter is that there has been a dramatic change in the nature of the student unrest since the late 1960s. There's been a sharp shift in the protest issues. In 1969, the three most frequent causes of unrest were Vietnam, minority rights, and rules of student conduct. In 1978, they were student fees, institutional facilities, and faculty or staff hiring and firing. The emphasis has changed from primarily external issues to seemingly more me-oriented internal campus issues.[15]

Changes in protest tactics have been at least as dramatic as shifts in the issues. What stands out here is the decline in use of tactics familiar from the sixties—building takeovers, strikes, demonstrations, and the destruction of property. What has taken its place are litigation and tactics ranging from lobbying and use of grievance procedures to educating the public and fellow students via seminars and research reports. These are activities more attuned to the current era, when students see less justification for violence, interruption of college classes, or even demonstrations on campus. These activities are also more practical, more individually oriented, more suitable to causes lacking popular support, and less risky.[16]

Student litigation and serious threats of lawsuits have increased on more than one-third of the nation's campuses (35 percent). Even more startling, at the most prestigious research universities, nearly three out of every four schools report increases.[17] In fact, student bodies at a number of institutions from coast to coast have hired staff lawyers or created legal services offices. This development has encouraged what might be called student-interest litigation. For example, at the University of Massachusetts, under the state's Freedom of Information Act, the student legal services office named all department chairpersons and deans in a suit attempting to obtain the release of student course questionnaires filled out by students and used by departments for evaluation purposes. The Student Litigation Organization at Pennsylvania State University filed a class-action suit seeking a refund for classes cancelled because of bad weather. And the student senate at Southern Oregon University, assisted by student governments at several other Oregon institutions, filed a suit charging that certain students given low grades had been evaluated unfairly and had not been duly informed of the grading criteria.[18]

Developments in student lobbying have been at least as far-reaching. The 1970s witnessed the rise of two nationwide student lobbies—Public Interest Research Groups (PIRGs) and state student associations. PIRGs, proposed by Ralph Nader in 1970 and endorsed by President Carter in 1979, are now found at 11 percent of American colleges and universities on campuses located in twenty-five states.[19] The theory behind the Public Interest Research Groups, which have more than 700,000 dues-paying undergraduate members nationwide, is that colleges and universities offer students theories of social change but provide no means for implementing them. PIRGs provide the structure and financial support through which students can step out of the classroom and work at reform activities, while training themselves in areas of research, government, and simple good citizenship.

State student associations, which have more than doubled in number since 1969, are found on 22 percent of the nation's campuses in thirty-nine states.[20] And since 1971, a national student lobby, now called the United States Student Association, has been active in Washington, D.C. These organizations behave just like any other lobbying group—they fight for legislation favorable to their constituents.

PIRGs and state student associations differ from the primary activist organizations of the 1960s. They are more eclectic and use a variety of tactics, including lobbying, litigation, the media, community organizing, and demonstrations. Many of these tactics were used much less or not at all in the 1960s, when protest depended more on mobilizing the masses.

Also, both organizations are more issue-oriented than ideological in bent. It is felt by PIRGs and student associations that the absence of a party line enables them to build a broad base of support, as individuals will work hard on the issues they care about, ranging from school costs and student representation to marijuana legalization and utilities pricing. The demand for an ideological commitment would turn away students who disagreed with even a few of the organization's goals.

PIRGs and state associations tend to be more pragmatic and less idealistic than their predecessors. As a former president of the City University of New York student association pointed out, in the 1960s students wanted "pie in the sky" and were willing to protest to get it even when they did not get what they wanted. Today, students are playing to win; they take whatever they can get and then push for more.

In addition, both types of organization are better funded and more politically sophisticated than previous student organizations. State student associations tend to rely upon enrollment-based fees from member campuses, while PIRGs, which use a variety of funding mechanisms, recommend the negative checkoff. That is, students are charged a refundable PIRG fee as part of their university tuition billing. They may decide not to pay this fee by placing a check mark next to a statement to that effect that accompanies the bill. This procedure works to increase funding, as an affirmative act is required to avoid the fee and as few parents notice the few dollars charged to support PIRGs among the much larger sums being requested. The PIRG and state association leaders interviewed expressed a very clear understanding of the importance of money: it pays for research, lobbying, litigation, professional staff, and a good many other activities that are much more effective than mass demonstrations or violence. As one state student lobbyist explained, "We represent voters and we don't have to drag them into the street to prove it to legislators. We know it and they know it, so it doesn't even have to be discussed. Instead, we discuss the issues and my opinion carries weight." Perhaps the best proof of this is the record of the California State College and University student lobby, which boasts that no legislation that is has publicly opposed has ever been enacted.

This constellation of factors explains why student unrest seems to so many to have passed on to the great barricades in the sky. To be sure, student protest has declined significantly in recent years. But it is important to note that what protest there is is less visible. It should also be noted, first, that activism today is concerned with a multiplicity of issues rather than the one or two common concerns of yesterday; second, that the issues tend to be local, varying from campus to campus and student to student, rather than national in scope as they were in the 1960s; and third, that student protest tactics are both more individual—litigation as opposed to strikes and sit-ins—and more peaceful—lobbying as opposed to building takeovers—than they were in the sixties. Unseen activity is being confused with nonexistent activity. Activism remains a tool for the student constituency.

Involvement in Institutional Governance

In the current era, yesterday's omnipresent demand for "student power" has vanished, and what seemed a preoccupation with campus governance and governance issues in the 1960s has become merely an auxiliary interest. Paradoxically, student attitudes about the role they should play in governance have changed very little between the two periods. Today's students want a slightly larger role in determining policy on admissions and faculty appointments and promotions than their predecessors, but they are willing to accept a somewhat smaller role in regulating degree requirements, course content, dormitory rules, and student discipline.[21]

Part of the explanation for the seeming conflict is that student participation in institutional governance has increased substantially since the sixties. When asked to compare the extent of student participation in campus governance in 1969 and 1978, seven out of ten student personnel officers said that it had increased (41 percent) or at least that it had not decreased (29 percent).[22]

In past years, committees were as integral to academic governance as gasoline to the internal combustion engine. Owing to a variety of factors, including the rise of faculty collective bargaining and a growing role for the states in managing higher education, the significance of committees is declining. However, it is here that students have made their greatest gains. For example, three out of four college and university presidents report that students now sit on their institution's educational policy committee, one of the most important planning bodies at any school and one that lies well beyond the pale of those matters to which student participation has been traditionally relegated. Incidentally, more than 60 percent of the presidents polled indicate that student participation in such committees has come about since 1970.[23]

In fact, visits to twenty-six college campuses revealed that students held seats on most committees at all but one of the schools. Budget and personnel committees were the two most frequent holdouts. A substantial minority of undergraduate student leaders (41 percent) were satisfied with this arrangement, while the rest pointed to student indifference, expressed generalized feelings that things could be better, or stated a preference for some such alternative as one person/one vote that would mean student domination of the university. The latter idea was seldom offered seriously and always recognized to be pie in the sky a la mode.[24] On the more humorous side, few students seemed to understand that their increased role in governance was recent or that others had fought hard for it. Several student body presidents complained bitterly or felt put upon, having to furnish their college with a never-ending supply of students to sit on "dinky committees." One threw his arms in the air and asked plaintively, "Where am I supposed to get them all? I'm no magician."

Hand in hand with increased participation in governance has come an increasingly influential role in establishing campus policy and operation. This was the opinion of over one-third (36 percent) of American college presidents. In fact, five out of six presidents believed that student government was at least as influential in 1978 as it was in 1969, if not more so.[25]

However, there is little evidence of undergraduate interest in or concern with student government. Median voter turnout in student elections hovers between 26 and 30 percent—approximately the same level as in 1969 (Carnegie Surveys, 1978). But, even if undergraduates have not given student governments their ballots, they have given them something at least as important—their money. Seventy-two percent of American colleges require students to pay a student activities fee, with a median price of $31 to $45 per year.[26] Collectively, this amounts to no less than $240 million each year, which is more than the annual state expenditure of Idaho, Montana, or Nevada. This kind of money can buy a great deal. It can be and it has been borrowed by institutions to tide them over during cash flow problems. It can be and it has been used to provide services that universities can no longer afford, owing to shrinking budgets. It can be and it has been used to fight colleges in the courts, in the legislatures, and in the media; in some cases, student resources exceed those the institution itself can commit. Also, it can be and it has been used to achieve ends that a college desires but itself lacks the political muscle to realize. For example, the Georgia State University student lobby is working hard to bring a law school and new facilities to its campus.

Money is making students more powerful despite restrictions on how it can be spent. Students are to a greater extent than ever calling the tune on campus. For example, the Florida state senate recently voted to give students who are charged a credit-based construction fee veto power over all building projects at the nine state universities in which their money is used. This authority previously belonged to the state regents.[27]

Off campus the same is true. Student money is being courted and in some cases it is even being listened to. For instance, a flurry of activity resulted when student governments at several California colleges and universities considered removing their money from the Bank of America because of its investments in racially segregated South Africa. Bank of America officials hurriedly trekked around the state to explain bank policies and urge students not to withdraw their accounts. When the bank said that it would not or could not sever its ties with South Africa, several schools, including San Jose State University, severed their ties with the bank.

Conclusion

Current college students are more powerful politically both on and off campus than any student generation of the past. The reasons are several:

- The doctrine of in loco parentis is moribund on most campuses, struck dead by the courts.

- The eighteen-year-old vote and the rise of student lobbies means more clout for students.

- The conclusion of the post-World War II era of growth and the onset of steady-state, hard economic and demographic times for colleges have produced an educational marketplace that favors the buyers of education (students) in contrast to the growth years which favored the sellers (institutions).

- Financial aid programs have been increasingly targeted at students rather than institutions, which strengthens the hand of the user of educational services to the detriment of the supplier. Moreover, high default rates on federally guaranteed loans have increased the U.S. government's interest in consumer problems.

- Relative to the 1960s, students have greater access to university officers and more opportunities to participate in institutional governance. Consequently, students are generally more knowledgeable about institutional affairs. A glance at current student newspapers and those of years past bears this out.

- The growth in enrollments of nontraditional students who are older, married, and employed means that more students have competing demands outside of college and that students must be more selective in their commitment of limited discretionary time and money. They are more consumerist in orientation.

- Students are more self-interested today and more politically astute.

- Public confidence in higher education has declined substantially since the 1960s

In short this is the first generation both to have the vote and to live in a time when in loco parentis is dead. Politically, student organizations like PIRGs and lobbies are more sophisticated and effective than any of the groups that preceded them. At the same time students have risen in public standing while higher education has declined. The ultimate irony, though, is that, as the base of student power expands with increasing enrollment, so does diversity, which brings to the current generation increasing division and less in common to work for politically, particularly outside the educational realm. The me-ism that divides students politically will pass with time, but it seems quite likely that the diversity will increase for the next decade, with a concomitant decline in student political coherence and effectiveness.

In aggregate, the college students of this nation might be described as a sleeping giant. But as individuals students are more powerful than ever before. And they are beginning to realize this. When college students are asked what advice they would give a high school senior planning to attend higher education, consumer advice tops their list. "You're doing the paying, make sure they give you what you want." More than ever before the college student is in the catbird seat. What will happen remains to be seen. In the continuing skirmishes between government and higher education, college students are unlikely to be a prominent ally of either combatant. They can be expected to support whomever is on their side on a particular issue. In fact, it would not be surprising if consumerism became the rallying cry of students for the next decade and the dominant theme governing college and university education, both on and off campus for a long time to come.

Notes

1. National Center for Educational Statistics, *Opening Fall Enrollment, 1979* (Washington, D.C.: U.S. Government Printing Office, 1979) and National Center for Educational Statistics, *Opening Fall Enrollment 1969* (Washington, D.C.: U.S. Government Printing Office, 1969).
2. Carnegie Council on Policy Studies in Higher Education, "National Undergraduate Survey" (Berkeley, 1976).
3. National Center for Educational Statistics, *Opening Fall Enrollment,* 1979, and National Center for Educational Statistics, *Opening Fall Enrollment,* 1969.
4. Carnegie Council on Policy Studies in Higher Education, "National Survey of Institutional Adaptations to the 1970's" (Berkeley, 1978).
5. J. Bachman et al., *Monitoring the Future: Questionnaire Response from the Nation's High School Seniors, 1978* (Ann Arbor: Institute for Social Research, 1980).
6. A.W. Astin et al., *The American Freshman: National Norms for Fall 1979* (Los Angeles: Cooperative Institutional Research Program, Laboratory for Research in Higher

Education, University of California, 1980) and J.A. Creager et al., *National Norms for Entering College Freshmen—Fall 1969* (Washington, D.C.: American Council on Education, 1969).

7. Carnegie Council, "National Undergraduate Survey."
8. T. White, *Breach of Faith: The Fall of Richard Nixon* (New York: Atheneum, 1975).
9. B. Fuller and J. Samuelson, "Student Votes: Do They Make a Difference?" (Washington, D.C.: U.S. Student Association, 1977) and G. Pomper, *The Election of 1976* (New York: McKay, 1977).
10. B. Fuller and J. Samuelson, "Student Votes."
11. Ibid.
12. D. Jacobson, *Student Voting Power* (Washington, D.C.: United States Student Association, 1977).
13. Carnegie Council, "Survey of Institutional Adaptions."
14. Gallup International, Inc., *Gallup Opinion Index: Report 1969* (Princeton, N.J.: Gallup International, Inc., 1969) and Carnegie Council, "National Undergraduate Survey."
15. Carnegie Council, "Survey of Institutional Adaptions."
16. Ibid. and Carnegie Council, "National Undergraduate Survey."
17. Carnegie Council, "Survey of Institutional Adaptions."
18. "Student Groups Fund Law Suits," *National On-Campus Report* (July 1979), p. 1.
19. Carnegie Council, "Survey of Institutional Adaptions."
20. Ibid.
21. Carnegie Council, "National Undergraduate Survey."
22. Ibid.
23. Ibid.
24. Ibid.
25. Ibid.
26. Ibid.
27. *National On-Campus Report,* (June 1979), p.1.

14

Presidents and Governing Boards
John W. Nason

"Any serious fundamental change in the intellectual outlook of human society must necessarily be followed by an educational revolution," wrote Alfred North Whitehead in the *Aims of Education*. The profound intellectual and cultural changes that have surfaced in the present century are evident to any observer with the slightest historical perspective. It should be equally obvious that those changes have produced an educational revolution, particularly in higher education. Indeed, many of the preceding authors in this volume have documented and illuminated the nature of that revolution. It was and is inevitable that changes in the nature of education, in the expectations and demands that people make of education, should have a profound impact on the governance and management of higher education.

Higher education in America is decidedly a mixed bag containing four-year and two-year institutions, undergraduate, graduate and professional schools, public, private and proprietary, some free standing, others integral members within a more or less unified system. The governance and management of such disparate types vary not only with the types but also within them. Nevertheless, they share many common characteristics and problems that can be usefully and intelligently discussed so long as it is understood that every generalization has its exceptions.[1]

The Classic Model

The governance of colleges and universities consists of the machinery by which decisions are made respecting the nature, purposes, and goals of the institution, and the policies by which goals, purposes, and nature are realized. In its classic form the president stands at the peak of a hierarchy. In descending ranks below the president are the administrative officers who take their cue from the president, the departmental chairmen largely responsible for instruction, the faculty concentrating on teaching and research but with a substantial voice in determining the curriculum, standards of academic performance, and broad educational policies, and finally the students who form the base of the pyramid and the *raison d'être* for the whole enterprise. The president, to be sure, derives his or here authority from the trustees, but they in turn are expected to rely on the president for guidance in all educational matters.

Such is, or was, the classic pattern, and one of the purposes of this chapter is to examine how it has changed under the impact of new social expectations and demands. To appreciate the full import of what has happened it is necessary to understand the role of the governing board. Outside of the United States and Canada there are few educational institutions with lay boards of trustees as part of their governing structure. In European countries (and most other countries have followed the European example) Ministries of Education control the universities. In a few places, such as Oxford and Cambridge, the university faculties are the dominant voice. In the United States the board of trustees or regents is in theory the final authority.

Practical and Legal Control

To understand the current role of governing boards it is important to distinguish between legal and practical control. In multi-campus or statewide systems individual institutions may have advisory boards that can be quite influential although lacking in final authority. The advisory boards for SUNY's four-year colleges and universities are an example. Among colleges and universities controlled by religious organizations boards of trustees are sometimes created to provide for a broader public voice in the institution's affairs while maintaining legal control in the religious denomination or order.

Practical control of the direction and policies of an institution is often to be found in hands other than those of the trustees. In some American colleges and universities faculty have played a dominant role. As professionals in the field of education, in contrast to laymen from the outside, many faculty believe that they ought to have the decisive voice and hold up Oxford and Cambridge as examples of the way universities ought to be controlled. There is evidence to suggest that the policies of some institutions are controlled by alumni, either through their elected representatives on the board or through pressure generated by threats to withdraw their support. Students have had more influence on higher education than is generally recognized, either through the erosion of unpalatable programs by passive resistance or, as in the 1960s, by violent demands for change.[2] Whether trustees have delegated their powers or had them usurped legal authority (with exceptions noted in the preceding paragraph) resides in the governing board that owns the institution and its assets and holds the mandate to administer its affairs for the benefit of those designated in the charter.

Shifts in Practical Control

The history of the governance of higher education reveals the shifting centers of authority. In the nineteenth century—the century in which the great majority of America's four-year colleges and universities were founded—trustees were largely in control, in fact as well as by law. It took conviction to create a college. It meant hard work and sacrificial giving. The men and women who composed those early boards may not have known what they were doing, i.e., what their fledgling institutions would some day amount to, but they knew what they wanted and they saw to it that faculty and students lived up to their standards. They set the policies and monitored their execution. Toward the end of the century when the initial fervor of the founders was burning less brightly in their successor trustees and when American business, from which the majority of the trustees were recruited, was dominated by the great captains of industry, a new breed of educational leader took over control. Eliot at Harvard, Gilman at Johns Hopkins, Harper at Chicago, White at Cornell, Butler at Columbia presided over their institutions with magisterial autocracy. They provided educational leadership to faculty and trustees and took unkindly to any opposition from either group.

With the establishment in 1915 of the American Association of University Professors the voice of the faculty in academic policy became much stronger. The competence of faculty in strictly academic matters had always been recognized, but it had been largely subordinated to decisions on educational policy made by others. Slowly at first and then with increasing vehemence the AAUP demanded a recognized place for faculty in academic governance. By the middle of the century governing boards had delegated many of their powers to the faculty—the control of the curriculum, standards for admission and for graduation, the selection of their present and future colleagues. To be sure, the trustees could in theory rescind the delegation of powers, but this proved difficult, if not impossible, in practice. The pendulum had swung very far.

Changes came rapidly in American society after World War II. They undermined the traditional pattern of higher education, creating problems with which faculty and indeed most educators seemed ill equipped to cope. Considerable confusion and chaos resuled, capped by the student revolts of the 1960s. In a sense the student demands for changes in the curriculum, in the grading system, in graduation requirements, in restrictions on their personal lives were persuasive because of the confusion and uncertainty that prevailed. In part, of course, they were merely one aspect of the revolt against authority. Students have an important contribution to make to the shaping of their colleges and universities, but the experience of the '60s makes clear that it should not be control.

Education and Cultural Values

The shift in control, summarily sketched above, has come full circle, and governing boards are well on their way to becoming once again what their name implies. The reasons for the resurgence of trustees are to be found in the changing nature of American society and, as an inevitable consequence, the changing nature of the academy. In the broadest sense of the term education is the process by which the older members of society seek to fashion the younger members into useful citizens. In shaping the attitudes and behavior of the younger generation, the older generation seeks to transfer and embody its own values. One of the paradoxes of higher education, especially liberal education, stems from the fact that the process of transferring values from one generation to another raises questions about the nature of those values. One of the most important contributions of higher education to our society is its constant challenge to and criticism of traditional or accepted ways of thinking and behaving. This is why academic freedom is so important. For most people challenges are at best uncomfortable and at worst threatening. They should, therefore, in their view be suppressed. This way leads to stagnation, and so it is essential that the university be a center for dissent, a protected marketplace for the free play of ideas.

The defense of the freedom of the university, which means in some sense its autonomy, however, must not blind us to its other function, namely, to insure the continuity and stability of society. As devices for transmitting values, attitudes, behavior patterns, educational institutions will inevitably reflect, sometimes enthusiastically and sometimes reluctantly, the nature of the society that supports and uses them. As that society changes, so will the institutions.

Impact of Social Change

Higher education in this country has been struggling to cope, as we have noted, with the changes following World War II. The growth in the educational establishment, the expectations and demands of vast numbers of students who see postsecondary education in some dim and hazy way as the gateway to impoved economic and social status, the switch from viewing education not as a privilege but as a right, together with the cost both to individual families and to the nation as a whole of financing the new and swollen dispensation, all these have weakened, if not destroyed, the traditional collegiate form of higher education.[3] The vast increase of federal support of higher education has created a new set of operating requirements. Federally financed scholarships and loans require an enormous amount of paperwork. With federal funds have come federal regulations respecting affirmative action, the hiring of minorities and women, equal treatment for women's athletics, facilities for the handicapped, new retirement regulations.

It is not surprising that the traditional form of governance has largely disintegrated under the cumulative effect of new conditions. The "collegial" form, in which trustees, presidents, and faculty worked closely together in an hierarchical pattern with appropriate division of labor, was always more honored than practiced. Indeed, many observers and critics viewed colleges and universities as "organized anarchies," in the descriptive phrase of Cohen and March.[4] Higher education was suddenly faced not with a reasoned choice of whom to educate, but with an overwhelming flood of applicants. A few independent institutions strong enought to resist public pressure held the line or grew very slowly. Publicly supported institutions had very limited choice; some could insist on certain minimum standards for admission while others coped as best they could with veterans, high school graduates, and older people compensating for the lack of earlier education.

In view of the magnitude of the task, management did a remarkable job, but it was a constant scramble; and in the process many of the larger issues of education were ignored. Presidents and the other top administrators were preoccupied with the very practical problems of finding faculty and classrooms, of housing and feeding, for more students each year. What it all added up to and where it would end were questions to be set aside for some nonexistent respite from daily emergencies. Nor were faculty of much help. Concerned with their own intellectual fields and with maintaining respectable standards of teaching and scholarship, they had little interest and less time for reviewing the problems of the institution as a total educational enterprise. Someone had to ask the important questions: where are we going? what kind of institution do we eally want to be? how will we ultimately pay the bill? Trustees began to find themselves more deeply involved in policy decisions than before.

In addition, various issues of student and faculty rights began in the 1960s to politicize campuses and ultimately to spill over into the courts. As the body legally responsible for the institution, the governing board found itself the target of damage suits brought by aggrieved students and faculty. In self-defense they needed to understand, and sometimes to correct, the ground rules on which debatable decisions were made. Was there provision for due process in cases of student discipline? Had there been a violation of implicit commitments in the refusal to renew an assistant professor's appointment? If trustees were to be held responsible, it was important that they *be* responsible, i.e., that they know what is going on, that they acquiesce in major policy decisions, that they insist on defensible ground rules, and that there be some notion of where the institution would be five or ten years in the future.

Erosion of Authority

Two pervasive changes in cultural attitudes contributed to the breakdown of traditional forms of governance and to the renewed responsibility of governing boards. The first was the spreading disrespect for authority characteristic of the postwar years and particularly acute in the 1960s. Whatever its cause—the shift to a younger population due to the "baby boom" following the war years, the self-consciousness of a youth culture, the threat to survival in a mismanaged world—all authority was challenged, in government, in the military, in religion, in business. "Don't trust anyone over thirty" became the slogan. On college and university campuses the authority of faculty to determine the curriculum, the content of courses, the quality of performance through grades was widely challenged, but the authority of the administration was the worst victim. Younger faculty frequently joined with students in opposing not just the content of administrative decisions, but the right of administrators to make them. In the organized anarchies anarchy threatened to dominate organization. In this context governing boards had no choice but to investigate what was happening and to back up (or replace) the administration. To be sure, the authority of the trustees themselves was questioned,[5] but they held legal power and they were in a sense above the fray. In recent years the national mood has begun to change. Respect for authority is once more evident. The involvement of governing boards, however, remains

Demand for Accountability

The second change has been the demand for accountability, a demand that is leveled at all our institutions. Since institutions affect people—their opportunities, the choices open to them, their way of living—institutions are clearly accountable for their policies and actions. Colleges and universities have always been held accountable. The operating questions are: to whom, and to what extent? The enormous expansion of higher education since World War II, the number of people involved, and the amount of money being spent have focused public attention on colleges and universities in ways rarely experienced when they served a much smaller part of the population. In independent colleges faculty and administrative officers are accountable to the governing boards as the embodiment or repository of the interests of the founders, donors, and those the colleges were created to serve. With the acceptance of public funds they are also accountable to federal and state governments.

The concept of accountability, however, bears most heavily on the tax-supported institutions. In an incisive and disturbing article entitled "Requiem or Renaissance for the New State College Trustees?" Homer Babbidge argues that the new preoccupation with accountability arises from diametrically opposed sources, one conservative and the other populist.[6] Upward accountability is represented by the concern of state governors and commissioners of education (and of federal officials responsible for affirmative action and other regulations) for thorough supervision, if not actual control, of the expenditure of the vast sums now channeled into state colleges and universities. Downward accountability results from the growing demand of taxpayers that their state colleges serve their particular interest, that they respond to the popular will. Both demands impact on the governing board as the accountable agency. The growth of statewide systems of higher education has been the chief device for focusing control in the state's executive offices, with consequences that we shall examine below. At the same time, since trustees and regents are being held accountable for what goes on in state colleges and universities, they have no choice but to concern themselves more intimately with the affairs of the institutions.

Standard Trustee Responsibilities

What kind of affairs should trustees and regents be concerned with? It is easy to draw up long lists of responsibilities.[7] Governing boards have always been expected to enhance the public relations of the institution by interpreting and defending its policies to the general public, by transmitting public concerns to administration and faculty, by the support inherent in the public stature and prestige of individual trustees. Trustees have traditionally been concerned with the bricks-and-mortar aspects of their institutions, compensating perhaps for their hands-off position with respect to educational matters by an active hands-on policy toward buildings and grounds.

Governing boards have always had the responsibility for selecting the chief administrative officer. Of all the board's responsibilities this is the most important. The president, as already noted, is by no means so powerful as commonly believed. Nevertheless, the president is more influential than any other individual in directing the course of the institution. The good president—meaning good for this institution at this juncture in its history—can under the worst conditions provide the stability needed to weather the storm and under good conditions provide the educational leadership necessary for improved education, enhanced stature, and greater national visibility.

There was a time when the president was handpicked by the chairman of the board or when boards could meet for dinner at a private club and agree upon a candidate. Modern conditions render such a procedure impossible. The job is too complex for simple, easy answers. The committee of selection must first decide which aspects of the president's job are most important. Does the institution need an educational innovator, a fund raiser, a conciliator, a practical administrator, someone with political influence in the state capitol? The composition of the committee of selection must be carefully considered, as it is essential that the new president take office with the good will and support of the various constituencies. Since the president will be held accountable for his or her actions, it is important that the criteria on which judgment will be based be made explicit at the start. Whether the president is appointed for an indefinite period "at the pleasure of the board" or for a finite term, his or her tenure in the post is not likely to extend much beyond ten years. The average tenure today is eight years. It therefore behooves the board to work out, at the time of appointment, the terms for retirement or resignation or forced departure.

Under modern conditions it is not surprising that the selection and appointment of new college and university presidents normally takes five to nine months and occasionally extends well over a year. The selection of a new president is a delicate and sensitive matter. It involves difficult individual judgments about abilities, personality, character, and experience. Such judgments can best be made in private with full assurance of confidentiality. The growing pressure to conduct all business in public, epitomized in its extreme form in various sunshine laws, greatly complicates the process of selection. The laws of some states permit confidential business to be conducted in private. States such as Florida and Minnesota that make no exceptions pay a substantial price in length of time and quality of candidates.

A second major board responsibility is to monitor the performance of the administrative team. There was a time when trustees, having selected the president, could turn over to him or her responsibility for running the institution. They saw their role as largely *reactive*—to approve the president's recommendations, to increase from time to time the compensation, to help when called upon with fund raising or legislative appropriations, to take independent action only when some crisis erupted calling for the defense or removal of the president. Today the problems of higher education defy the capacity of any one man or woman. A high quality of teamwork is essential for effective administration. The president must pick the team, the members of which should be responsible directly to him or her. The board needs to know who the members are, to be satisfied with their competence, and to insist that their loyalties belong to the president. Divided authority, administrative end runs, political infighting can reduce university management to a shambles. The president, with inherited and often highly entrenched staff, subject to unconscionable pressures from within and without, may need support and indeed guidance from the board.

Quite apart from the question of administrative efficiency the modern college or university president needs to be able to turn to the trustees for guidance and comfort. Where else can the president turn? Sometimes to the faculty, though this will depend on the climate on the campus and the extent to which the president has established some kind of personal relations with members of the faculty. Even where such personal relations exist there is the ever-present danger that the president will be seen as playing favorites. Faculty tend to view any palace guard with misgivings. Sometimes the president will want to bring a difficult and unresolved question to the board as a whole for full discussion; more often he or she will turn to the board chairman for private discussion and counsel. The chairman should be prepared to reverse the initiative and on behalf of the board to encourage the president not to exhaust himself or herself in unremitting struggles, to get away from the campus for recuperation and for perspective. Presidents need help, both human and professional. Having picked the president, the board serves itself and the institution badly if it fails to help the president do the best possible job.

The board also needs to make sure that the president is carrying out the policies adopted by the board. As a professional educator the president will propose to the new board major educational policies that the board then approves. Having approved them, the board needs to know that they are in effect and are working. The board needs to know that progress is being made in the areas that had originally been agreed to be most important. If conditions change and new needs arise, the board must decide whether the president can shift gears, be buttressed by someone who can cope satisfactorily, or be replaced by a new president with different talents. Such an assessment is never easy, and colleges and universities are currently experimenting with various methods of making an appraisal of administrative performance. These range the spectrum from highly informal to very formal. There are advantages to each.[8]

Mission and Long-Range Planning

The policies approved by the board should be consistent with the nature and mission of the institution, but that is a bit difficult if the mission itself is not clear. The gradual erosion of the religious drive which inspired many nineteenth-century small colleges has left many of them with vaguely worded statements about their concern for the moral and intellectual development of students. The pressures on many state colleges and universities to serve any and every concern expressed by some group of citizens have produced academic cafeterias without any central or unifying set of principles. Change is inevitable, and colleges and universities must accommodate themselves to the changes in order to survive. But the mission of the true university must be more than survival. In a decade when enrollments are almost certain to decline and when energy costs and inflation are creating havoc with balanced budgets, the temptations to try this or to add that become very strong. What look like short-term additions to income may end up being long-term disasters. Faculty and administration ought to be thinking about the mission of the institution and how it can best be formulated; but for the most part faculty are too concerned with their research and teaching to take time for broader issues, and administrative officers are too busy putting out brush fires. It remains for the governing board to insist on a statement of mission, to ask where the institution is going, to demand a set of long-range plans that, however roughly, will give some notion of where they will be ten years hence. Trustees are rarely in a position to draft such a statement. It is, however, their responsibility to insist that it be done. Only then can policies be clearly judged on their consistency with long-term goals.

While not the only reason for taking the long view, the financial squeeze that nearly every college and university is feeling is a very important one. Higher education at the beginning of the decade of the '80s is in serious financial trouble. Never adequately financed under stable conditions, colleges and universities, public and private, are highly vulnerable to inflation and soaring energy costs. The steady growth (except for the period of the Great Depression) throughout the first three-quarters of this century provided some additional funds each year for new buildings, better salaries, more books and magazines in the libraries, a wider range of extracurricular programs, more and better student services. That growth has now come to an end, or so it appears. Total enrollments may not decline as anticipated, but they are unlikely to grow. Unless and until inflation is brought under control, institutions face the constantly rising cost of standing still. Student fees may keep pace with the rise in inflation, but they do not begin to pay for the cost of education. Unless private philanthropy and government support match inflation, colleges and universities will have declining purchasing power. Some have already folded; others will close their doors in the years ahead. And for all it will be a struggle to maintain quality.

Balancing the Budget

These circumstances place a heavy responsibility on governing boards. They must see that bills are paid. Either they must insist that expenses be cut to fit anticipated income or they must raise the additional money necessary to cover anticipated expenses. Some institutions will survive for a period by living off capital. Some will meet their payrolls by disregarding the needs of the physical plant. Some may even tide themselves over by borrowing funds against a hoped for brighter future. The board "owns" the institution with all its assets and its liabilities. The board is ultimately responsible for its debts. The board must, therefore, not only examine the current budget with an eagle eye, but must also demand projections for at least the next five years.

Balancing the budget is not an exercise to be undertaken for its own sake. It is a means to an educational end, and those who juggle the figures need to be fully cognizant of the relative value of the programs that they are proposing to fund or to excise. They need further to be sensitive to the human factor—the legitimate expectations of the students who elected to enroll, the moral as well as legal commitments to long-time employees, the obligation of the tax-supported and/or tax-exempt institution to whatever community it has sought to serve. In those halcyon days (did they ever really exist?) when income and expense were reasonably assured and stable from one year to the next, budget decisions could be left to the president. The board's role was to satisfy itself that income would match expenditures. Similar behavior in these troubled and turbulent times would be abdication of board responsibility.

Educational Policies

The plain fact is that whoever controls the budget determines the educational program. Those cold budget figures are a front for the vital life of the institution. Should economies by effected by changing the student/faculty ratio from 12:1 to 15:1 or even 20:1? Should classics and modern language instruction be sacrificed as less important or less "productive"? What price will the institution pay if it eliminates intercollegiate football—a notoriously expensive program, but in some universities the source of support for other athletics? What will be the long-run consequences of a failure to increase faculty salaries to keep up with inflation or of a reduction in standards of admission to attract more students? These are the decisions on which the budget is based. If trustees are genuinely concerned about the finances, then they must become involved in important *educational* judgments.

For a long time conventional academic wisdom held that trustees should stay out of the educational issues of the institution. Their concerns should focus on the physical plant, the public relations, investment of endowment, fund raising, and a once-over-lightly review of the budget. There are those on college and university campuses who still believe that trustees should not "meddle" in what is none of their business. Any realistic view of the place of higher education in modern American society leads to a diametrically opposite position. Only by knowing their institution and by becoming involved in its central policy decisions can a governing board meet its full responsibility.

Autonomy vs. System

One further responsibility of trustees deserves special attention because it is being threatened by current trends. Most countries have followed the European pattern of centralized control of higher education through a Ministry of Education or its equivalent. One of the great strengths of the American system has been its pluralism—its large, seemingly cluttered, often confusing network of individual institutions, public and private, two year and four year, undergraduate and graduate, teaching and research. Each had originally its own governing board composed of people concerned for its mission and welfare.

Lay boards served obviously useful purposes in guiding and protecting the early colleges created by private initiative. While eager to accept public as well as private funds, they considered themselves independent of government control and interference—a position confirmed by the famous Dartmouth College case and the Supreme Court decision of 1819.[9] When state colleges and universities began to multiply in the second half of the nineteenth century, the desire to keep them free from political influence, particularly partisan political influence, led to the creation of boards of trustees or of regents for them as well. Public institutions must be accountable for the use of public funds. "Thus," writes Homer Babbidge in the article already referred to, "while political accountability has always been a reality of public higher education, boards of trustees, their members appointed on the basis of merit with staggered terms, have been seen as a device for removing colleges and universities at least one step from direct political abrasion. The delicate equilibrium thus maintained between accountability and autonomy so admired by educators has been the genius of American public higher education. And trusteeship has been the principal stabilizing mechanism."[10]

The "delicate equilibrium" described by Babbidge has been severely damaged by political and economic developments of the past quarter-century. Higher education in America has functioned so well in part because lay boards protected the institutions from outside interference, but in recent years it has been a losing battle.

Private colleges and universities still retain a considerable amount of autonomy, but their freedom of action is being steadily eroded by the requirements attendant on federal grants. Most of those requirements are in the public interest, which includes the interest of the institutions. Bureaucracies, however, can become excessive. They represent external interference in the policies and management of the institution—annoying but relatively harmless under the best circumstances, destructive of the institution's autonomy under the worst. Even state coordinating boards, with power to plan but not to mandate change, can bring pressure on private colleges and universities that judge that they can ignore recommendations only at their peril.

Public institutions find themselves in an ever tighter bind. Twenty-eight states now have coordinating boards whose mandates extend over the statewide need for postsecondary education, the resources available to meet those needs, and the rational allocation of those resources among existing or still-to-be-created institutions. The dizzy growth of postsecondary education, the need for coordination and planning, the bitter struggle among existing state colleges and universities for public funds, the popular demand for more and different education on the one hand and justification for the increasing expenditures on the other, all these are factors encouraging the establishment of statewide *systems* of higher education. Indeed, the very size and complexity of the educational establishment make systems virtually inevitable. For all their drawbacks it is unlikely that we shall ever return to the freewheeling pattern of an earlier day.[11]

Trustees within a System

In statewide or multi-campus systems trustees tend to gravitate to opposite poles. The trustees or regents comprising the system's board have greatly enlarged responsibilities. They must be concerned for the system as a whole and not for a single institution. They become remote, impersonal, concerned with policies applicable to all the members of the system. Their loyalties belong not to Upstate U or Downstate U, but to The University of the State. Often they have no time to visit the constituent campuses. The trustees of an individual college or university can supplement the information provided by the president with information gained through other channels—faculty contacts, student newspapers, attendance at campus events. The regents of the state system must rely on the chancellor or chief executive officer of the system for their information. The issues they face are important; their decisions, often momentous. But the colors and smells, the successes and defeats of direct involvement are missing. Both they and the institutions are the poorer as a result.

In most systems there will be boards for individual institutions as well. Some still have significant authority and can make a real contribution to the nature and performance of the college or university. Some have limited responsibilities, such as an active role in the selection of the president. Some are advisory only, though even under these conditions their role can vary. Being often seen as window dressing, they come to see themselves as nothing more. They are chosen or appointed, however, to serve as a bridge between the institution and the community. As concerned trustees they can help the president at times of local crisis. They can warn him or her of community feelings and demands; they can interpret campus activities and decisions to the outside community. They can counsel with the president, providing aid, comfort, and encouragement when most needed. Under most statewide governing or coordinating systems their responsibilities have been reduced. The need for their help, however, has not, and they can still play a very effective role if they will.

Leadership and Ambiguity

How have the "acids of modernity" in Lippmann's famous phrase affected the role of college and university presidents? They have eroded his, or her, authority. The same forces that have enhanced the role of trustees have undermined the power and position of the president. The once benign father figure, the outstanding scholar, preacher, speaker, the educator/ statesman to whom society turned for public leadership is a vanishing, if not vanished, species.

College and university presidents have not been reticent in describing their uprisings and downsittings. There is a substantial literature dealing with their recent plight. Cohen and March, in their study for the Carnegie Commission on Higher Education already referred to, take a quizzical, if not jaundiced, view of the profession. Some presidents see themselves as managers of the store, labor union negotiators, mediators among competing factions, budget balancers, glorified office boys. They clearly view themselves as expendable, and some have argued that they should assume that they will wear out their welcome or exhaust their capital of good will within relatively few years.

Are these the reverberations of discouragement or realistic analyses of present and future prospects? Let there be no doubt that the president's job has changed. The very complexity of the modern university tends to isolate administrative officers in their cubicles as they try to cope with the flood of requirements and paperwork resulting from a multitude of government regulations. Their freedom of administrative movement is drastically curtailed. Time was when the president could use his or her best judgment in selecting a new dean or department chairman or faculty member. Now it is a complicated matter of advertising, interviewing, committee operation, steps to meet affirmative action requirements, resolution of conflicting opinions on the best choice. The spread of faculty unions has introduced a new dimension. Codes of conduct must be devised and published. Actions must follow prescribed rules. It is a job that provides no time for scholarship and little leisure for contemplation.

All these frustrations are exacerbated when presidents must function within the restrictions of a system. Instead of advising a board on educational policy, defending some institutional practice or seeking counsel from a group of directly concerned lay trustees, the president must deal with the chief executive officer of the system. With luck he or she may occasionally appear before the system board, but only briefly, and it is apt to be an appearance before strangers rather than friends. The chancellor, president, or executive officer of the system may have been a university president and must certainly have had some practical experience in education; but managerial skill, political connection, and loyalty to the governor are likely to be important in the appointment. He or she will want to run a smooth operation with lieutenants, i.e., local presidents, who will accept orders and not protest. The university president who argues vigorously for what he or she believes will not be popular. A low profile may be the price of survival.

What are the prospects for the future? Will the position of university president no longer attract the best people? It continues to be the single most important job within the educational establishment. It is a job calling for educational leadership, and those presidents do themselves and their institutions a disservice who fail to see themselves as providing leadership. It is no place for the timid or the hesitant. The final reward is the satisfaction of doing an important and difficult task well.[12]

Just as American society has shaped our educational system, so our colleges and universities have shaped and will continue to shape our society. How those institutions are managed is therefore a vitally important issue for our society. Both society and the institutions deserve the best contribution that governing boards and presidents can provide.

Notes

1. In spite of their number and growing importance, proprietary institutions are omitted from discussion.

2. See Frederick Rudolph, *The American College and University—A History* (New York: Alfred A. Knopf, 1962), especially chap. 8.

3. The data on increasing enrollments and the changed composition of student bodies are voluminous and familiar. One of the more perceptive interpretations of the phenomena is to be found in Martin Trow, "Reflections on the Transition from Mass to Universal Higher Education" *Daedalus* 99 (Winter 1970).

4. Michael D. Cohen and James G. March, *Leadership and Ambiguity—The American College President* (New York: McGraw-Hill, 1974).

5. Note, for example, the position taken by a group of Princeton University students in the report of a Special Committee entitled *The Governing of Princeton University* (1970), cited in James Harvey, "College Trustees," *ERIC Research Currents* (June 1971), reprinted in *AGB Notes* 2 (September, 1971): "The issue is not whether the trustees are doing their job well. The issue is that there is no justification for such a group of men controlling the destiny of an institution and a community in which they have no legitimate place. The University is a community of students and faculty, not businessmen."

6. Homer D. Babbidge, Jr., "Requiem or Renaissance for the New State College Trustees?" *AGB Reports* 17 (July/August 1975).

7. See, for example, John W. Nason, *The Future of Trusteeship—The Role & Responsibilities of College & University Boards* (Washington, D.C.: Association of Governing Boards, 1974); also his "Responsibilities of the Governing Board," chap. 3 in Richard T. Ingram and Associates, *Handbook of College and University Trusteeship* (San Francisco: Jossey-Bass, 1980).

8. The types of assessment and their relative merits are discussed in John Nason, *Presidential Assessment—A Challenge to College and University Leadership* (Washington, D.C.: Association of Governing Boards, 1980).

9. See Rudolph, *American College and University,* pp. 207-12.

10. Babbidge, "Requiem or Renaissance," p. 37.

11. Illuminating discussions of this development are to be found in two publications of the New York-based International Council for Educational Development: *Higher Education: From Autonomy to Systems,* edited by James A. Perkins and Barbara Baird Israel (1972); and the four articles by Alan Pifer, John Shea, David Henry, and Lyman Glenny constituting *Systems of Higher Education: United States* (1978).

12. In his recent book, *At the Pleasure of the Board* (Washington, D.C.: American Council on Education, 1980), Joseph Kauffman, a former president now turned professor and consultant in higher education, analyzes in positive and constructive fashion the problems of the modern college president. His last chapter, "The President and Educational Leadership," provides a strong note of hope and encouragement.

15

Stress and the Academic Dean
Donald J. McCarty and I. Phillip Young

Sharp shifts in external and internal environmental influences sometimes
precipitate radical revisions in organizational roles without much evident
understanding of the consequences. All too often many individuals who are
greatly affected by these changes are somehow shielded from what is actually happening; it is so reassuring to retain the beliefs and expectations of a
different time. Unless a dramatic upheaval takes place, things appear to be
normal enough.

So it is with the role of deans and other senior administrators in higher
education today. Participants in the higher educational enterprise, particularly professors, became accustomed in the sixties and seventies to a
reasonably privileged status. Resources to support their ventures were
generally available from some funding source. Moreover, the professoriate
was extraordinarily mobile, a moderately solid performance guaranteed
tenure and promotion, opportunities for engaging in entrepreneurial activities of various kinds were plentiful, and favorable workloads could be
negotiated.

The mind-set of the dean or senior administrator in the sixties and seventies was also expansive. The general public seemed to revere higher education, student enrollment kept steadily increasing, and public and nonpublic

269

subventions were generous. Admittedly, the student riots of the period raised some discontent but they had little effect on a professor's academic life. So the dean had a relatively easy time. Protecting the faculty was symbolically important but the threats were minor. A considerable amount of budgetary discretion permitted the dean to build new programs and to facilitate the work of faculty members in a number of positive ways. The accent was on growth; these were the golden years.

Contrast this enterprising environment with what deans have to face today. Budgets are declining, programs are being phased out, professors are becoming immobile, tenure and promotion are now difficult to obtain, legislatures are more recalcitrant, donors less responsive, and administrators in central administrative posts are steadily increasing their surveillance.

Current deans know that many professors still expect to receive the bounties of the recent past and that this level of consciousness changes slowly. It is the dean who is expected to protect the faculty from these incursions. Trying to sensitize academics to these new realities is a sensitive and unpleasant task. Many deans have done so up to the present by making budgetary cuts in areas like student services and physical plant where the lives of professors are not directly touched. This temporizing will not suffice much longer; deeper cuts will have to be undertaken for the accent now is on containment.

The purpose of this essay, then, is to discuss the general role of deans and senior administrators in the context of academic institutions as they are likely to be in the eighties and to speculate about how these individuals will be influenced by differing internal pressures within the academy and by the manifold external constituencies bearing down on them from the society at large. This essay will attempt to place the present role of dean in a historical context, to indicate what some of the main issues in deaning are all about, and to suggest different ways in which deans may cope with the challenge of their post. The central thesis to be proposed is that deaning in the eighties will be quite a different undertaking than it was in the sixties and seventies because the societal pressures are of an entirely different order.

Let us begin by pointing out that academic deans and senior administrators in higher education settings today are subjected to conflicts that would be difficult to resolve in the best of circumstances. Professors in colleges and universities like to function with a great deal of discretion and autonomy and with minimal direct supervision. We are further aware that it is hard to quantify the effect of the total higher education process on students, let alone the effect of individual professors on them. This situation tends to irritate the citizenry who call for clear accountability and more visible results from the expensive enterprise called higher education.[1]

Many outsiders seem to sense that higher educational institutions lack close internal coordination, especially of the content and methods of what is primarily one of their main activities—teaching. A number of these critics believe that the techniques of rational bureaucratic management would likely enhance productivity (student learning) with greater efficiency and with more public accountability. The bureaucratic concept has appeal because it emphasizes hierarchy and planned order. Principles like division of labor, delegation of authority, impartial rules, dependable communication, and coordination of the whole are seen as providing the building blocks for a sound organizational structure.[2] Of course, the desire of the academic to function as independently as possible runs counter to the coordination and control maxims of management science.

Why colleges and universities resist these bureaucratic management models and seem to prefer a form of semicontrolled anarchy is not well understood or appreciated by many outside constituencies. To state as some theorists do that the goals of higher education are inchoate and indefinite and therefore immune to systematic evaluative measures seems self-serving and does not appear to strike the right chord in the minds of the citizenry.[3] Though it may appear cynical at first blush, Clark Kerr's argument that there is a need to maintain some confusion about the multiple goals of the multiversity in order for them all to coexist may be more appropriate in the present milieu.[4] For it is becoming increasingly obvious that the affairs of academe must often be resolved by essentially political means as in other kinds of lesser enterprises. We in higher education are no longer granted the luxury of defining our own purposes in isolation from the desires of American society.

Highlighting the significant alternation in the way society currently looks at universities is the fact that college or university administrators are now held responsible for implementing decisions to which they have given no advice or consent and which may be contrary to their own personal values. Implementing decisions that allocate or reallocate scarce resources becomes extraordinarily onerous when they are made at the board, legislative, or executive level and are justified by overt political rationales. Formula budget reductions, affirmative action compliance, and detailed procedural guidelines all indicate increasing demands for conformity to systems and processes that have long been considered antithetical to the elevated purposes of higher education.

These sustained attempts to standardize university administration are seen negatively by academicians. Establishing formal rules as the modal response for problem resolution increases the probability that some regulations will not be honored to the letter. Such conformity flies in the face of faculty autonomy as ordinarily defined. The level of hierarchy and control needed to insure compliance may be so great as to prove counterproductive.

For example, rules and regulations governing staff travel may be enforced so restrictively in the attempt to apprehend an occasional cheat that the upshot is a guarantee of an irritating loss to the traveler on every voucher submitted. Such policies definitely discourage unnecessary travel;

likewise, they increase the probability that the legitimate goals of ordinary staff travel are unlikely to be realized either. Professors are not so well paid that they are willing to subsidize their own travel on organizational pursuits. No matter how pure the original intent of the regulations, this end result is the classic example of the negative impact of centralized oversight mechanisms.

Ten to twenty years ago academic deans on most campuses were reputed to be administrative figures not easily to be trifled with and they seemed to manage the affairs of their college with a minimum of external interference. In those days their signature on a travel voucher was all that was required. It now appears that the position of senior administrator or dean is becoming weaker and less appealing as the role expectations become more numerous, complex, and conflicting.[5] This leads us to a brief historical review of the evolution of the dean's role.

Evolution of the Dean's Role

There seems in the main to be agreement that academic deans fulfill similar roles regardless of their respective institutions. Miller[6] implied such a consensus concerning the dean's role when he indicated that all educational institutions face common problems regardless of the type or size of the institution. Even though deans or other senior administrators may all experience some of the same problems, evidence suggests that the issues and duties associated with the position have changed through the years. When deans emerged as an extension to the presidential role their tasks consisted primarily of three fundamental roles: (1) considering the ends and means of education, (2) selecting faculty, and (3) preparing budgets.[7] Gould[8] furthered the list to include (4) curriculum work, (5) promotion decisions, (6) committee work, (7) faculty relations, and (8) evaluation of personnel. These roles were again expanded by Miller[9] to encompass (9) collective bargaining and (10) accountability involving cost effective analyses. It seems that few tasks have been removed or delegated to others from a role that has moved historically from an extension of the university presidency to a precarious middle management position.[10]

Financial Issues

Research findings indicate that the greatest area of disagreement among deans, central administrators, departmental chairpersons, and faculty focuses on the dean's participation in personnel and fiscal affairs.[11] Faculty and department chairpersons prefer that the dean not become too heavily involved in these crucial responsibilities. However, both deans and central administrators believe that these areas are precisely those where the dean should exercise initiative. In view of the lack of slack resources in university coffers in these times and because of belligerent legislative and executive concerns about the excessive costs of financing higher education the dean may receive directions from central administration that require severe cutbacks in both personnel and fiscal affairs. How do deans cope, accustomed as they are to operating in a collegial setting rather than a line and staff relationship, when the inevitable impasses arise over matters of people and money?

According to the formulations of Meyer and Rowan the dean should avoid the temptation to coordinate and control work activities more rigorously in order to solve such problems.[12] Rather the dean needs to learn to relax in order to preserve the confidence and good faith of the faculty. Attempting to enforce conformity through inspection, monitoring output quality closely, evaluating the efficiency of various units, and trying to unify and coordinate goals are certain to lead to value conflicts and in the process the dean will lose the legitimacy of office needed to be effective.

Meyer and Rowan believe that deans are dealing with professionals who have been delegated the right to perform teaching, research, and service activities on their own and beyond the purview of the dean.[13] Therefore, human relations skills or the ability to get along with other people takes ascendancy. The wise dean is the one who stresses the ceremonial myths of the college or university that bind the participants together rather than set them apart. Structurally, the dean allows units to decouple from each other; integration or unity of purpose is not emphasized. Tension is thereby reduced.

For example, the dean who subscribed to this frame of reference would let individual departments pursue their own interests within reason and would not attempt to build tight and unified policy statements for the college. Instead, the dean would preserve the formal structure of the organization by carrying out day-to-day routine activities in an orderly fashion. The main thrust, however, would be to preserve morale and encourage high performance through the stressing of the ceremonial myths of the organization. Displays of unity around such abstract goals as the dedication of faculty members to the "search for truth" or to "the borders of the campus are the borders of the state" are of benefit not only to internal participants but also to external constituents as well. Deans definitely should not try to uncover unsavory events and deviations through inspection and evaluation for such revelations injure the image of the unit.

Meyer and Rowan have provided an insightful analysis that suggests that deans need to develop their human and political skills to a high level.[14] This same point is sometimes made in a different fashion by deans who write about their experiences. Jackson did not hesitate to say that he never made public the real details of his budget, particularly the discretionary funds.[15]

In most institutions deans have substantial budgets, and it is well known that a budget is spent in a surprisingly different manner than the printed format may indicate. What this means is that deans have substantial degrees of freedom to alter spending patterns without seeking advice from traditional faculty committees.

In most colleges and universities there are suitable provisions and numerous points of contact between administration and faculty in the budgetary sequence, including mechanisms to handle retrenchment decisions should they be required. The truth of the matter is that the dean or senior administrator charged with resource allocation and personnel matters has a considerable amount of confidential information at hand that cannot be easily shared without revealing confidences or embarrassing individuals publicly. However, if faculty members are to play a meaningful role in the process of making these kinds of decisions, administrators must make the underlying facts available to the faculty so that informed choice can be made. Without a steady flow of accurate information from those who have it to those who need it, joint decision making cannot be successful. Since much of this "factual" data is privileged information of a highly personal sort, which cannot easily be dispensed in open forums, the tendency is for the dean to make as many budgetary decisions as possible in secret with as little fanfare as possible.

Perrow may not be far wrong when he suggests that organizations become tools in the hands of their masters.[16] It is the dean, perhaps in consultation with other senior administrators, who decides whether or not to award a new position to a particular department. It is the dean again who states that funds are just not available to increase the supplies and expense allotment of a particular department. Amazingly, deans are seldom challenged in these budgetary decisions. In curricular matters or highly visible academic policy issues, of course, the dean is plainly constrained by faculty opinion.

Stress, therefore, comes not so much from balancing the role expectations of divergent groups and individuals but from the loneliness of the command post. If, as we are suggesting, deans make most of the critical budgetary and personnel decisions, there is the psychological pressure of not knowing whether things will work out as expected. Were these the right decisions? Time might tell but the passage of years obliterates the memory and few recall which particular dean made what decisions. Perhaps because of the illusion that faculty governance made those choices anyway, evaluation of the worth of a particular dean and his volitions will never surface.

Recruitment of Minorities

Meyer and Rowan's ideas take on greater cogency when we examine the role stress emanating from recruitment of minorities.[17] This objective has been set by federal mandate and its implementation often falls heavily on the office of the dean. Inspection of how well recruitment of minorities is proceeding asserts societal control while undermining the assumption that everyone in academe is acting with competence and in good faith. Deans are expected to buffer dicta of this kind so that internal college morale does not suffer.

The dean knows that a substantial contingent of his or her faculty do not believe that ethnic background and sex should play a role in faculty selection. Rather, academic promise and achievement are the only criteria, and anything less undermines the search for truth, mistreats the most qualified faculty candidates, and cheats the students. Another substantial contingent will take the position that previous deprivation must be righted and that a search for a qualified female or minority candidate is appropriate. For this latter group, it is not necessary to select the most promising academic in the talent pool but only an acceptable minority or female person.

In any event, ceremonially, the dean must emphasize that his or her college is moving toward the goal of recruiting more minorities so, at least, the intent of good faith is maintained. This action defuses external accountability measures of a punitive kind, such as absolute quotas, and enables the college to grapple with the issue in its own patterned way. Stresses of this genre separate the dean from others in the college and from persons outside as well; displaying confidence while feeling unsure that you can bring about the required results is role ambiguity of the first magnitude.

Rewarding Faculty

Rewarding faculty is another internal role demand of considerable consequence. In the decentralized world of the college and university as we have known it, salary increases have been greatly influenced by faculty committees effectively removing the most obvious reward from the dean's control. In fact, it has been the academic department that bestowed most of the meaningful rewards that academics covet. Departments ordinarily have exercised almost complete control over the initial selection of new faculty members and over the promotion to higher ranks, including tenure. Assignment to office space, the appointment of graduate assistants, the awarding of travel funds, the distribution of ordinary supplies, negotiations about teaching load, and similar decisions have usually been decided at the departmental level, within, of course, the limits authorized by the dean and local institutional traditional practices.

If all the awards of real importance are made at the departmental level, what rewards are left for the dean to dispense? As always, the power is more subtle than hierarchical. Many of the decisions previously mentioned do need at least tacit approval from the dean and the veto power may sometimes be used, if only sparingly. At least the threat to use it is there, which makes the dean's approbation worth something. The dean is obviously a good ally to have if a faculty member is seeking support for sabbaticals, chaired professorships, research and foundation grants, recommendations for positions elsewhere, and any number of other similar benefits. To the extent that recognition is a key motivator the dean may appoint certain faculty members to important committees, seek them out for confidential advice, acknowledge their contributions whenever occasions permit, and engage in a myriad of other positive gestures of approval.[18] But when all is said and done, for the most part, professors are free to ignore the dean's blandishments for they know that the rewards of the most surpassing value are made at the departmental level. When rewards are limited, status positions are weakened, and that is the situation most senior administrators face.

Rewarding faculty is one place where new societal pressures have already begun to establish a completely different perspective from what we have been used to. Unionization of faculty members is on the increase and is likely to be stepped up if state legislatures and boards of trustees try to balance budgets in these inflationary times by offering inadequate salary increases to faculty or by enforcing the other more stringent measures that seem to be on the horizon.

Unions argue for equalization in salaries and they attack the subjective aspect to merit raises. Once union contracts stipulate the exact procedures required in personnel matters of this sensitivity, the role of the dean will become more of an enforcer of the contract and new interaction patterns between deans and faculty will have to be discovered. Here is a prime example of how changing environmental factors impinge on the shared government mechanism long associated with higher education institutions.

Outside Activities of Faculty

Supervising outside professional activities is complicated because of the implication of coercive power. As Meyer and Rowan indicate, faculty members seek to minimize inspection and evaluation by both internal managers and external constituents.[19] Newspaper reports acknowledge that professors on occasion violate their good faith compact and misuse funds or make too much money in outside professional activities that are not a part of regular responsibilities. Should the dean have known about these activities in advance and done something about them?

It is highly probable that most deans are aware of the petty peccadillos of their faculty members. The grapevine is an effective communication device in the higher education enterprise and a person holding a central position in the communication network is bound to hear most of the gossip.

Deans are aware that they are not expected to perform as members of the Federal Bureau of Investigation. They are expected to correct gross abuses but not go looking for sinners. Moreover, the individuals who have the funds to mismanage are often cosmopolitans and leading researchers with conceivably greater academic images than their deans.[20] Usually college administrators do not want their contact with a leading academic figure on their faculty to be focused on items like questionable travel vouchers, so the upshot is that surveillance is low key. The role conflict may come when a particular college administrator has his or her own personal values offended or when deans have to balance the value of supporting one of their professors with a national reputation against the displeasure of other faculty members who resent the special consideration given this "star."

Needless to say, external authorities expect the monitoring of grant and contract activities to be supervised closely in the bureaucratic mode, a response that the senior administrator is hard pressed to render. If irregularities are discovered, it is the dean who appears incompetent if not venal.

Political Relationships

Colleges and universities, at least in their idealized state, are expected to be relatively free from the pushing and hauling attributed to crass politicization. A community of scholars where concern for teaching and learning is paramount ought to be a setting where rational thought should predominate. And for the most part it probably does.

Deans, though, have to view their units as political entities with internal and external relationships. If following Karpik the dean sees his or her college as a political system, it becomes apparent that professors are political actors with their own needs, objectives, and strategies to achieve those objectives.[21] Professors, however, do not interpret their behavior in these terms. If professors informally caucus before a departmental meeting to hammer out a position, they consider the activity to be part of shared governance. They do not recognize that they are engaging in developing a coalition, identifying a collective objective, and devising a strategy to achieve that objective. They instinctively realize that they have to have the votes to win and they search for them but they do not call this effort the building of a dominant coalition. Those who labor in this way usually have a full understanding of the history behind the issue at stake. In short, they are consummate politicians. Hazard Adams has described in great detail how sophisticated academic politicians are, mainly because they refuse to categorize what they do as political.[22]

But the dean can ill afford not to play the political game. The dean cannot be constantly victimized by dominant coalitions who decide what direction the college is going to take unless, of course, the dean is part of that coalition. But the dean should be careful to avoid the image of the manipulator. What this means in operational terms is that deans need to have enough political savvy to recognize dominant coalitions when they see them and devise a way to work with them or against them so that the interests of the college are best served.

External Relationships

Colleges or schools within universities become matched with their environments by technical and exchange interdependencies of innumerable kinds. It is the dean who must orchestrate these connections for a particular college. There are general targets and there are specific targets.

The most powerful voices outside the higher education institution itself cannot be denied access to the decision-making process inside the institution. Such interest groups as the state legislature and the governor's office, in the case of state universities, and the organized alumni, in the case of private universities, regularly impact on academic society. Agencies of the federal government plying their own missions in research, health science, affirmative action, and the like also become systematically linked to various interests.

Every college also has a special constituency it must nurture. The professions of agriculture, engineering, business, law, medicine, and the like have peculiar interests and deans must relate to them.

Clearly, the decision making of the large academic institution is heavily shaped by the intensity of the demands placed on it by these diverse interest groups. Theorists like Perrow have doubted that the ponderous, shared government mechanism of academe is equal to this kind of task; he has argued that these mounting outside pressures have weakened the traditional faculty participation in these matters.[23]

For the massive size of today's academic institution militates against the effective use of faculty governing bodies on "hot" issues; in the elongated hierarchies of contemporary universities, key decisions are often made by faceless officials in central administration, removed some four or five echelons from the professor's classroom.[24] The upshot is that administrators of one kind or another make most of the major decisions, albeit by cloaking them in ritualistic language or by obscuring the actual process within the bureaucratic maze they administer.

Still, the expectation is that there should be wide participation by faculty members in the affairs of the university and that administrators should be open to suggestions, criticism, and change. When it is not possible to find the time and means to develop mutual cooperation and shared authority in the ideal sense, administrators may feel guilty in pursuing objectives and making choices that are primarily their own. Thus, role conflict and ambiguity may be endemic to their positions, and the resultant stress inescapable.

Role Overload

A recent book by Henry Mintzberg has taken a careful look at role overload by executives.[25] He found that administrators feel compelled to perform a great quantity of work at any unrelenting pace. Moreover, their activities are characterized by brevity, variety, and fragmentation. Interruptions are commonplace and most of the time is spent in verbal contact.

Time pressures and job demands of this intensity certainly contribute to role overload in higher education. Deans probably feel that they must attend meetings and functions, even when these are not all that significant, in order to demonstrate personal interest, to fly the flag, so to speak. The upshot is that the college dean's priorities are not set by the relative importance of each individual task, but by the necessity to deal with those things that are required as part of the job. Deadlines become the stimulus for action. The collegial nature of university administration is of little help, for each and every professor wants to deal with the dean directly, not an associate or assistant dean.

Interactions with Higher Level Administrators

When internal strain threatens the cohesiveness of an organization, as is likely to be the case for universities during the eighties, deans have difficulty in maintaining a purchase on their problems. In such a volatile situation it stands to reason that deans must operate from a position of power, and this can only be obtained by support from higher-level administrators.

Blau has pointed out that leadership derives from the exchange process in which the leader acquires political capital by doing something for superordinates.[26] Deans instinctively realize this elementary principle. When requests come down they must be responded to in a fashion that engenders confidence. Over time an able dean should have built up a reserve of good will that can be utilized when needed. To put it simply, if they need a favor they can get it.

Deans cannot afford to seem weak to their superiors nor can they appear to their subordinates to be accommodating to the most demanding groups while ignoring the interests of others. This is a difficult tightrope to walk and it is exacerbated when declining budgets reduce degrees of freedom.

Complicating the issue is the exponential expansion of junior administrators at the higher levels of academe. Time was when the dean could deal directly with the president of the university or like official on matters of import. Now, the expansion of administrative oversight means that deans deal with a variety of representatives often much younger and less experienced but still part of the superordinate hierarchy. Bad marks from junior administrators who report regularly to the top official do not strengthen the reputation of the dean. The dean knows that it is essential to make decisions without compromising basic principles. Deprived of direct access to the status leader on delegated matters, deans must make peace with a variety of overseers who are looking for points of weakness in their performance.

Deans know that the college entrusted to their care can only prosper if their superior is willing to provide the necessary resources. Some deans have it easier than others because they lead a unit like agriculture in a land-grant university, which is virtually untouchable even in hard times. Even in such an enviable position, the strictures of hierarchy demand a minimum amount of loyalty to your superior. Deans, in short, are highly dependent on how they are perceived by their immediate superiors. Seldom are deans successful who see their role as transmitting all the requests of faculty to higher levels routinely. Administrators, whether in higher education or elsewhere, anticipate that their principal line administrators will assume some of the noxious burden of saying "no" to entreaties.

Furthermore, these interactions between deans and their superiors are private encounters. The dean conceivably could argue heatedly and determinedly for a position or could be entirely acquiescent to demands. In any event the dependent nature of the transaction encourages a certain measure of conformity to the wishes of higher level authorities. To do otherwise is to endanger the close working relationship that needs to exist.

Of course, central administrators are subject to increasing mandates from outside sources themselves. State legislatures may order position freezes and other noxious restrictions or boards of trustees may require policies on sexual harassment and the like that must be complied with. The tendency, everywhere, is to institute more and more compliance measures from outside the academy and middle-level administrators are continuously expending their energies in minimizing the negative effect of these demands on the lives of the professors who ultimately must make the higher education enterprise go.

Leadership Options for Deans

Role stress for the dean, then, is something that must be lived with. If they are not unusually astute, deans in complex institutions, who are necessarily somewhat distanced from peers, subordinates, and superordinates, may also become little more than spectators in the campus power politics. One option to relieve stress of this kind might be to engage in dramaturgy.[27] Incumbency guarantees a certain symbolic respect in the academic world; the responsibilities of a dean are often ill understood, and the individual who is able to dramatize his or her own competence is likely to be viewed with approbation. While it may not be possible to revise the curriculum of the college or to reorganize its internal governing structure, it is possible to give the impression of forcefulness, scholarliness, and the ability to cope. What symbol can be more reassuring than the dean who seems to know what to do and is willing to act?

The dean who does not meddle with faculty prerogatives, who plays the role of facilitator, who knows how to preside effectively at meetings, who seems genuinely interested in the enhancement of the college is likely to have a successful tenure as long as the symbols of office are maintained. Impartiality by the dean in serving others, rather than scheming to remake a school or college according to a preconceived plan, is preferred by most academicians. Successful deans in these turbulent times may well be those who emphasize style in their administrative work. Faculties do demand the proper maintenance of the symbols of their institutions and it is the wise dean who responds to this expectation eagerly and well.

Another alternative always open to a dean is to resign. This removes the stress from the individual occupant of the role though it does not affect the nature of the role itself; the successor will be subject to the same congeries of forces that engaged the energies of his or her predecessor. Besides it is a little belittling to leave one's post under a cloud, for resignation may seem like surrender. Therefore, to the dean, the desire to tough it out becomes paramount, barring an offer too good to refuse, such as a cherished appointment that colleagues would perceive as ample reason for casting aside deanly responsibilities. Resignation does not become the easy alternative that it is reputed to be; returning to an academic department when one's scholarly skills may have eroded is not a glorious prospect. That deans persist and try to struggle with their lot seems entirely understandable.

The experienced dean knows, of course, that role conflicts and role ambiguity come with the territory. Moreover, hostility when it is directed at the dean is hardly ever personal; it is directed at the position not the person. For even the most contrary of professors realizes that a modicum of administrative coordination is needed; understanding that fact, however, does not inhibit those professors who perceive they have been slighted in some way from registering disapproval vociferously. On the other hand, veteran deans have been through many volatile sessions over the years and they are well aware that time heals most conflicts, whether they were imagined or real. What seemed so overwhelming an issue this year is likely to be forgotten or at least partially resolved by the next. Stress can be reduced, then, by the insight that pressure situations have a way of losing their own momentum in due course and that remaining relaxed and reasonably openminded throughout the strife is likely to lead to beneficial results. This view is championed by March and Olsen, who argue that some problems do not have solutions and that rational analytic models sometimes are not helpful.[28] For them it is far better for the administrator in these instances to rely on experience, intuition, insight, or luck. It should be heartening for the dean to realize that conflict is sometimes real and not susceptible to resolution by ordinary means.

Deans like other role occupants come in all shapes, sizes, and significances. Some deans, therefore, may decide to reduce stress by taking the initiative and try to shape their jobs as they see fit, rather than serving all the daily demands thrust upon them. Cohen, March, and Olsen have a prescription for leaders with this bent.[29] They suggest that since time is scarce, the willingness to spend time on an issue of concern increases the likelihood of the dean being present when things happen. If deans are not successful the first time, they should persist. The mix of individuals that decided things yesterday may not return today. The preferred strategy, then, is to overload the system. When time is scarce, an overload on the system produces decisions that are more in the control of relatively full-time administrative participants, of which the dean is clearly one. The dean should manage the time of others by providing them opportunities to engage their energies elsewhere while the dean tries to achieve his or her particular goals.

Obviously, some of these latter recommendations must be taken with tongue-in-cheek; still, the thrust of the argument has merit. Deans are full-time administrators, they have access to financial and human resources, and they are expected to make at least some modests proposals for change. If they decide to focus on a limited number of issues that they consider important, the probability of achieving modest gains in those areas is reasonably good. Deans are not impotent unless they allow themselves to be.

If one were to accept the thrust of most of the essays written about the need for the college administrator to maintain autonomy and academic freedom for the professoriate at all costs, even in the face of stubbornness and eccentricity of the most shameless sort, why would a worthy person seek such a baleful post? While candidates for these roles seem plentiful enough, is it not the ambitious politician who never loved academic life in the first place or the innocent faculty member lured into the responsibility under duress who succumbs?

Or is faculty autonomy all that one-sided in the end? Hazard Adams has clarified the issue cogently by offering two antinomies pertaining to the administration's relations with faculty: (1) the faculty is the university; the faculty are employees of the university, and (2) the administration is the master of the faculty; the administration is the servant of the faculty.[30] He argues that faculty wish and do not wish strong leadership but that they must recognize that both halves of these antinomies are true; each separately is false.

This latter statement puts the twin issues of autonomy and accountability in their proper perspective. The citizenry needs to appreciate that for the faculty to declare itself to be the university can be a commitment to the search for truth for the sake of the glory of society in general but the opposite view is equally true. Faculty are paid salaries and are responsible to the people who pay even though the nature of the higher education enterprise might permit limited oversight. The second antinomy suggests that the administrator must anticipate faculty desires but that does not mean that the only responsibility is to put into effect what the faculty proposes.

Fortunately, these two contrasting ideas, autonomy and accountability, are attended to by the average dean as a matter of course. Deans are invariably chosen from the faculty usually by mechanisms that guarantee considerable faculty participation. Candidates who emerge from such a screening process are likely to have extreme sensitivity to faculty feelings and to the idea of the university that faculty ordinarily profess. Deans do understand the need to balance freedom with order and their considerable experience as faculty members has taught then how it is done.

For it must be remembered that colleges and universities are highly stabilized and ritualized structures that are much more dependent on ceremonial and political congruence with their environments than on any aspect of technical efficiency.[31]

Therefore, deans who understand their responsibilities fully are the ones who likely will enjoy their work the most, for they will be aware that they are making an essential contribution. Colleges and universities cannot prosper without deans who care and who appreciate both the strengths and limitations of their role.

To conclude, the eighties offer enormous challenges to middle managers like deans. We have indicated that in the sixties and seventies college and university administration did achieve its own internal consistency, admittedly by avoiding the excesses of machine bureaucracy.

The situation is now substantially different; the tendency for governments and private bodies to assume increasingly direct control over universities is apparent. Such pressures result in more centralization and formalization; the drive toward machine bureaucracy seems inexorable. Standards are being imposed from outside and this serves to upset the delicate balance inside academe. When deans are forced to deny tenure to enterprising young scholars because of financial limitations, faculty are likely to become discouraged and concerned about their own positions. Yet the performance of scholars, as that of all other professions, depends primarily on their skills and training and a nurturant and secure environment in which to fully develop. The worst way to correct deficiencies in professional activity is through control by externally developed standards and procedures.

What the new configurations promise to be are still problematic. What is assured is that the role of deans in higher education is due for a transformation.

Notes

1. Stanley O. Ikenberry, "The Organizational Dilemma," *The Journal of Higher Education* 43 (January 1972), pp. 23-34.
2. Peter M. Blau and W. Richard Scott, *Formal Organizations* (San Francisco: Chandler, 1962).
3. James G. March and Johan P. Olsen, *Ambiguity and Choice in Organizations* (Bergen, Norway: Universitetsforlaget, 1976).
4. Clark Kerr, *The Uses of the University* (Cambridge, Mass.: Harvard University Press, 1963).
5. Stanley Salmen, *Duties of Administrators in Higher Education* (New York: Macmillan, 1971).
6. Richard I. Miller, "The Academic Dean," *Intellect* 102 (January 1974), pp. 231-234.
7. Laurence R. Veysey, *The Emergence of the American University* (Chicago: University of Chicago Press, 1965).
8. John W. Gould, *The Academic Deanship* (New York: Institute of Higher Education, Teachers College, Columbia University, 1964).
9. Miller, "The Academic Dean."
10. William R. Dill, "The Deanship: An Unstable Craft," in *The Dilemma of the Deanship,* Daniel E. Griffiths and Donald J. McCarty, eds. (Danville, Ill.: Interstate Printers and Publishers, 1980).
11. Edward L. Dejnoska, "The Dean of Education: A Study of Selected Role Norms," *Journal of Teacher Education* 29 (September/October 1978), pp. 81-84.
12. John W. Meyer and Brian Rowan, "Institutionalized Organizations: Formal Structure as Myth and Ceremony," *American Journal of Sociology* 83 (September 1977), pp. 340-362.
13. Ibid., p. 358.
14. Ibid., pp. 340-362.
15. Philip W. Jackson, "Lonely at the Top: Observations on the Genesis of Administrative Isolation," *School Review* 85 (May 1977), pp. 425-433.
16. Charles Perrow, *Complex Organizations: A Critical Essay* (Glenview, Ill : Scott, Foresman & Co., 1972).
17. Meyer and Rowan, "Institutionalized Organizations," pp. 340-362.
18. Frederick Herzberg, Bernard Mausner, and Barbara Snyderman, *The Motivation to*

Work (New York: John Wiley, 1959).

19. Meyer and Rowan, "Institutionalized Organizations," pp. 340-362.

20. Alvin W. Gouldner, "Cosmopolitans and Locals: Toward an Analysis of Latent Social Roles," *Administrative Science Quarterly* 2 (December 1957), pp. 281-306.

21. Lucian Karpik, ed., *Organization and Environment: Theory, Issues, and Reality* (London: Sage Publications, 1978).

22. Hazard Adams, *The Academic Tribes* (New York: Liveright, 1976).

23. Perrow, *Complex Organizations.*

24. John J. Corson, *The Governance of Colleges and Universities* (New York: McGraw-Hill, 1975).

25. Henry Mintzberg, *The Nature of Managerial Work* (New York: Harper and Row, 1973).

26. Peter M. Blau, *Exchange and Power in Social Life* (New York: Wiley, 1964).

27. Murray Edelman, *The Symbolic Uses of Politics* (Urbana, Ill.: University of Illinois Press, 1964).

28. March and Olsen, *Ambiguity and Choice in Organizations.*

29. Michael D. Cohen, James G. March, and Johan P. Olsen, "A Garbage Can Model of Organizational Choice," *Administrative Science Quarterly* 17 (March 1972), pp. 1-23.

30. Adams, *Academic Tribes.*

31. Marshall W. Meyer, *Environment and Organizations* (San Francisco: Jossey-Bass, 1978).

Part 4
Concluding Perspectives

16

The Insulated Americans: Five Lessons From Abroad

Burton R. Clark

In thinking about postsecondary education, Americans tend to remain isolated and insular. The reasons are numerous: Ours is the largest national system; we know this massive complex is the system most widely acclaimed since the second quarter of this century; we are geographically separated from the other major national models; we have many unique features; and we are busy and have more pressing things to do in Montana as well as in New York than to ask how the Austrians and Swedes do it. But there is a great deal to learn about ourselves by learning about the experiences of others in this important sector of society, and it is wise that we learn in advance of the time when events force us to do so.

To use an analogy: American business could have studied the Japanese way of business organization, and the German way, and even the Swedish way a quarter of a century ago instead of waiting until virtually forced to do so in the 1970s by worsening competitive disadvantage and deepening worker discontent. Cross-national thinking encourages the long view in which, for once, we might get in front of our problems. We might even find out what not to do while there is still time not to do it. The perspectives that

Reprinted with permission from *Change* (November 1978).

I draw from comparative research indicate that we are now making changes that not only deny the grounds on which we have been successful to date but will probably lead to arrangements that will seriously hamper us in the future.

To help develop a broad analytical framework within which legislators, chief executive officers, educational officials, faculty, and others can make wiser decisions in postsecondary education, I will set forth some rudimentary ideas in the form of five lessons from abroad. The basic points are interconnected. The first three of these lessons are largely "do nots" or warnings, and they set the stage for the last two, which are affirmations of what should remain central in our minds as we think about leadership and statesmanship in postsecondary education.

Central bureaucracy cannot effectively coordinate mass higher education. Many nations have struggled for a long time to coordinate higher education by means of national administration, treating postsecondary education as a subgovernment of the national state. The effort has been to achieve order, effectiveness, and equity by having national rules applied across the system by one or more national bureaus. France has struggled with the possibilities and limitations of this approach for a century and a half, since Napoleon created a unitary and unified national system of universities. And Italy has moved in this direction for over a century, since the unification of the nation.

Many of the well-established systems of this kind, in Europe and elsewhere, have not only a nationalized system of finance, but also: (a) much nationalization of the curriculum, with common mandated courses in centrally approved fields of study; (b) a nationalized degree structure, in which degrees are awarded by the national system and not by the individual university or college; (c) a nationalized personnel system, in which all those who work for the university are members of the civil service and are hired and promoted accordingly; and (d) a nationalized system of admissions, in which federal rules determine stude it access as well as rights and privileges. Such features naturally obtain strongly in Communist-controlled state administrations, such as East Germany and Poland, where the dominant political philosophy affirms strong state control, based on a hierarchy of command. In some countries, such as West Germany, heavy reliance on central bureaucracy takes place at the state or provincial level of government rather than at the federal level, but often the results are no less thorough.

Back in the days of "elite" higher education, when the number of students and teachers was small, this approach worked to some degree—and we now know why. A bargain was struck, splitting the power between the bureaucrats at the central level and the professors at each institution. There were few middlemen—no trustees, since private individuals were not be be trusted with the care of a public interest, and not enough campus administrators to constitute a separate force. Professors developed the personal and collegial forms of control that provided the underpinnings for personal and group freedom in teaching and research. They elected their own deans and rectors and kept them on a short-term basis. Hence the professors were the power on the local scene, with the state officials often remote, even entombed hundreds of miles away in a Kafkaesque administrative monument. State administration sometimes became a bureaucracy for its own sake, a set of pretenses behind which oligarchies of professors were the real rulers, nationally as well as locally. The public was always given to understand that there was single-system accountability, while inside the structure power was so fractured and scattered that feudal lords ruled sectors of the organizational countryside. In general, this was the traditional European mode of academic organization—power concentrated at the top (in a central bureaucratic staff) and at the bottom (in the hands of chaired professors), with a weak middle at the levels of the university and its major constituent parts.

But the unitary government pyramid has become increasingly deficient over the last 25 years as expansion has enlarged the composite of academic tasks as well as the scale of operations. As consumer demand grows, student clienteles are not only more numerous but more varied. As labor force demands proliferate, the connections to employment grow more intricate. As demands for knowledge multiply, inside and outside the academic occupations, the disciplines and fields of knowledge increase steadily in number and kind. The tasks that modern higher education is now expected to perform differ in kind from those demanded traditionally in other sectors of public administration, and the challenge is to find the structure best suited for these new roles. There is a need to cover knowledge in fields that stretch from archeology to zoology, with business, law, physics, psychology, you name it, thrown in. Across the gamut of fields, knowledge is supposed to be discovered—the research imperative—as well as transmitted and distributed—the teaching and service imperatives. On top of all this has come an accelerated rate of change which makes it all the more difficult for coordinators, who tend to be generalists, to catch up with and comprehend what the specialists are doing.

Clearly, a transition from elite to mass higher education requires dramatic changes in structured state and national systems. The success of mass higher education systems will increasingly depend on: (a) plural rather than singular reactions, or the capacity to face simultaneously in different directions with contradictory reactions to contradictory demands; (b) quicker reactions, at least by some parts of the system, to certain demands; and (c) a command structure that allows for myriad adaptations to special contexts and local conditions. A unified system coordinated by a state bureaucracy is not set up to work in these ways. The unitary system resists differentiated and flexible approaches.

In such countries as Sweden, France, and Italy, many reformers in and out of government are now beginning to realize this, so that the name of their game at this point in history is decentralization—efforts to disperse academic administration to regions, local authorities, and campuses. But this is extremely difficult to do through planned, deliberate effort. Federal officials with firmly fixed power do not normally give it away—abroad any more than in the United States—especially if the public, the legislature, and the chief executive still hold them responsible. But at least things are changing; responsible people in many countries have become convinced that the faults of unitary coordination far outweigh the virtues, and they are looking for ways to break up central control. They are almost ready to take seriously that great admirer of American federalism, De Tocqueville, who maintained over a century ago that while countries can be successfully governed centrally, they cannot be successfully administered centrally. There is surely no realm other than higher education where this principle more aptly applies.

Meanwhile, the United States, historically blessed with decentralization and diversity, within states as well as among them, is hankering after the promised virtues: economy, efficiency, elimination of overlap, less redundancy, better articulation, transferability, accountability, equity, and equality. Our dominant line of reform since World War II has been to impose on the disorder of a market system of higher education new levels of coordination that promise administered order. We continue to do this at an accelerating rate. In fact, if our current momentum toward bureaucratic centralism is maintained, first at the state level and then at the national, we may see the day when we catch up with our friends abroad or even pass them as they travel in the direction of decentralization.

Unless strong counterforces are brought into play, higher education at the state level will increasingly resemble a ministry of education. Administrative staffs will grow, and the powers of central board and staff will shift increasingly from weakly proffered advice toward a primary role in the allocation of resources and in the approval of decisions for the system as a whole. Legislators, governors, and anyone else looking for a source to berate, blame, or whatever will increasingly saddle the central board and staff with the responsibility for economy, efficiency, equity, and all the other goals. And the oldest organizational principle in the world tells us that where there is responsibility, the authority should be commensurate. The trend toward central political and bureaucratic coordination is running strong. Just how strong can be easily seen if we compare state structures of coordination between 1945 and 1975. Robert Berdahl, Lyman Glenny, and other experts on state coordination have noted that in the 1960s alone a remarkably rapid centralization took place, with the states shifting from structures of little or no formal coordination to coordinating boards with regulatory powers.

To see just how fast such an evolutionary trend can change matters at the national level in a democratic nation, we have only to observe Great Britain. Like us, the British were long famous for institutional autonomy. As government money increasingly became the sole source of support, they devised the ingenious University Grants Committee (UGC), which, between 1920 and 1965, became the foremost world model for how to have governmental support without governmental control. But things have changed in the last decade. UGC, which initially received its moneys directly from the treasury and doled out lump sums with few questions asked, now must work with and under the national education department.

The national department has always supervised and sponsored the nonuniversity sector, which operates without a buffer commission. But recently it has become a more aggressive instrument of national educational policy as determined by the party in power and senior administrators in the department. Along with the UGC, it has been swept along toward a stronger regulatory role. Now, in the mid-1970s, central offices in Britain ask all kinds of questions of the institutions, favor one sector at the expense of another, tell some colleges previously out of their purview to close their doors, and suggest to other universities and colleges that they ought not attempt A, B, and C if they hope to maintain the good will of those who must approve the next budget. Britain is still far from having a continental ministry of education, but evolution in that direction has recently been rapid. For the best of short-run reasons, the central administrative machinery is becoming the primary locus of power.

Our own centralization is first taking place at the state level. This allows for diversity and competition among the state systems, some outlet for personnel and students when any one system declines or otherwise becomes particularly unattractive, and the chance for some states to learn from the successes and failures of others. Apparently, it can pay sometimes to be an attentive laggard. But we are certainly heading in the direction of bureaucratic coordination. Most important, our central offices at the national level have adopted a different posture in the mid-1970s from one or two decades earlier. We have already bowed to the quaint notion of taking away federal moneys flowing to an institution when it fails to obey a particular federal rule. Such an approach characterizes the sternest type of relationship between government and higher education in democratic countries with national ministries of education.

Our national policy will ricochet around on such matters for some years to come, while federal officials learn to fit the punishment to the crime. But the new world of national coordination into which we are moving rapidly was made perfectly clear by Secretary of Health, Education, and Welfare Joseph Califano, in a speech at the 1977 meeting of the American Council on Education. In front of an audience of hundreds of university and college presidents, he pointed out that since a recent bit of legislation opposed by academics was now national law, they would have to "comply," and he would have to "enforce." From the market to the minister in a decade! Others in Washington, inside or outside of government, feel free these days to speak of "federal supervision of education" (see Samuel Halperin, "The Federal Future in Education," *Change,* February 1978). Where one stands depends largely upon where one sits, and those who sit in Washington, consumed by national responsibilities and limited to a view from the top, will generally stand on formal coordination, by political and bureaucratic means, of national administration.

In short, we could learn from our friends on the European continent who are now realizing that their national and often unified administrative structures can't cope with mass higher education. Particularly, we could take a lesson from the British, who evolved rapidly in the last decade toward dependence on central bodies as an answer to the immediate demands of economy and equity. But as matters now stand, it appears that we will not do so. Rather we seem determined to learn the hard way, from brute experience.

The greatest single danger in the control of higher education is a monopoly of power, for two good reasons: A monopoly expresses the concerns and perspectives of just one group, shutting out the expression of other interests; and no one group is wise enough to solve all the problems. The history of higher education exhibits monopolies and near monopolies by various groups. Students in some medieval Italian universities, through student guilds, could hire and fire professors and hence obtain favors from them. Senior faculty in some European and English universities during the last two centuries were answerable to no one and hence could sleep for decades. Trustees in some early and not-so-early American colleges could and did fire presidents and professors for not knowing the number of angels dancing on the head of the ecclesiastical pin, or, within our lifetime, for simply smoking cigarettes and drinking martinis. Autocratic presidents in some American institutions, especially teachers colleges, ran campuses as personal possessions; and state bureaucratic staffs and political persons in Europe and America, past and present, democratic and nondemocratic, have often been heavily dominant.

A monopoly of power can be a useful instrument of change: Some states in Western Europe, normally immobilized in higher education, have effected large changes only when a combination of crisis events and a strong ruler produced a temporary monopoly, e.g., France in 1968 under DeGaulle. But the monopoly does not work well for long. It soon becomes a great source of rigidity, resisting change and freezing organization around the rights of just a few.

In the increasingly complex and turbulent organizational environment of the remaining quarter of this century, no small group will be smart enough to know the way. This holds even for the central bureaucratic and planning staffs, who are most likely to evolve into near monopolies of control. State and party officials in East European countries have been finding out that they cannot, from on high and by themselves, effect even so simple an exercise as manpower planning—allotting educational places according to labor force targets. They have been forced by their errors to back off from total dominance and to allow more room for the academic judgments of professors and the choices of students. As mentioned earlier, various countries in Western Europe are attempting to halt and reverse a long trend of centralization in order to move decision making out to the periphery, closer to participants and to the realities of local operating conditions.

All organized systems of any complexity are replete with reciprocal ignorance. The expert in one activity will not know the time of day in another. The extent of ignorance is uncommonly high in systems of higher education, given the breadth of subjects they cover. The chief state higher education officer may not be able to do long division, let alone high-energy physics, while the professor of physics, until retrained and reoriented, is ignorant in everyday matters of system coordination. Here is a fundamental feature of modern organized life: While higher education has been moving toward the formation of large hierarchies traditionally associated with business firms and government agencies, those organizations have been driven to greater dependence on the judgment of authorities in different parts of the organization as work becomes more rooted in expertise. That authority flows toward expert judgment is evident in such mechanisms as peer review and committee evaluation. The organized anarchy of the university remains a useful model of how to function as those at the nominal top become more ignorant.

Another great danger in the control of higher education is domination by a single form of organization. No single form will suffice in mass higher education. Here again some of our European counterparts have been fundamentally unlucky and we can learn from their misfortune. The European university has been around for eight centuries, predating in most locales the nation states that now encompass it. Over the centuries, the assumption grew that genuine higher education meant university education, and that made it difficult to bring other forms into being or to give them prestige. Thus, some nations were swept into mass education with only the nationally supported public university legitimated as a good place to study. As a result, since 1960, this dominant form has been greatly overloaded, with large numbers of students and faculty making more and more heterogeneous demands. This has weakened the traditional function of the university— basic research. In many European countries it is now problematic whether most basic research will remain within the university as teaching time drives out research time and as governments sponsor and protect the science they think they need by placing it in research institutes outside the university systems. Differentiation of form has to occur, but it will happen the hard way in those countries where one form has enjoyed a traditional monopoly.

In the United States, we are in fairly good shape on this score, despite recent worry about homogenization. We have at least five or six major sectors or types of institutions, and the best efforts to classify our 3,000 institutions reveal no less than a dozen or more categories, taking into account extensive differences among the hundreds of places now called universities, the still greater number called colleges, and the 1,000 community colleges. Here no single form dominates the system. But we may have cause to worry about voluntary and mandated convergence.

Institutional differentiation is the name of the game in the coordination of mass higher education. Lesson four is the flip side of lesson three, but the point is so fundamental that it can stand restatement. It answers the most important, substantive question in high-level system coordination and governmental policy: Will and should our universities and colleges become more or less alike? The pressure of the times in nearly all countries is heavily toward institutional uniformity. Yet cross-national comparison tells us that differentiation is the prime requirement for system viability.

One of the great pressures for institutional uniformity derives from the search for equality and equity. For a long time in this country the notion of what constitutes educational equality has been broadening. At first, equality of access simply meant equal chances of getting into a limited number of openings—selection without regard to race, color, or creed. This changed to a position that there should be no selection, that the door should be open to all. But while this idea was developing, a differentiated arrangement of colleges and universities was also taking shape. Everyone could get into the system, but not into all its parts: We differentiated among the roles of the community college, the state college, and the state university, made differential selection an important part of the process, and allowed private colleges and universities to do business as they pleased. This saved us from some of the deleterious effects of letting everyone in. Now the idea of equality is being carried a step further as observers and practitioners take critical note of our institutional unevenness. The effort will grow to extend the concept of educational equality to mean equal treatment for all. To make this possible, all institutions in a system should be equated.

Europeans have already had considerable experience with this idea. It has been embedded in those systems comprising a set of national universities and not much else. The French, Italians, and others have made a sustained attempt to administer equality by formally proclaiming and often treating the constituent parts of the system as equal in program, staff, and value of degree. Still, back in the days when selection was sharp at the lower levels, only 5 percent or less graduated from the upper secondary level and were thereby guaranteed a university place of their choosing. But mass elementary and now mass secondary education have virtually eliminated the earlier selection in some countries and radically reduced it in others. As a result, much larger numbers have come washing into the old undifferentiated university structure, like a veritable tide, with all entrants expecting governmentally guaranteed equality of treatment. There has been no open way of steering the traffic, or of differentiating, which is surely the grandest irony for a national system founded on rational, deliberate administrative control.

This European version of open-door access has recently generated enormous conflict within almost all the European systems. Unless some way is found to distinguish and differentiate, everyone who wants to go to medical school has the right to attend; everyone who wants to go to the University of Rome will continue to go there—when they last stopped counting, it was well above 150,000; and the French apparently had over 200,000 at the University of Paris before a deep crisis forced them to break that totality into a dozen and one parts. Ideally, more degree levels, with appropriate underpinnings, will also have to develop, since the heterogeneous clientele, with its more uneven background and varied aptitude, needs programs of different length and different stopping places. But to attempt to effect selection, assignment, and barriers now, precisely at the time when the doors have finally swung open, is morally outrageous to the former have-nots and to the political parties, unions, and other groups that articulate their interests. The battle rages on the national stage, with virtually all education-related ideologies and interests brought into play. In America, we have been saved from this by a combination of decentralization and differentiation.

Other strong pressures for institutional uniformity come from within higher education systems themselves. One is a voluntary movement of sectors, now referred to as academic drift, toward the part that has highest prestige and offers highest rewards. The English have had trouble resisting such convergence, since the towering prestige of Oxford and Cambridge has induced various institutions to drift toward their style. In addition, administered systems tend toward mandated convergence. Within the European unitary systems, this is expressed in the thousand and one details of equating salaries, teaching loads, laboratory spaces, and sabbatical leaves. Have-nots within the system become pressure groups to catch up with the haves (e.g., in America, state college personnel seek equality with university personnel). Then, too, impartial and fair administration demands system-wide classifications of positions and rewards, with salaries for everyone going up or down by the same percentage. From Warsaw to Tokyo there is a strong tendency in public administration generally to expand and contract in this fashion, equalizing and linking the costs, with the result that future costs become more restrictive.

Since the historical development of our institutions has presented America with the necessary differentiation, a central task is to maintain it by legitimating different institutional roles. We have been relatively successful in initiating tripartite structures within our state systems, but cannot manage to fix this division. A classic case is the unstable role of the state college. In one state after another, the state colleges will not stay where they are supposed to, according to plan, but at a blinding rate—that is, within a decade or two—take on some or all of the functions of universities, alerting their printers to the change in title that soon will be lobbied through the legislature. In contrast, the two-year colleges have accepted their distinctive role and—outside of Connecticut and a few other backward states—have prospered in it.

This has been in the face of predictions, a quarter century ago, that two-year colleges would renounce their obviously undesirable role and evolve into four-year institutions. That convergence was cut off at the pass, more by the efforts of community college people themselves than by weakly manned state offices. There came into being a community college philosophy and a commitment to it, notably in the form of a "movement." Some leaders even became zealots, true believers, glassy eyes and all. Around the commitment, they developed strong interest groups with political muscle. Today, no one's patsy, they have a turf, the willingness and ability to defend it, and the drive and skill to explore such unoccupied territory as recurrent education and lifelong learning to see how much they can annex. When did we last hear about a state college movement? If the name of the game is institutional differentiation, the name of differentiation is legitimation of institutional roles.

Planning and autonomous action are both needed as mechanisms of differentiation, coordination, and change. The difference between the acceptance of roles and the trend toward convergence, both here and abroad, suggests that we cannot leave everything to the drift of the marketplace. Unless the anchorage is there for different roles, institutions will voluntarily converge. Clearly defined roles stand the best chance of surviving. A strong state college was never far from a weak university in the first place. It took only the addition of a few more PhDs to the faculty and a little more inching into graduate work in order to say: Why not us? Teachers colleges were once quite different from universities, but as the former evolved into comprehensive state colleges, their institutional role became fuzzier and harder to stabilize. In contrast, our two-year units were inherently different from universities. Perhaps the rule is: Organizational species that are markedly different can live side by side in a symbiotic relation; species that are similar, with heavily overlapping functions, are likely to conflict, with accommodation then often taking the form of convergence on a single type.

Distinct bases of support and authority seem to contribute to the stability of differentiated roles. The French have a set of institutions, the *Grandes*

Ecoles, that continue to be clearly separated from the universities; many of them are supported by ministries other than the ministry of education. In Britain, teachers colleges until recently were a distinctive class of institutions, operating under the control of local educational authorities. Now that the national department of education has been sitting on them, their separate and distinct character is undergoing erosion. In the United States, the community colleges worked out their separate identity primarily under local control. They came into higher education from a secondary school background and, straddling that line, have often been able to play both sides of the street. This local base has afforded some protection.

So if we must plan and coordinate at higher levels, as we must to some degree, then we should be deliberately attempting to separate and anchor institutional roles. And as formal coordination takes over, multiple sources of sponsorship and supervision will be the best guarantee of institutional diversity. Multiple agencies protect multiple types and check and balance each other. A power market of competing agencies will replace the market of competing institutions.

But not all developments must be planned. A higher order of statesmanship is to recognize the contribution—past, present, and future—of autonomous action and organic growth. There are numerous reasons for pointing our thinking in this direction. One is the basis for our relative success: The strength and preeminence of American higher education is rooted in an unplanned disorderliness that has permitted different parts to perform different tasks, adapt to different needs, and move in different directions of reform. "The benefits of disorder" (see *Change,* October 1976) ought not be inadvertently thrown away as we assemble permanent machinery for state and national coordination.

There is another reason for putting great store in emergent developments. Whether we can effectively plan diversity remains highly problematic. The arguments for planned diversity are strong. State higher education officials surely can point to some successes in the last two decades, as in the case of new campuses in the New York state system that have distinguishing specialties. But we must not congratulate ourselves too soon, since our immature central staffs have not had time yet to settle down as enlarged central bureaucracies loaded with responsibilities, expectations, and interest group demands.

Our central coordinating machinery has not been in place long enough to become the gathering spot for trouble. But the news from abroad on such matters is not promising. The experience of other countries suggests that the balance of forces in and around a central office, especially in a democracy, may not permit planned differentiation to prevail over planned and unplanned uniformity. One of the finest administrators in Europe—Ralf Dahrendorf, now head of the London School of Economics—recently addressed himself to "the problems expansion left behind" in continental and

British higher education and saw as central the need to distinguish, to differentiate. He confessed that he had reluctantly come to the conclusion that deliberate differentiation is a contradiction in terms. Why? Because in the modern world the pressures to have equal access to funds, equal status for all teachers, and so on, are too strong.

People who are held responsible for getting things done are, by the nature of their roles, inclined to value and trust deliberate effort over spontaneously generated developments. But it is the better part of reality to recognize what sociologists have long seen as the imposing weight of the unplanned. As put by Dahrendorf in taking the long view in Britain and continental Europe: "The more one looks at government action, the more one understands that most things will not be done anyway, but will happen in one way or another."

Our central procedural concern ought to be the relative contribution of planned and autonomous actions, especially in regard to differentiation. Both are needed and both are operative, so we need to assess different mixtures of the two. With current combinations tilting toward controlled action, we need to add support to the organic side. We shall need to be increasingly clever about planning for unplanned change, about devising the broad frameworks that encourage the system's constituents to generate, on their own, changes that are creative and adaptive to local contexts.

In the changing relation between higher education and government, higher education is becoming more governmental. It moves inside government, becomes a constituent part of government, a bureau within public administration. On this, perspectives from abroad are invaluable, since we are the laggards who can look down the road that others have already traveled. No small point from abroad is transferable, since context is everything, but the larger portraits of relations should catch our attention, principally to stimulate our thinking about options, potentialities, and limits.

Lessons from abroad help us construct longer time frames through which to analyze the character of our institutions. For example, in considering the problem of a new U.S. Department of Education, we need to ask what it will look like a decade, a quarter century, a half century hence, when it is many times larger in personnel, greatly extended in scope, vertically elaborated in echelons, and well established as a bureaucratic arm of the state alongside Agriculture, Labor, and Commerce. Up to this point, the largest advanced democratic country to attempt to order higher education by means of a national department has been France, a country one fourth the size of the United States, where the effort has been crowned with failure and the name of reform is decentralization. We will be the first nation to attempt to "supervise" 3,000 institutions in a country of over 200,000,000 people by means of double pyramids in which a national department is placed over the state structures, with both levels exercising surveillance over private as well as public institutions. Before taking that step, we need to gain more perspective on what we are doing.

Especially under the time constraints of governmental policy making, our canons of judgment nearly always suffer from overconcentration on immediate problems and short-run solutions. Comparative vision helps to correct these defects, thus reducing the probability of unanticipated, unwanted consequences. Anyone who studies other countries intensively will have seen futures that do not work.

17

Conclusion
Robert O. Berdahl and Philip G. Altbach

A Sense of Perspective

If the preceding chapters have accomplished anything, they ought to have helped create a sense of perspective. Clearly Part One, focusing on the conceptual framework, offered abundant evidence to illustrate that the issues of autonomy, academic freedom, and accountability are not new to academe, but that some of their current and emerging dimensions are. If "financial exigency" acts as a temptation for institutions to use it as a means of ridding themselves of unorthodox faculty members, then eternal vigilance to guard academic freedom will be necessary. If state legislative performance audit committees can demand that universities and colleges define their outputs in measurable terms to allow more precise evaluation, these institutions must consider their strategies carefully. If a court of law can order a professor to jail for his refusal to reveal his vote on a tenure matter, then (irrespective of the merits of the case) we've come a long way from Metzger's "localized institution" governing itself in isolated splendor. Duryea's and Metzger's chapters, then, provided background from which to appreciate the more contemporary perspectives of McConnell and Slaughter.

By the same token, Stadtman's essay on the evolution of American higher education in the 1970s provided a valuable backdrop for Kerr and Gade to explore the emerging issues that universities and colleges will have to confront in the coming years. While we have largely been preoccupied with *process* issues, it is useful to be reminded of the major substantive concerns that will have to be handled by those processes. Enrollment declines, fiscal problems, faculty reallocation, and other controversial matters will all have to be dealt with in the coming decade.

The emphasis in Part Two shifted from the conceptual concerns of the opening section to a detailed exposition of the major external constituencies that act to influence and/or control the actions of universities and colleges. Here the focus was more on the rationales behind the roles of state and federal governments, the courts, and the variety of private and voluntary associations. In a sense, Millett, McGuiness, Hobbs, and Harcleroad have served as quasi-advocates for the legitimacy of the roles that their respective constituencies play in American higher education. It remains for the reader to decide in each case whether the relations in question are in rough balance or whether they need adjustment either toward more autonomy or more accountability.

Part Three then shifted the focus to the ways in which the various internal constituencies have responded to the increasing external pressures. Nason reported a certain reassertion of lay board authority and stronger presidential leadership in the face of demands for retrenchment and increased accountability. Altbach pointed to a faculty apparently less sure of its professional status in an "industry" under heavy pressure, with some portions hoping to recoup through external collective bargaining what they felt they had lost internally through changes in power relationships.

McCarty and Young's analysis of the changing role of deans reflects the ambivalence one might expect from the preceding two categories: deans are increasingly torn between an identification with senior administration or with the faculty. They are finding their *primary* ties with the former, but at the cost of some of the discretionary powers they formerly wielded.

Finally, Levine has shown how the student community has turned to political channels external to the university and college to find more forceful expression for student views. At a time when this volume confirms the increasing role of the state and federal governments, it seems quite logical for the student movement to widen its efforts to include those citadels of power.

Where Do We Go from Here?

Is the academy really in a state of crisis, or are things being exaggerated for dramatic effect?

While the word "crisis" is often used, it is our view that we are in the midst of an unprecedented situation. In addition, we view the combination of enrollment decline, federal and state budget cuts and general fiscal austerity, and much more demanding accountability measures as placing universities and colleges that have grown used to expansion in students and budgets under far greater than normal strain.

Some voices—from greatly respected sources—counsel universities and colleges to take more careful stock of their essential identities and to consider what operating freedoms they must have to achieve those identities. They must then try to arrive at explicit understandings with surrounding public authorities to honor such relationships. Shils, in an essay on "Government and University" addresses this concern as involving

> interdependence and conflict of government and universities, with what each owes the other and what each owes to values which are inherent in its own distinctive nature and which are not necessarily harmonious with the values of the other. I would aim at a "constitution" of university and state according to the idea of each.[1]

Shils's essay is essentially concerned with relations between the major research universities and the U.S. federal government, but his plea for a clearer consensus of values and orientations could be extended to all postsecondary education.

In a vastly different context, Lord Ashby made a similar point. He observed that the African universities that had been founded by the British in their former colonies suffered from a unique dilemma. They inherited a written university charter from the British. But African social and educational conditions made this charter constricting, illogical, and in part inappropriate.[2] Ashby urged that the universities rethink their charters and agree on those essential aspects of governance that they must be prepared to defend. (The smaller the list, he points out, the easier it will be to reach agreement.) Then, at a time *other* than that of a crisis in university-state relations, university personnel would open discussions with state officials about an accommodation concerning university/state relationships. Finally, after such an agreement, the academic community should have the courage and the determination to oppose as forcefully as necessary any violations of the agreement.

While Ashby's proposal was addressed to certain African universities, our earlier chapters have revealed some parallel ambiguities in American universities' current relations with their governments. Thus, the Carnegie Commission in 1973 offered the following recommendation:

> Coordinating agencies at the state level should seek to establish, in cooperation with public and private institutions of higher education, guidelines defin-

ing areas of state concern and areas of institutional independence that avoid detailed control.[3]

The Commission reasoned that although campuses had "largely occupied" "by default" the "substantial sphere of ambiguity in the past," governmental authority was expanding and moving into those areas. "The ambiguities that once were an asset are now a liability. Greater precision of understanding is now highly desirable."[4]

Not all agree, however. Stephen Bailey, former Vice President of the American Council on Education, argued:

> at heart we are dealing with a dilemma we cannot rationally wish to resolve. The public interest would not...be served if the academy were to enjoy an untroubled immunity. Nor could the public interest be served by the academy's being subjected to an intimate surveillance. Whatever our current discomforts because of a sense that the state is crowding us a bit, the underlying tension is benign.[5]

Bailey then dissented from the concordat approach, saying that "the precise border between the state and the academy is, and must be kept, fuzzy. For if a precise delineation is sought,...the state has more than the academy of what it takes to draw the line."[6]

But if Bailey cautions not to define limits, in another address he urges that the academy should seek to understand the difference between the *efficiency* that is owed to Caesar and *effectiveness* that is owed "to God." Furthermore, he warns that sometimes efficiency is the enemy of effectiveness and when this is so, the academy must resolutely defend the greater value.[7]

We have, in this volume, proposed no panaceas. Rather, we have attempted to illustrate how the intersection between higher education and society functions at a time of considerable stress for academic institutions and those who work in them. The relationship is complex and involves external constituencies such as government, the courts, and others and all of the internal communities that make up an academic institution. In addition, the imponderables of enrollment declines, budget cuts, and changing student interests are added to an already complex situation. If this volume has not provided clear solutions, at least it has raised important questions. Even more, it has suggested ways of approaching the relationship between higher education and society.

Notes

1. *Newsletter of The International Council on the Future of the University*, 3, no. 5 (1976).

2. Eric Ashby, *Universities: British, Indian, African* (Cambridge, Mass.: Harvard University Press, 1966).

3. Carnegie Commission, *Governance of Higher Education* (New York: McGraw-Hill, 1973), p. 29.

4. Ibid., pp. 28-29.

5. Stephen Bailey, "Education and the State," in *Education and the State,* John Hughes ed., (Washington, D.C.: American Council on Education, 1974).

6. Ibid.

7. Stephen Bailey, "The Limits of Accountability" (remarks at New York Regents Trustees' Conference, New York, N.Y., February 8, 1973).

Bibliography

This selected bibliography is intended to provide a listing of key materials related to the topics considered in this volume. It has been prepared with the assistance of the contributors to this volume, who have provided the references in their areas of expertise. The stress is on a short list of the most important writings, mainly recent materials, concerning these topics. The bibliography is intended to provide a preliminary guide to further reading and research, rather than a comprehensive listing of material. We have arranged our listings according to the main topics considered in the book.

P.G. Altbach
R.O. Berdahl

General References: Higher Education in American Society

Adelman, Howard. *The Holiversity.* Toronto: New Press, 1973.

Ashby, Eric. *Any Person, Any Study: An Essay on Higher Education in the*

United States. New York: McGraw-Hill, 1971.

Ben-David, Joseph. *Trends in American Higher Education.* Chicago: University of Chicago Press, 1972.

Carnegie Commission. *Priorities for Action: Final Report of the Carnegie Commission on Higher Education.* New York: McGraw-Hill, 1973.

Carnegie Council on Policy Studies in Higher Education. *Three Thousand Futures: The Next Twenty Years for Higher Education.* San Francisco: Jossey-Bass, 1980.

Carnegie Foundation for the Advancement of Teaching. *More Than Survival.* San Francisco: Jossey-Bass, 1975.

Dressel, Paul. *The Autonomy of Public Colleges.* New Directions for Institutional Research, no. 26. San Francisco: Jossey-Bass, 1980.

Finn, Chester E. Jr. *Scholars, Dollars and Bureaucrats.* Washington, D.C.: Brookings Institution, 1978.

Hook, Sidney; Kurtz, Paul; and Todorovich, Miro. *The University and the State.* Buffalo, N.Y.: Prometheus Books, 1978.

Jencks, Christopher and Riesman, David. *The Academic Revolution.* Chicago: University of Chicago Press, 1977.

Kerr, Clark. *The Uses of the University.* New York: Harper and Row, 1972.

Parsons, Talcott and Platt, Gerald M. *The American University.* Cambridge, Mass.: Harvard University Press, 1973.

Perkins, James, ed. *Higher Education: From Autonomy to Systems.* New York: International Council for Educational Development, 1972.

Rudolph, Frederick. *Curriculum: A History of the American Undergraduate Course of Study Since 1636.* San Francisco: Jossey-Bass, 1977.

Wolff, Robert Paul. *The Ideal of the University.* Boston: Beacon Press, 1969.

Historical Overview

Brody, Alexander. *The American State and Higher Education.* Washington, D.C.: American Council on Education, 1935.

Cobban, A.B. *The Medieval Universities.* London: Methuen, 1975.

Duryea, E.D. *Prologue to the American System of Higher Education: Higher Learning in Western Culture.* Occasional Paper, no. 4. Buffalo, N.Y.: Department of Higher Education, State University of New York at Buffalo, 1979.

Gellhorn, Ernest and Boyer, Barry B. "Government and Education: The University as a Regulated Industry." *Arizona State Law Journal,* (1977).

Herbst, Jurgen. "The First Three American Colleges: Schools of the Reformation." *Perspectives in American History* 8 (1972).

Hofstadter, Richard and Smith, Wilson, eds. *American Higher Education: A Documentary History.* Chicago: University of Chicago Press, 1961.

Metzger, Walter P. "Origins of the Association." *AAUP Bulletin* 55 (Summer 1965), pp. 229-237.

Nevins, Allan. *The State Universities and Democracy.* Urbana, Ill.: University of Illinois Press, 1962.

Reeves, Marjorie. "The European University from Medieval Times." In *Higher Education: Demand and Response.* Edited by W.R. Niblett. San Francisco: Jossey-Bass, 1970, pp. 61-84.

Veysey, Laurence. *The Emergence of the American University.* Chicago: University of Chicago Press, 1965.

Autonomy and Accountability

Astin, Alexander W.; Bowen, Howard R.; and Chambers, Charles M. *Evaluating Educational Quality: A Conference Summary.* Washington,

D.C.: Council on Postsecondary Education, 1979.

Bowen, Howard R. *Investment in Learning.* San Francisco: Jossey-Bass, 1977.

————. *The Costs of Higher Education.* San Francisco: Jossey-Bass, 1980.

Carnegie Foundation for the Advancement of Teaching. *The States and Higher Education: A Proud Past and A Vital Future.* San Francisco: Jossey-Bass, 1976.

Clark, Burton R., and Youn, Ted I.K. *Academic Power in the United States: Comparative Historical and Structural Perspectives.* Washington, D.C.: American Association for Higher Education, 1976.

Dressel, Paul L. *The Autonomy of Public Colleges.* San Francisco: Jossey-Bass, 1980.

Folger, John K., ed. *Increasing the Public Accountability of Higher Education.* San Francisco: Jossey-Bass, 1977.

Kaplin, William A. *The Law of Higher Education.* San Francisco: Jossey-Bass, 1978.

Lenning, Oscar T. *The Outcomes Structure: An Overview and Procedures for Applying It In Postsecondary Education Institutions.* Boulder, Colo.: National Center for Higher Education Management Systems, 1977.

Selden, William K. *Accreditation and the Public Interest.* Washington, D.C.: The Council on Postsecondary Education, 1976.

Academic Freedom

Brubacher, John S., and Rudy, Willis. *Higher Education in Transition: A History of American Colleges and Universities, 1636-1976.* New York: Harper and Row, 1976.

Furner, Mary O. *Advocacy and Objectivity: The Professionalization of Social Science, 1865-1905.* Lexington, Ky.: University of Kentucky Press, 1975.

Hofstadter, Richard and Metzger, Walter P. *The Development of Academic Freedom in the United States.* New York: Columbia University Press, 1957.

Joughlin, Louis, ed. *Academic Freedom and Tenure: A Handbook of the AAUP.* Madison, Wis.: University of Wisconsin Press, 1969.

McIver, Robert. *Academic Freedom in Our Time.* New York: Columbia University Press, 1955.

Metzger, Walter P. "Academic Tenure in America: A Historical Essay." In *Academic Tenure: Report of the Commission.* San Francisco: Jossey-Bass, 1973, pp. 93-105.

Pincoffs, Edmund L., ed. *The Concept of Academic Freedom.* Austin, Tex.: University of Texas Press, 1975.

Slaughter, Sheila. "The Danger Zone: Academic Freedom and Civil Liberties." *Annals of the American Academy of Political and Social Science* 448 (March 1980): 46-61.

Current and Emerging Issues

Bowen, Howard R. *Investment in Learning: The Individual and Social Value of American Higher Education.* San Francisco: Jossey-Bass, 1977.

Carnegie Council on Policy Studies in Higher Education. *Giving Youth A Better Chance: Options for Education, Work, and Service.* San Francisco: Jossey-Bass, 1979.

_____. *Three Thousand Futures: The Next Twenty Years for Higher Education.* San Francisco: Jossey-Bass, 1980.

Glenny, Lyman A. "Demographic and Related Issues for Higher Education in the 1980s." *Journal of Higher Education* 51 (1980): 363-380.

Mayhew, Lewis B. *Surviving the Eighties: Strategies and Procedures for Solving Fiscal and Enrollment Problem.* San Francisco: Jossey-Bass, 1979.

Ohio Board of Regents. *A Strategic Approach to the Maintenance of Institutional Financial Stability and Flexibility in the Face of Enrollment Instability or Decline.* Washington, D.C.: Academy for Educational Development, 1979.

Smith, Bruce L.R., and Karlesky, Joseph J. *The State of Academic Science: The Universities in the Nation's Research Effort.* New York: Change Magazine Press, 1977. Vol. I: Summary of Major Findings; Vol. II: Working Papers.

Stadtman, Verne A. *Academic Adaptations: Higher Education Prepares for the 1980s and 1990s.* San Francisco: Jossey-Bass, 1980.

State Governments

Andersen, Charles J., compiler. *1980 Fact Book for Academic Administrators.* Washington, D.C.: American Council on Education, 1980.

Benezet, Louis T. *Private Higher Education and Public Funding.* Washington, D.C.: American Association for Higher Education, 1976.

Berdahl, Robert O. *Statewide Coordination of Higher Education.* Washington, D.C.: American Council on Education, 1971.

Breneman, David W., and Finn, Chester E., Jr., eds. *Public Policy and Private Higher Education.* Washington, D.C.: Brookings Institution, 1978.

Carnegie Commission on Higher Education. *The Capitol and the Campus.* New York: McGraw-Hill, 1971.

_____. *Priorities for Action.* New York: McGraw-Hill, 1973.

Carnegie Commission on Policy Studies in Higher Education. *The States and Private Higher Education.* San Francisco: Jossey-Bass, 1977.

_____. *Three Thousand Futures.* San Francisco: Jossey-Bass, 1980.

Carnegie Foundation for the Advancement of Teaching. *The States and Higher Education.* San Francisco: Jossey-Bass, 1976.

Committee on Government and Higher Education. *The Efficiency of Free-*

dom. Baltimore, Md.: Johns Hopkins University Press, 1959.

Cowley, W.H. *Presidents, Professors and Trustees.* Edited by Donald T. Williams, Jr. San Francisco: Jossey-Bass, 1980.

Dressel, Paul L. *The Autonomy of Public Colleges.* New Directions for Institutional Research. San Francisco: Jossey-Bass, 1980.

Education Commission of the States. *Challenge: Coordination and Governance in the '80s.* Denver, Colo.: Education Commission of the States, 1980.

Glenny, Lyman A. *Autonomy of Public Colleges.* New York: McGraw-Hill 1959.

Harcleroad, Fred F., ed. *Administration of Statewide Systems of Higher Education.* Iowa City: American College Testing Program, 1975.

Lee, Eugene C., and Bowen, Frank M. *Managing Multicampus Systems.* San Francisco: Jossey-Bass, 1975.

McCoy, Marilyn and Halstead, D. Kent. *Higher Education Financing in the Fifty States: Interstate Comparisons Fiscal Year 1976.* Washington, D.C.: U.S. Government Printing Office, 1979.

Millett, John D. *Financing Higher Education in the United States.* New York: Columbia University Press, 1952.

Moos, Malcolm and Rourke, Francis E. *The Campus and the State.* Baltimore, Md.: Johns Hopkins University Press, 1959.

National Commission on United Methodist Higher Education. *Endangered Service: Independent Colleges, Public Policy, and the First Amendment.* Nashville, Ky.: National Commission, 1976.

Sloan Commission on Government and Higher Education. *A Program for Renewed Partnership.* Cambridge, Mass.: Ballinger, 1980.

Task Force of the National Council of Independent College and Universities. *A National Policy for Private Higher Education.* Washington, D.C.: Association of American Colleges, 1974.

The Federal Government and Postsecondary Education

History of Federal Role

Honey, John C., and Hartle, Terry W. *Federal-State-Institutional Relationships in Postsecondary Education.* Syracuse, N.Y.: Syracuse University Research Corporation, 1975.

Rainsford, George. *Congress and Higher Education in the Nineteenth Century.* Knoxville: University of Tennessee, 1972.

Rivlin, Alice. *The Role of the Federal Government in Financing Higher Education.* Washington, D.C.: Brookings Institution, 1961.

Policy Process

Finn, Chester E. *Education and the Presidency.* Lexington, Mass.: D.C. Heath, 1978.

Gladieux, Lawrence E. "What Has Congress Wrought?" *Change,* October 1980: 25-31.

Wolanin, Thomas R., and Gladieux, Lawrence E. *Congress and the College.* Lexington, Mass.: D.C. Heath, 1977.

Regulations and Higher Education

Bender, Louis W. *Federal Regulations and Higher Education.* Washington, D.C.: American Association for Higher Education, 1977.

Frances, Carol and Coldren, Sharon L. *The Costs of Implementing Federally Mandated Social Programs at Colleges and Universities.* Washington, D.C.: American Council on Education, 1976.

Sloan Commission on Government and Higher Education. *A Program for Renewed Partnership.* Cambridge, Mass.: Ballinger, 1980.

Other Publications

Breneman, Davis W., and Finn, Chester E., Jr., eds. *Public Policy and Private Higher Education*. Washington, D.C.: Brookings Institution, 1978.

Finn, Chester E., Jr. *Scholars, Dollars and Bureaucrats*. Washington, D.C.: Brookings Institution, 1978.

Legal Aspects

Edwards, Harry T. *Higher Education and the Unholy Crusade Against Governmental Regulation*. Cambridge, Mass.: Institute for Educational Management, Harvard University, 1980.

Edwards, Harry T., and Nordin, Virginia Davis. *Higher Education and the Law*. Cambridge, Mass.: Institute for Educational Management, Harvard University, 1979.

Edwards, Harry T., and Nordin, Virginia Davis. *An Introduction to the American Legal System*. Cambridge, Mass.: Institute for Educational Management, Harvard University, 1980.

Hobbs, Walter C., ed. *Government Regulation of Higher Education*. Cambridge, Mass.: Ballinger, 1978.

Hollander, Patricia A. *Legal Handbook for Educators*. Boulder, Colo.: Westview Press, 1978.

Dick, Howard A.E. *State Aid to Private Higher Education*. Charlottesville, Va.: Michie, 1977.

Kaplin, William A. *The Law of Higher Education: Legal Implications of Administrative Decision Making*. San Francisco: Jossey-Bass, 1978.

_____. *The Law of Higher Education 1980*. San Francisco: Jossey-Bass, 1980.

The Sloan Commission on Government and Higher Education. *A Program for Renewed Partnership*. Cambridge, Mass.: Ballinger, 1980.

Young, Parker D. *The Yearbook of Higher Education Law 1977...1980.* Topeka, Kans.: National Organization on Legal Problems of Education, 1977-1980.

Private Constituencies

Cheit, Earl F., and Lobman, Theodore E. *Foundations and Higher Education.* Berkeley, Calif.: Carnegie Council on Policy Studies in Higher Education, 1979.

Cosand, Joseph, et. al. *Higher Education's National Institutional Membership Association.* Ann Arbor, Mich.: Center for the Study of Higher Education, University of Michigan, 1980.

Harcleroad, Fred. *Accreditation: History, Process and Problems.* Washington, D.C.: American Association for Higher Education/ERIC Clearinghouse on Higher Education, Washington, 1981.

_____. "Effects of Regional Agencies and Voluntary Associations." In *Improving Academic Management: A Handbook of Planning and Institutional Research.* Edited by Paul Jedamus and Marvin Peterson. San Francisco: Jossey-Bass, 1980.

_____. *Voluntary Organizations in America and the Development of Educational Accreditation.* Washington, D.C.: Council on Postsecondary Accreditation, 1980.

Moore, Raymond S. *Consortiums in American Higher Education: 1965-66.* Washington, D.C.: U.S. Government Printing Office, 1968.

Orlans, Harold. *Private Accreditation and Public Eligibility.* Lexington, Mass.: D.C. Heath, 1975.

Selden, William K. *Accreditation: A Struggle Over Standards in Higher Education.* New York: Harper, 1960.

Trivett, David. *Accreditation and Institutional Eligibility.* Washington, D.C.: American Association for Higher Education, 1976.

Academic Profession

Altbach, Philip G., ed. *Comparative Perspectives on the Academic Profession.* New York: Praeger, 1977.

Altbach, Philip G., and Slaughter, Sheila, eds. "The Academic Profession." *Annals of the American Academy of Political and Social Science* 448 (March 1980): pp. 1-150.

Anderson, Charles and Murray, John, eds. *The Professors.* Cambridge, Mass.: Schenkman, 1971.

Ladd, E.C., Jr. and Lipset, S.M. *The Divided Academy: Professors and Politics.* New York: McGraw-Hill, 1975.

Lewis, Lionel. *Scaling the Ivory Tower: Merit and Its Limits in Academic Careers.* Baltimore, Md.: Johns Hopkins University Press, 1975.

Schulman, Carol Herrnstadt. *Old Expectations, New Realities: The Academic Profession Revisited.* Washington, D.C.: American Association for Higher Education, 1979.

Shils, Edward. "The Academic Ethos Under Strain." *Minerva* 13 (Spring 1975): 1-37.

Trow, Martin, ed. *Teachers and Students.* New York: McGraw-Hill, 1975.

Wilson, Logan. *American Academics: Then and Now.* New York: Oxford University Press, 1979.

The College Student

Altbach, P. *Student Politics in America: A Historical Analysis.* New York: McGraw-Hill, 1974.

Astin, A.W., et al. *The American Freshman: Norms for Fall 1979.* Los Angeles: Cooperative Institutional Research Program, 1980.

Fuller, B., and Samuelson, J. *Student Votes: Do They Make A Difference?* Washington, D.C.: U.S. Student Association, 1977.

Jacobson, D. *Student Voting Power.* Washington, D.C.: U.S. Student Association, 1978.

Lamont, L. *Campus Shock.* New York: Dutton, 1979.

Levine, A. *When Dreams and Heroes Die: A Portrait of Today's College Students.* San Francisco: Jossey-Bass, 1980.

Lipset, S.M. *Rebellion in the University.* Chicago: University of Chicago Press, 1976.

Wohl, R. *The Generation of 1914.* Cambridge, Mass.: Harvard University Press, 1970.

Yankelovich, D. *The New Morality: A Profile of American Youth in the 1970's.* New York: McGraw-Hill, 1974.

_____. *The Changing Values on Campus: Political and Personal Attitudes of Today's College Students.* New York: Washington Square Press, 1972.

Presidents and Governing Boards

Carnegie Commission on Higher Education. *The Governance of Higher Education: Six Priority Problems.* New York: McGraw-Hill, 1973.

Cohen, Michael D., and March, James G. *Leadership and Ambiguity: The American College President.* New York: McGraw-Hill, 1974.

Corson, John. *The Governance of College and Universities.* Rev. ed. New York: McGraw-Hill, 1975.

Cowley, W.H. *Presidents, Professors and Trustees.* San Francisco: Jossey-Bass, 1980.

Hodgkinson, Harold L. *College Governance - The Amazing Thing is That It Works At All.* Washington, D.C.: Report No. 11 of ERIC Clearinghouse on Higher Education.

Ingram, Richard T., ed. *Handbook of College and University Trusteeship.* San Francisco: Jossey-Bass, 1980.

Kauffman, Joseph F. *At the Pleasure of the Board.* Washington, D.C.: American Council on Education, 1980.

Nason, John W. *The Future of Trusteeship.* Washington, D.C.: Association of Governing Boards, 1974.

Perkins, James A., ed. *The University as an Organization.* New York: McGraw-Hill, 1973.

Rauh, Morton A. *The Trusteeship of Colleges and Universities.* New York: McGraw-Hill, 1969.

Zwingle, J.L. *Effective Trusteeship.* Washington, D.C.: Association of Governing Boards, 1975.

Senior Administrators

Adams, Hazard. *The Academic Tribes.* New York: Liveright, 1976.

Corson, John J. *The Governance of Colleges and Universities.* New York: McGraw-Hill, 1975.

Gould, John W. *The Academic Deanship.* New York: Institute for Higher Education, Teachers College, Columbia University, 1964.

Griffiths, Daniel E., and McCarty, Donald J., eds. *The Dilemma of the Deanship.* Danville, Ill.: The Interstate Printers and Publishers, 1980.

Jackson, Philip W. "Lonely at the Top: Observations on the Genesis of Administrative Isolation." *School Review* 85 (May 1977): 425-433.

Kapel, David E., and Dejnoska, Edward L. "The Educational Deanship: A Further Analysis." *Research in Higher Education* 10 (April 1979): 99-112.

Meyer, John W., and Rowan, Brian. "Institutionalized Organizations: Formal Structure as Myth and Ceremony." *American Journal of Sociology* 83 (September 1977): 340-362.

Salmen, Stanley. *Duties of Administrators in Higher Education.* New York: Macmillan, 1971.

Comparative Perspectives

Altbach, Philip G. *Comparative Higher Education.* London: Mansell, 1979.

————. *Comparative University Reform.* Washington, D.C.: American Association for Higher Education, 1981.

Ashby, Eric. *Universities: British, Indian, African.* Cambridge, Mass.: Harvard University Press, 1966.

Ben-David, Joseph. *Centers of Learning: Britain, France, Germany, United States.* New York: McGraw-Hill, 1977.

Ben-David, Joseph and Zloczower, Awarham. "Universities and Academic Systems in Modern Societies." *European Journal of Sociology* **3** (1962): 45-84.

Bereday, George Z.F. *Universities for All.* San Francisco: Jossey-Bass, 1973.

Burn, Barbara; Altbach, P.G.; Kerr, Clark; and Perkins, James. *Higher Education in Nine Countries.* New York: McGraw-Hill, 1971.

Driver, Christopher. *The Exploding University.* Indianapolis, Ind.: Bobbs-Merrill, 1971.

Niblett, W.R., and Butts, R.F., eds. *Universities Facing the Future.* San Francisco: Jossey-Bass, 1972.

Ross, Murray. *The University.* New York: McGraw-Hill, 1976.

Stone, Lawrence, ed. *The University in Society.* Princeton, N.J.: Princeton University Press, 1974.

Van de Graaff, John, et al. *Academic Power: Patterns of Authority in Seven National Systems of Higher Education.* New York: Praeger, 1978.

Contributors

PHILIP G. ALTBACH is Professor of Higher Education and Chairman and Professor in the Department of Social Foundations of Education at the State University of New York at Buffalo, He is also Director of the Comparative Education Center. He is North American Editor of *Higher Education,* an international journal, and editor of the *Comparative Education Review.* Among his recent publications are *Comparative University Reform* (1981), *Publishing in the Third World* (1980), and *Comparative Education* (1981).

ROBERT O. BERDAHL is Professor of Higher Education and Director of the Institute for Higher and Adult Education at the University of Maryland at College Park. He has been Chairman of the Department of Higher Education at the State University of New York at Buffalo and has served as President of the Association for the Study of Higher Education. He has written widely on university-state relations in the United States and Britain.

BURTON R. CLARK is Allan Cartter Professor of Education and Professor of Sociology at the University of California, Los Angeles. He has written *Academic Power in Italy, The Open Door College,* and other books. He directs a research project concerning the international aspects of higher education.

E.D. DURYEA is Professor of Higher Education and Chairman of the Department of Higher Education, State University of New York at Buffalo. Following his doctorate from Stanford University in 1948, his professional career has included both service in major administrative positions and teaching in the field of higher education. His scholarly focus has combined organization and administration and the history of higher education. Among his publications is *Faculty Unions and Collective Bargaining.* He is currently working on a history of governing boards and corporate authority in higher education.

MARIAN L. GADE is a Research Associate at the Center for Studies in Higher Education at the University of California at Berkeley. She works with Clark Kerr under the auspices of the Carnegie Foundation for the Advancement of Teaching.

FRED F. HARCLEROAD is Professor and was Founding Director of the Center for the Study of Higher Education at the University of Arizona.

WALTER C. HOBBS is Associate Professor of Higher Education at the State University of New York at Buffalo. He is a sociologist and also holds a law degree. His recent research interests have been in the area of the legal aspects of higher education. He is editor of *Government Regulation of Higher Education.*

CLARK KERR is President Emeritus of the University of California. He served as Director and Chairman of the Carnegie Commission on Higher Education and the Carnegie Council on Policy Studies in Higher Education from 1967 until 1979. He currently serves on the boards of several organizations, including the International Council for Educational Development and the Work in America Institute. He is the author of a number of books, among them the classic *The Uses of the University.*

ARTHUR LEVINE is Senior Fellow at the Carnegie Foundation for the Advancement of Teaching. He is author of several books, including *When Dreams and Heroes Died: A Portrait of Today's College Students* and *Reform of Undergraduate Education.* Dr. Levine holds the Ph.D. from the State University of New York at Buffalo.

DONALD J. McCARTY is Professor of Educational Administration at the

University of Wisconsin, Madison, where he served as Dean of the School of Education. His most recent book, co-edited with Daniel Griffiths, is *The Dilemma of the Deanship.*

T.R. McCONNELL is Professor Emeritus of Education at the University of California at Berkeley. He has served as dean of Cornell College, dean of the College of Science, Literature and the Arts at the University of Minnesota and as Chancellor of the University of Buffalo. In 1957, he organized the Center for the Study of Higher Education at Berkeley. He is co-author, with K.P. Mortimer, of *Sharing Authority Effectively: Participation, Interaction and Discretion.*

AIMS C. McGUINNESS, JR. is Assistant Executive Director for Intergovernmental and Organizational Relations, Education Commission of the States. He has served as executive assistant to the Chancellor of the University of Maine. He is co-author of *The Changing Image of Postsecondary Education.*

WALTER METZGER is Professor of History at Columbia University. He has written widely on the question of academic freedom and is co-author of *The Development of Academic Freedom in the United States.*

JOHN D. MILLETT is President Emeritus of Miami University (Ohio) and Chancellor Emeritus of the Ohio Board of Regents. He has also served as an officer of the Academy for Educational Development. Author of a number of books in higher education, he is currently serving as Professor of Educational Leadership at Miami University.

JOHN W. NASON served as President of Swarthmore College (1940-53), as President of the Foreign Policy Association (1953-62) and of Carleton College (1962-70). He is author of *The Future of Trusteeship, Presidential Assessment,* and other publications.

SHEILA SLAUGHTER is Assistant Professor of Higher Education at the State University of New York at Buffalo. She has served on the faculty of Virginia Polytechnic Institute and State University and has been assistant to the President of a community college in Massachusetts. She has co-edited several volumes, including *Academic Supermarkets* and *Perspectives on Publishing.*

VERNE A. STADTMAN is Vice-President of the Carnegie Foundation for the Advancement of Teaching in Washington, D.C. He was formerly associate director of the Carnegie Council on Policy Studies in Higher

Education. He is co-editor of *Academic Transformations*

I. PHILLIP YOUNG is Assistant Professor of Educational Administration at the University of Wisconsin, Madison. He has served as an assistant superintendent of schools and has a research interest in personnel.

PAPERBACKS AVAILABLE FROM PROMETHEUS BOOKS

CRITIQUES OF THE PARANORMAL

____ESP & Parapsychology: A Critical Re-evaluation *C.E.M. Hansel* $8.95

____Extra-Terrestrial Intelligence *James L. Christian, editor*   6.95

____Objections to Astrology *L. Jerome & B. Bok*   3.95

____The Psychology of the Psychic *D. Marks & R. Kammann*   8.95

____Philosophy & Parapsychology *J. Ludwig, editor*   8.95

____Paranormal Borderlands of Science *Kendrick Frazier, editor* $12.95

HUMANISM

____Ethics Without God *K. Nielsen*   6.95

____Humanist Alternative *Paul Kurtz, editor*   5.95

____Humanist Ethics *Morris, Storer, editor*   9.95

____Humanist Funeral Service *Corliss Lamont*   2.95

____Humanist Manifestos I & II   1.95

____Humanist Wedding Service *Corliss Lamont*   2.95

____Humanistic Psychology *Welch, Tate, Richards, editors*   9.95

____Moral Problems in Contemporary Society *Paul Kurtz, editor*   5.95

____Voice in the Wilderness *Corliss Lamont*   5.95

____A Secular Humanist Declaration   1.95

LIBRARY OF LIBERAL RELIGION

____Facing Death and Grief *George N. Marshall*   7.95

____Living Religions of the World *Carl Hermann Voss*   4.95

PHILOSOPHY & ETHICS

____Art of Deception *Nicholas Capaldi*   5.95

____Beneficent Euthanasia *M. Kohl, editor*   10.95

____Esthetics Contemporary *Richard Kostelanetz, editor*   10.95

____Exuberance: A Philosophy of Happiness *Paul Kurtz*   3.00

____Fullness of Life *Paul Kurtz*   5.95

____Freedom of Choice Affirmed *Corliss Lamont*   4.95

____Humanhood: Essays in Biomedical Ethics *Joseph Fletcher*   7.95

____Journeys Through Philosophy *N. Capaldi & L. Navia, editors*   11.95

____Philosophy: An Introduction *Antony Flew*   6.95

____Thinking Straight *Antony Flew*   5.50

____Worlds of Plato & Aristotle *Wilbur & Allen, editors*   6.95

____Worlds of the Early Greek Philosophers *Wilbur & Allen, editors*   7.95

____Animal Rights and Human Morality *Bernard Rollin*   9.95

____A Secular Humanist Declaration *drafted by Paul Kurtz*   1.95

____Worlds of Hume and Kant *Wilbur & Allen, editors*   7.95

____Problem of God *Peter A. Angeles*   8.95

____Invitation to Philosophy *Capaldi, Kelly, Navia, editors*   11.95

____Infanticide and the Value of Life *Marvin Kohl, editor*   7.95

____Responsibilities to Future Generations *Ernest Partridge, editor*   9.95

____Reverse Discrimination *Barry Gross, editor*   8.95

____Introductory Readings in the Philosophy of Science *Klemke, Hollinger, Kline, editors*   11.95

____Ethics and the Search for Values *L. Navia and E. Kelly, editors*   12.95

SEXOLOGY

____The Frontiers of Sex Research *Vern Bullough, editor*   7.95

____New Bill of Sexual Rights & Responsibilities *Lester Kirkendall*   2.95

____New Sexual Revolution *Lester Kirkendall, editor*   5.95

____Philosophy & Sex *Robert Baker & Fred Elliston, editors*   6.95

____Sex Without Love: A Philosophical Exploration *Russell Vannoy*   7.95

____Sexual Practices and the Medieval Church *Bullough and Brundage, editors*   9.95

THE SKEPTIC'S BOOKSHELF

____Classics of Free Thought *Paul Blanshard, editor*   5.95

____Critiques of God *Peter Angeles, editor*   8.95

____What About Gods? (for children) *Chris Brockman*   3.95

____Atheism: The Case Against God *George H. Smith*   6.95

____Atheist Debater's Handbook *B.C. Johnson*   10.95

SOCIAL ISSUES

____Age of Aging: A Reader in Social Gerontology *Monk, editor*   8.95

The books listed above can be obtained from your book dealer
or directly from Prometheus Books.
Please check off the appropriate books.
Remittance must accompany all orders from individuals.
Please include $1.25 postage and handling for first book,
.50 for each additional book ($3.00 maximum).
(N.Y. State Residents add 7% sales tax)

Send to _____

(Please type or print clearly)

Address _____

City _____ State_____ Zip_____

Amount Enclosed_____

Prometheus Books
700 E. Amherst St.
Buffalo, New York 14215